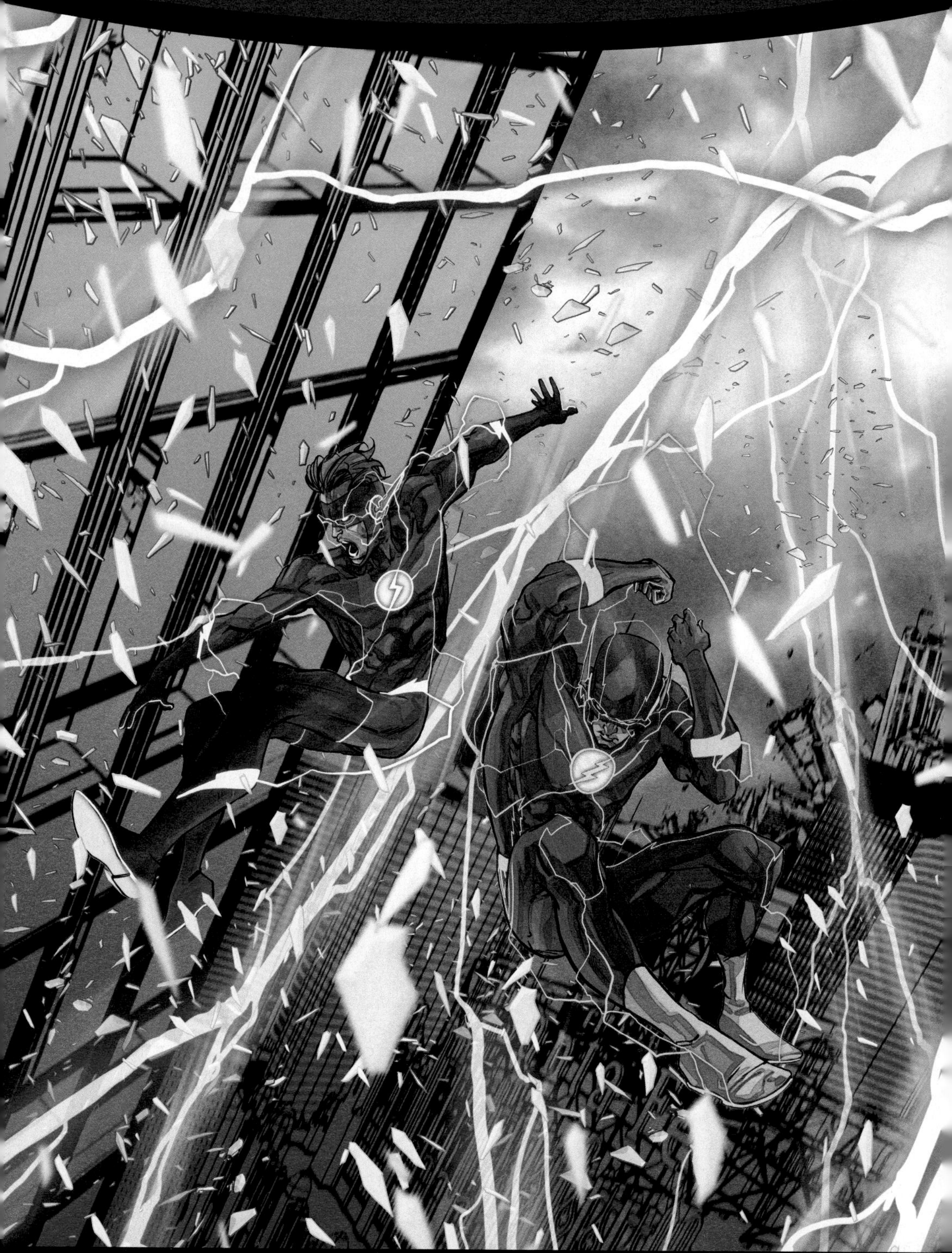

THE FLASH

VOL.7 PERFECT STORM

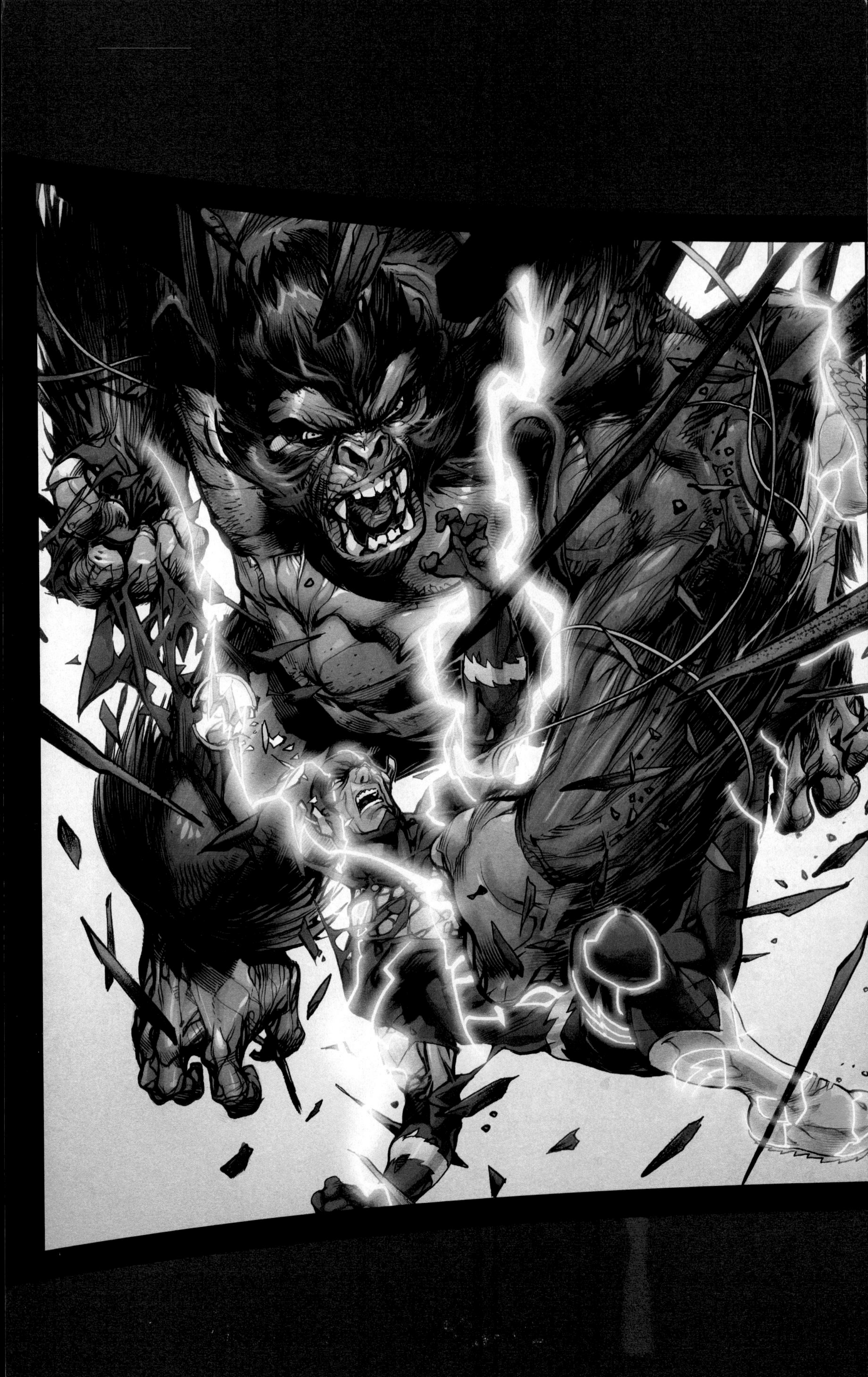

THE FLASH
VOL.7 PERFECT STORM

JOSHUA WILLIAMSON
writer

CARMINE DI GIANDOMENICO
CARLOS D'ANDA ✳ DAN PANOSIAN ✳ CHRISTIAN DUCE
artists

IVAN PLASCENCIA ✳ **LUIS GUERRERO** ✳ **HI-FI**
colorists

STEVE WANDS
letterer

CARMINE DI GIANDOMENICO and **IVAN PLASCENCIA**
collection cover artists

SUPERMAN created by **JERRY SIEGEL** and **JOE SHUSTER**
By special arrangement with the Jerry Siegel family

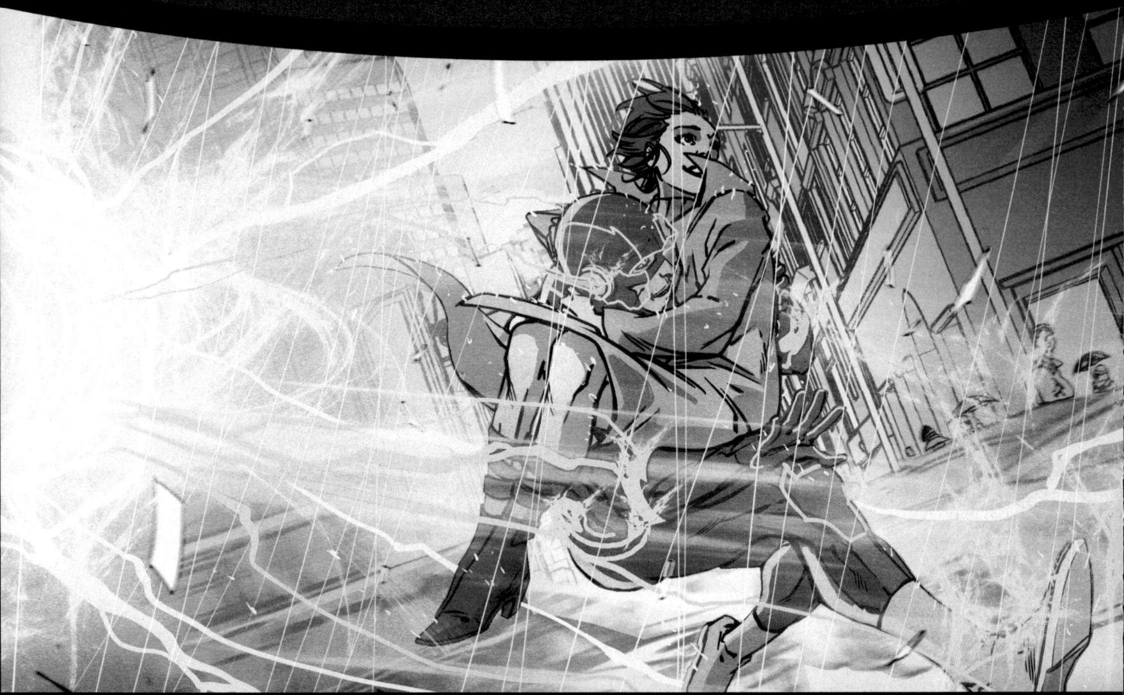

REBECCA TAYLOR Editor - Original Series * **ANDREW MARINO** Assistant Editor - Original Series
JEB WOODARD Group Editor - Collected Editions * **ERIKA ROTHBERG** Editor - Collected Edition
STEVE COOK Design Director - Books * **MONIQUE NARBONETA** Publication Design

BOB HARRAS Senior VP - Editor-in-Chief, DC Comics
PAT McCALLUM Executive Editor, DC Comics

DIANE NELSON President * **DAN DiDIO** Publisher * **JIM LEE** Publisher * **GEOFF JOHNS** President & Chief Creative Officer
AMIT DESAI Executive VP - Business & Marketing Strategy, Direct to Consumer & Global Franchise Management
SAM ADES Senior VP & General Manager, Digital Services * **BOBBIE CHASE** VP & Executive Editor, Young Reader & Talent Development
MARK CHIARELLO Senior VP - Art, Design & Collected Editions * **JOHN CUNNINGHAM** Senior VP - Sales & Trade Marketing
ANNE DePIES Senior VP - Business Strategy, Finance & Administration * **DON FALLETTI** VP - Manufacturing Operations
LAWRENCE GANEM VP - Editorial Administration & Talent Relations * **ALISON GILL** Senior VP - Manufacturing & Operations
HANK KANALZ Senior VP - Editorial Strategy & Administration * **JAY KOGAN** VP - Legal Affairs * **JACK MAHAN** VP - Business Affairs
NICK J. NAPOLITANO VP - Manufacturing Administration * **EDDIE SCANNELL** VP - Consumer Marketing
COURTNEY SIMMONS Senior VP - Publicity & Communications * **JIM (SKI) SOKOLOWSKI** VP - Comic Book Specialty Sales & Trade Marketing
NANCY SPEARS VP - Mass, Book, Digital Sales & Trade Marketing * **MICHELE R. WELLS** VP - Content Strategy

THE FLASH VOL. 7: PERFECT STORM

DC Comics, 2900 West Alameda Ave., Burbank, CA 91505
Printed by LSC Communications, Kendallville, IN, USA. 8/24/18. First Printing.
ISBN: 978-1-4012-8452-7

Library of Congress Cataloging-in-Publication Data is available.

PEFC Certified
Printed on paper from sustainably managed forests, controlled sources
PEFC/29-31-337
www.pefc.org

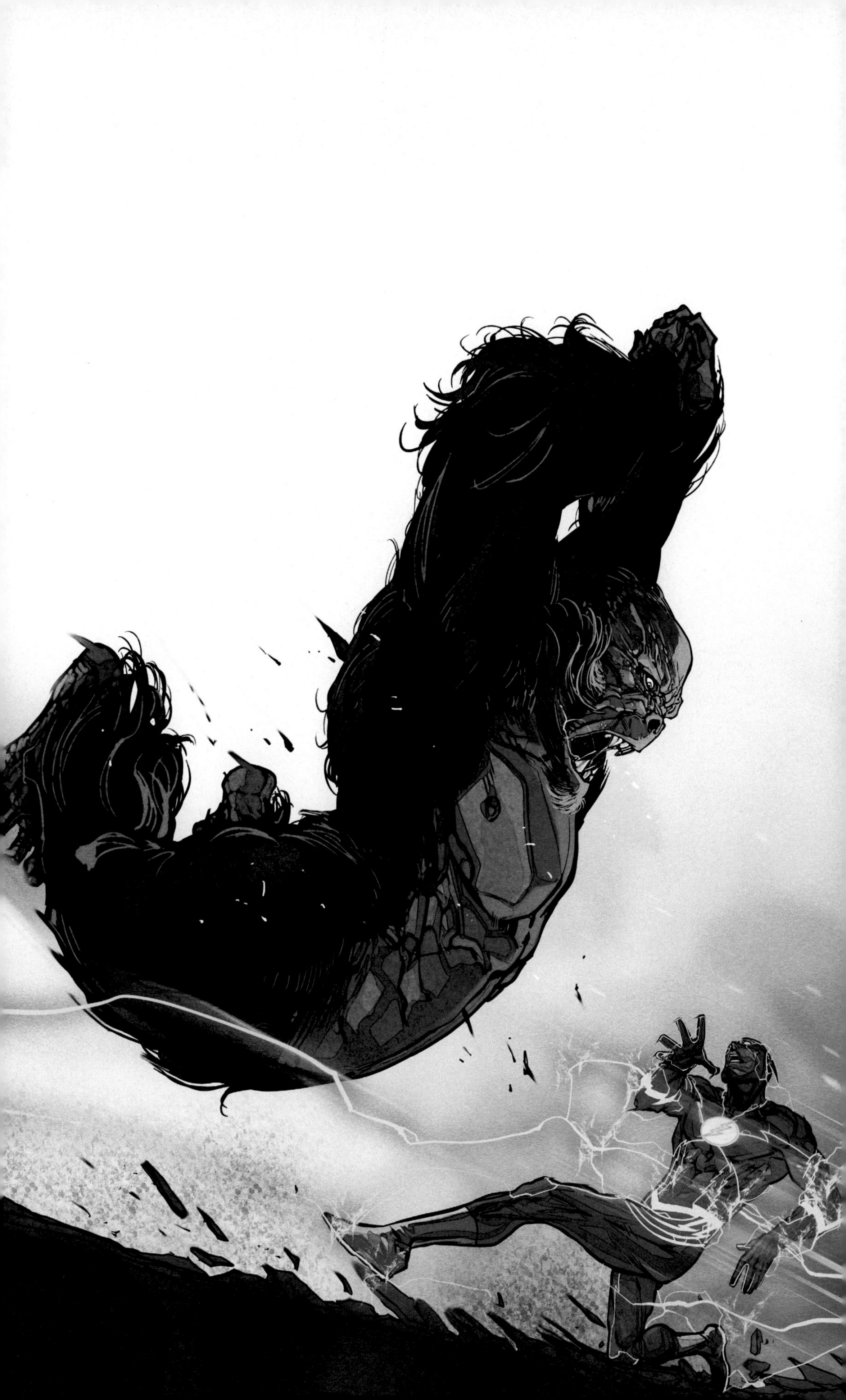

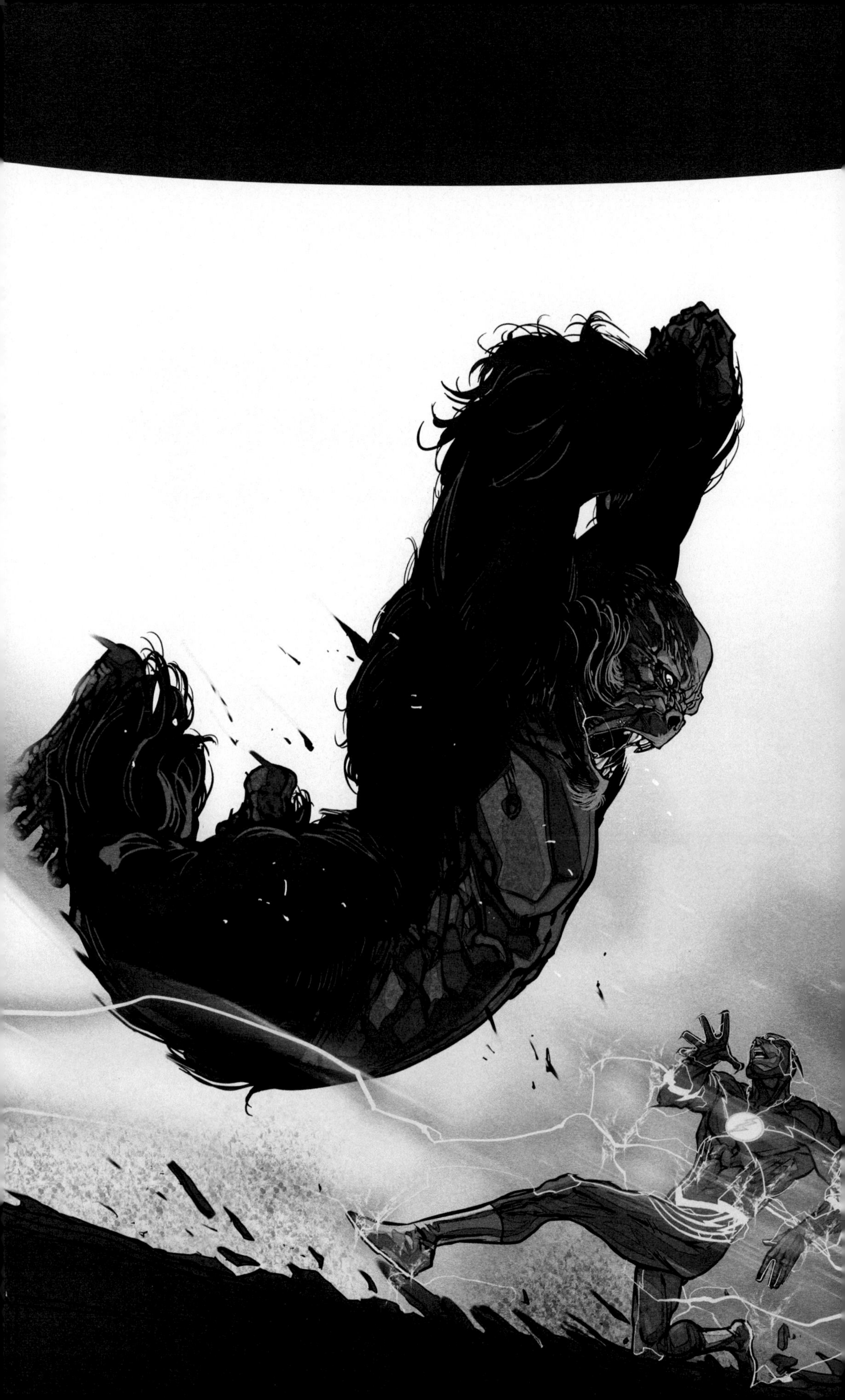

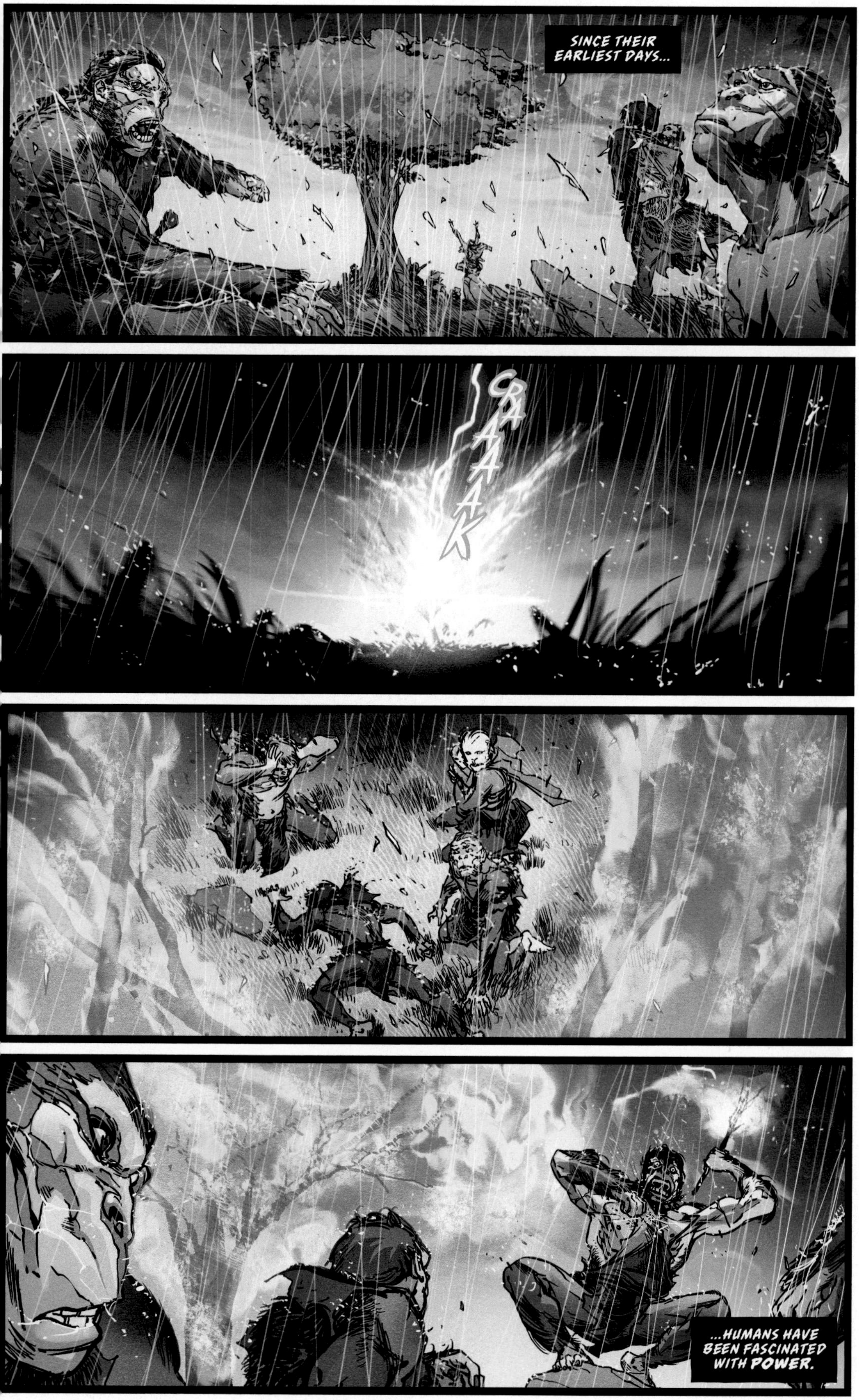
SINCE THEIR EARLIEST DAYS...
CRAAAAAK
...HUMANS HAVE BEEN FASCINATED WITH POWER.

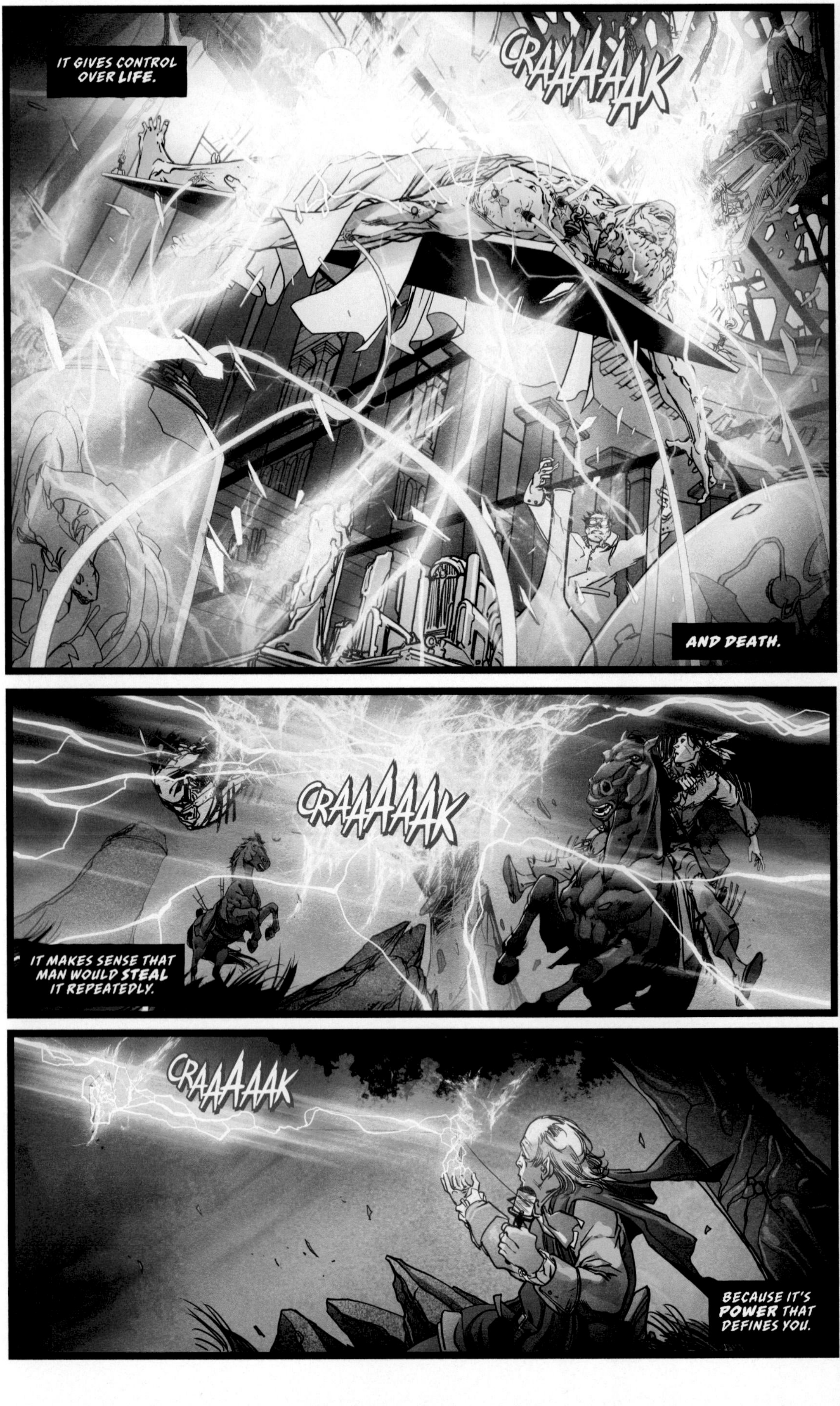
IT GIVES CONTROL OVER LIFE.
CRAAAAAK
AND DEATH.
CRAAAAAK
IT MAKES SENSE THAT MAN WOULD STEAL IT REPEATEDLY.
CRAAAAAK
BECAUSE IT'S POWER THAT DEFINES YOU.

DC COMICS

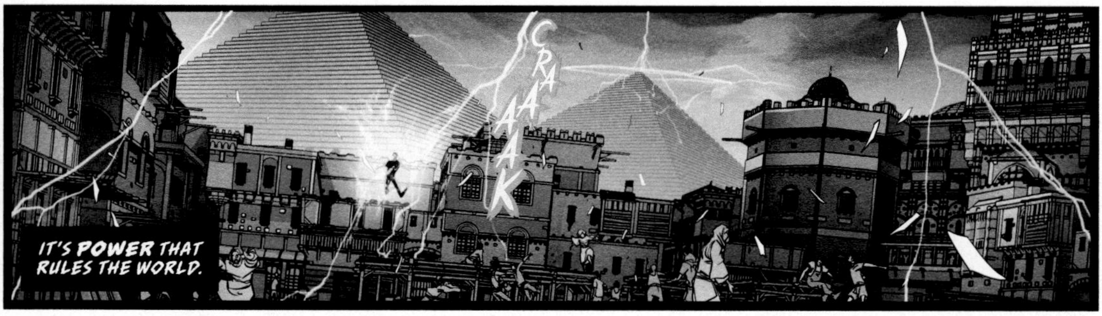
CRAAAAK
IT'S POWER THAT RULES THE WORLD.

PROUDLY PRESENTS...

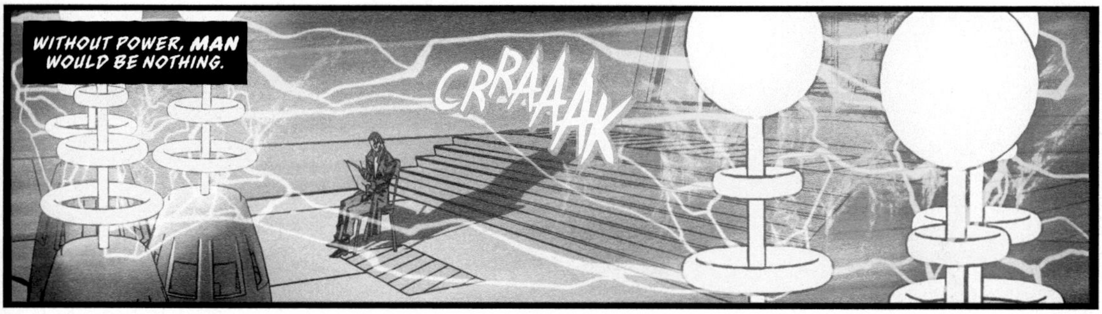
WITHOUT POWER, MAN WOULD BE NOTHING.
CRRAAAK

THE 700TH ISSUE OF...

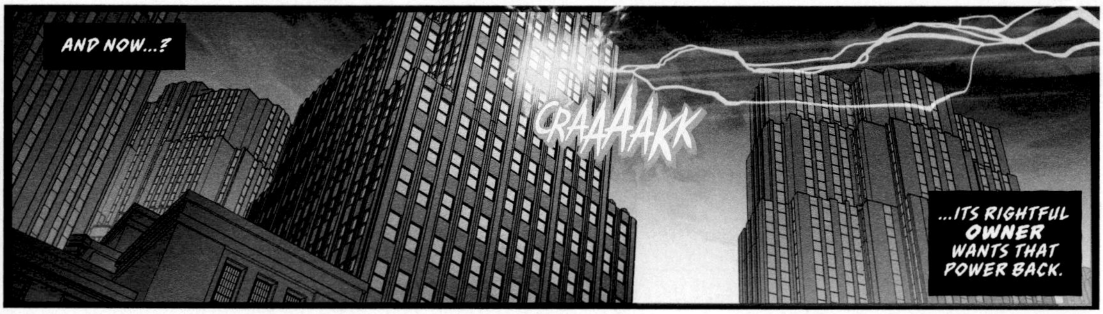
AND NOW...?
CRAAAAKK
...ITS RIGHTFUL OWNER WANTS THAT POWER BACK.

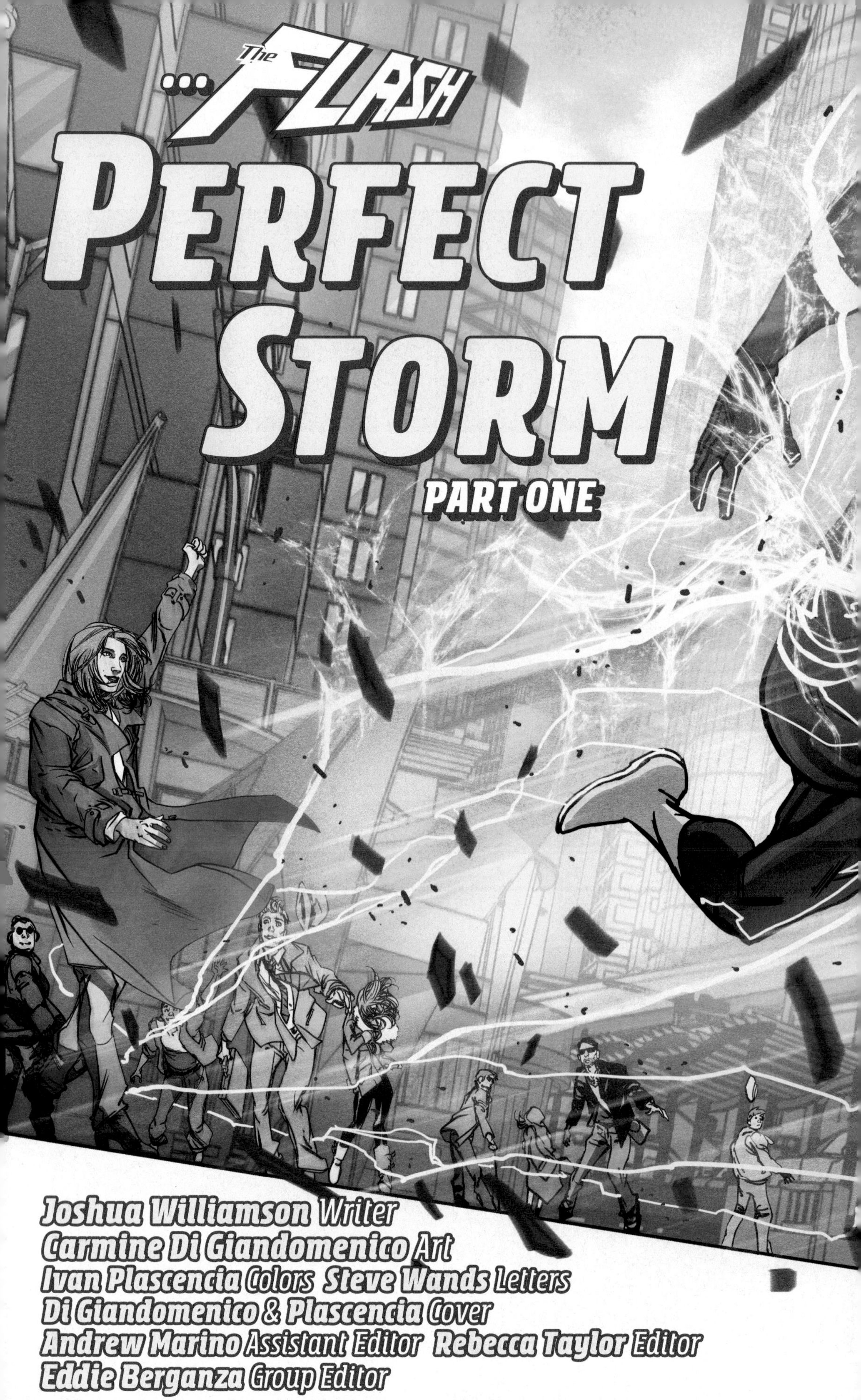
The FLASH
PERFECT STORM
PART ONE

Joshua Williamson Writer
Carmine Di Giandomenico Art
Ivan Plascencia Colors **Steve Wands** Letters
Di Giandomenico & Plascencia Cover
Andrew Marino Assistant Editor **Rebecca Taylor** Editor
Eddie Berganza Group Editor

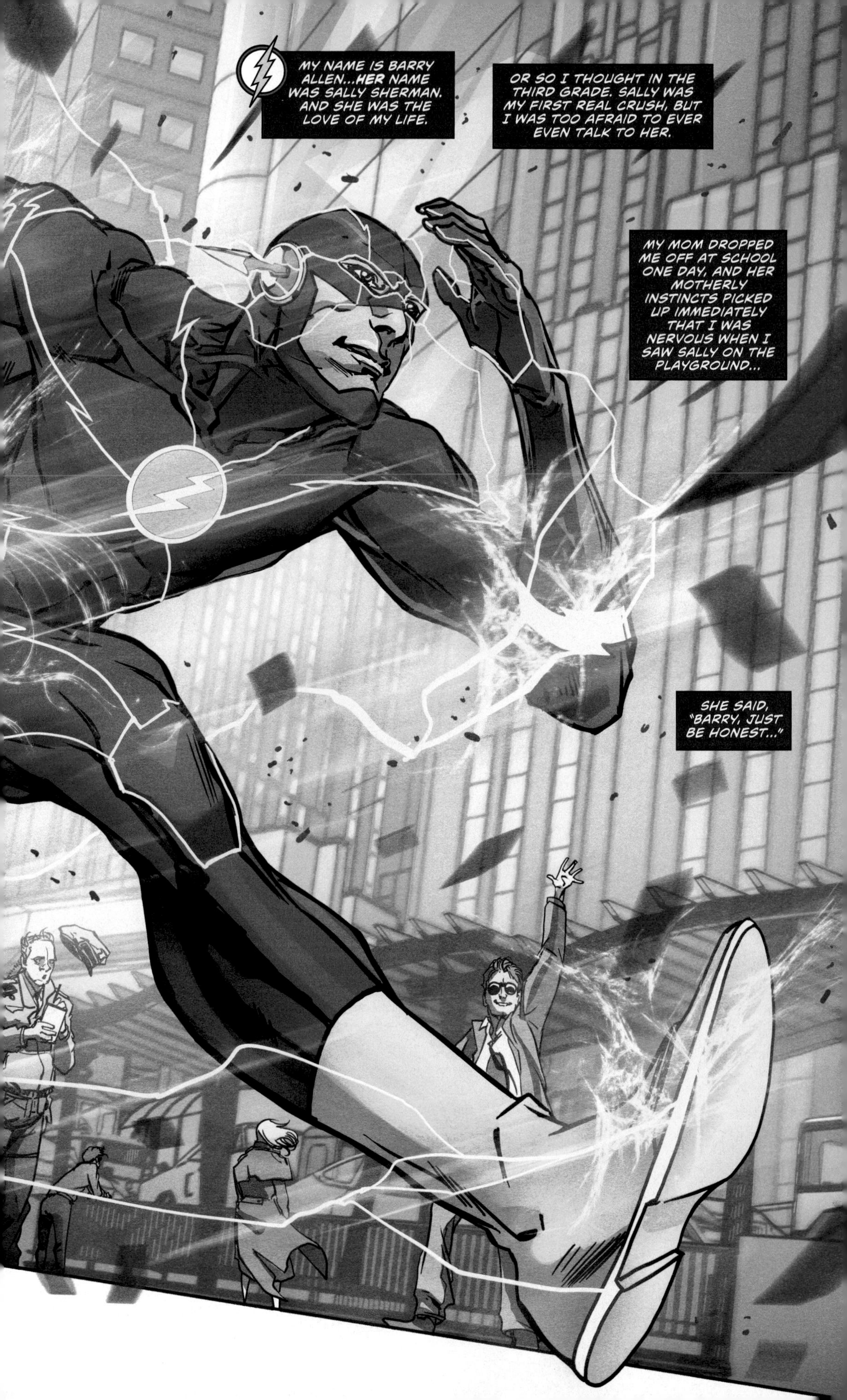
MY NAME IS BARRY ALLEN...HER NAME WAS SALLY SHERMAN. AND SHE WAS THE LOVE OF MY LIFE.
OR SO I THOUGHT IN THE THIRD GRADE. SALLY WAS MY FIRST REAL CRUSH, BUT I WAS TOO AFRAID TO EVER EVEN TALK TO HER.
MY MOM DROPPED ME OFF AT SCHOOL ONE DAY, AND HER MOTHERLY INSTINCTS PICKED UP IMMEDIATELY THAT I WAS NERVOUS WHEN I SAW SALLY ON THE PLAYGROUND...
SHE SAID, "BARRY, JUST BE HONEST..."

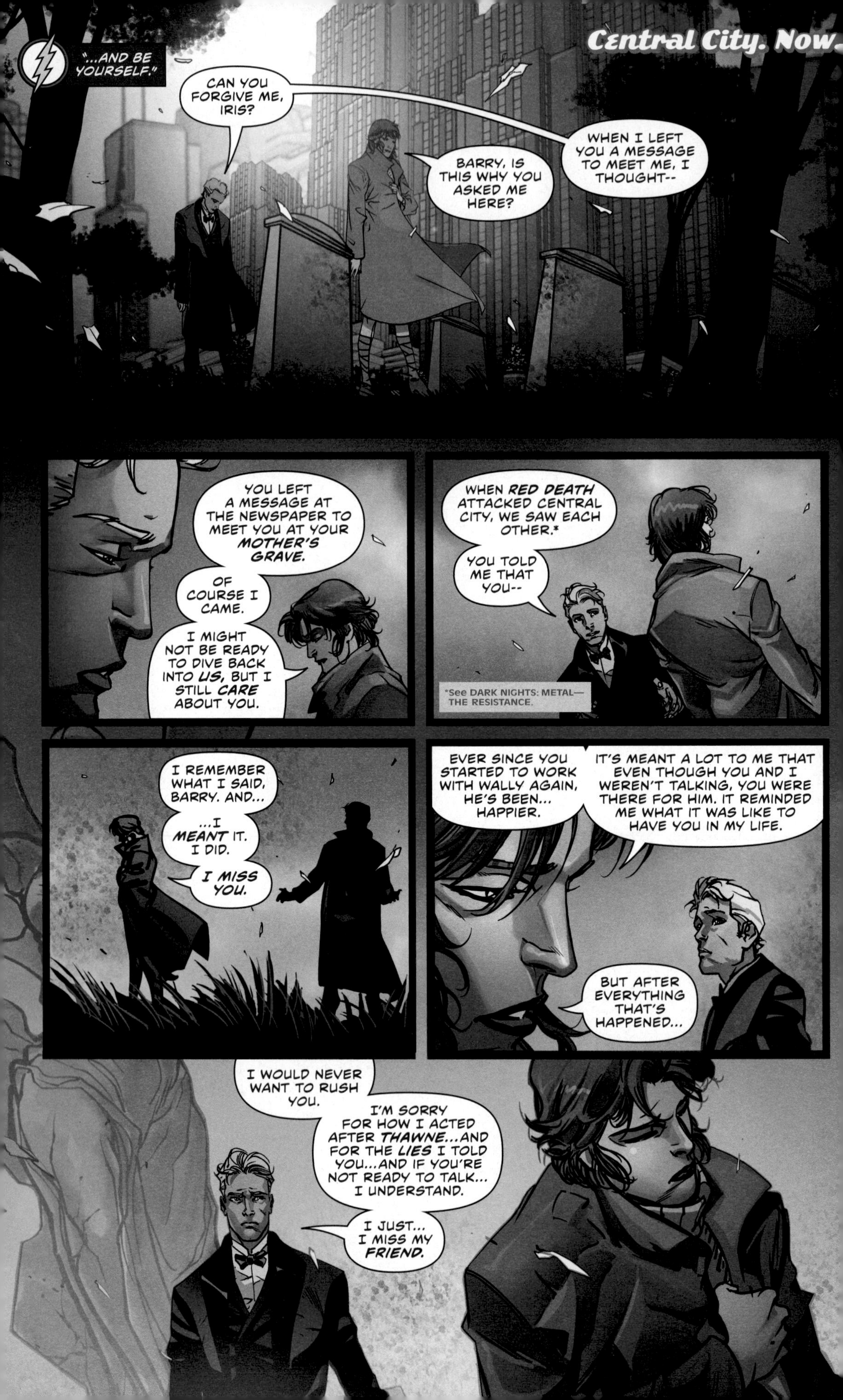
Central City. Now.
"...AND BE YOURSELF."
CAN YOU FORGIVE ME, IRIS?
BARRY, IS THIS WHY YOU ASKED ME HERE?
WHEN I LEFT YOU A MESSAGE TO MEET ME, I THOUGHT--
YOU LEFT A MESSAGE AT THE NEWSPAPER TO MEET YOU AT YOUR MOTHER'S GRAVE.
OF COURSE I CAME.
I MIGHT NOT BE READY TO DIVE BACK INTO US, BUT I STILL CARE ABOUT YOU.
WHEN RED DEATH ATTACKED CENTRAL CITY, WE SAW EACH OTHER.*
YOU TOLD ME THAT YOU--
*See DARK NIGHTS: METAL— THE RESISTANCE.
I REMEMBER WHAT I SAID, BARRY. AND...
...I MEANT IT. I DID.
I MISS YOU.
EVER SINCE YOU STARTED TO WORK WITH WALLY AGAIN, HE'S BEEN... HAPPIER.
IT'S MEANT A LOT TO ME THAT EVEN THOUGH YOU AND I WEREN'T TALKING, YOU WERE THERE FOR HIM. IT REMINDED ME WHAT IT WAS LIKE TO HAVE YOU IN MY LIFE.
BUT AFTER EVERYTHING THAT'S HAPPENED...
I WOULD NEVER WANT TO RUSH YOU.
I'M SORRY FOR HOW I ACTED AFTER THAWNE...AND FOR THE LIES I TOLD YOU...AND IF YOU'RE NOT READY TO TALK... I UNDERSTAND.
I JUST... I MISS MY FRIEND.

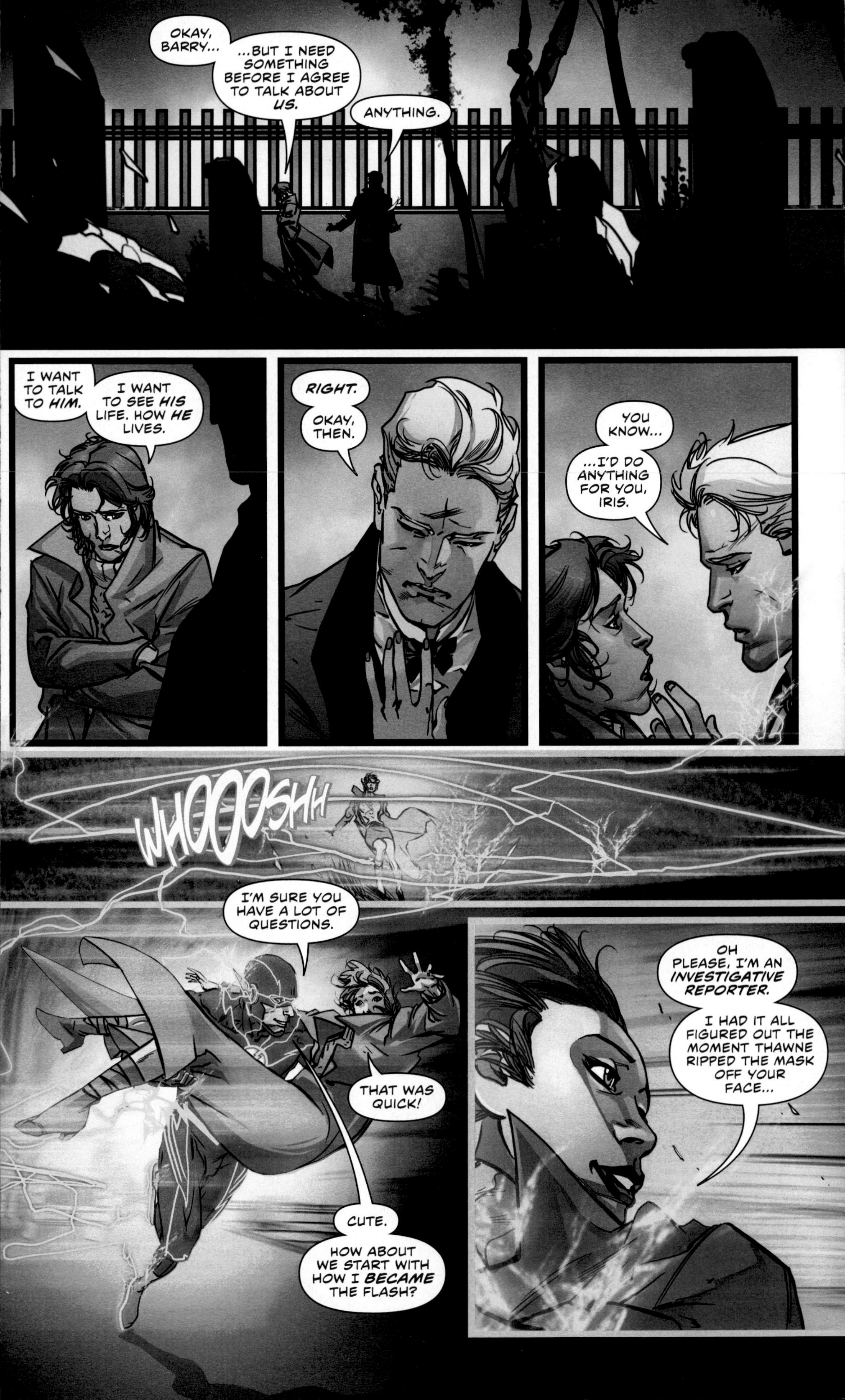
OKAY, BARRY...
...BUT I NEED SOMETHING BEFORE I AGREE TO TALK ABOUT US.
ANYTHING.
I WANT TO TALK TO HIM.
I WANT TO SEE HIS LIFE. HOW HE LIVES.
RIGHT.
OKAY, THEN.
YOU KNOW...
...I'D DO ANYTHING FOR YOU, IRIS.
WHOOOSHH
I'M SURE YOU HAVE A LOT OF QUESTIONS.
THAT WAS QUICK!
CUTE.
HOW ABOUT WE START WITH HOW I BECAME THE FLASH?
OH PLEASE, I'M AN INVESTIGATIVE REPORTER.
I HAD IT ALL FIGURED OUT THE MOMENT THAWNE RIPPED THE MASK OFF YOUR FACE...

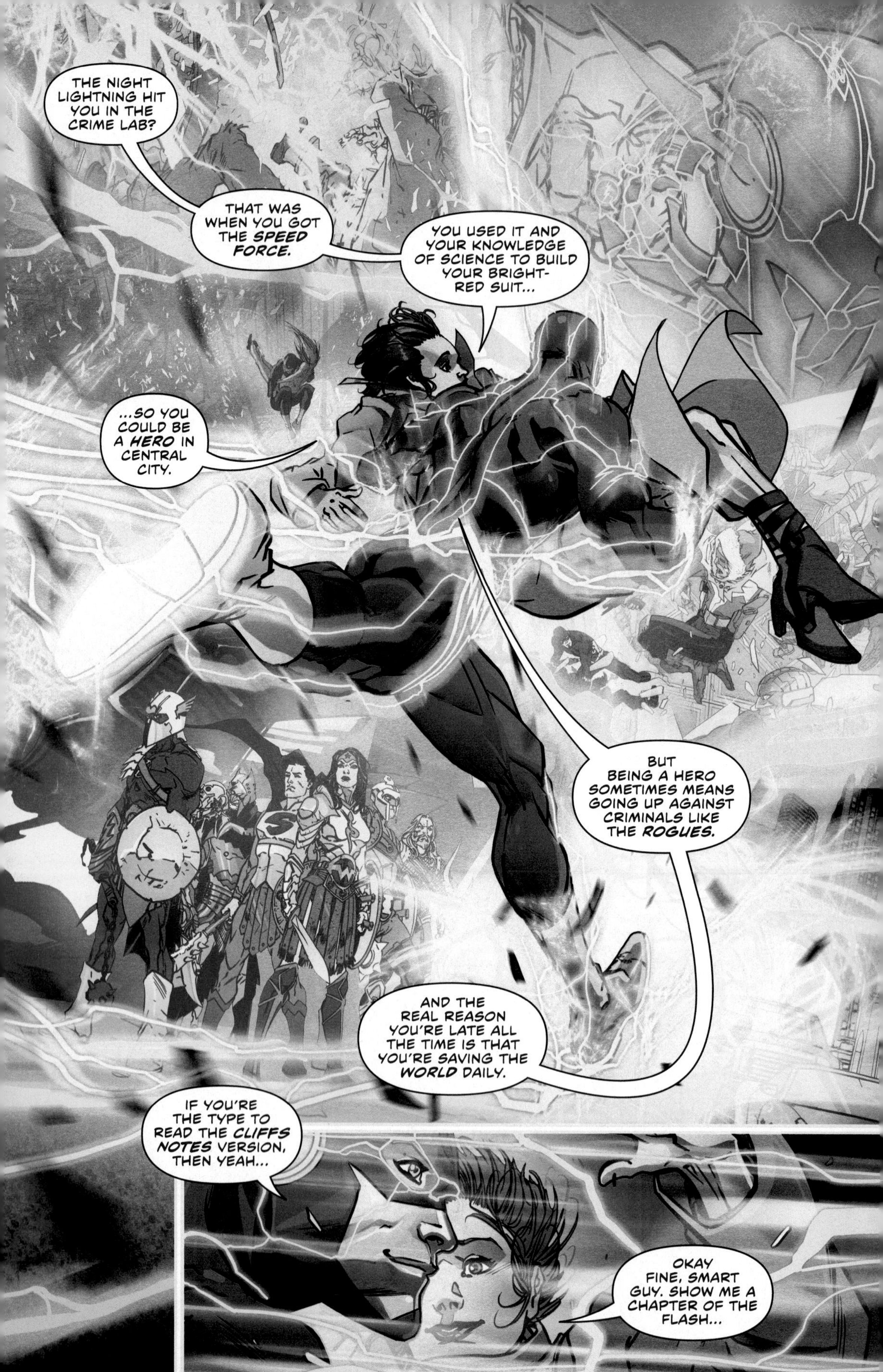
THE NIGHT LIGHTNING HIT YOU IN THE CRIME LAB?
THAT WAS WHEN YOU GOT THE *SPEED FORCE.*
YOU USED IT AND YOUR KNOWLEDGE OF SCIENCE TO BUILD YOUR BRIGHT-RED SUIT...
...SO YOU COULD BE A *HERO* IN CENTRAL CITY.
BUT BEING A HERO SOMETIMES MEANS GOING UP AGAINST CRIMINALS LIKE THE *ROGUES.*
AND THE REAL REASON YOU'RE LATE ALL THE TIME IS THAT YOU'RE SAVING THE *WORLD* DAILY.
IF YOU'RE THE TYPE TO READ THE *CLIFFS NOTES* VERSION, THEN YEAH...
OKAY FINE, SMART GUY. SHOW ME A CHAPTER OF THE FLASH...

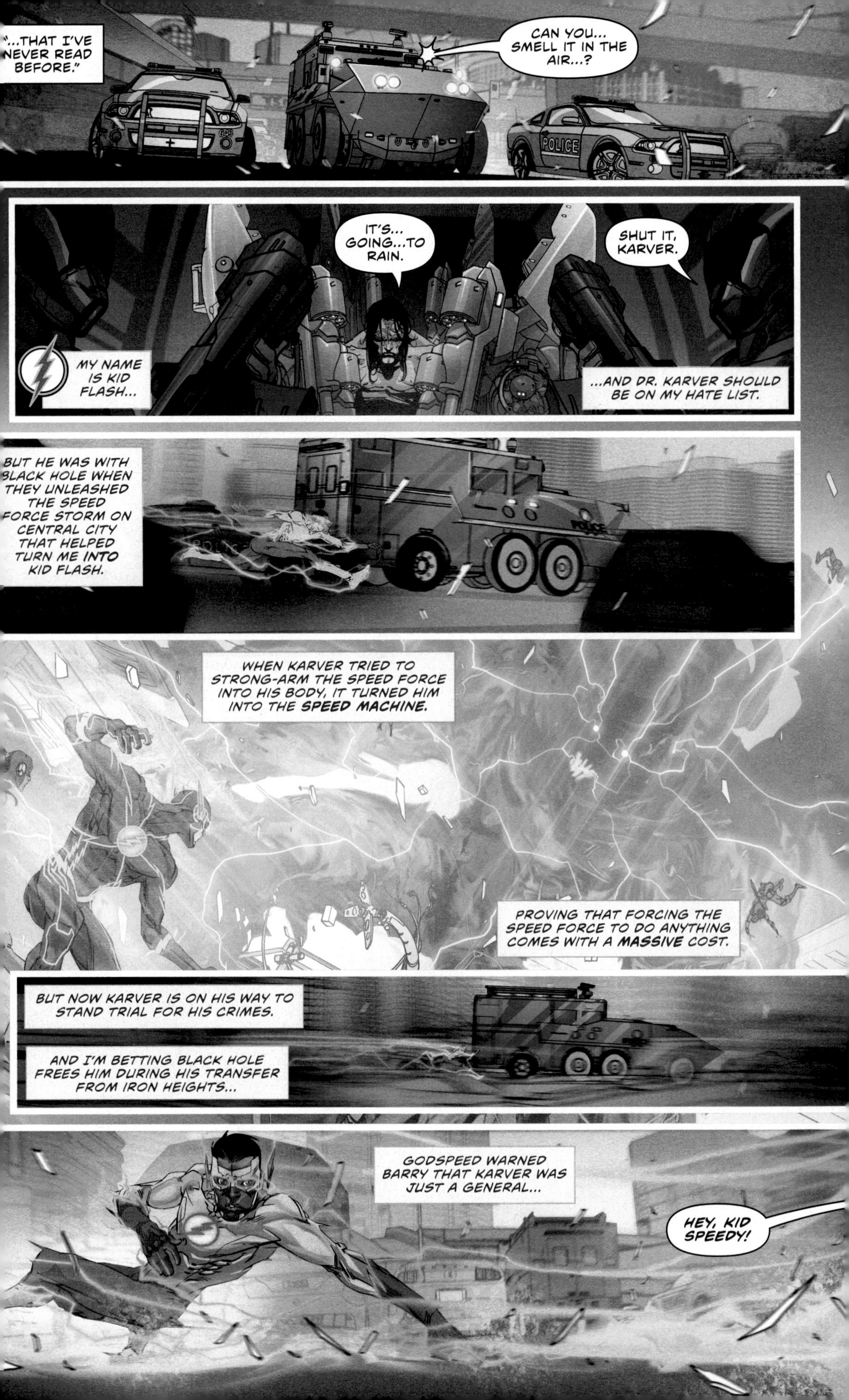
"...THAT I'VE NEVER READ BEFORE."
CAN YOU... SMELL IT IN THE AIR...?
POLICE
IT'S... GOING...TO RAIN.
SHUT IT, KARVER.
MY NAME IS KID FLASH...
...AND DR. KARVER SHOULD BE ON MY HATE LIST.
BUT HE WAS WITH BLACK HOLE WHEN THEY UNLEASHED THE SPEED FORCE STORM ON CENTRAL CITY THAT HELPED TURN ME INTO KID FLASH.
WHEN KARVER TRIED TO STRONG-ARM THE SPEED FORCE INTO HIS BODY, IT TURNED HIM INTO THE SPEED MACHINE.
PROVING THAT FORCING THE SPEED FORCE TO DO ANYTHING COMES WITH A MASSIVE COST.
BUT NOW KARVER IS ON HIS WAY TO STAND TRIAL FOR HIS CRIMES.
AND I'M BETTING BLACK HOLE FREES HIM DURING HIS TRANSFER FROM IRON HEIGHTS...
GODSPEED WARNED BARRY THAT KARVER WAS JUST A GENERAL...
HEY, KID SPEEDY!

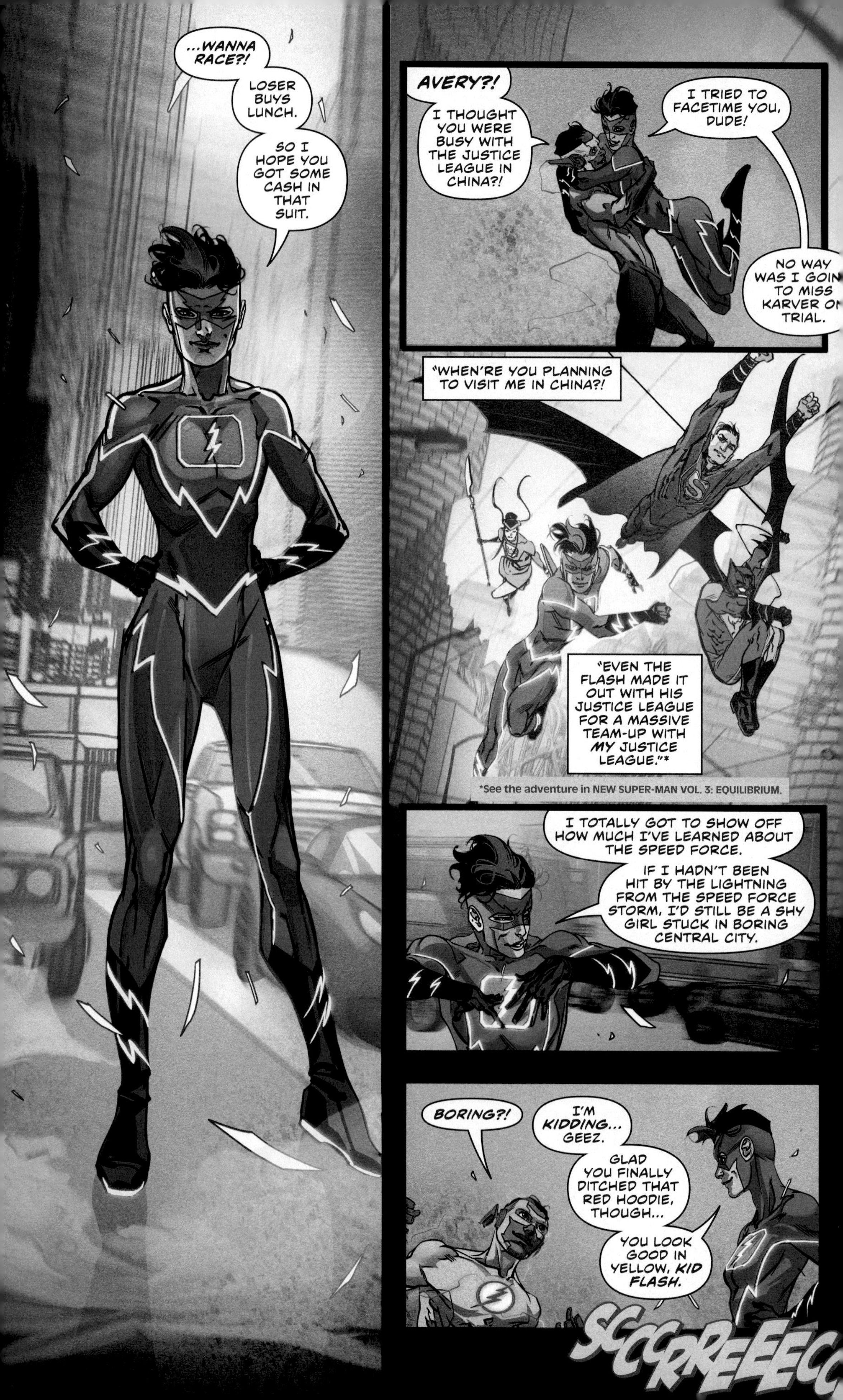
...WANNA RACE?!
LOSER BUYS LUNCH.
SO I HOPE YOU GOT SOME CASH IN THAT SUIT.
AVERY?!
I THOUGHT YOU WERE BUSY WITH THE JUSTICE LEAGUE IN CHINA?!
I TRIED TO FACETIME YOU, DUDE!
NO WAY WAS I GOIN TO MISS KARVER O TRIAL.
"WHEN'RE YOU PLANNING TO VISIT ME IN CHINA?!
"EVEN THE FLASH MADE IT OUT WITH HIS JUSTICE LEAGUE FOR A MASSIVE TEAM-UP WITH MY JUSTICE LEAGUE."*
*See the adventure in NEW SUPER-MAN VOL. 3: EQUILIBRIUM.
I TOTALLY GOT TO SHOW OFF HOW MUCH I'VE LEARNED ABOUT THE SPEED FORCE.
IF I HADN'T BEEN HIT BY THE LIGHTNING FROM THE SPEED FORCE STORM, I'D STILL BE A SHY GIRL STUCK IN BORING CENTRAL CITY.
BORING?!
I'M KIDDING... GEEZ.
GLAD YOU FINALLY DITCHED THAT RED HOODIE, THOUGH...
YOU LOOK GOOD IN YELLOW, KID FLASH.
SCCCRREEEECC

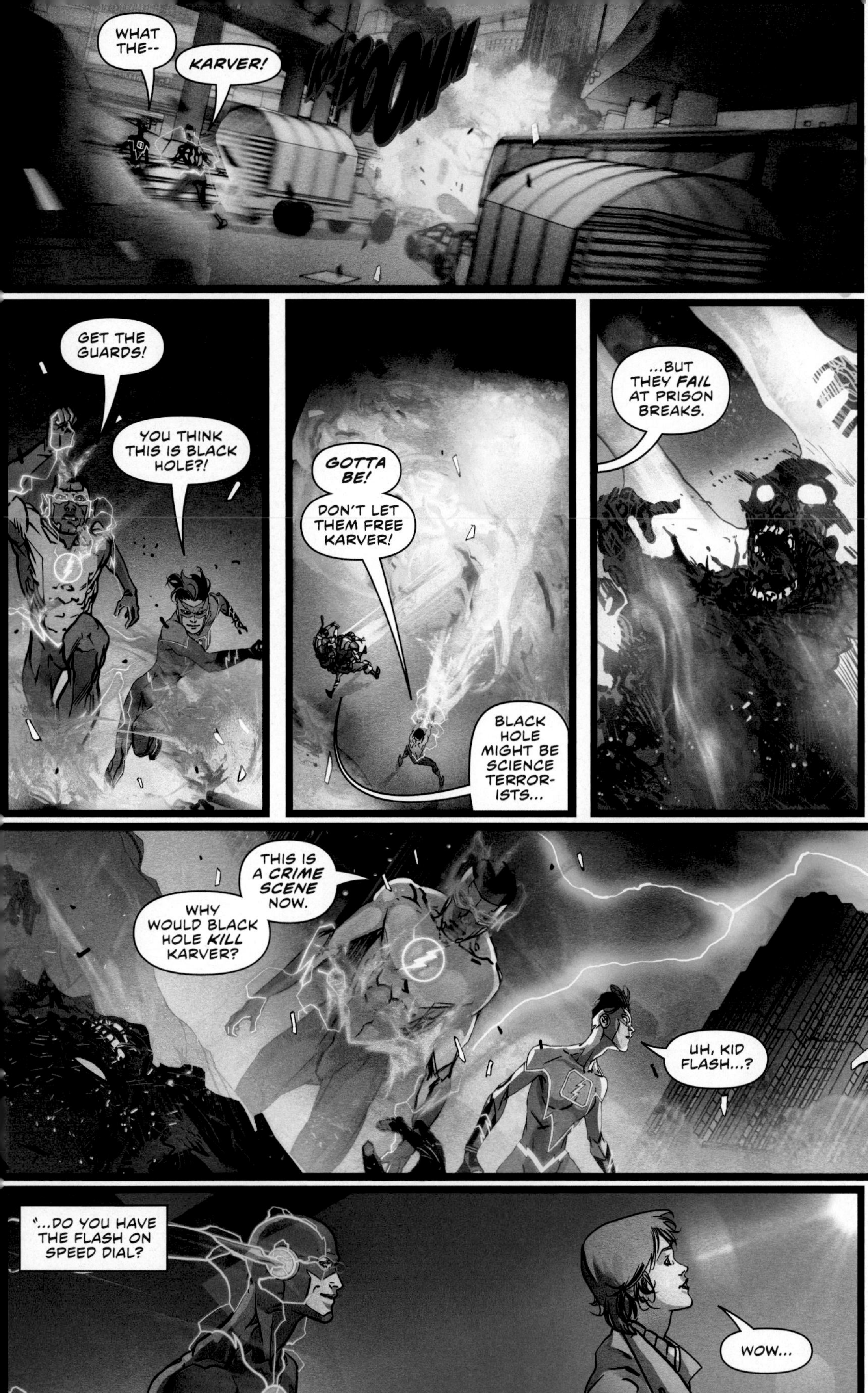

WHAT THE--
KARVER!
GET THE GUARDS!
YOU THINK THIS IS BLACK HOLE?!
GOTTA BE!
DON'T LET THEM FREE KARVER!
BLACK HOLE MIGHT BE SCIENCE TERROR-ISTS...
...BUT THEY FAIL AT PRISON BREAKS.
THIS IS A CRIME SCENE NOW.
WHY WOULD BLACK HOLE KILL KARVER?
UH, KID FLASH...?
"...DO YOU HAVE THE FLASH ON SPEED DIAL?
WOW...

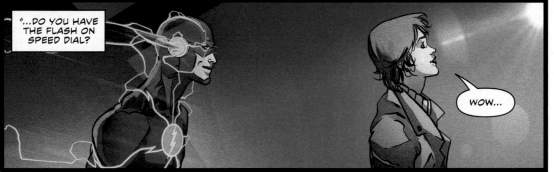

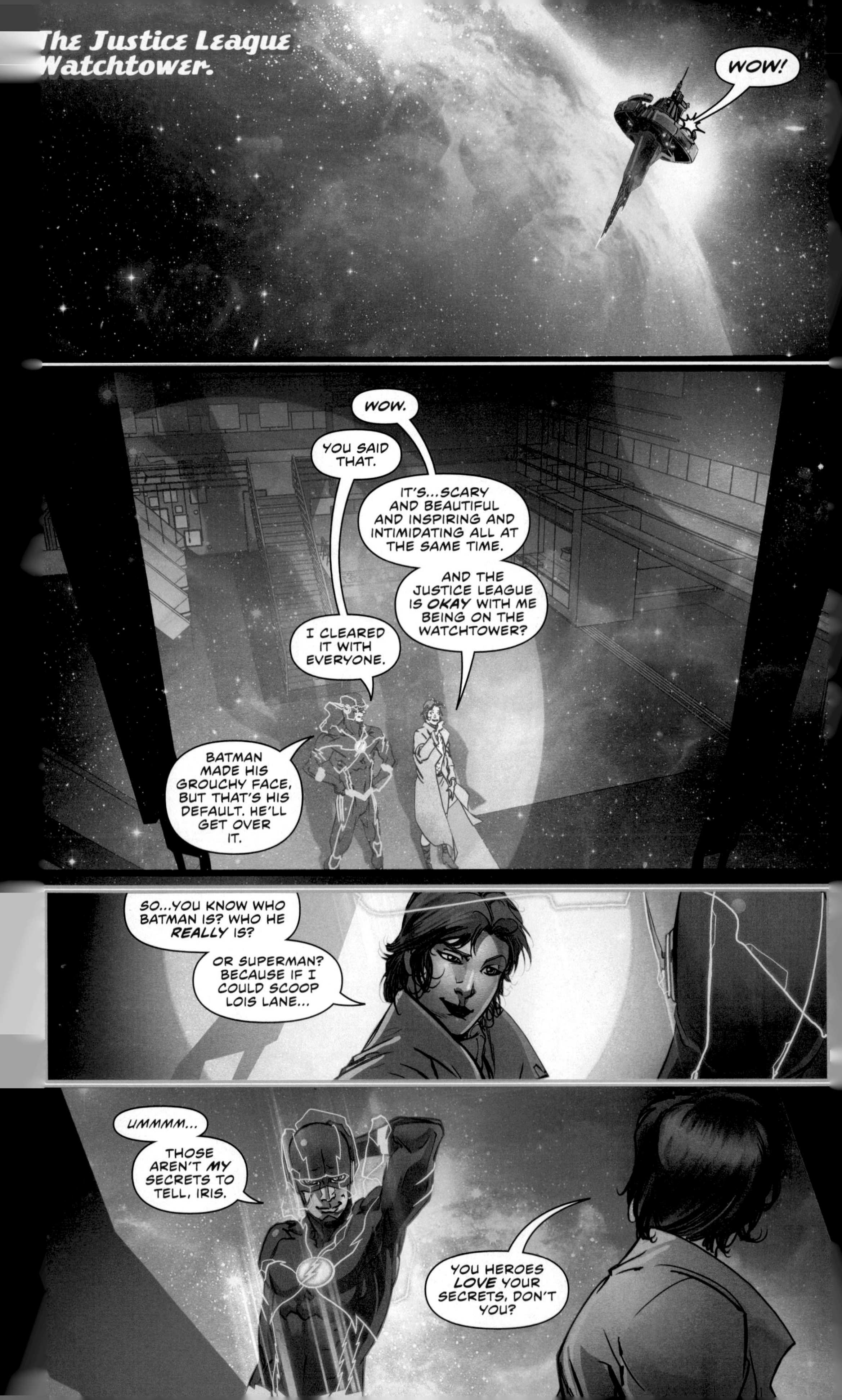
The Justice League Watchtower.
WOW!
WOW.
YOU SAID THAT.
IT'S...SCARY AND BEAUTIFUL AND INSPIRING AND INTIMIDATING ALL AT THE SAME TIME.
AND THE JUSTICE LEAGUE IS OKAY WITH ME BEING ON THE WATCHTOWER?
I CLEARED IT WITH EVERYONE.
BATMAN MADE HIS GROUCHY FACE, BUT THAT'S HIS DEFAULT. HE'LL GET OVER IT.
SO...YOU KNOW WHO BATMAN IS? WHO HE REALLY IS?
OR SUPERMAN? BECAUSE IF I COULD SCOOP LOIS LANE...
UMMMM...
THOSE AREN'T MY SECRETS TO TELL, IRIS.
YOU HEROES LOVE YOUR SECRETS, DON'T YOU?

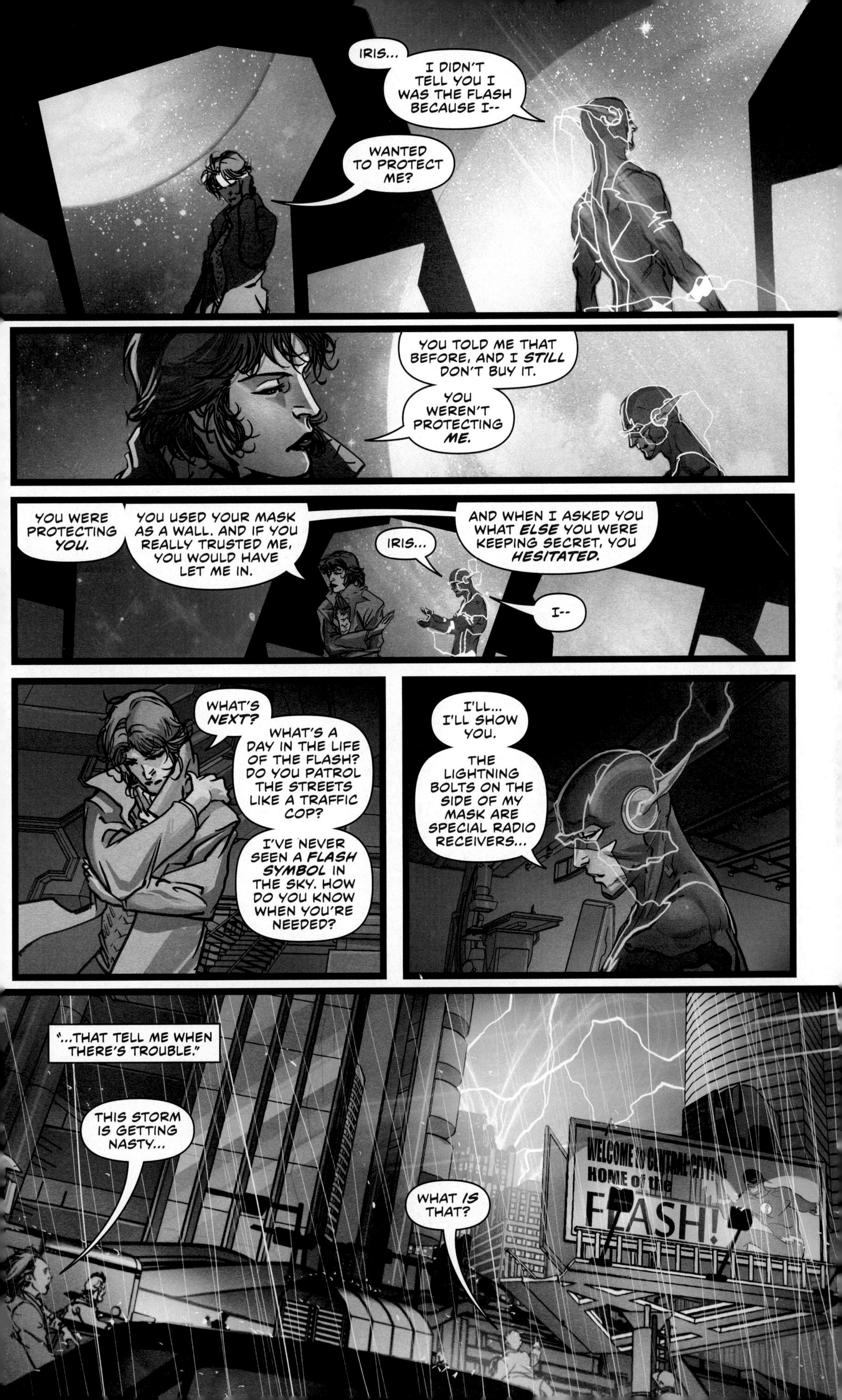

IRIS...
I DIDN'T TELL YOU I WAS THE FLASH BECAUSE I--
WANTED TO PROTECT ME?
YOU TOLD ME THAT BEFORE, AND I STILL DON'T BUY IT.
YOU WEREN'T PROTECTING ME.
YOU WERE PROTECTING YOU.
YOU USED YOUR MASK AS A WALL. AND IF YOU REALLY TRUSTED ME, YOU WOULD HAVE LET ME IN.
IRIS...
AND WHEN I ASKED YOU WHAT ELSE YOU WERE KEEPING SECRET, YOU HESITATED.
I--
WHAT'S NEXT?
WHAT'S A DAY IN THE LIFE OF THE FLASH? DO YOU PATROL THE STREETS LIKE A TRAFFIC COP?
I'VE NEVER SEEN A FLASH SYMBOL IN THE SKY. HOW DO YOU KNOW WHEN YOU'RE NEEDED?
I'LL... I'LL SHOW YOU.
THE LIGHTNING BOLTS ON THE SIDE OF MY MASK ARE SPECIAL RADIO RECEIVERS...
"...THAT TELL ME WHEN THERE'S TROUBLE."
THIS STORM IS GETTING NASTY...
WHAT IS THAT?
WELCOME TO CENTRAL CITY HOME of the FLASH!

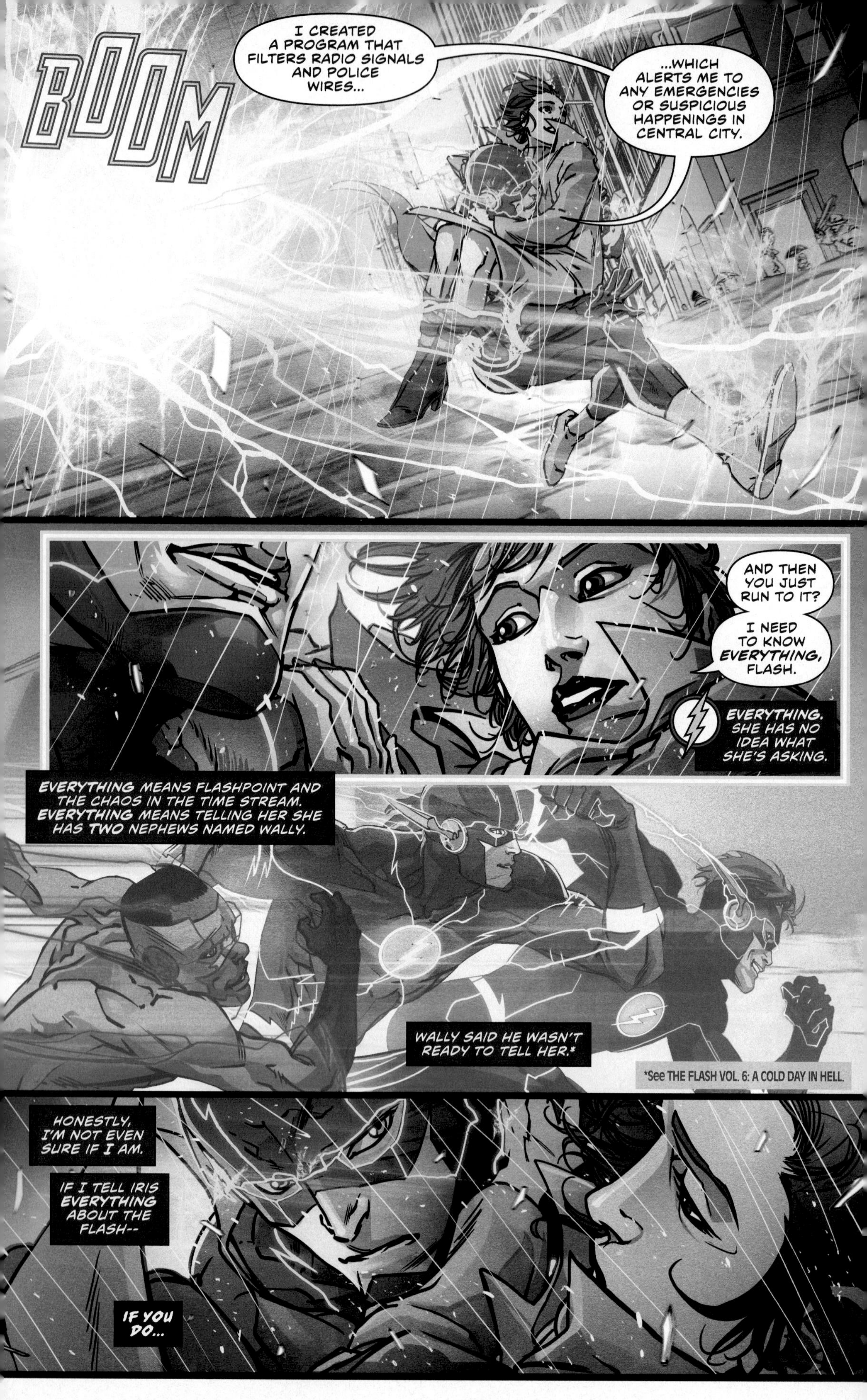
BOOM
I CREATED A PROGRAM THAT FILTERS RADIO SIGNALS AND POLICE WIRES...
...WHICH ALERTS ME TO ANY EMERGENCIES OR SUSPICIOUS HAPPENINGS IN CENTRAL CITY.
AND THEN YOU JUST RUN TO IT?
I NEED TO KNOW EVERYTHING, FLASH.
EVERYTHING. SHE HAS NO IDEA WHAT SHE'S ASKING.
EVERYTHING MEANS FLASHPOINT AND THE CHAOS IN THE TIME STREAM. EVERYTHING MEANS TELLING HER SHE HAS TWO NEPHEWS NAMED WALLY.
WALLY SAID HE WASN'T READY TO TELL HER.*
*See THE FLASH VOL. 6: A COLD DAY IN HELL.
HONESTLY, I'M NOT EVEN SURE IF I AM.
IF I TELL IRIS EVERYTHING ABOUT THE FLASH--
IF YOU DO...

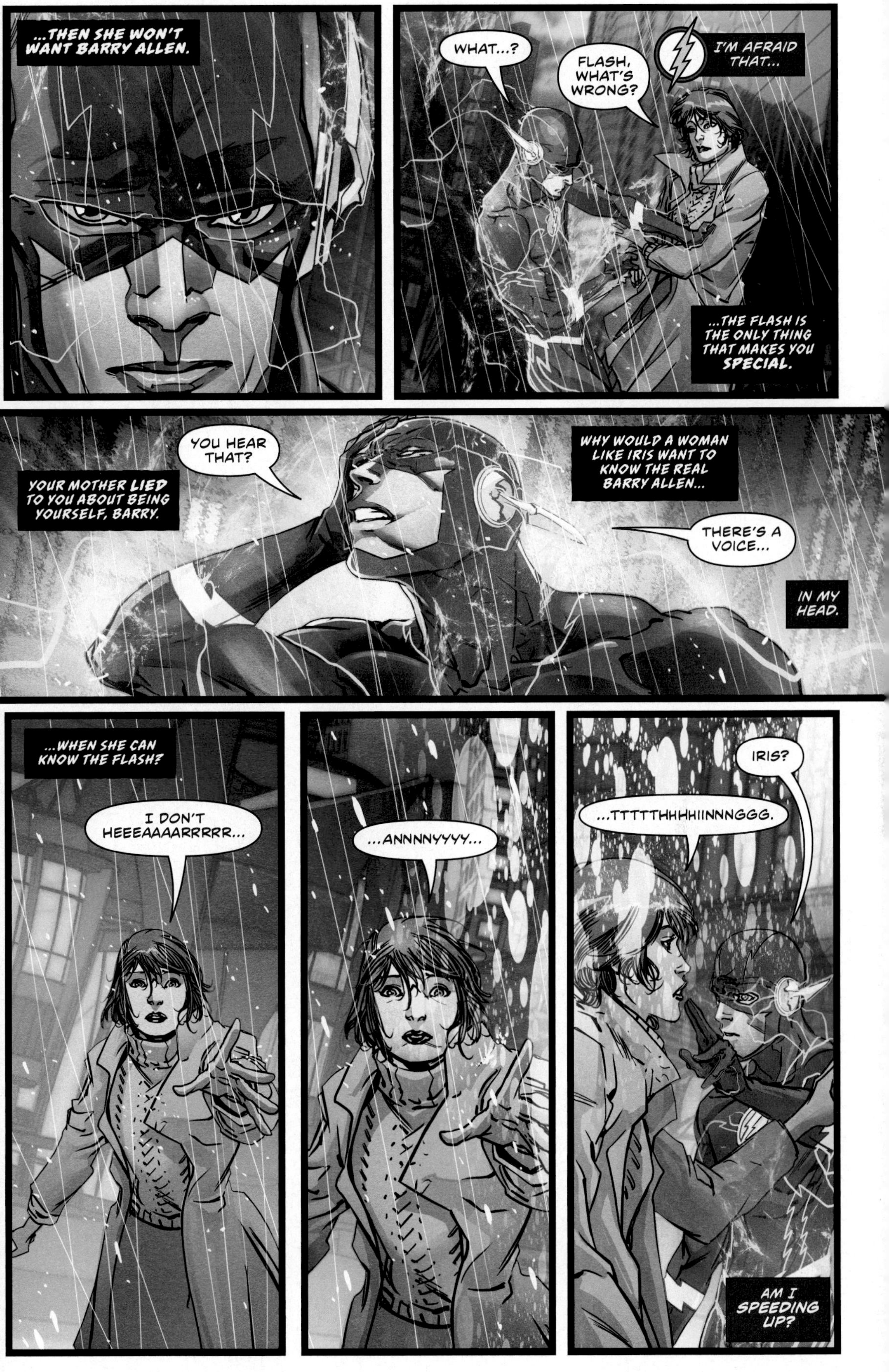
...THEN SHE WON'T WANT BARRY ALLEN.
WHAT...?
FLASH, WHAT'S WRONG?
I'M AFRAID THAT...
...THE FLASH IS THE ONLY THING THAT MAKES YOU SPECIAL.
YOUR MOTHER LIED TO YOU ABOUT BEING YOURSELF, BARRY.
YOU HEAR THAT?
WHY WOULD A WOMAN LIKE IRIS WANT TO KNOW THE REAL BARRY ALLEN...
THERE'S A VOICE...
IN MY HEAD.
...WHEN SHE CAN KNOW THE FLASH?
I DON'T HEEEAAAARRRRR...
...ANNNNYYYY...
IRIS?
...TTTTTHHHHIINNNGGG.
AM I SPEEDING UP?

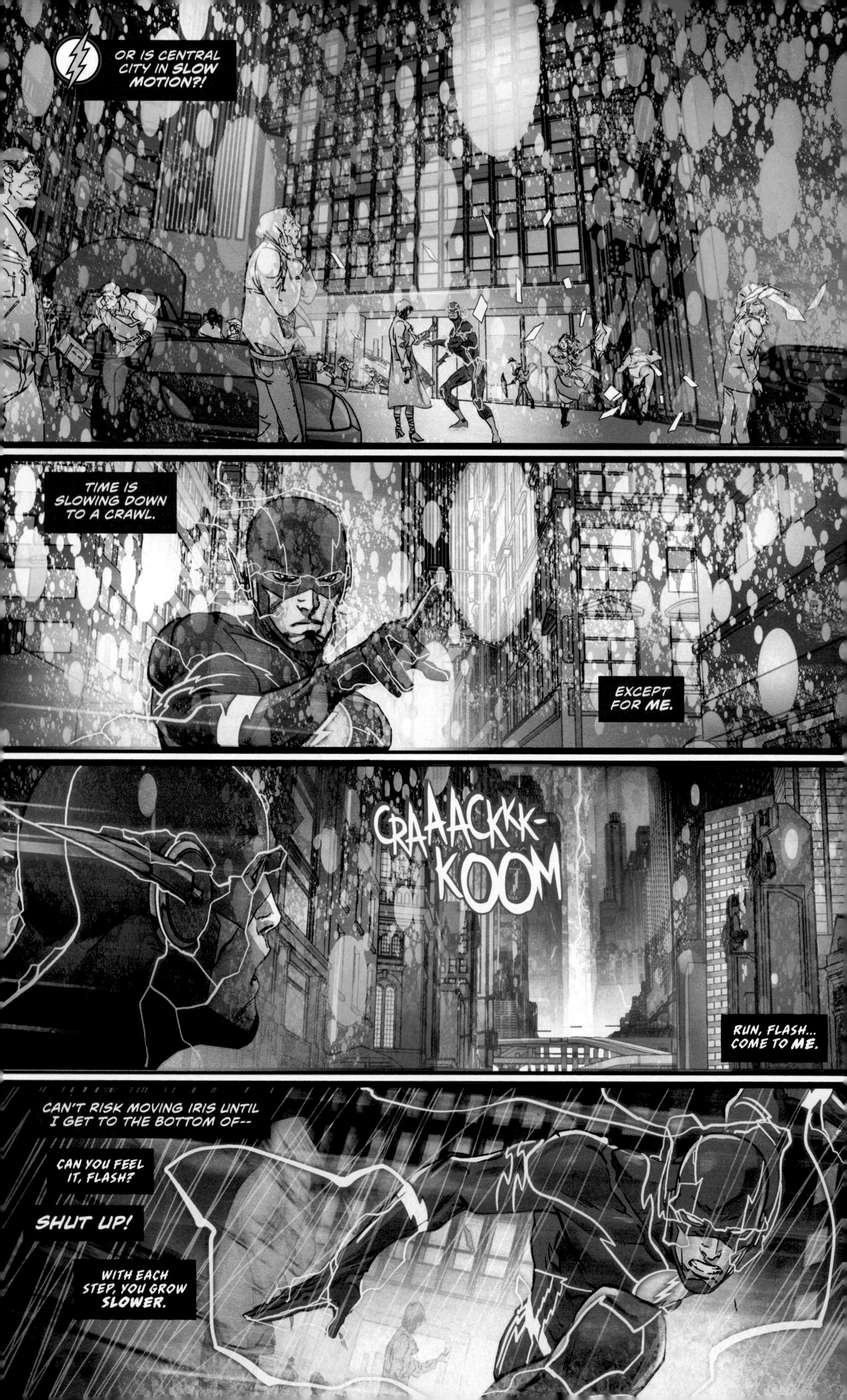
OR IS CENTRAL CITY IN SLOW MOTION?!
TIME IS SLOWING DOWN TO A CRAWL.
EXCEPT FOR ME.
CRAAACKKK-KOOM
RUN, FLASH... COME TO ME.
CAN'T RISK MOVING IRIS UNTIL I GET TO THE BOTTOM OF--
CAN YOU FEEL IT, FLASH?
SHUT UP!
WITH EACH STEP, YOU GROW SLOWER.

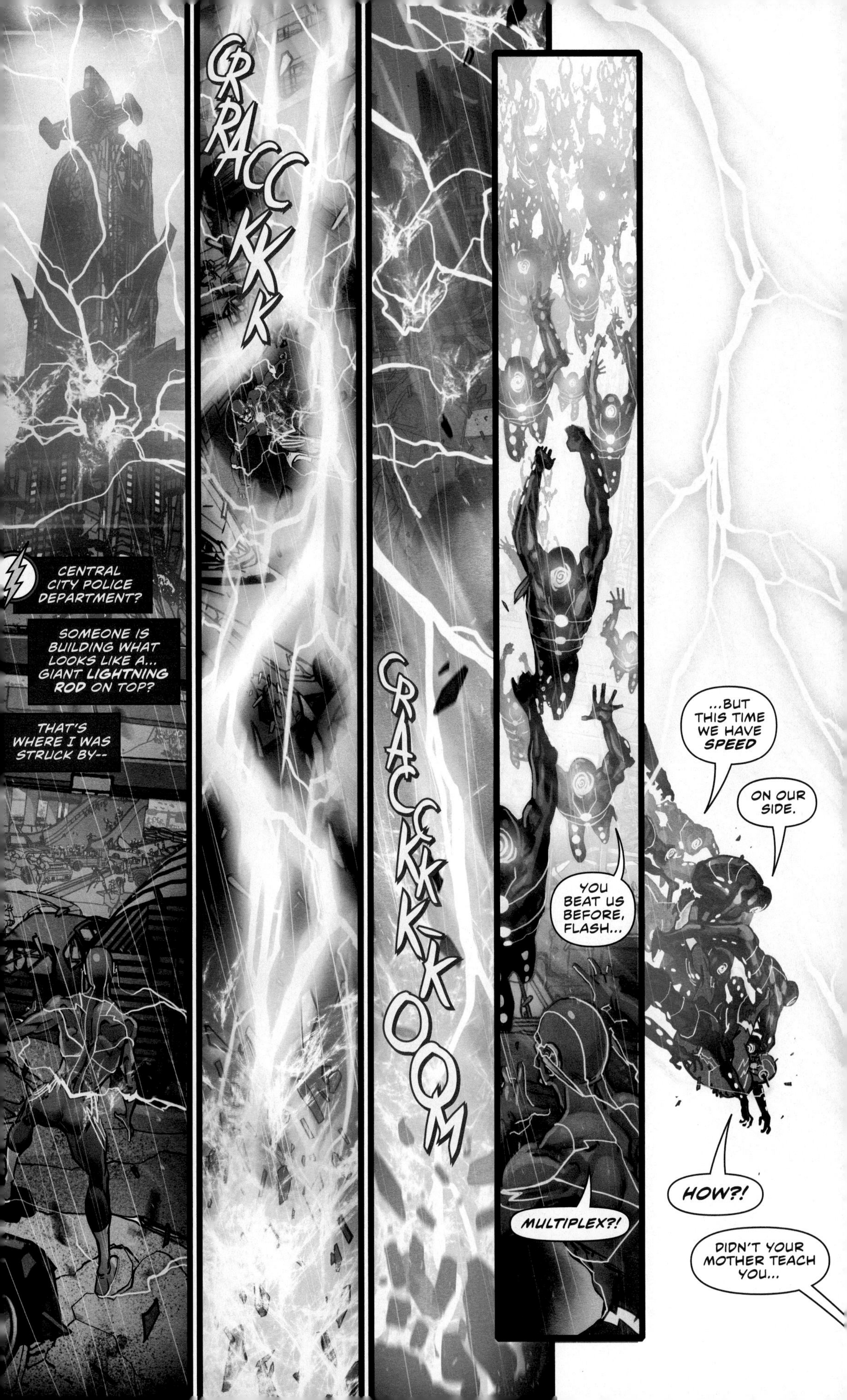
CENTRAL CITY POLICE DEPARTMENT?
SOMEONE IS BUILDING WHAT LOOKS LIKE A... GIANT LIGHTNING ROD ON TOP?
THAT'S WHERE I WAS STRUCK BY--
CRRACCKKKK
CRACCKKKKOOM
YOU BEAT US BEFORE, FLASH...
...BUT THIS TIME WE HAVE SPEED
ON OUR SIDE.
MULTIPLEX?!
HOW?!
DIDN'T YOUR MOTHER TEACH YOU...

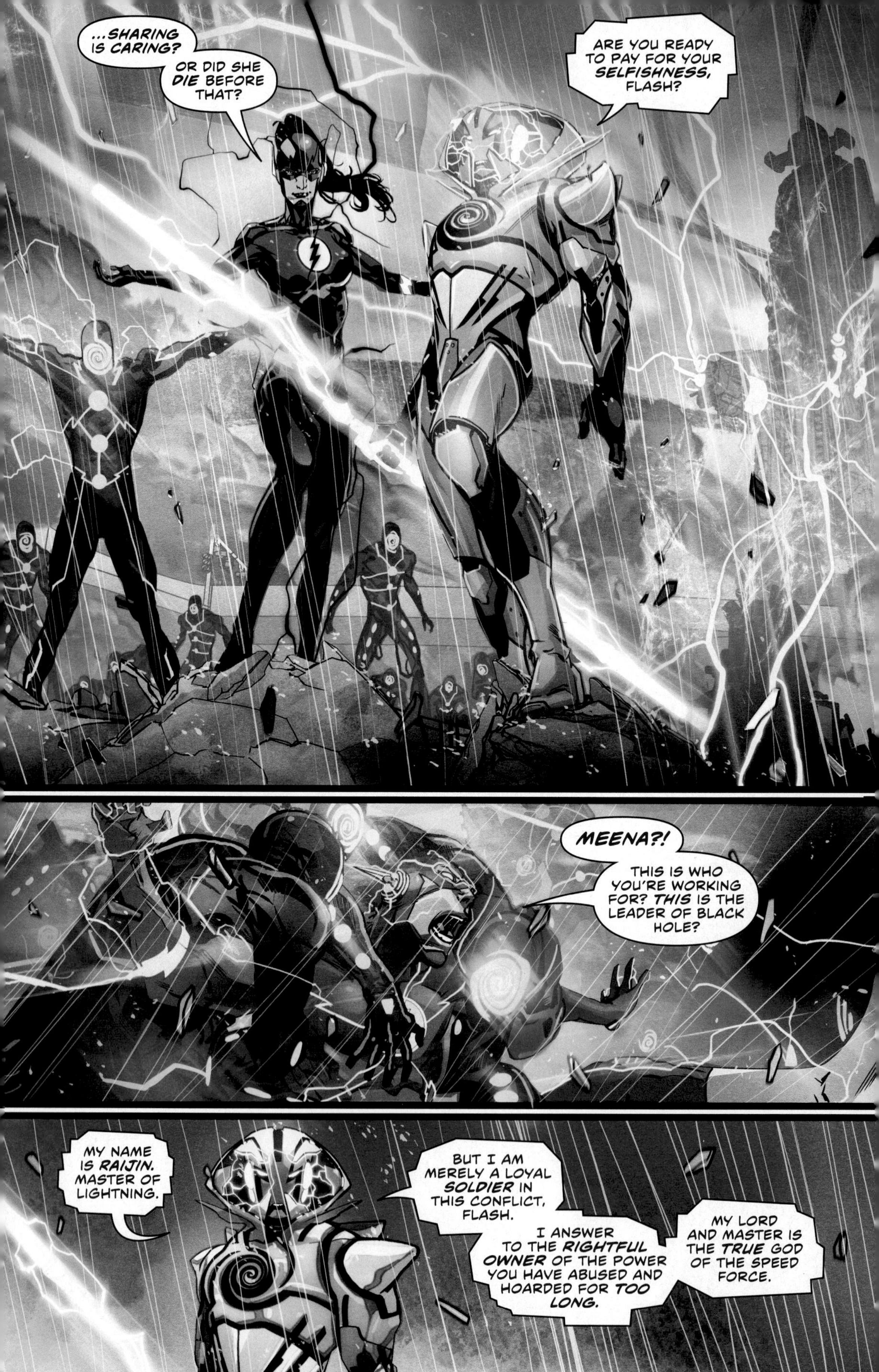
...SHARING IS CARING?
OR DID SHE DIE BEFORE THAT?
ARE YOU READY TO PAY FOR YOUR SELFISHNESS, FLASH?
MEENA?!
THIS IS WHO YOU'RE WORKING FOR? THIS IS THE LEADER OF BLACK HOLE?
MY NAME IS RAIJIN. MASTER OF LIGHTNING.
BUT I AM MERELY A LOYAL SOLDIER IN THIS CONFLICT, FLASH.
I ANSWER TO THE RIGHTFUL OWNER OF THE POWER YOU HAVE ABUSED AND HOARDED FOR TOO LONG.
MY LORD AND MASTER IS THE TRUE GOD OF THE SPEED FORCE.

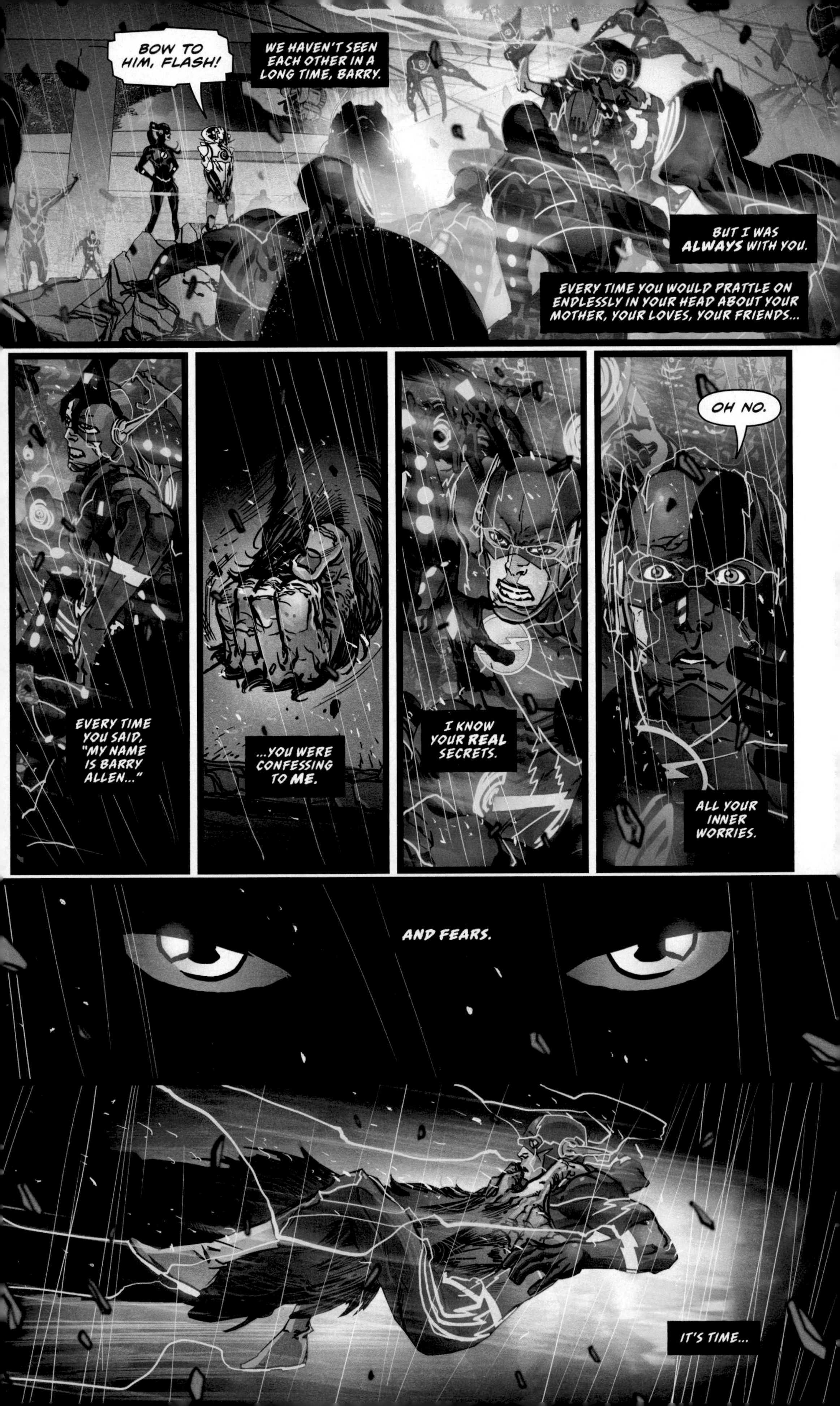
BOW TO HIM, FLASH!
WE HAVEN'T SEEN EACH OTHER IN A LONG TIME, BARRY.
BUT I WAS ALWAYS WITH YOU.
EVERY TIME YOU WOULD PRATTLE ON ENDLESSLY IN YOUR HEAD ABOUT YOUR MOTHER, YOUR LOVES, YOUR FRIENDS...
EVERY TIME YOU SAID, "MY NAME IS BARRY ALLEN..."
...YOU WERE CONFESSING TO ME.
I KNOW YOUR REAL SECRETS.
OH NO.
ALL YOUR INNER WORRIES.
AND FEARS.
IT'S TIME...

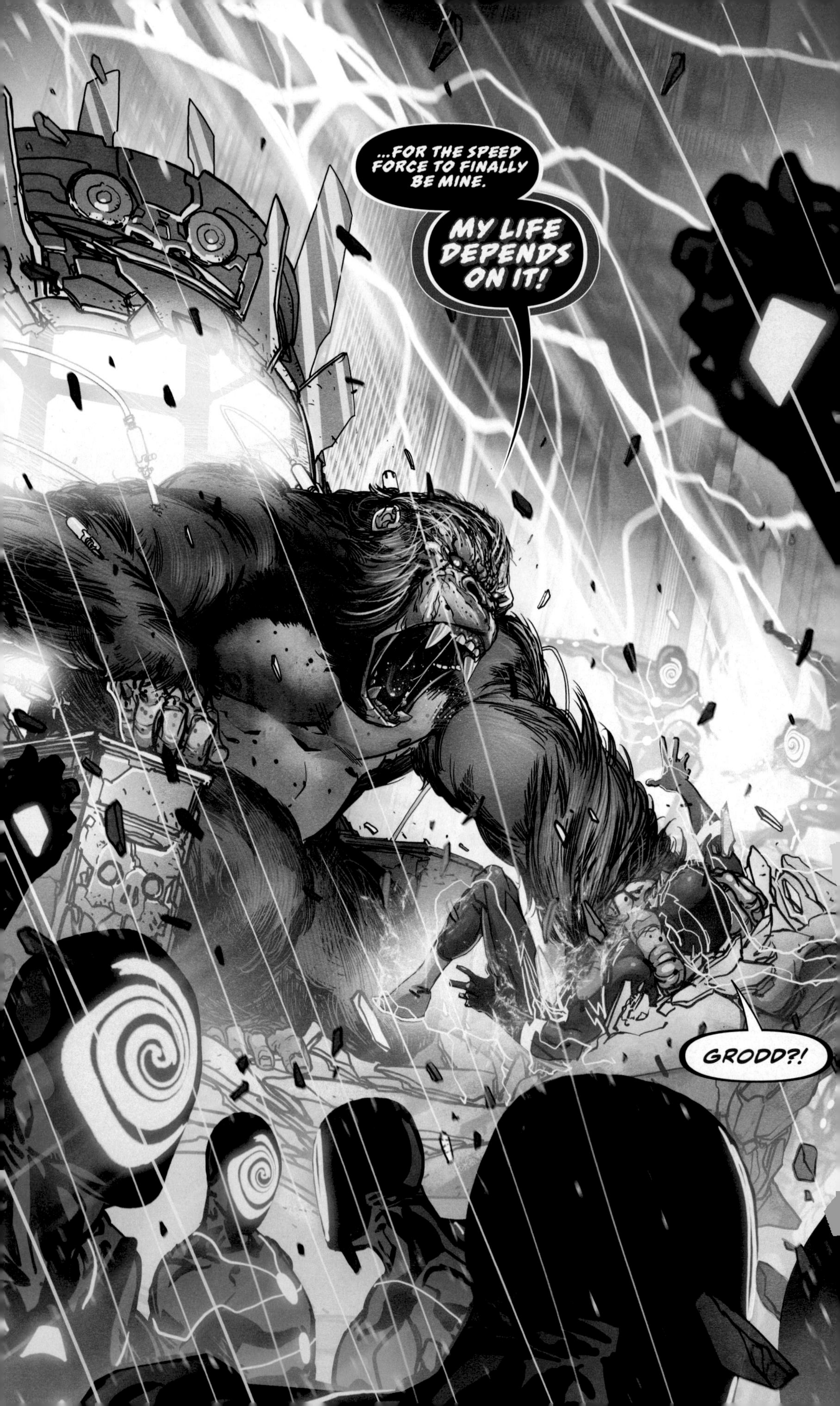
...FOR THE SPEED FORCE TO FINALLY BE MINE.
MY LIFE DEPENDS ON IT!
GRODD?!

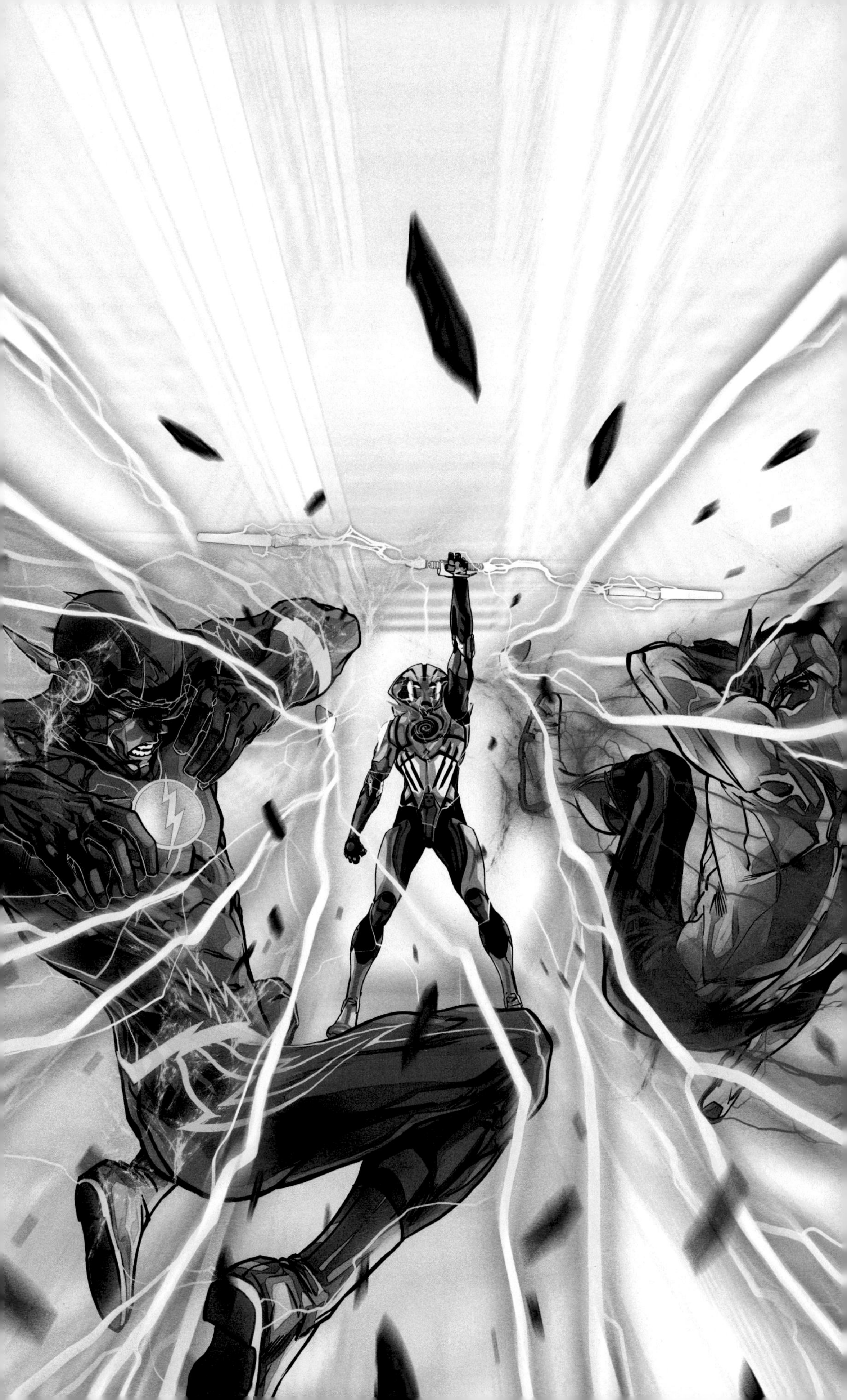

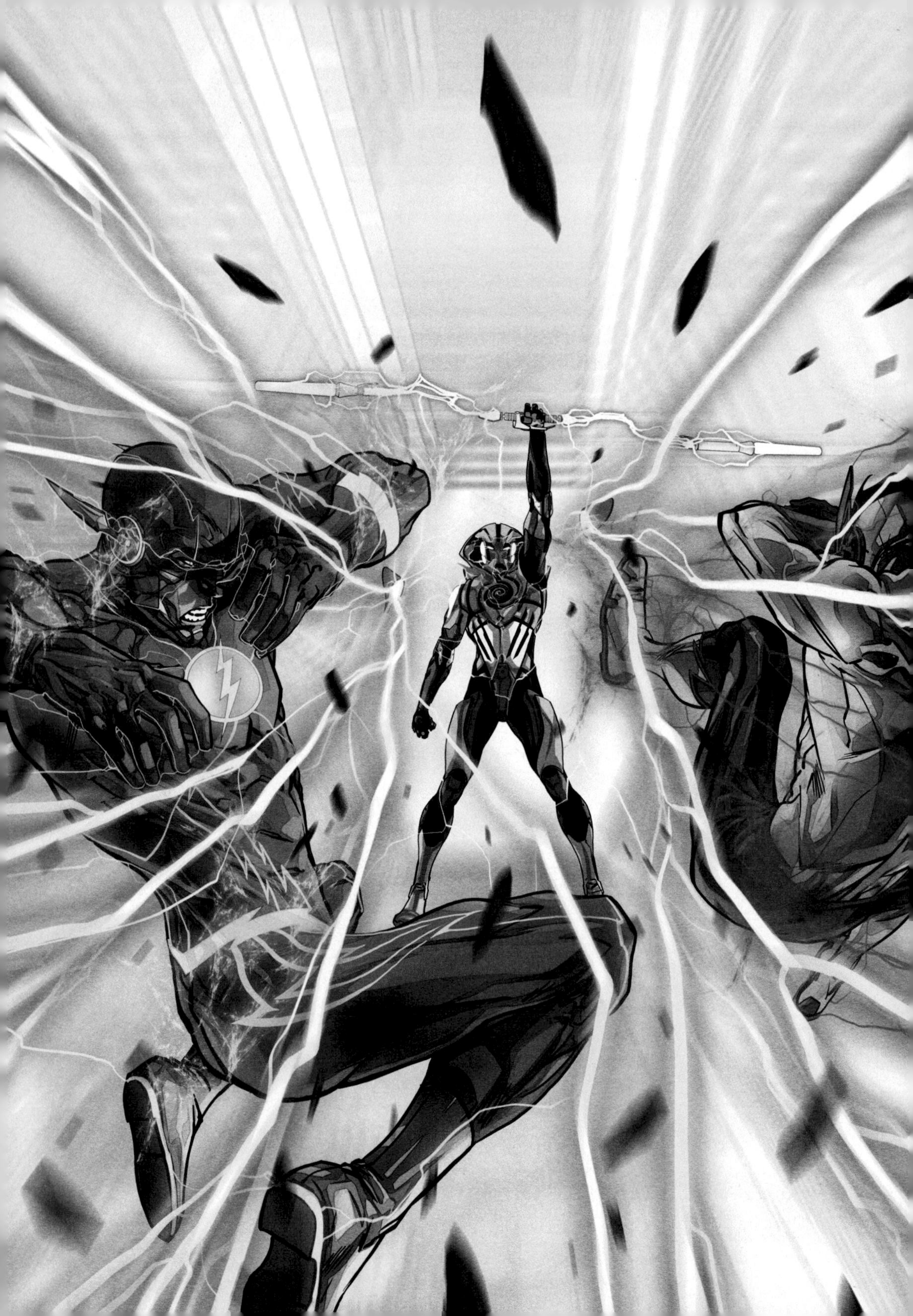

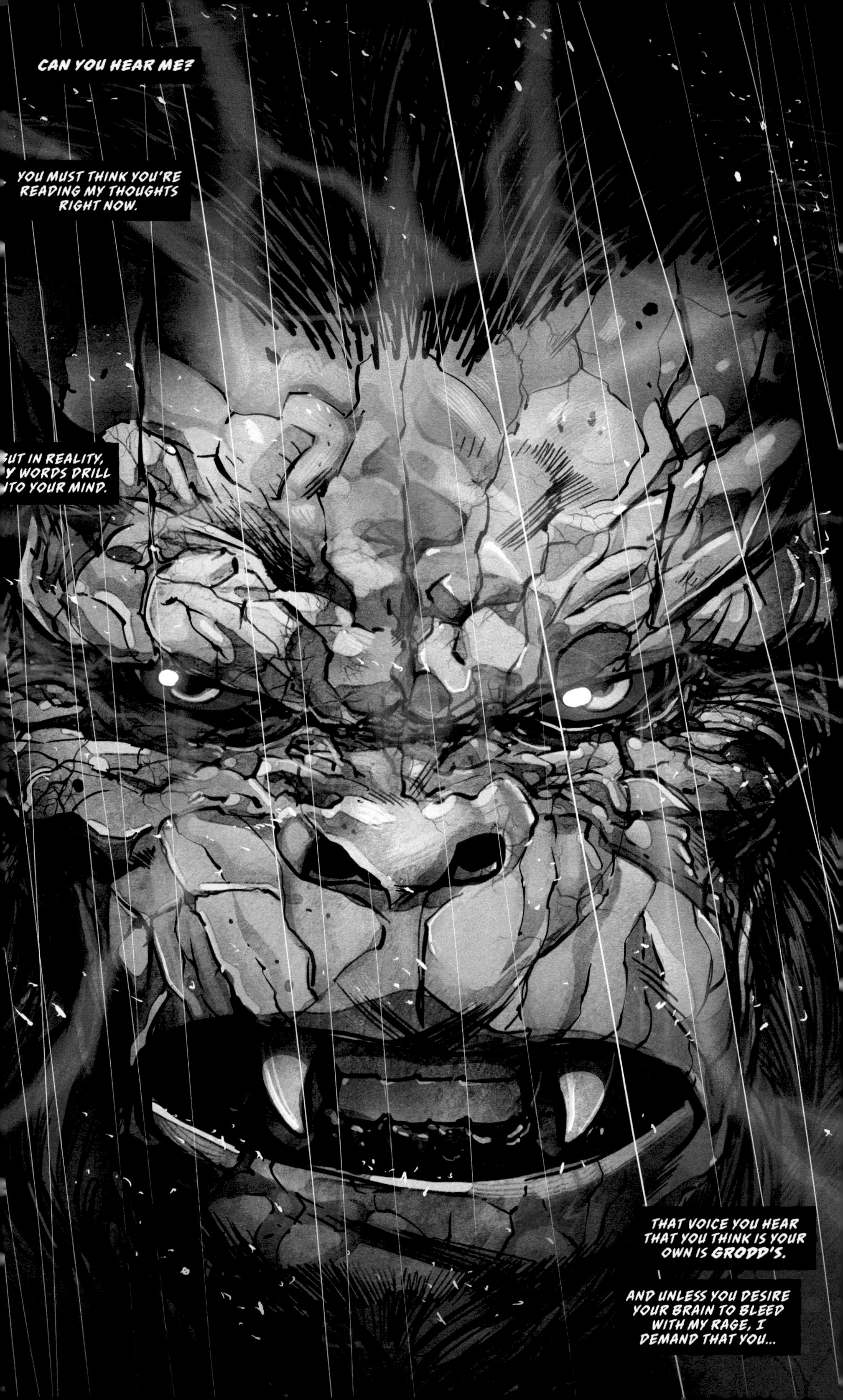
CAN YOU HEAR ME?
YOU MUST THINK YOU'RE READING MY THOUGHTS RIGHT NOW.
UT IN REALITY, Y WORDS DRILL TO YOUR MIND.
THAT VOICE YOU HEAR THAT YOU THINK IS YOUR OWN IS GRODD'S.
AND UNLESS YOU DESIRE YOUR BRAIN TO BLEED WITH MY RAGE, I DEMAND THAT YOU...

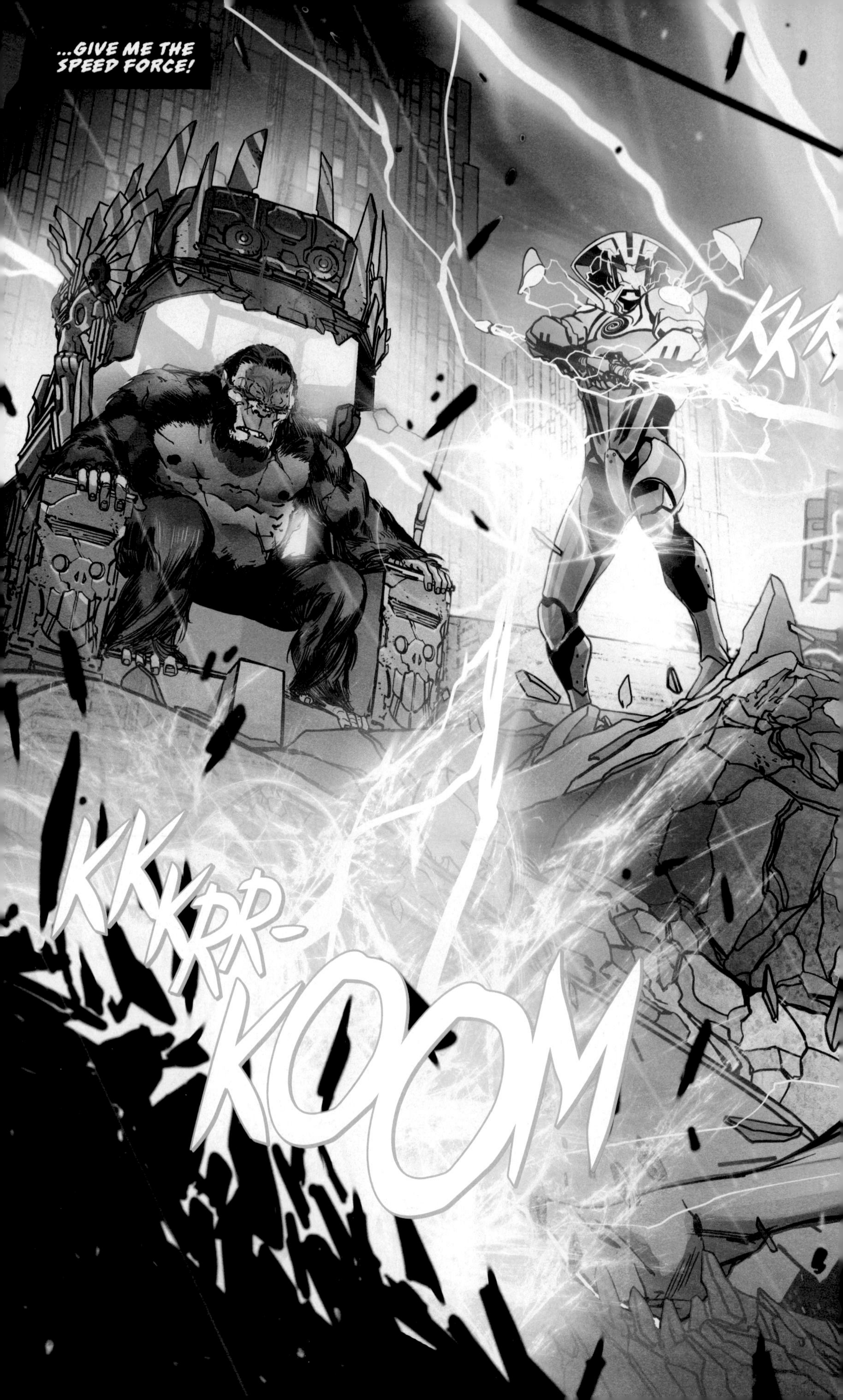
...GIVE ME THE SPEED FORCE!
KKKRR-
KKKRR-KOOM

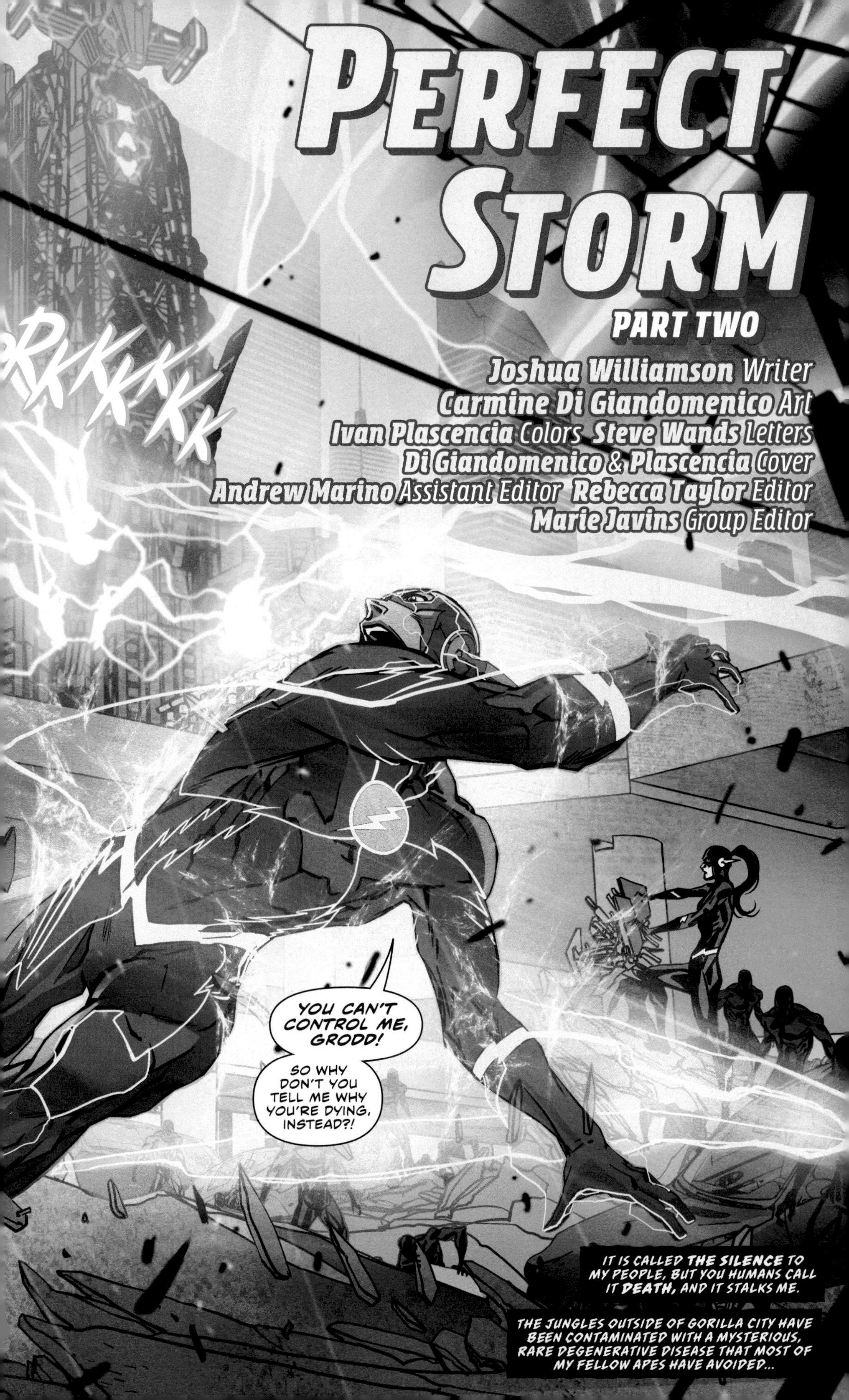
PERFECT STORM
PART TWO
Joshua Williamson Writer
Carmine Di Giandomenico Art
Ivan Plascencia Colors Steve Wands Letters
Di Giandomenico & Plascencia Cover
Andrew Marino Assistant Editor Rebecca Taylor Editor
Marie Javins Group Editor
RKKKKKK
YOU CAN'T CONTROL ME, GRODD!
SO WHY DON'T YOU TELL ME WHY YOU'RE DYING, INSTEAD?!
IT IS CALLED THE SILENCE TO MY PEOPLE, BUT YOU HUMANS CALL IT DEATH, AND IT STALKS ME.
THE JUNGLES OUTSIDE OF GORILLA CITY HAVE BEEN CONTAMINATED WITH A MYSTERIOUS, RARE DEGENERATIVE DISEASE THAT MOST OF MY FELLOW APES HAVE AVOIDED...

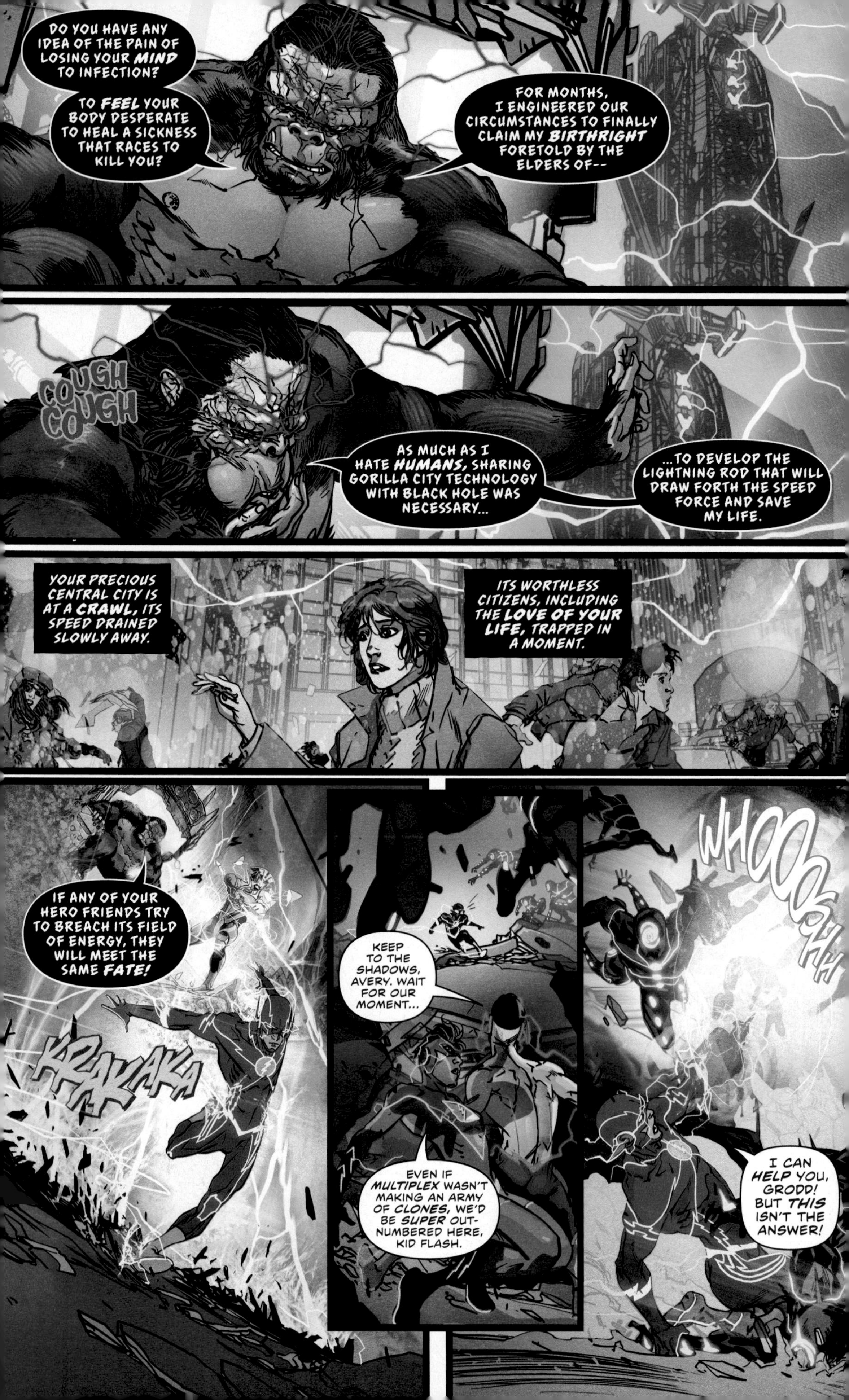
DO YOU HAVE ANY IDEA OF THE PAIN OF LOSING YOUR MIND TO INFECTION?
TO FEEL YOUR BODY DESPERATE TO HEAL A SICKNESS THAT RACES TO KILL YOU?
FOR MONTHS, I ENGINEERED OUR CIRCUMSTANCES TO FINALLY CLAIM MY BIRTHRIGHT FORETOLD BY THE ELDERS OF--
COUGH COUGH
AS MUCH AS I HATE HUMANS, SHARING GORILLA CITY TECHNOLOGY WITH BLACK HOLE WAS NECESSARY...
...TO DEVELOP THE LIGHTNING ROD THAT WILL DRAW FORTH THE SPEED FORCE AND SAVE MY LIFE.
YOUR PRECIOUS CENTRAL CITY IS AT A CRAWL, ITS SPEED DRAINED SLOWLY AWAY.
ITS WORTHLESS CITIZENS, INCLUDING THE LOVE OF YOUR LIFE, TRAPPED IN A MOMENT.
IF ANY OF YOUR HERO FRIENDS TRY TO BREACH ITS FIELD OF ENERGY, THEY WILL MEET THE SAME FATE!
KRAKAKA
KEEP TO THE SHADOWS, AVERY. WAIT FOR OUR MOMENT...
EVEN IF MULTIPLEX WASN'T MAKING AN ARMY OF CLONES, WE'D BE SUPER OUT-NUMBERED HERE, KID FLASH.
WHOOOOSHH
I CAN HELP YOU, GRODD! BUT THIS ISN'T THE ANSWER!

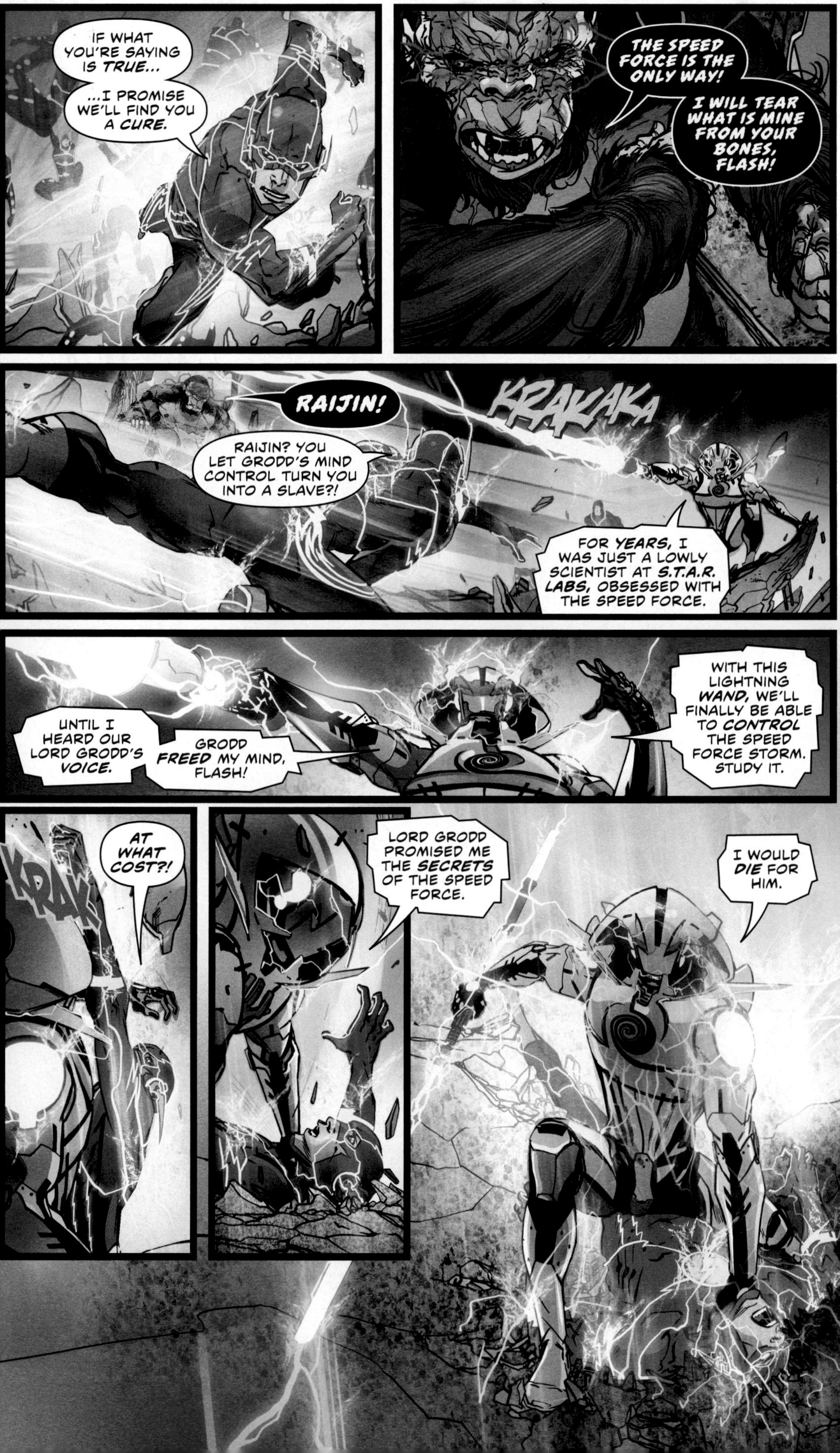

IF WHAT YOU'RE SAYING IS TRUE...
...I PROMISE WE'LL FIND YOU A CURE.
THE SPEED FORCE IS THE ONLY WAY!
I WILL TEAR WHAT IS MINE FROM YOUR BONES, FLASH!
RAIJIN!
KRAKAKA
RAIJIN? YOU LET GRODD'S MIND CONTROL TURN YOU INTO A SLAVE?!
FOR YEARS, I WAS JUST A LOWLY SCIENTIST AT S.T.A.R. LABS, OBSESSED WITH THE SPEED FORCE.
UNTIL I HEARD OUR LORD GRODD'S VOICE.
GRODD FREED MY MIND, FLASH!
WITH THIS LIGHTNING WAND, WE'LL FINALLY BE ABLE TO CONTROL THE SPEED FORCE STORM. STUDY IT.
KRAK
AT WHAT COST?!
LORD GRODD PROMISED ME THE SECRETS OF THE SPEED FORCE.
I WOULD DIE FOR HIM.

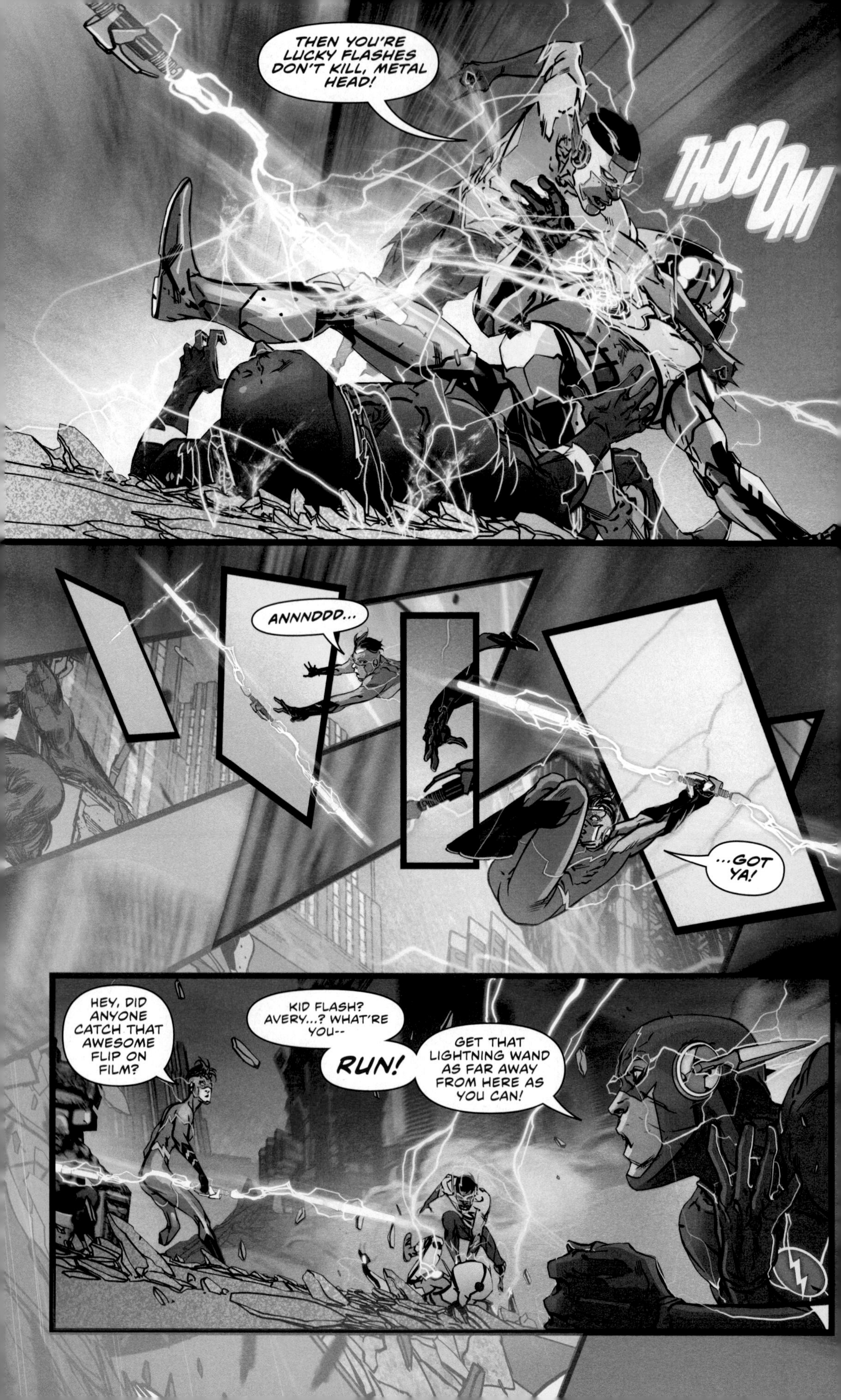
THEN YOU'RE LUCKY FLASHES DON'T KILL, METAL HEAD!
THOOOOM
ANNNDDD...
...GOT YA!
HEY, DID ANYONE CATCH THAT AWESOME FLIP ON FILM?
KID FLASH? AVERY...? WHAT'RE YOU--
RUN!
GET THAT LIGHTNING WAND AS FAR AWAY FROM HERE AS YOU CAN!

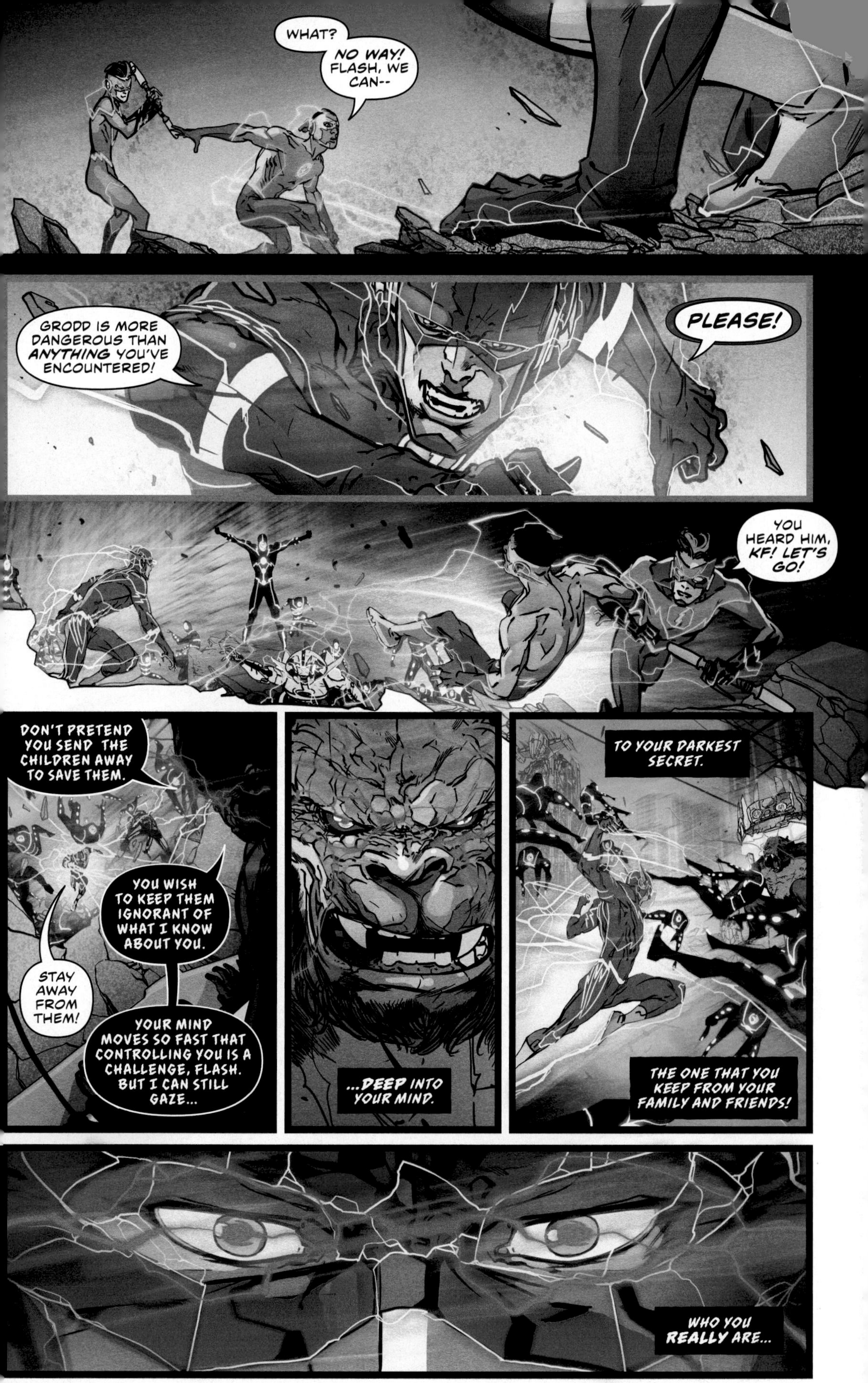
WHAT?
NO WAY! FLASH, WE CAN--
GRODD IS MORE DANGEROUS THAN ANYTHING YOU'VE ENCOUNTERED!
PLEASE!
YOU HEARD HIM, KF! LET'S GO!
DON'T PRETEND YOU SEND THE CHILDREN AWAY TO SAVE THEM.
YOU WISH TO KEEP THEM IGNORANT OF WHAT I KNOW ABOUT YOU.
STAY AWAY FROM THEM!
YOUR MIND MOVES SO FAST THAT CONTROLLING YOU IS A CHALLENGE, FLASH. BUT I CAN STILL GAZE...
...DEEP INTO YOUR MIND.
TO YOUR DARKEST SECRET.
THE ONE THAT YOU KEEP FROM YOUR FAMILY AND FRIENDS!
WHO YOU REALLY ARE...

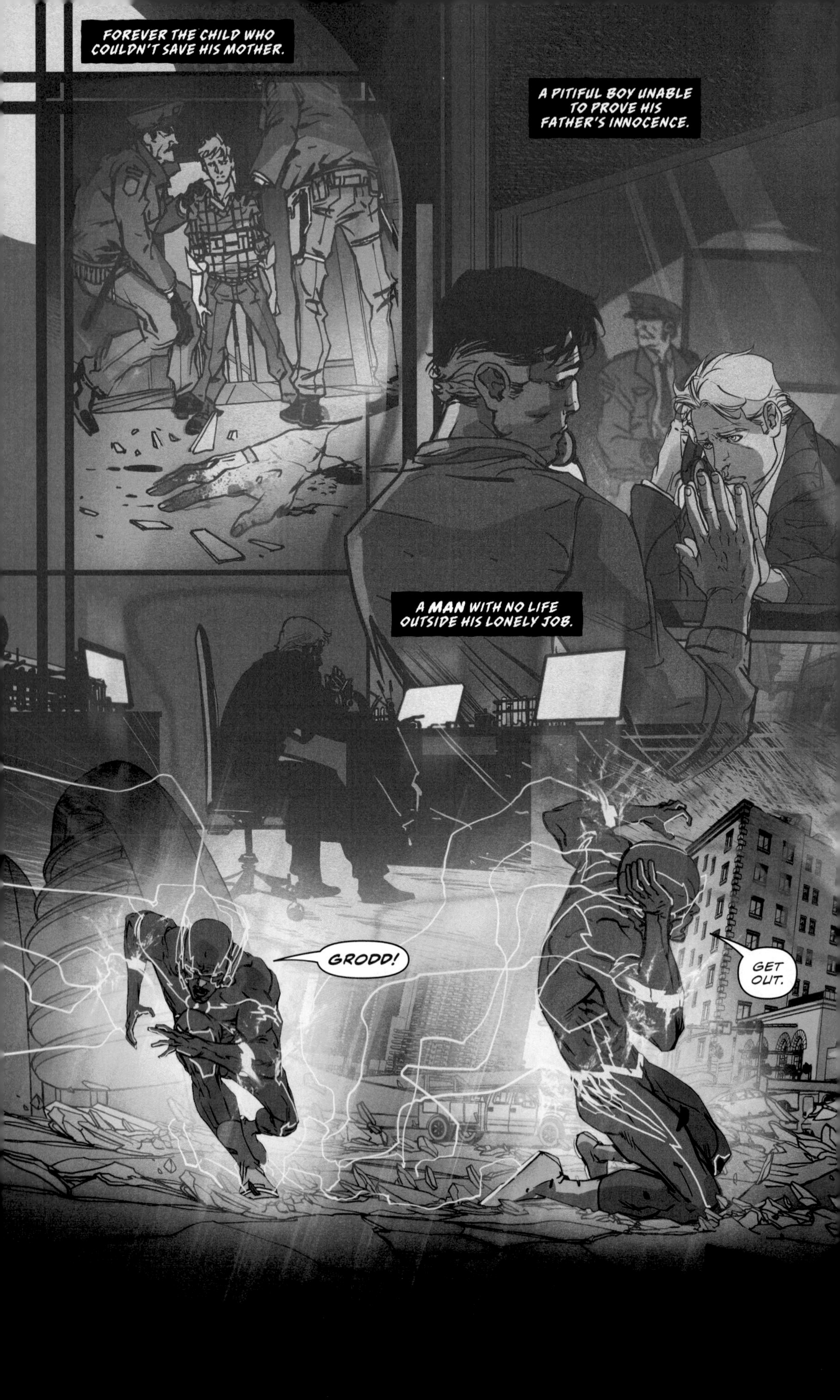
FOREVER THE CHILD WHO COULDN'T SAVE HIS MOTHER.
A PITIFUL BOY UNABLE TO PROVE HIS FATHER'S INNOCENCE.
A MAN WITH NO LIFE OUTSIDE HIS LONELY JOB.
GRODD!
GET OUT.

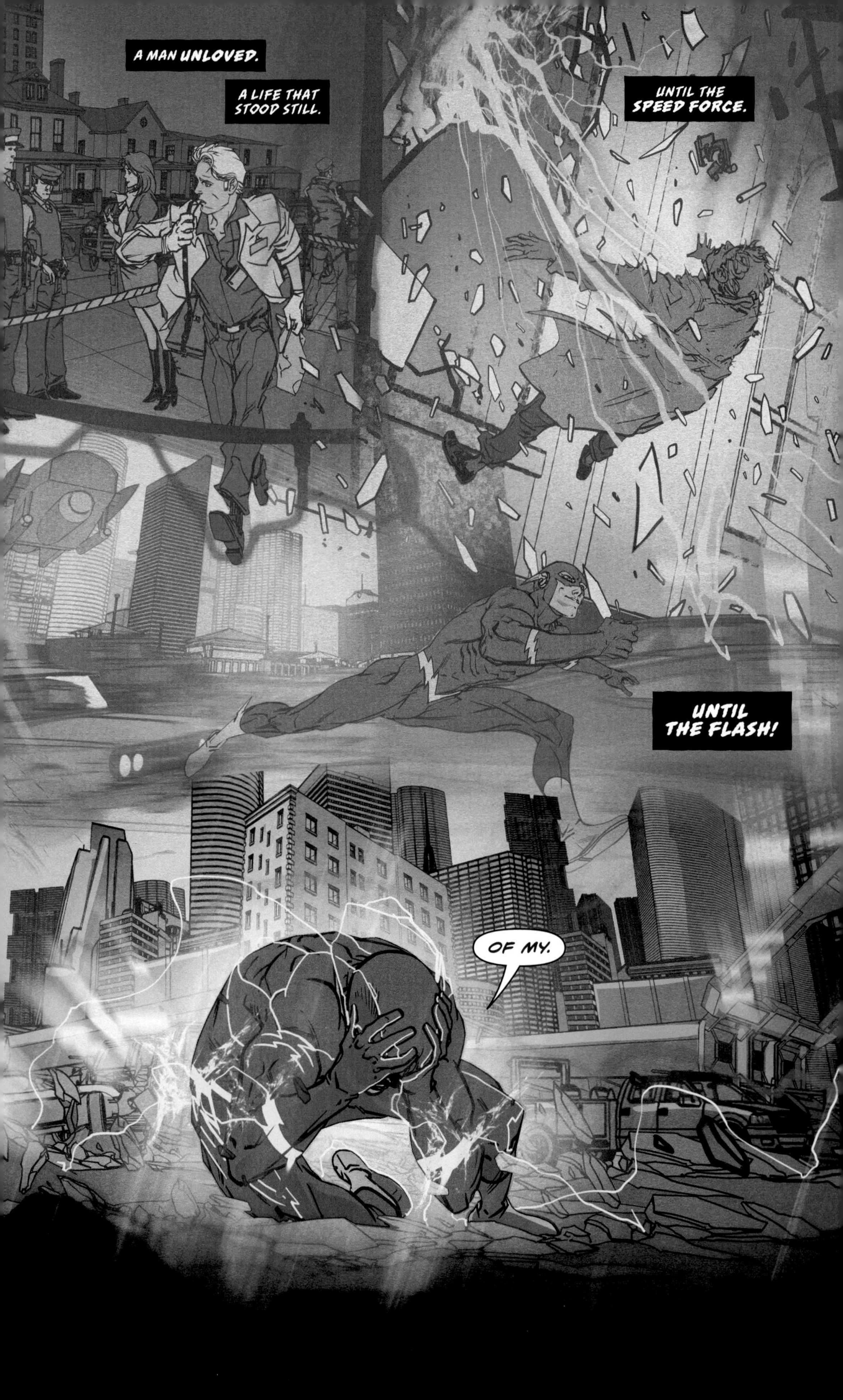
A MAN UNLOVED.
A LIFE THAT STOOD STILL.
UNTIL THE SPEED FORCE.
UNTIL THE FLASH!
OF MY.

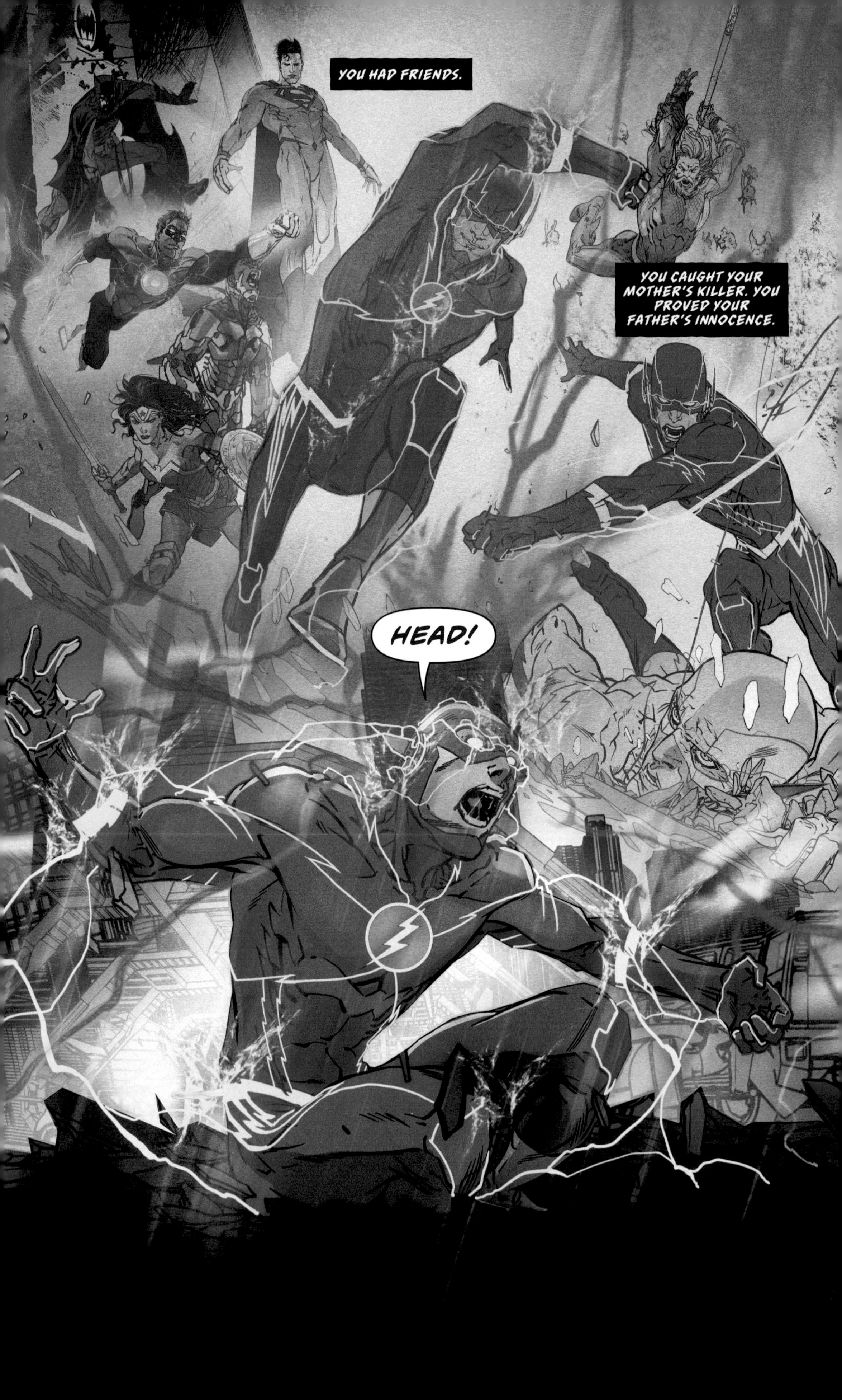
YOU HAD FRIENDS.
YOU CAUGHT YOUR MOTHER'S KILLER. YOU PROVED YOUR FATHER'S INNOCENCE.
HEAD!

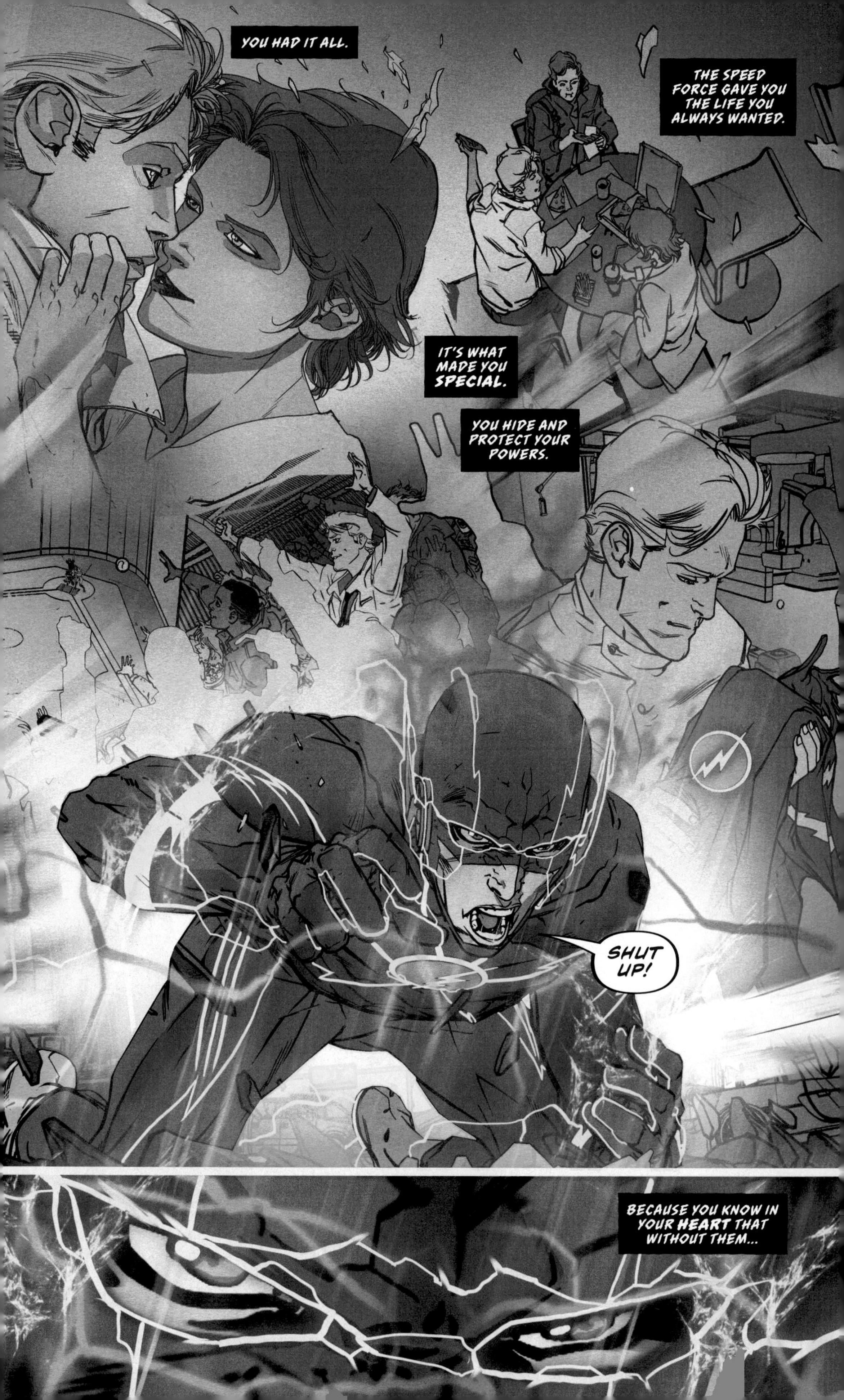
YOU HAD IT ALL.
THE SPEED FORCE GAVE YOU THE LIFE YOU ALWAYS WANTED.
IT'S WHAT MADE YOU SPECIAL.
YOU HIDE AND PROTECT YOUR POWERS.
SHUT UP!
BECAUSE YOU KNOW IN YOUR HEART THAT WITHOUT THEM...

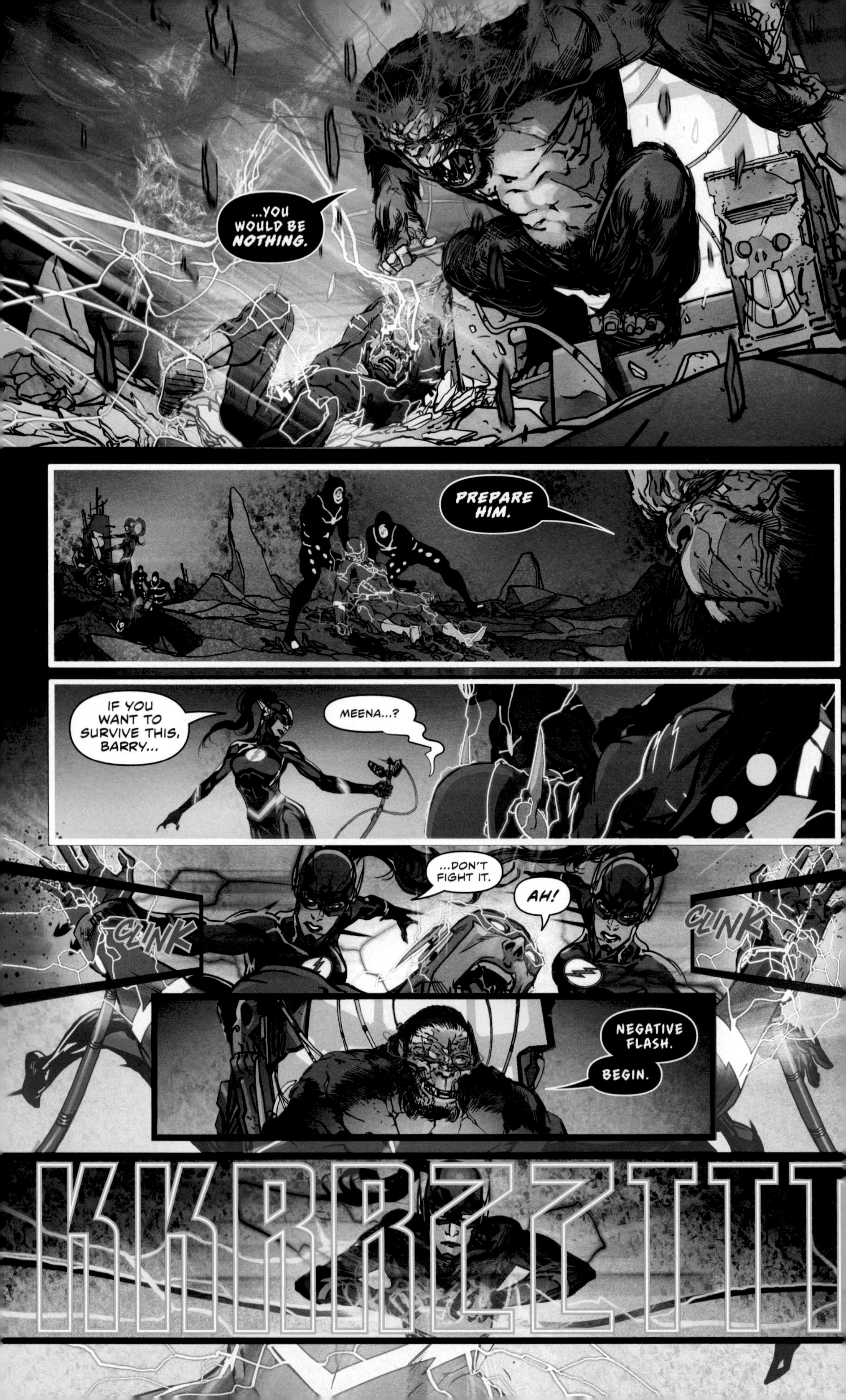
...YOU WOULD BE NOTHING.
PREPARE HIM.
IF YOU WANT TO SURVIVE THIS, BARRY...
MEENA...?
...DON'T FIGHT IT.
AH!
CLINK
CLINK
NEGATIVE FLASH.
BEGIN.
KKRRZZTTT

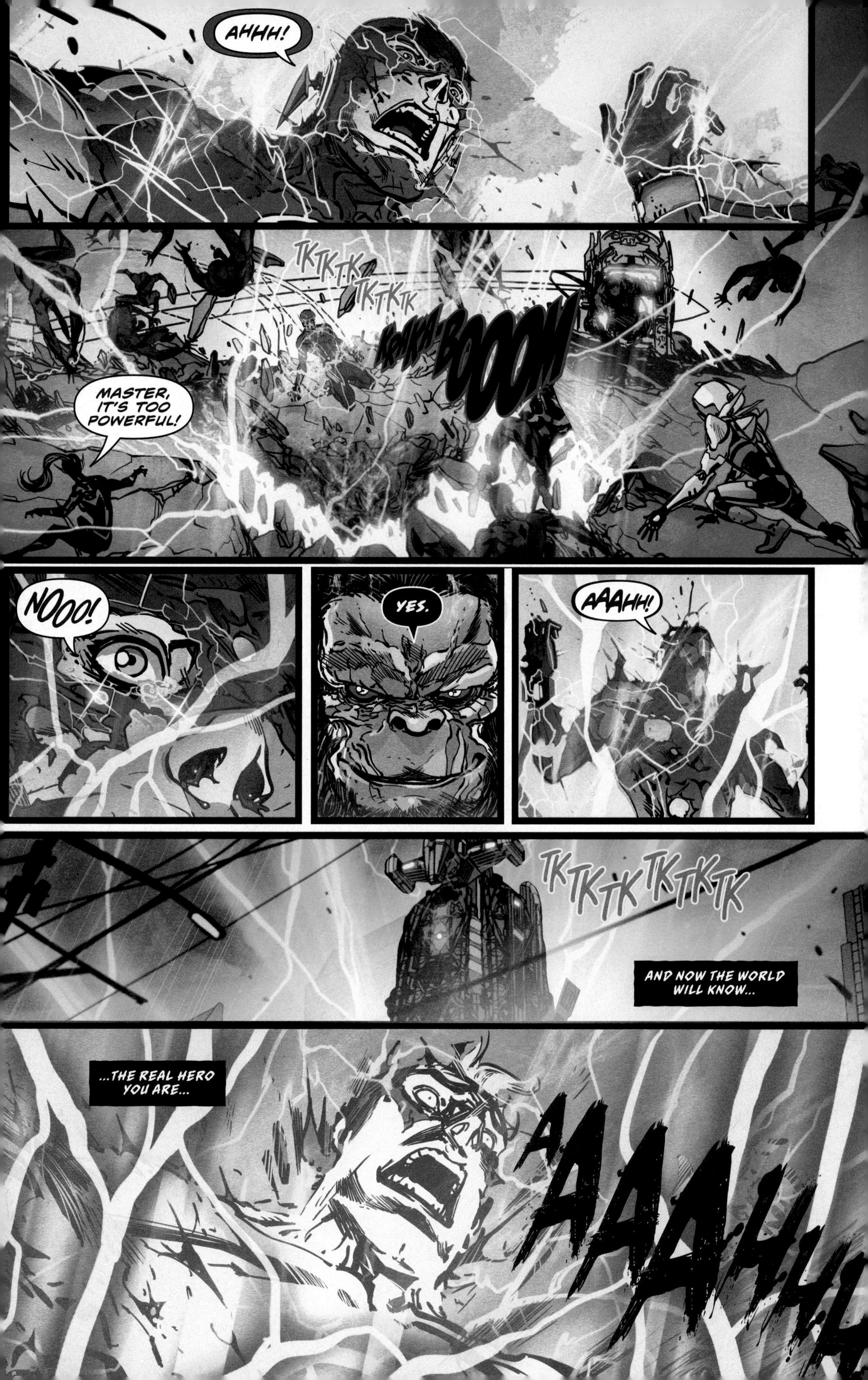
AHHH!
TKTKTK TKTKTK
KRAKH-BOOOM
MASTER, IT'S TOO POWERFUL!
NOOO!
YES.
AAAHH!
TKTKTK TKTKTK
AND NOW THE WORLD WILL KNOW...
...THE REAL HERO YOU ARE...
AAAAHH

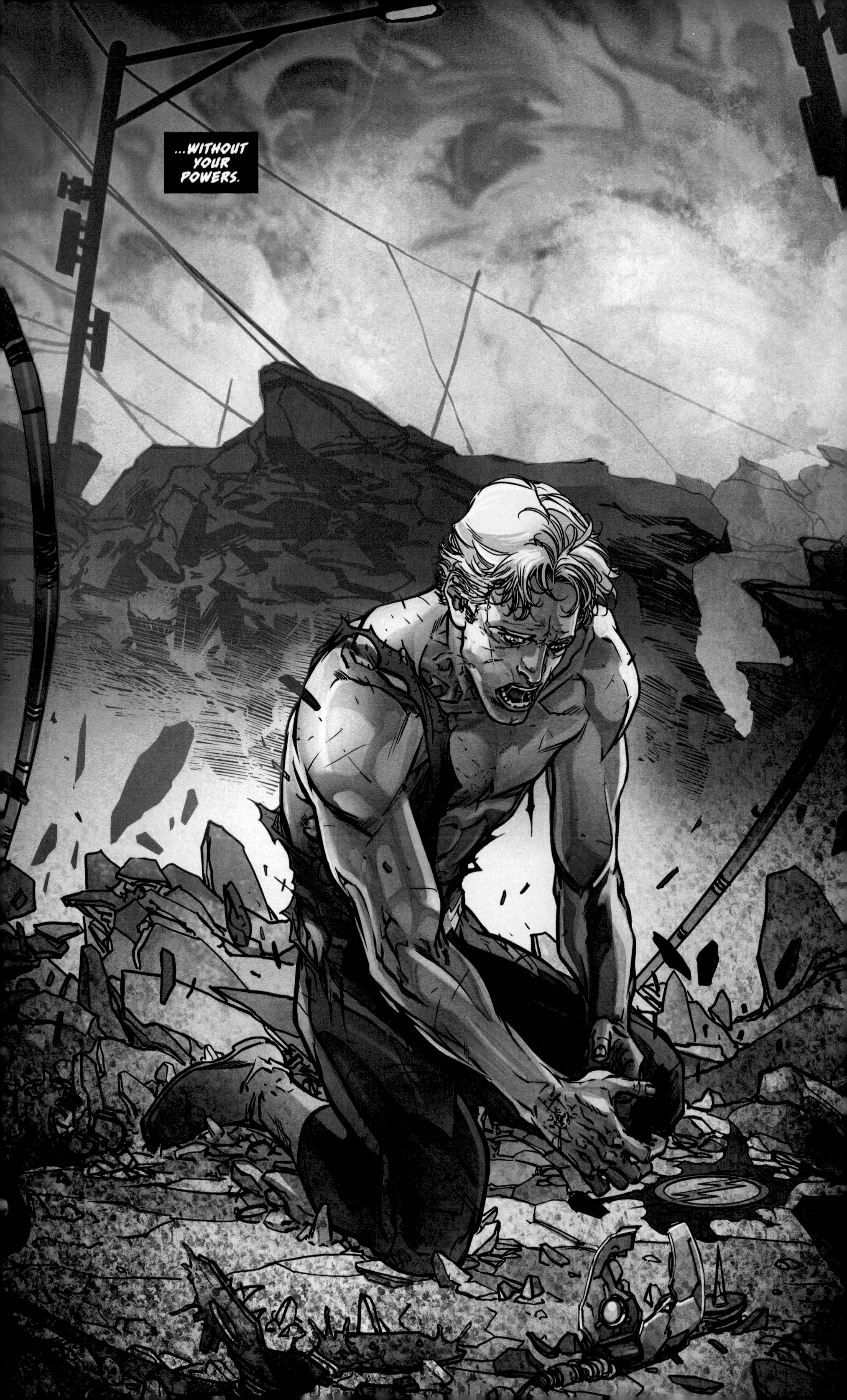
...WITHOUT YOUR POWERS.

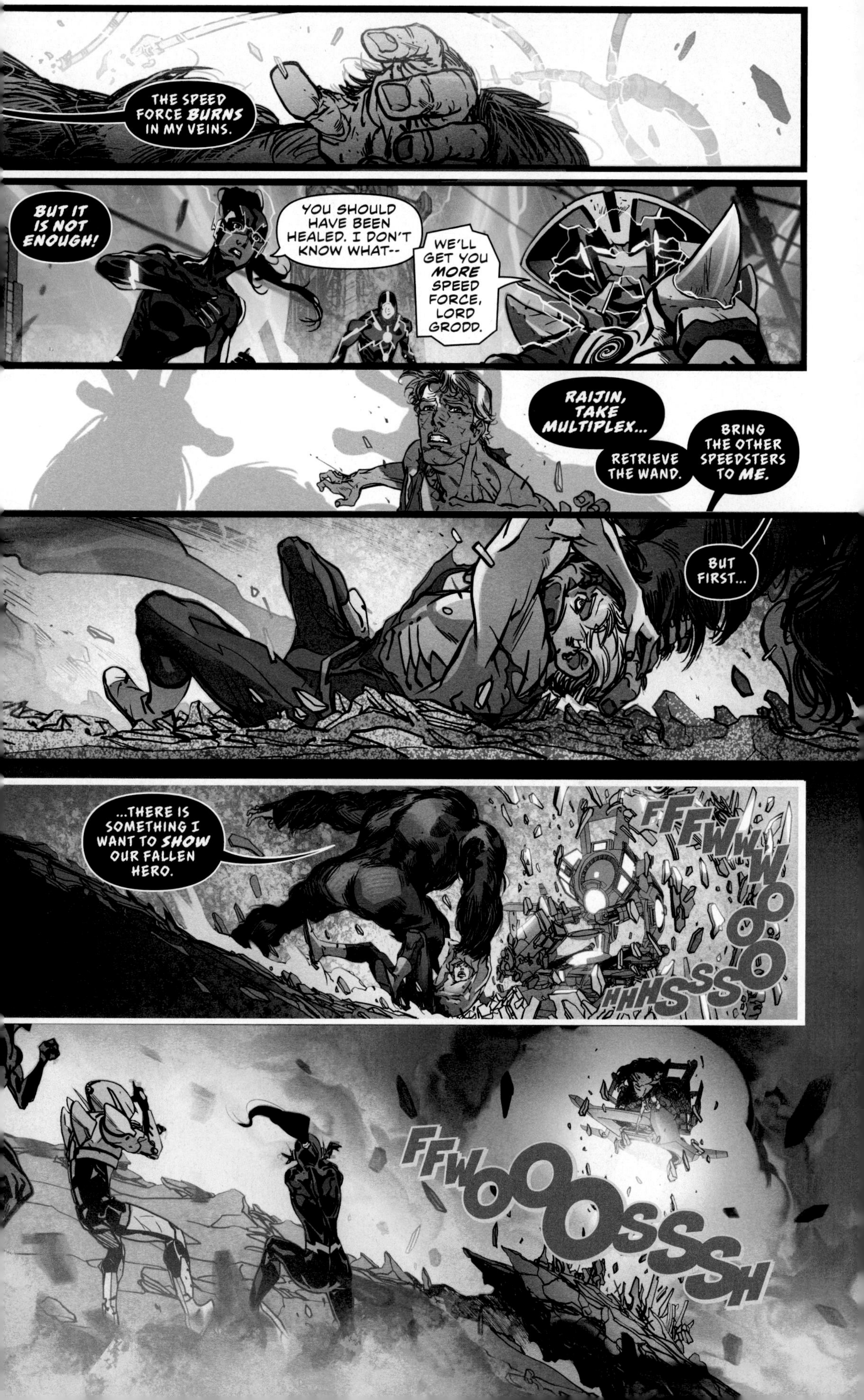
THE SPEED FORCE BURNS IN MY VEINS.
BUT IT IS NOT ENOUGH!
YOU SHOULD HAVE BEEN HEALED. I DON'T KNOW WHAT--
WE'LL GET YOU MORE SPEED FORCE, LORD GRODD.
RAIJIN, TAKE MULTIPLEX...
RETRIEVE THE WAND.
BRING THE OTHER SPEEDSTERS TO ME.
BUT FIRST...
...THERE IS SOMETHING I WANT TO SHOW OUR FALLEN HERO.
FFFWWWWOOOOHHHSSSS
FFWOOOOSSSSH

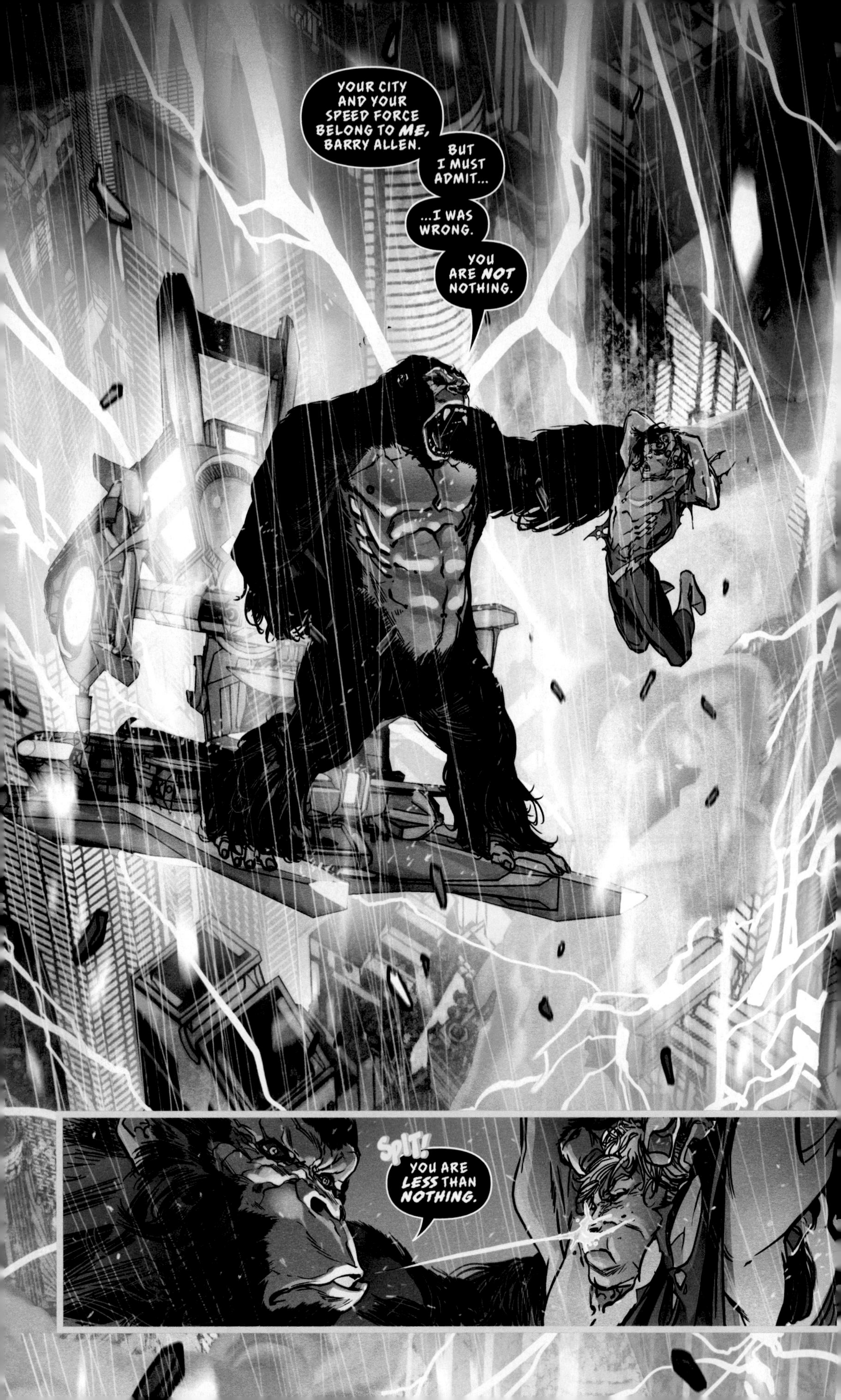
YOUR CITY AND YOUR SPEED FORCE BELONG TO *ME*, BARRY ALLEN.
BUT I MUST ADMIT...
...I WAS WRONG.
YOU ARE *NOT* NOTHING.
SPIT!
YOU ARE *LESS* THAN *NOTHING*.

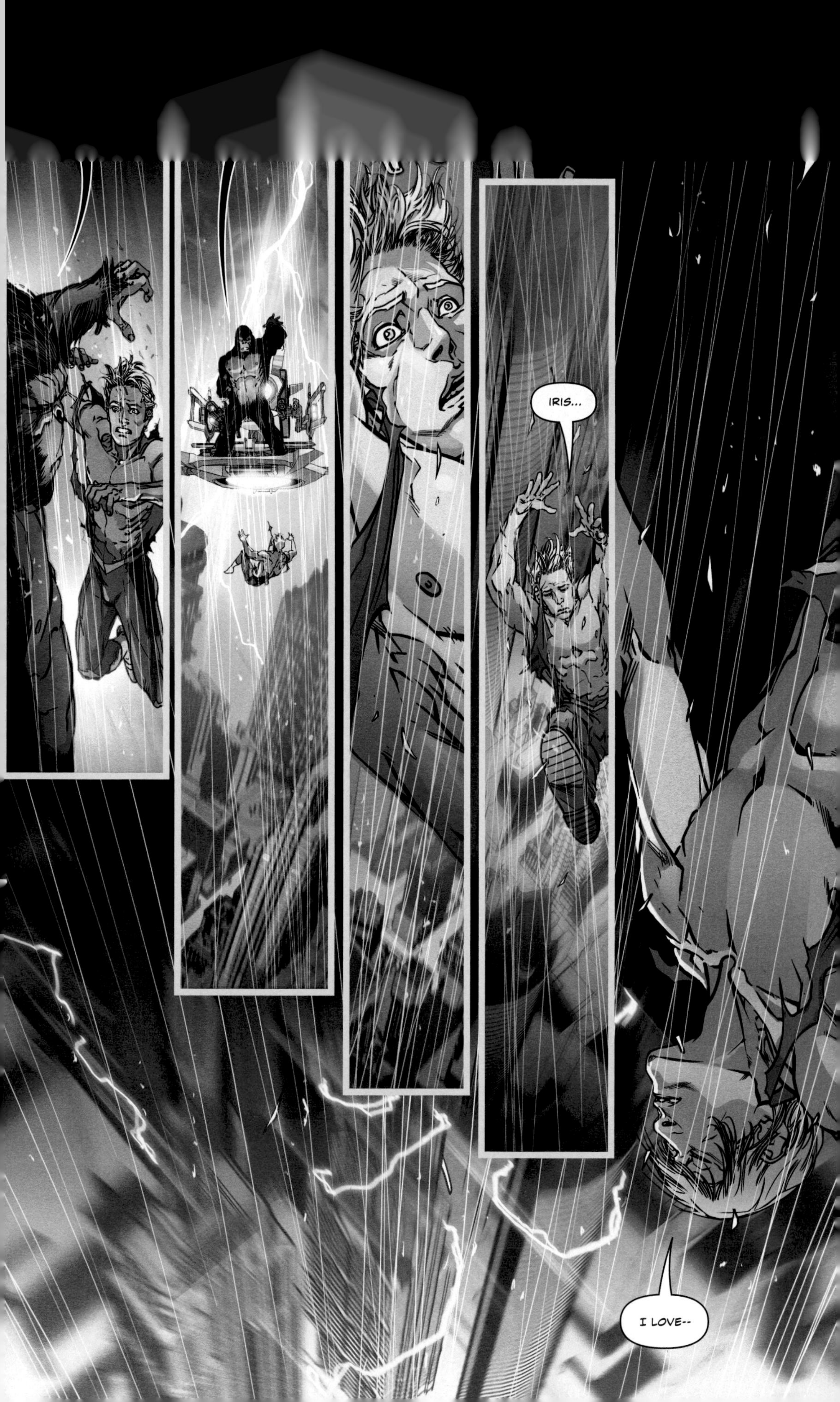
IRIS...
I LOVE--

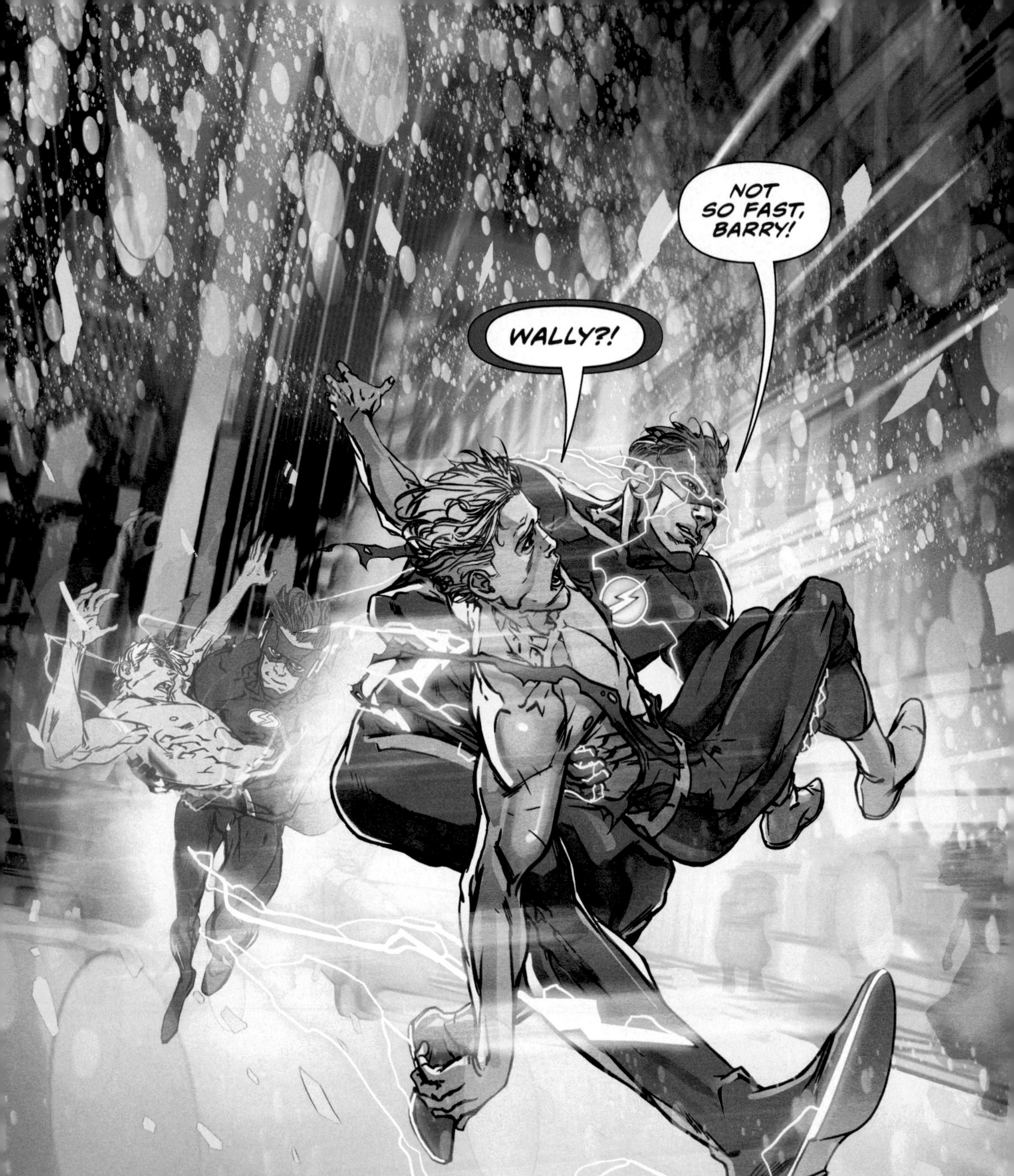
NOT SO FAST, BARRY!
WALLY?!

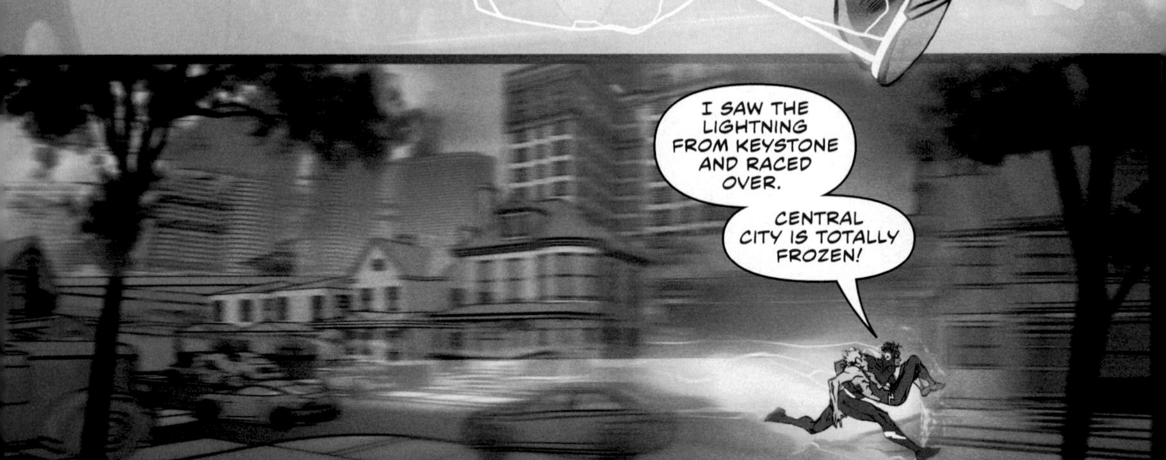
I SAW THE LIGHTNING FROM KEYSTONE AND RACED OVER.
CENTRAL CITY IS TOTALLY FROZEN!

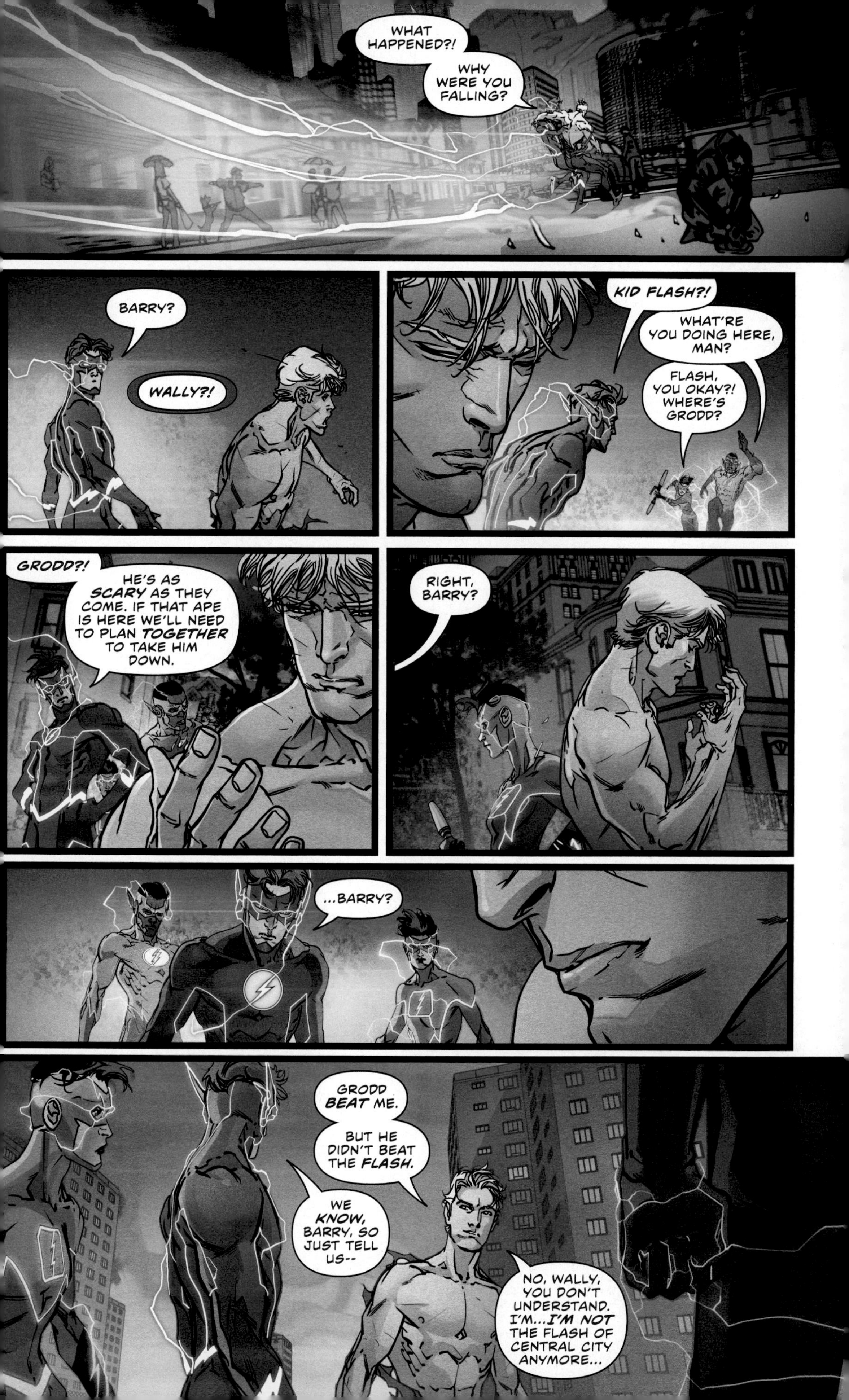
WHAT HAPPENED?!
WHY WERE YOU FALLING?
BARRY?
WALLY?!
KID FLASH?!
WHAT'RE YOU DOING HERE, MAN?
FLASH, YOU OKAY?! WHERE'S GRODD?
GRODD?!
HE'S AS SCARY AS THEY COME. IF THAT APE IS HERE WE'LL NEED TO PLAN TOGETHER TO TAKE HIM DOWN.
RIGHT, BARRY?
...BARRY?
GRODD BEAT ME.
BUT HE DIDN'T BEAT THE FLASH.
WE KNOW, BARRY, SO JUST TELL US--
NO, WALLY, YOU DON'T UNDERSTAND. I'M...I'M NOT THE FLASH OF CENTRAL CITY ANYMORE...

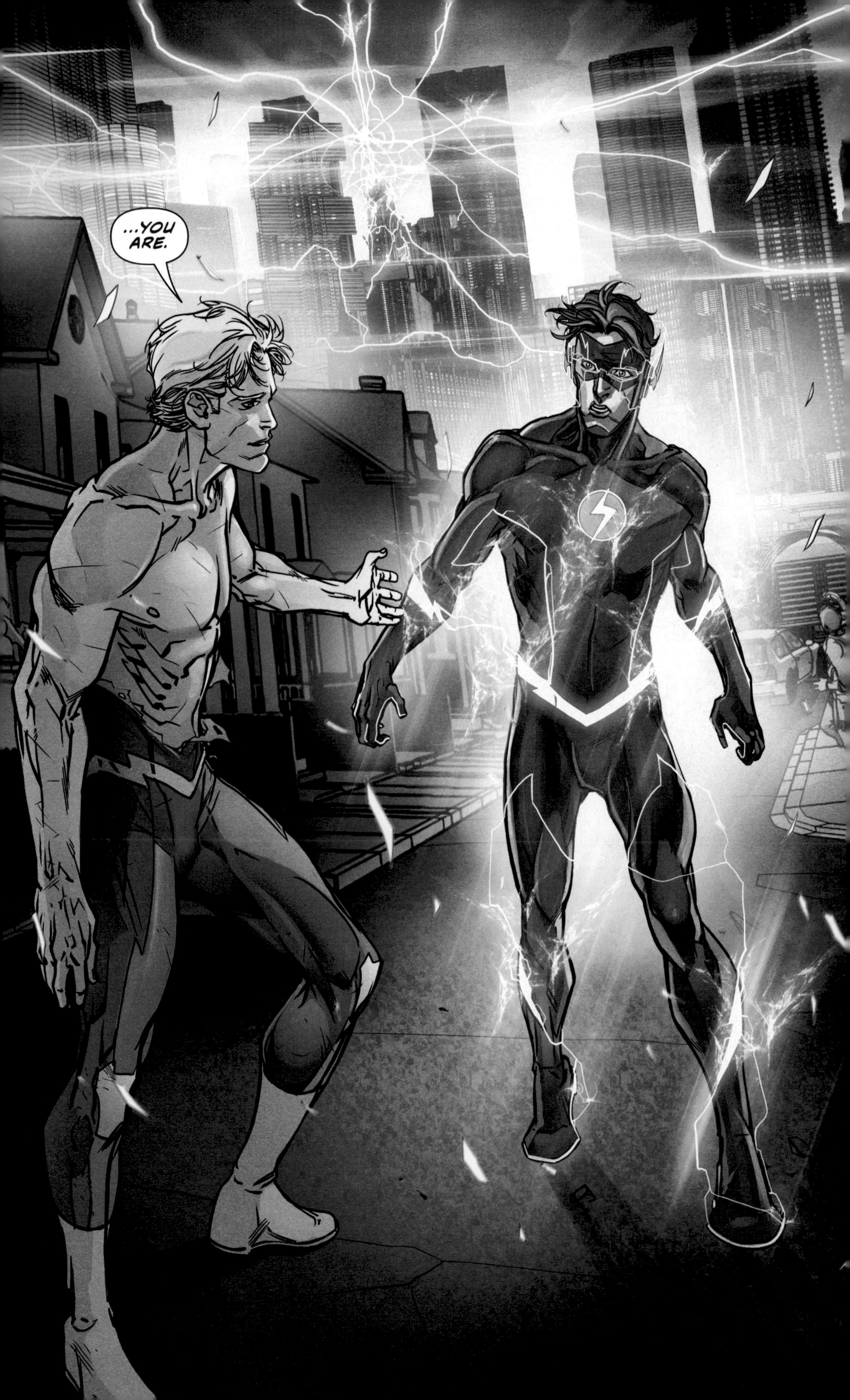
...YOU ARE.

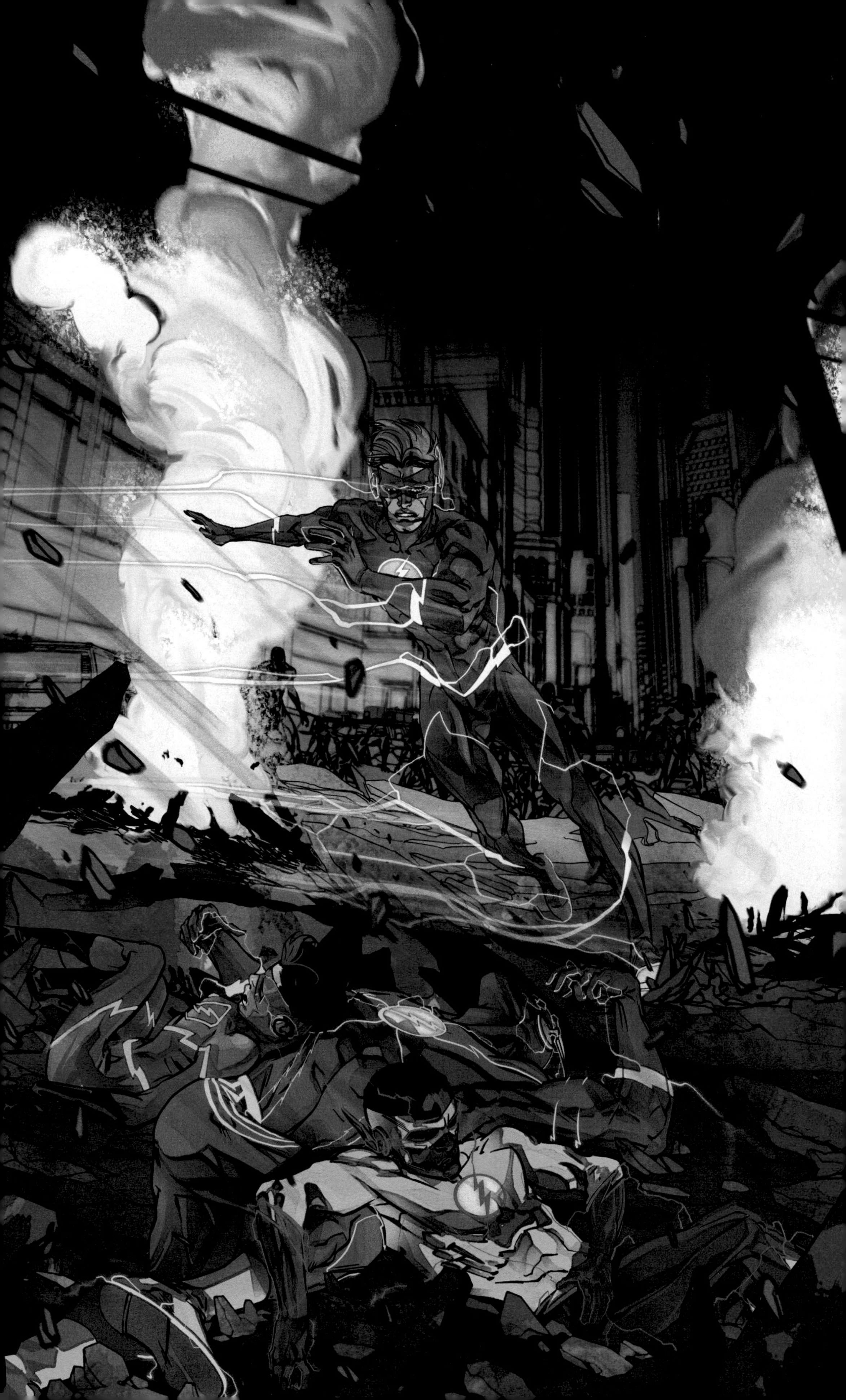

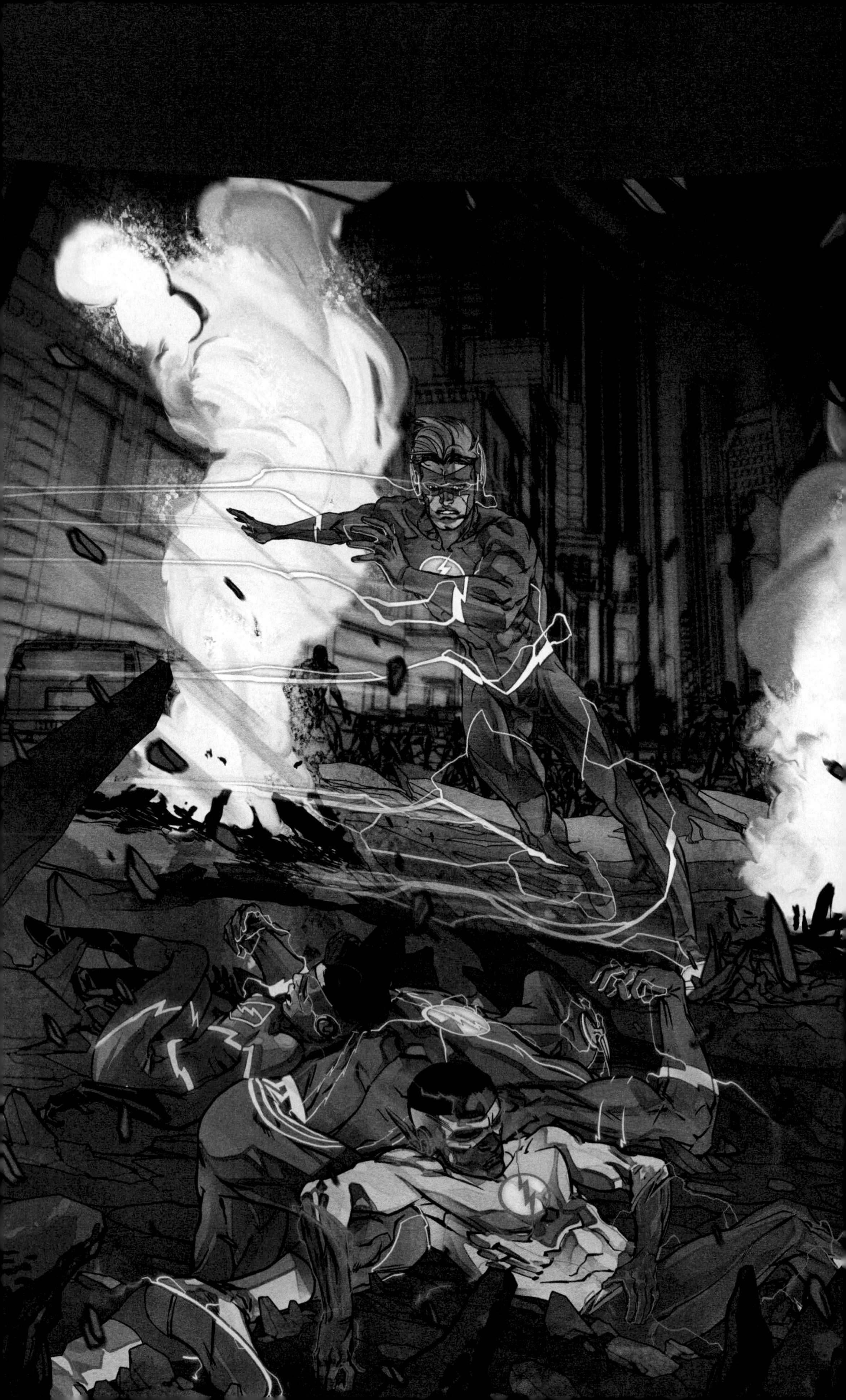

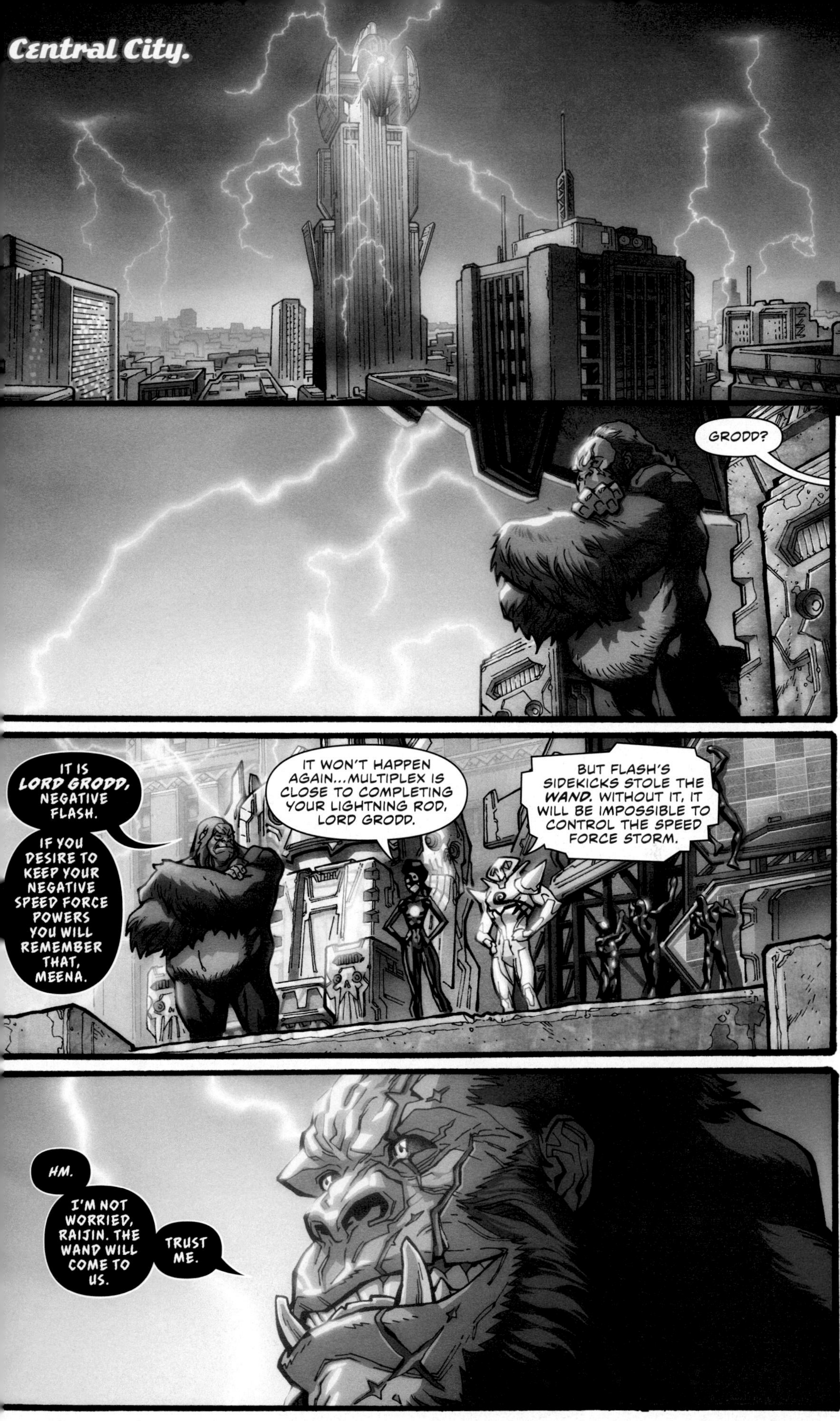
Central City.
GRODD?
IT IS LORD GRODD, NEGATIVE FLASH.
IF YOU DESIRE TO KEEP YOUR NEGATIVE SPEED FORCE POWERS YOU WILL REMEMBER THAT, MEENA.
IT WON'T HAPPEN AGAIN...MULTIPLEX IS CLOSE TO COMPLETING YOUR LIGHTNING ROD, LORD GRODD.
BUT FLASH'S SIDEKICKS STOLE THE WAND. WITHOUT IT, IT WILL BE IMPOSSIBLE TO CONTROL THE SPEED FORCE STORM.
HM.
I'M NOT WORRIED, RAIJIN. THE WAND WILL COME TO US.
TRUST ME.

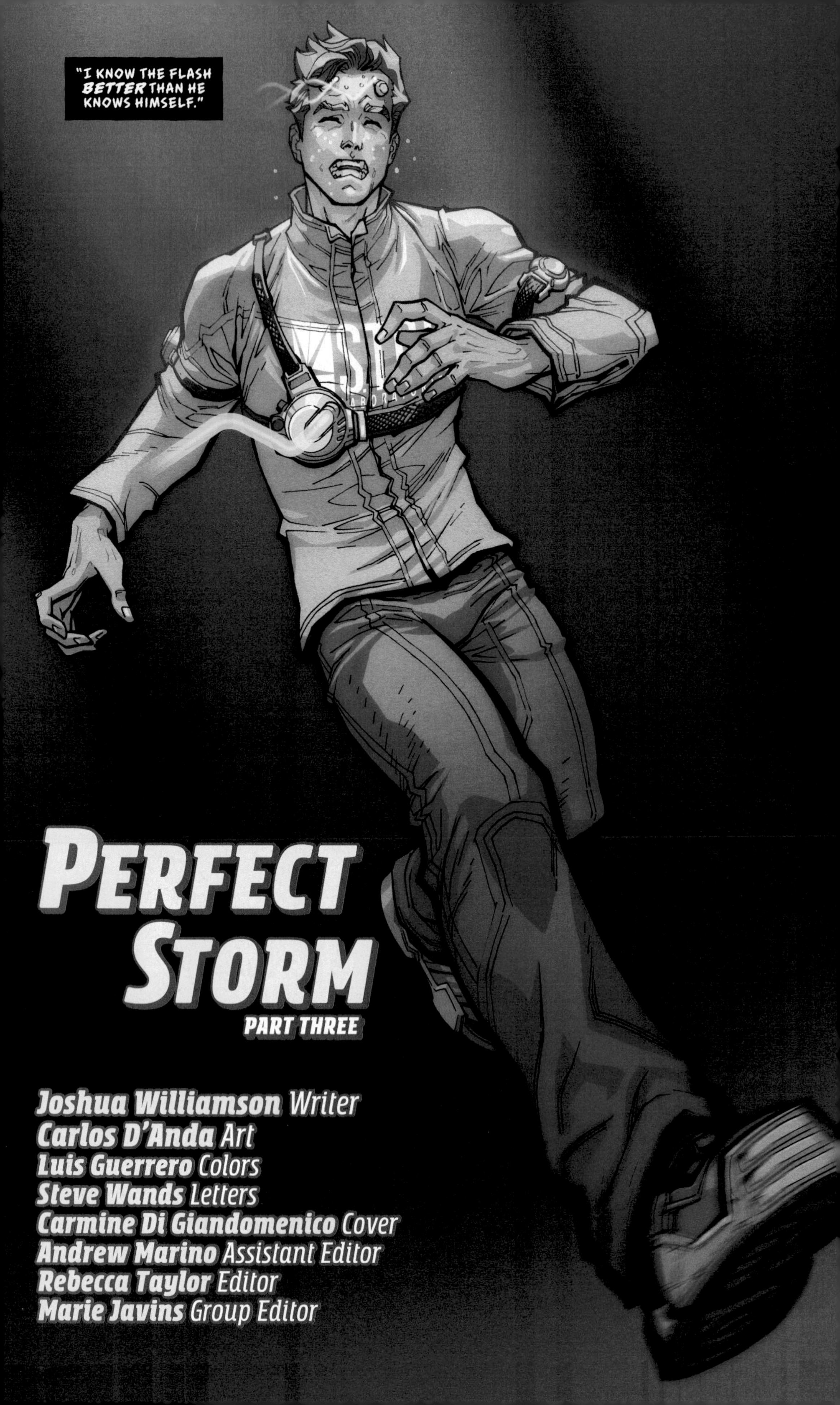
"I KNOW THE FLASH BETTER THAN HE KNOWS HIMSELF."

PERFECT STORM

PART THREE

Joshua Williamson Writer
Carlos D'Anda Art
Luis Guerrero Colors
Steve Wands Letters
Carmine Di Giandomenico Cover
Andrew Marino Assistant Editor
Rebecca Taylor Editor
Marie Javins Group Editor

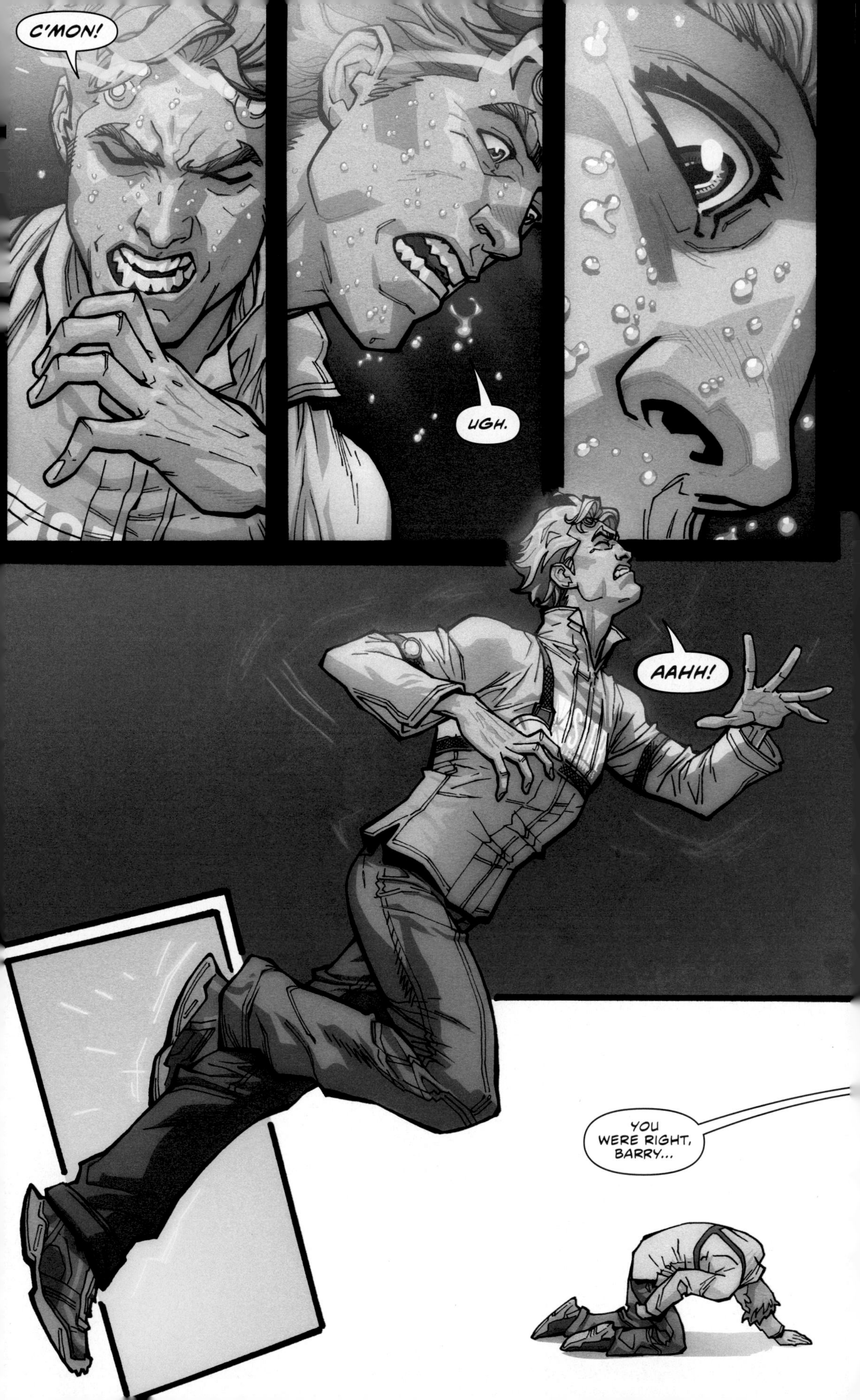
C'MON!
UGH.
AAHH!
YOU WERE RIGHT, BARRY...

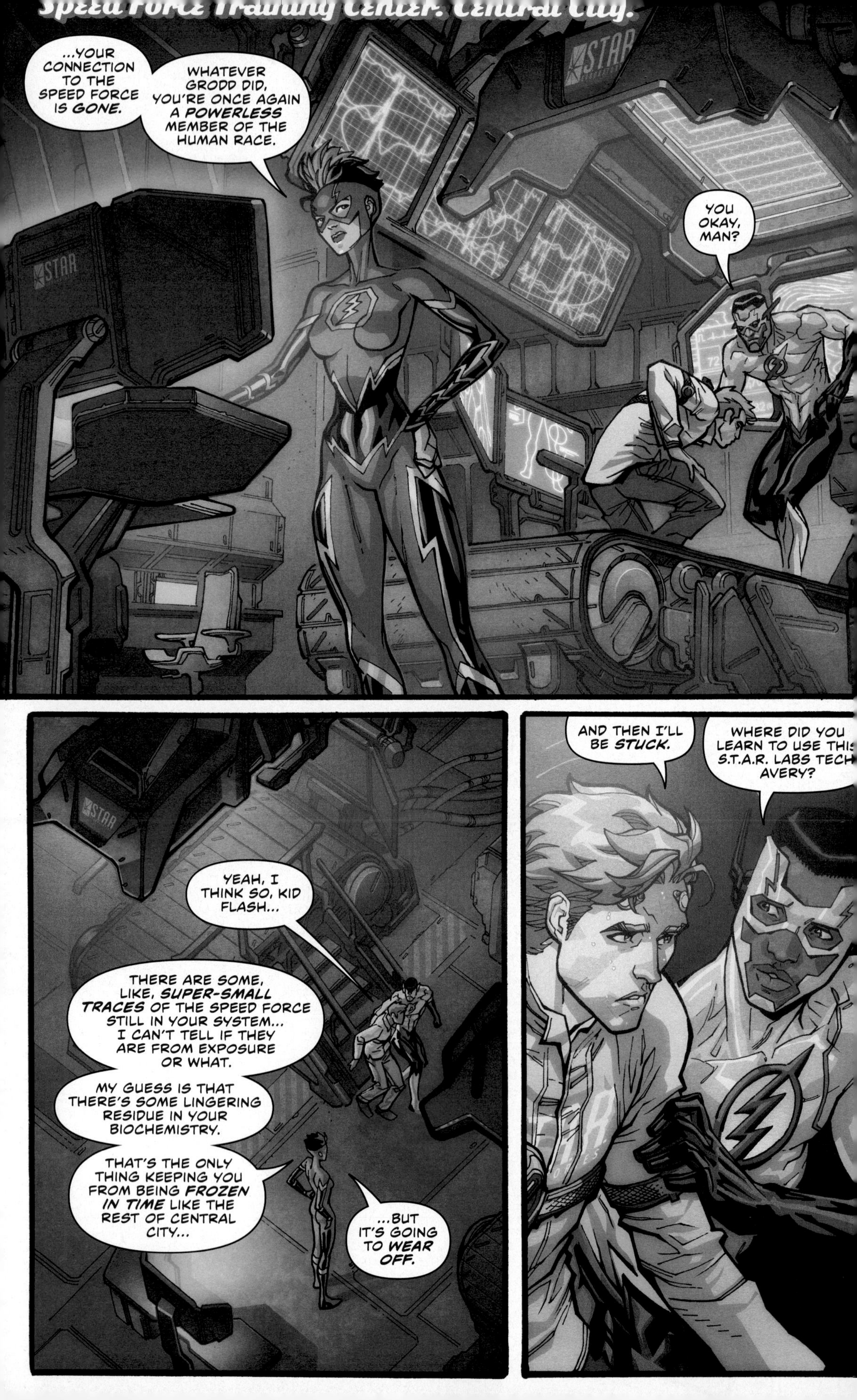
Speed Force Training Center. Central City.
...YOUR CONNECTION TO THE SPEED FORCE IS GONE.
WHATEVER GRODD DID, YOU'RE ONCE AGAIN A POWERLESS MEMBER OF THE HUMAN RACE.
YOU OKAY, MAN?
YEAH, I THINK SO, KID FLASH...
THERE ARE SOME, LIKE, SUPER-SMALL TRACES OF THE SPEED FORCE STILL IN YOUR SYSTEM... I CAN'T TELL IF THEY ARE FROM EXPOSURE OR WHAT.
MY GUESS IS THAT THERE'S SOME LINGERING RESIDUE IN YOUR BIOCHEMISTRY.
THAT'S THE ONLY THING KEEPING YOU FROM BEING FROZEN IN TIME LIKE THE REST OF CENTRAL CITY...
...BUT IT'S GOING TO WEAR OFF.
AND THEN I'LL BE STUCK.
WHERE DID YOU LEARN TO USE THIS S.T.A.R. LABS TECH AVERY?

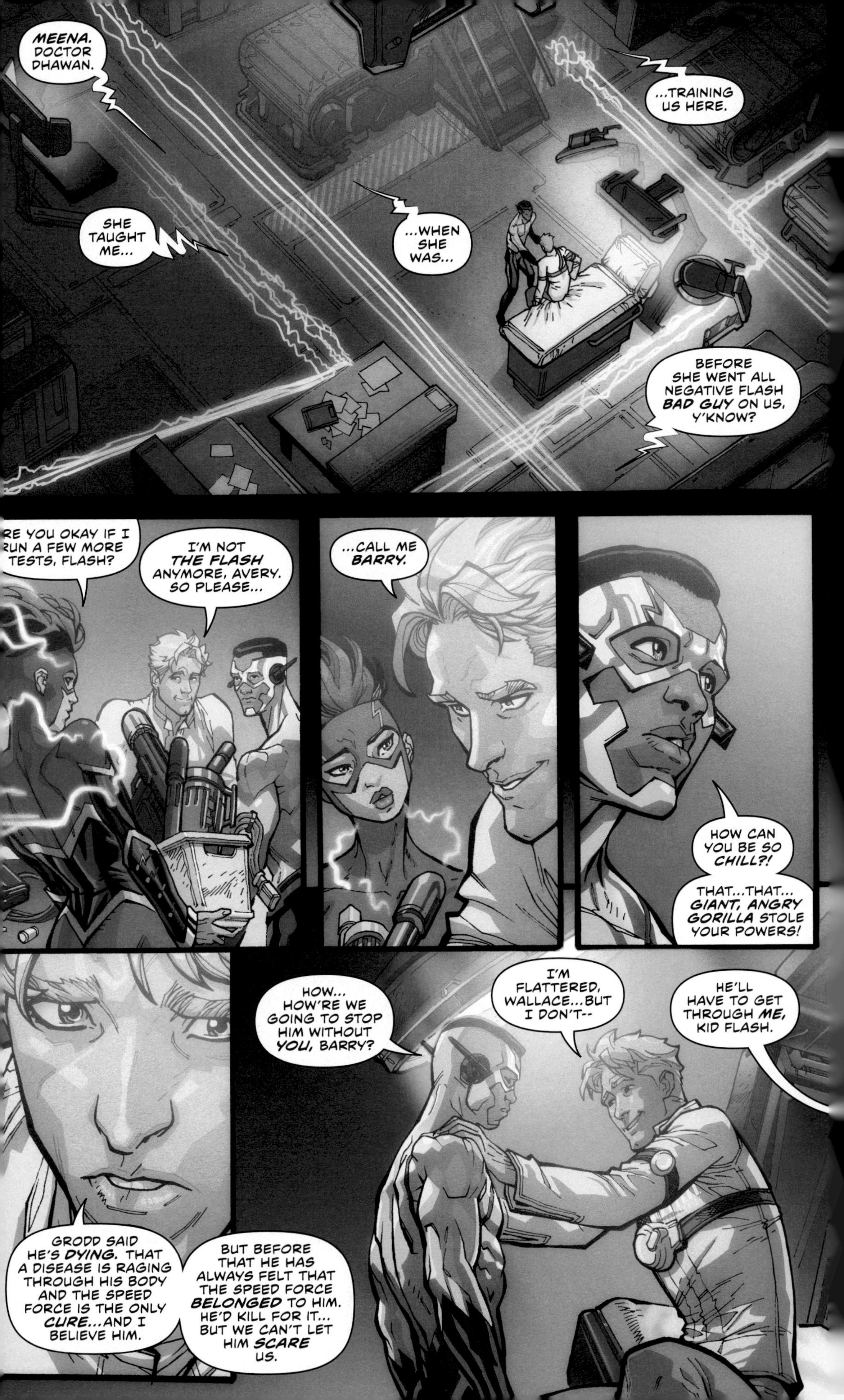
MEENA. DOCTOR DHAWAN.
SHE TAUGHT ME...
...WHEN SHE WAS...
...TRAINING US HERE.
BEFORE SHE WENT ALL NEGATIVE FLASH BAD GUY ON US, Y'KNOW?
RE YOU OKAY IF I RUN A FEW MORE TESTS, FLASH?
I'M NOT THE FLASH ANYMORE, AVERY. SO PLEASE...
...CALL ME BARRY.
HOW CAN YOU BE SO CHILL?!
THAT...THAT... GIANT, ANGRY GORILLA STOLE YOUR POWERS!
HOW... HOW'RE WE GOING TO STOP HIM WITHOUT YOU, BARRY?
I'M FLATTERED, WALLACE...BUT I DON'T--
HE'LL HAVE TO GET THROUGH ME, KID FLASH.
GRODD SAID HE'S DYING. THAT A DISEASE IS RAGING THROUGH HIS BODY AND THE SPEED FORCE IS THE ONLY CURE...AND I BELIEVE HIM.
BUT BEFORE THAT HE HAS ALWAYS FELT THAT THE SPEED FORCE BELONGED TO HIM. HE'D KILL FOR IT... BUT WE CAN'T LET HIM SCARE US.

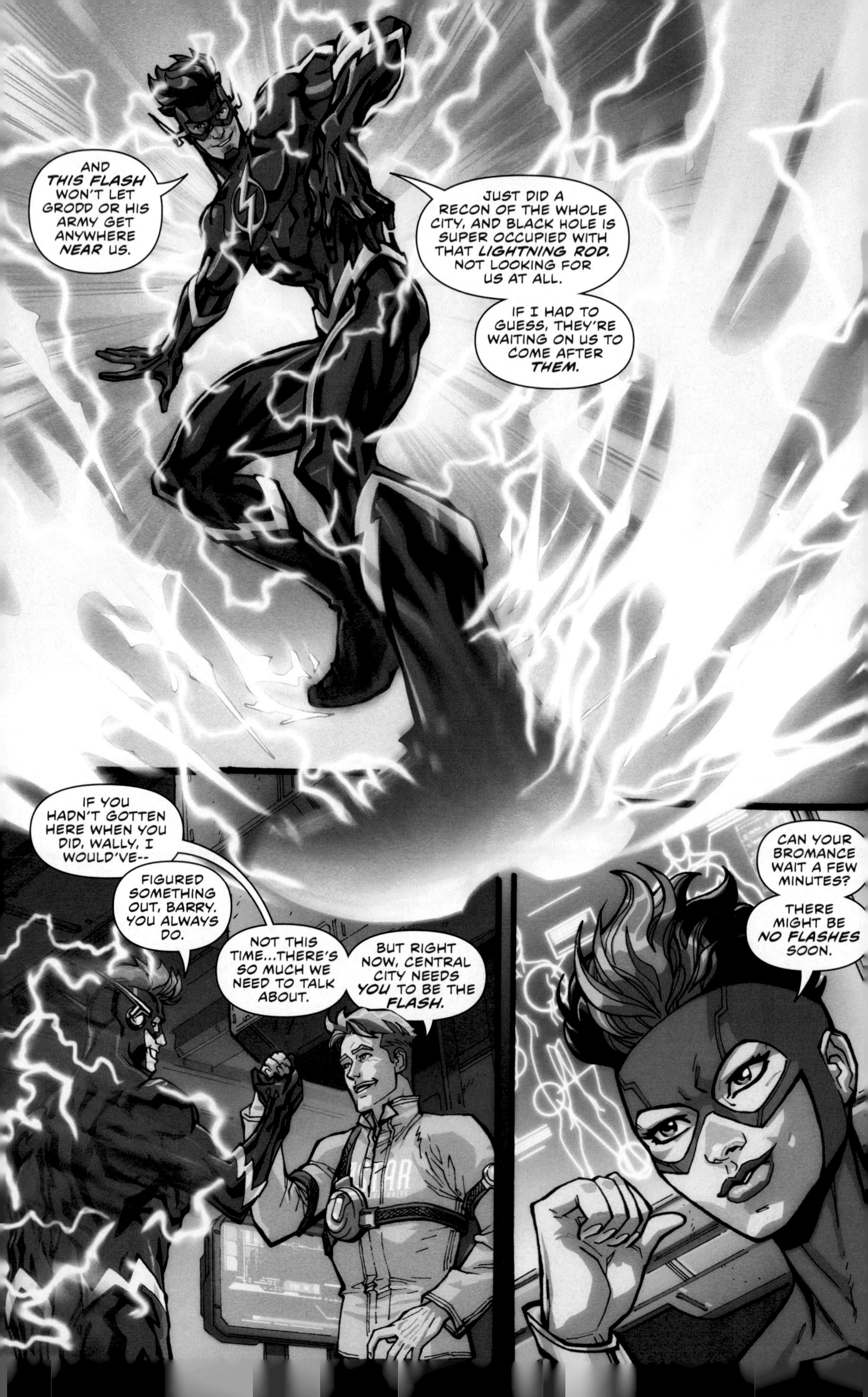
AND THIS FLASH WON'T LET GRODD OR HIS ARMY GET ANYWHERE NEAR US.
JUST DID A RECON OF THE WHOLE CITY, AND BLACK HOLE IS SUPER OCCUPIED WITH THAT LIGHTNING ROD. NOT LOOKING FOR US AT ALL.
IF I HAD TO GUESS, THEY'RE WAITING ON US TO COME AFTER THEM.
IF YOU HADN'T GOTTEN HERE WHEN YOU DID, WALLY, I WOULD'VE--
FIGURED SOMETHING OUT, BARRY. YOU ALWAYS DO.
NOT THIS TIME...THERE'S SO MUCH WE NEED TO TALK ABOUT.
BUT RIGHT NOW, CENTRAL CITY NEEDS YOU TO BE THE FLASH.
CAN YOUR BROMANCE WAIT A FEW MINUTES?
THERE MIGHT BE NO FLASHES SOON.

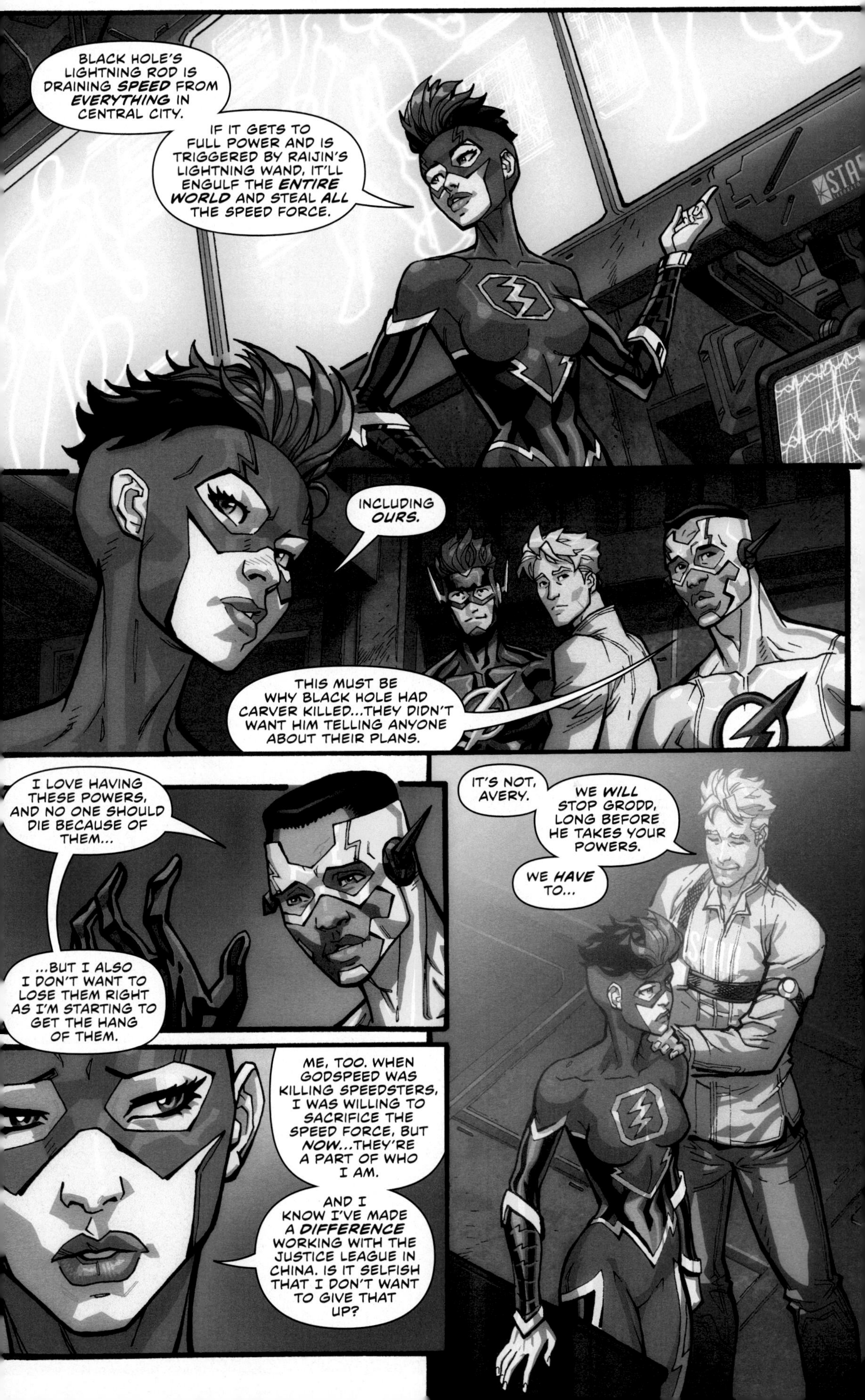

BLACK HOLE'S LIGHTNING ROD IS DRAINING *SPEED* FROM *EVERYTHING* IN CENTRAL CITY.
IF IT GETS TO FULL POWER AND IS TRIGGERED BY RAIJIN'S LIGHTNING WAND, IT'LL ENGULF THE *ENTIRE WORLD* AND STEAL *ALL* THE SPEED FORCE.
INCLUDING *OURS.*
THIS MUST BE WHY BLACK HOLE HAD CARVER KILLED...THEY DIDN'T WANT HIM TELLING ANYONE ABOUT THEIR PLANS.
I LOVE HAVING THESE POWERS, AND NO ONE SHOULD DIE BECAUSE OF THEM...
...BUT I ALSO I DON'T WANT TO LOSE THEM RIGHT AS I'M STARTING TO GET THE HANG OF THEM.
ME, TOO. WHEN GODSPEED WAS KILLING SPEEDSTERS, I WAS WILLING TO SACRIFICE THE SPEED FORCE, BUT *NOW*...THEY'RE A PART OF WHO I AM.
AND I KNOW I'VE MADE A *DIFFERENCE* WORKING WITH THE JUSTICE LEAGUE IN CHINA. IS IT SELFISH THAT I DON'T WANT TO GIVE THAT UP?
IT'S NOT, AVERY.
WE *WILL* STOP GRODD, LONG BEFORE HE TAKES YOUR POWERS.
WE *HAVE* TO...

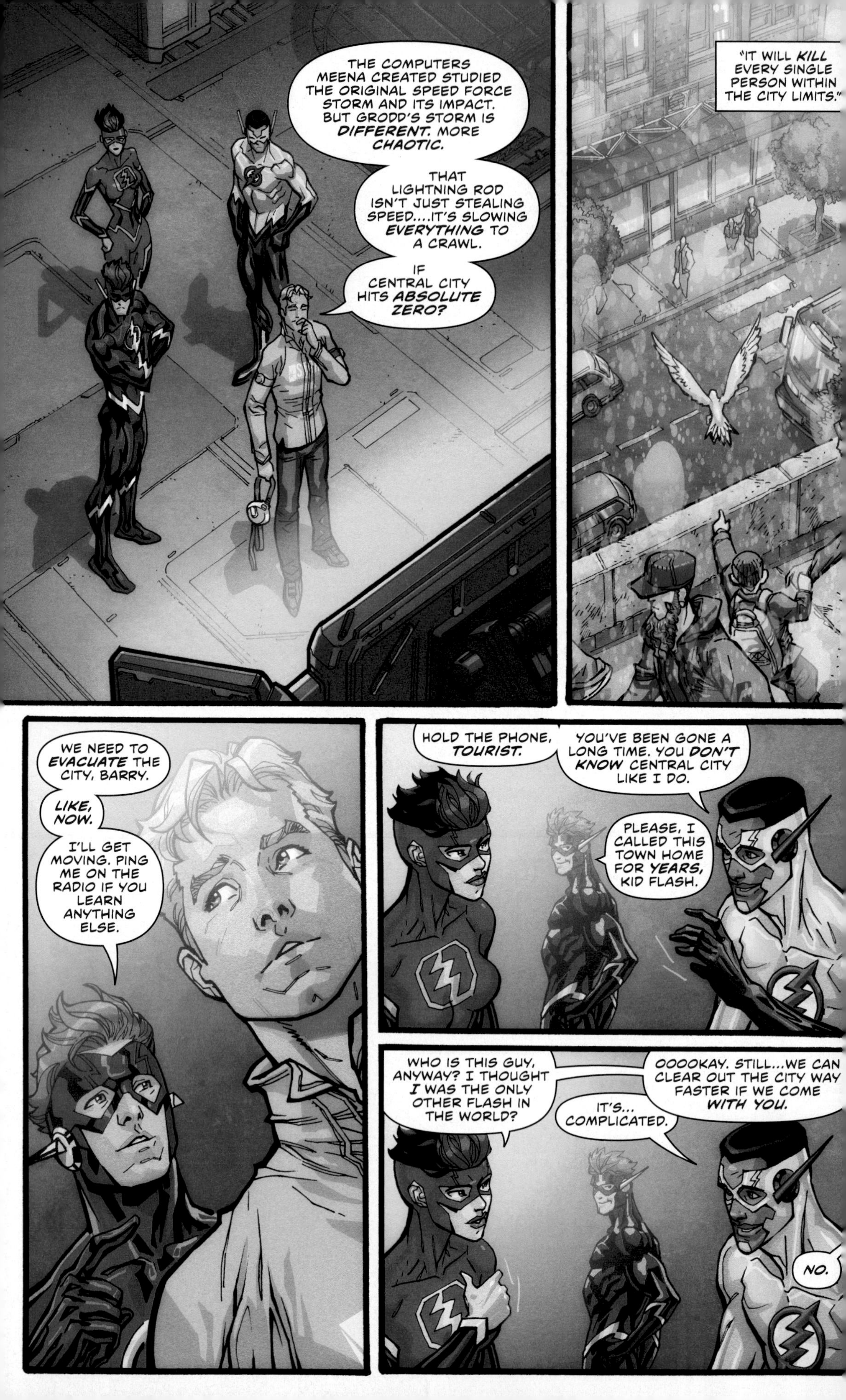

THE COMPUTERS MEENA CREATED STUDIED THE ORIGINAL SPEED FORCE STORM AND ITS IMPACT. BUT GRODD'S STORM IS *DIFFERENT.* MORE *CHAOTIC.*
THAT LIGHTNING ROD ISN'T JUST STEALING SPEED....IT'S SLOWING *EVERYTHING* TO A CRAWL.
IF CENTRAL CITY HITS *ABSOLUTE ZERO?*
"IT WILL *KILL* EVERY SINGLE PERSON WITHIN THE CITY LIMITS."
WE NEED TO *EVACUATE* THE CITY, BARRY.
LIKE, NOW.
I'LL GET MOVING. PING ME ON THE RADIO IF YOU LEARN ANYTHING ELSE.
HOLD THE PHONE, *TOURIST.*
YOU'VE BEEN GONE A LONG TIME. YOU *DON'T KNOW* CENTRAL CITY LIKE I DO.
PLEASE, I CALLED THIS TOWN HOME FOR *YEARS,* KID FLASH.
WHO IS THIS GUY, ANYWAY? I THOUGHT *I* WAS THE ONLY OTHER FLASH IN THE WORLD?
IT'S... COMPLICATED.
OOOOKAY. STILL...WE CAN CLEAR OUT THE CITY WAY FASTER IF WE COME *WITH YOU.*
NO.

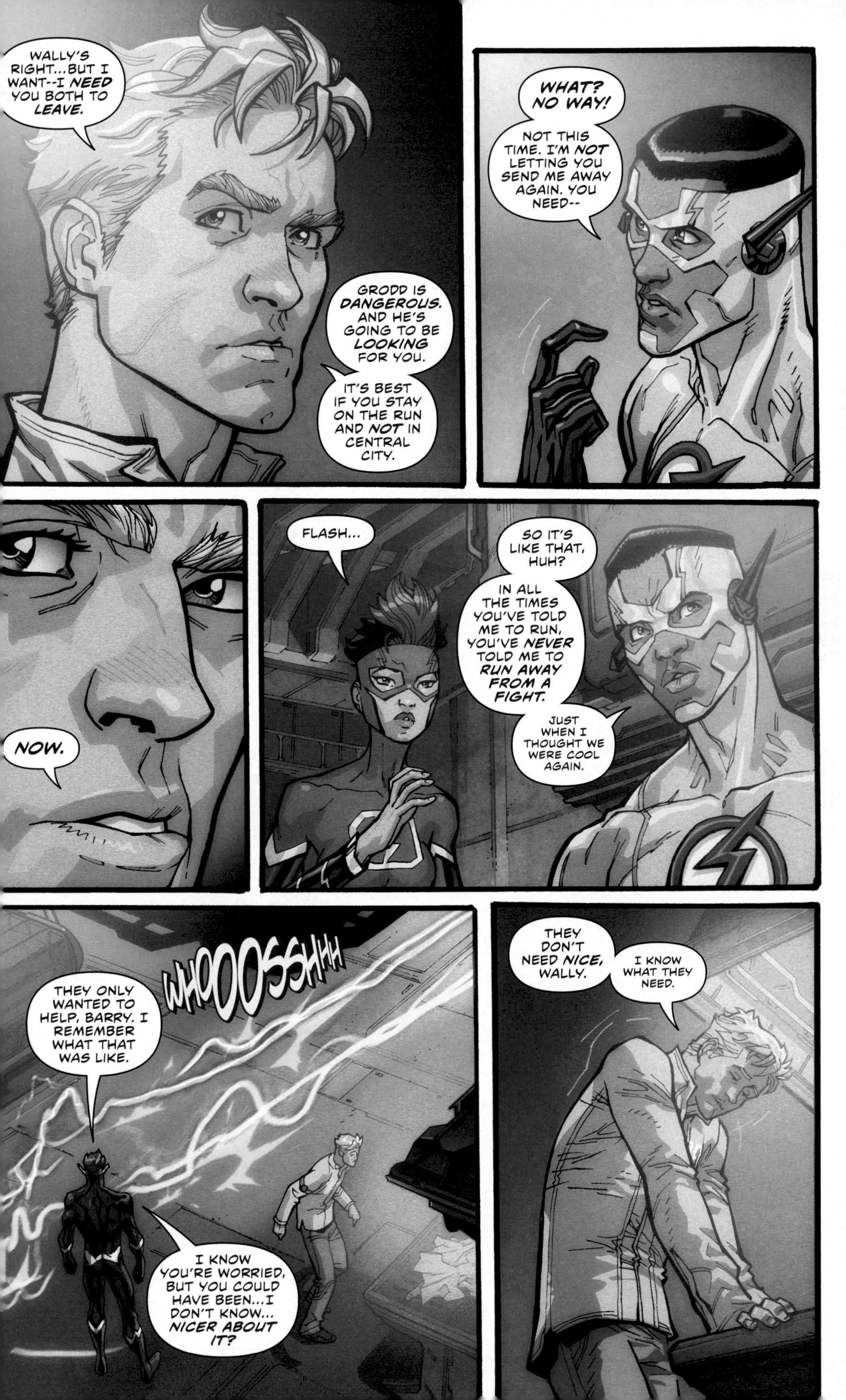
WALLY'S RIGHT...BUT I WANT--I NEED YOU BOTH TO LEAVE.
GRODD IS DANGEROUS. AND HE'S GOING TO BE LOOKING FOR YOU.
IT'S BEST IF YOU STAY ON THE RUN AND NOT IN CENTRAL CITY.
WHAT? NO WAY!
NOT THIS TIME. I'M NOT LETTING YOU SEND ME AWAY AGAIN. YOU NEED--
NOW.
FLASH...
SO IT'S LIKE THAT, HUH?
IN ALL THE TIMES YOU'VE TOLD ME TO RUN, YOU'VE NEVER TOLD ME TO RUN AWAY FROM A FIGHT.
JUST WHEN I THOUGHT WE WERE COOL AGAIN.
WHOOOSSHHH
THEY ONLY WANTED TO HELP, BARRY. I REMEMBER WHAT THAT WAS LIKE.
I KNOW YOU'RE WORRIED, BUT YOU COULD HAVE BEEN...I DON'T KNOW... NICER ABOUT IT?
THEY DON'T NEED NICE, WALLY.
I KNOW WHAT THEY NEED.

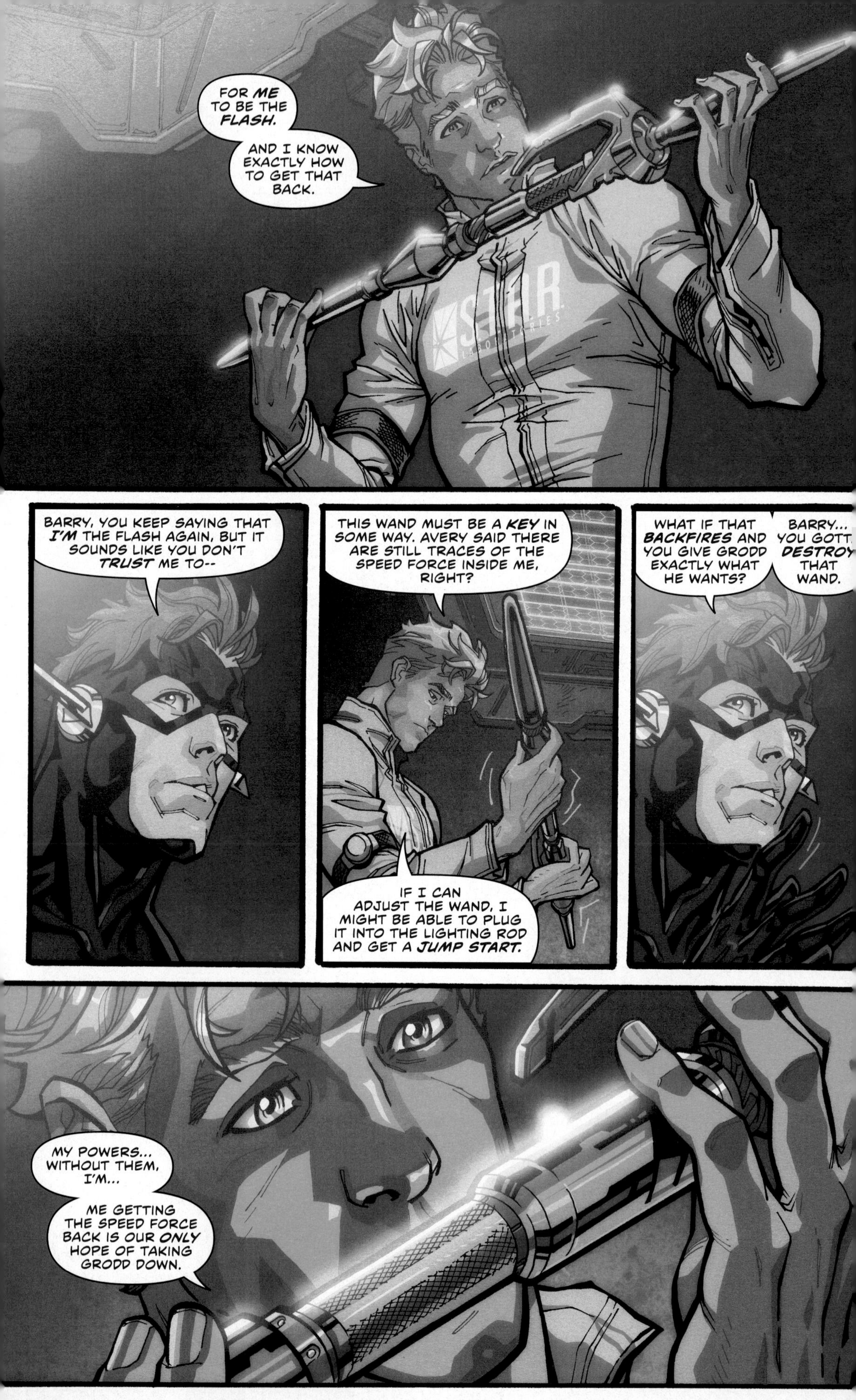
FOR ME TO BE THE FLASH.
AND I KNOW EXACTLY HOW TO GET THAT BACK.
BARRY, YOU KEEP SAYING THAT I'M THE FLASH AGAIN, BUT IT SOUNDS LIKE YOU DON'T TRUST ME TO--
THIS WAND MUST BE A KEY IN SOME WAY. AVERY SAID THERE ARE STILL TRACES OF THE SPEED FORCE INSIDE ME, RIGHT?
IF I CAN ADJUST THE WAND, I MIGHT BE ABLE TO PLUG IT INTO THE LIGHTING ROD AND GET A JUMP START.
WHAT IF THAT BACKFIRES AND YOU GIVE GRODD EXACTLY WHAT HE WANTS?
BARRY... YOU GOTT DESTROY THAT WAND.
MY POWERS... WITHOUT THEM, I'M...
ME GETTING THE SPEED FORCE BACK IS OUR ONLY HOPE OF TAKING GRODD DOWN.

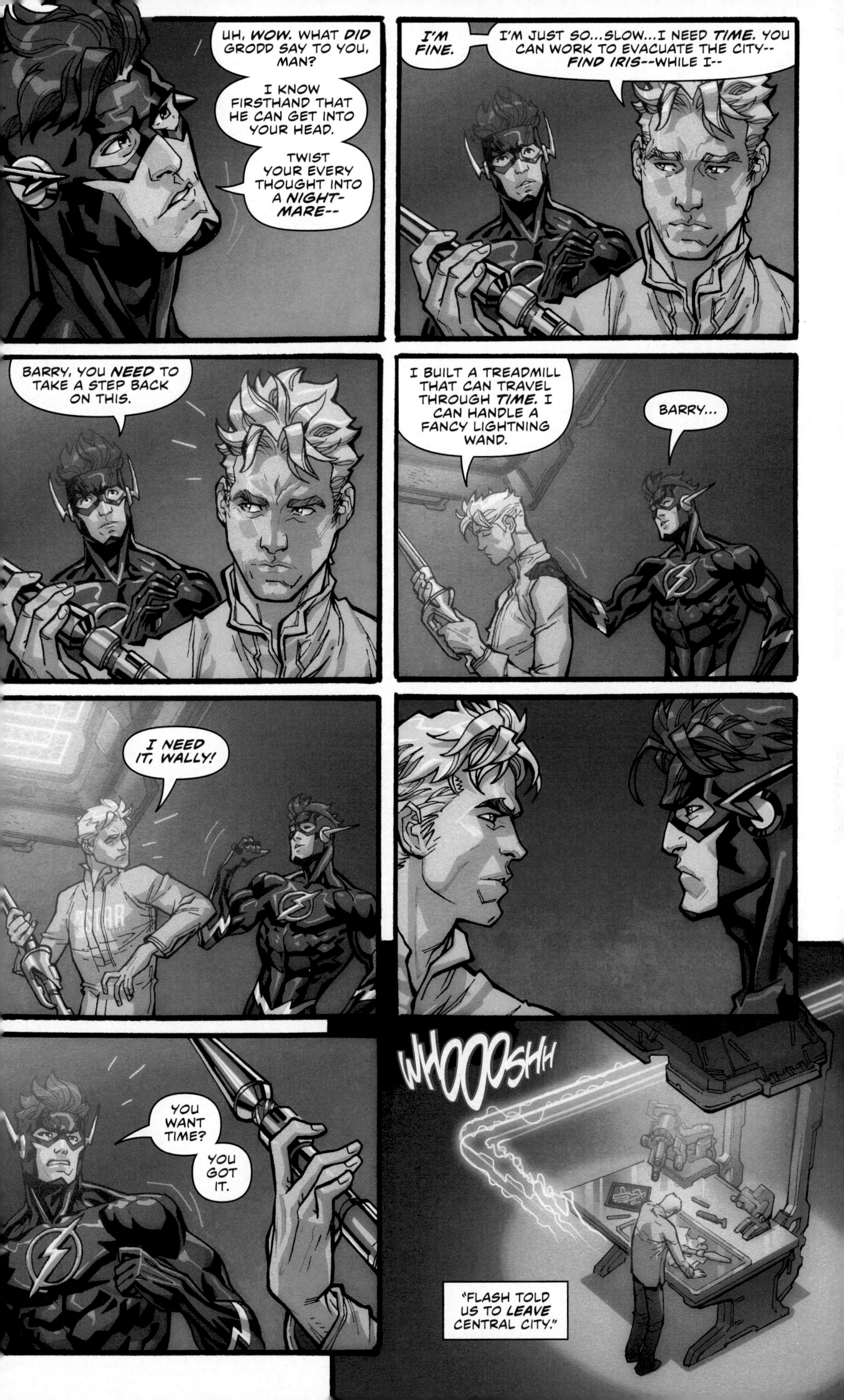
UH, WOW. WHAT DID GRODD SAY TO YOU, MAN?
I KNOW FIRSTHAND THAT HE CAN GET INTO YOUR HEAD.
TWIST YOUR EVERY THOUGHT INTO A NIGHT-MARE--
I'M FINE.
I'M JUST SO...SLOW...I NEED TIME. YOU CAN WORK TO EVACUATE THE CITY--FIND IRIS--WHILE I--
BARRY, YOU NEED TO TAKE A STEP BACK ON THIS.
I BUILT A TREADMILL THAT CAN TRAVEL THROUGH TIME. I CAN HANDLE A FANCY LIGHTNING WAND.
BARRY...
I NEED IT, WALLY!
YOU WANT TIME?
YOU GOT IT.
WHOOOSHH
"FLASH TOLD US TO LEAVE CENTRAL CITY."

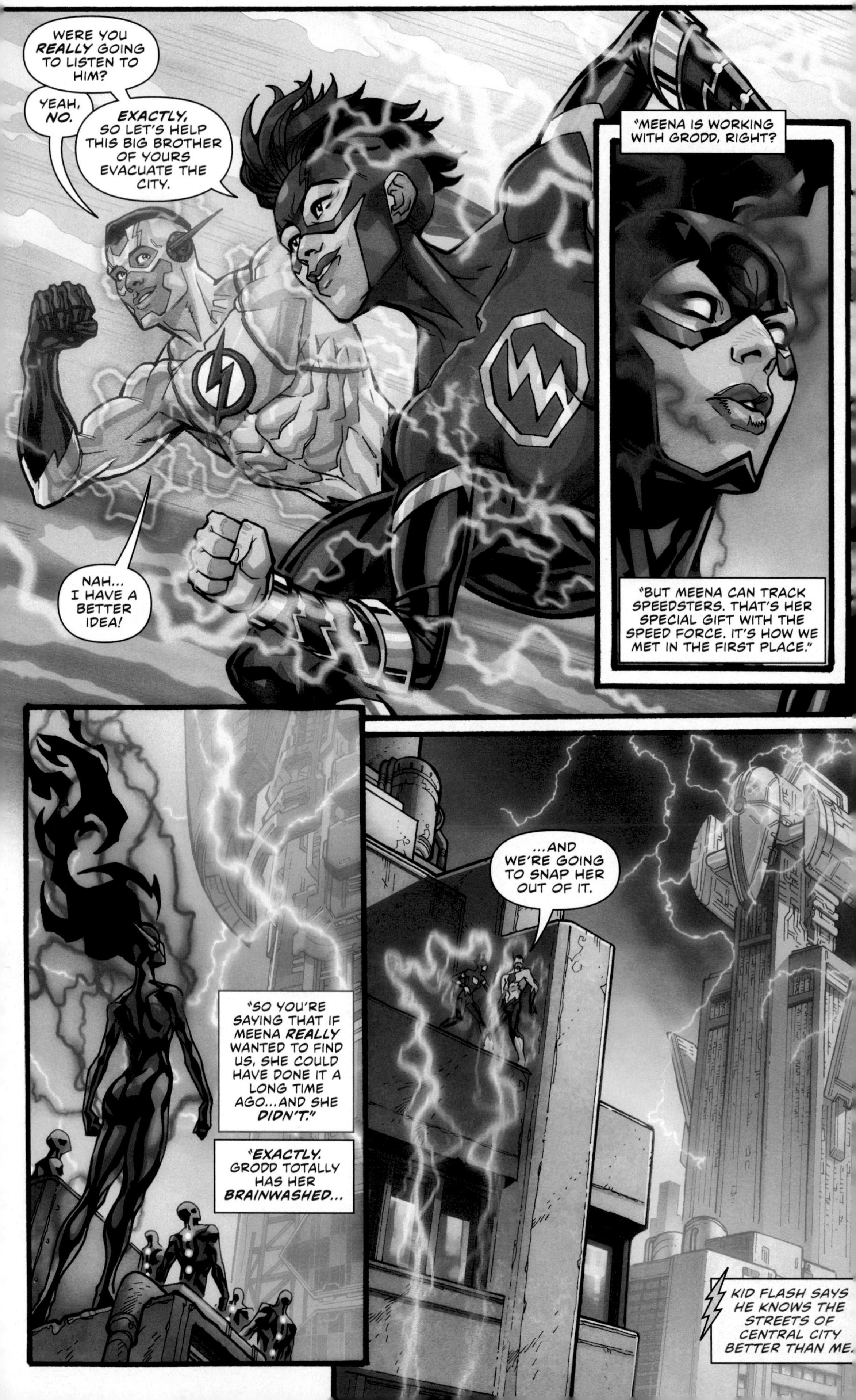

WERE YOU REALLY GOING TO LISTEN TO HIM?
YEAH, NO.
EXACTLY, SO LET'S HELP THIS BIG BROTHER OF YOURS EVACUATE THE CITY.
"MEENA IS WORKING WITH GRODD, RIGHT?
NAH... I HAVE A BETTER IDEA!
"BUT MEENA CAN TRACK SPEEDSTERS. THAT'S HER SPECIAL GIFT WITH THE SPEED FORCE. IT'S HOW WE MET IN THE FIRST PLACE."
"SO YOU'RE SAYING THAT IF MEENA REALLY WANTED TO FIND US, SHE COULD HAVE DONE IT A LONG TIME AGO...AND SHE DIDN'T."
"EXACTLY. GRODD TOTALLY HAS HER BRAINWASHED...
...AND WE'RE GOING TO SNAP HER OUT OF IT.
KID FLASH SAYS HE KNOWS THE STREETS OF CENTRAL CITY BETTER THAN ME.

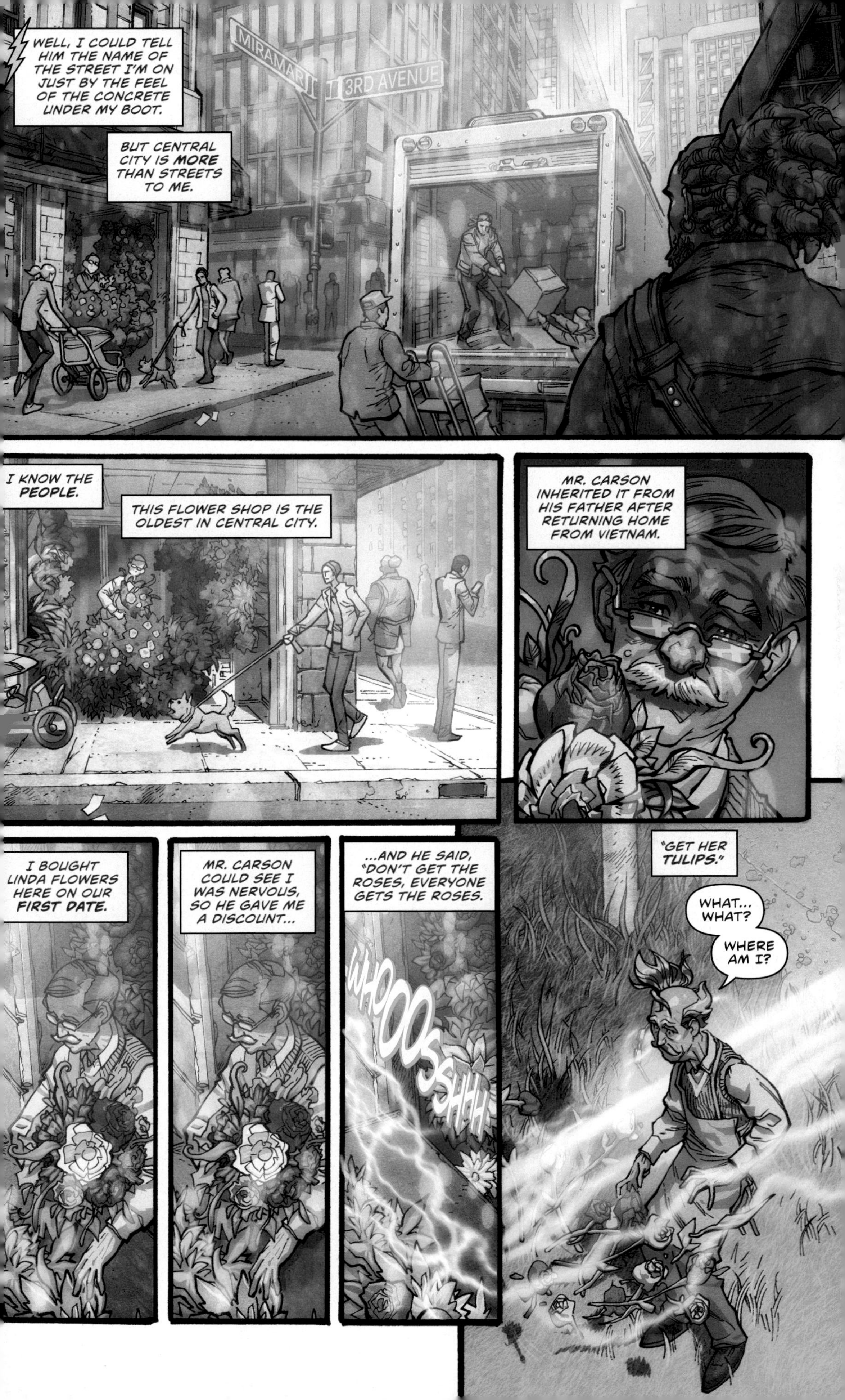
WELL, I COULD TELL HIM THE NAME OF THE STREET I'M ON JUST BY THE FEEL OF THE CONCRETE UNDER MY BOOT.
MIRAMAR
3RD AVENUE
BUT CENTRAL CITY IS MORE THAN STREETS TO ME.
I KNOW THE PEOPLE.
THIS FLOWER SHOP IS THE OLDEST IN CENTRAL CITY.
MR. CARSON INHERITED IT FROM HIS FATHER AFTER RETURNING HOME FROM VIETNAM.
I BOUGHT LINDA FLOWERS HERE ON OUR FIRST DATE.
MR. CARSON COULD SEE I WAS NERVOUS, SO HE GAVE ME A DISCOUNT...
...AND HE SAID, "DON'T GET THE ROSES, EVERYONE GETS THE ROSES.
WHOOOSSHHH
"GET HER TULIPS."
WHAT... WHAT?
WHERE AM I?

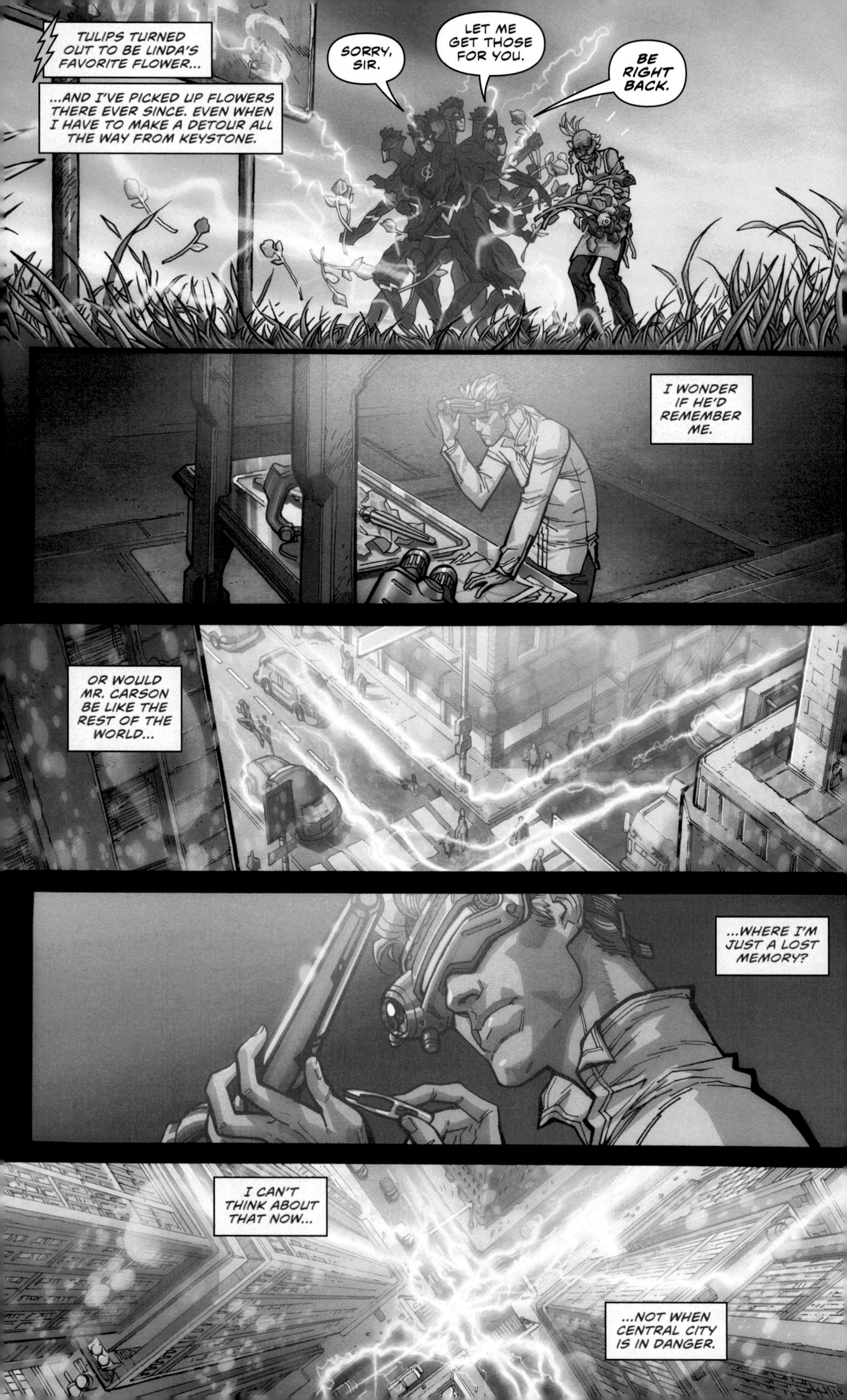
TULIPS TURNED OUT TO BE LINDA'S FAVORITE FLOWER...
...AND I'VE PICKED UP FLOWERS THERE EVER SINCE. EVEN WHEN I HAVE TO MAKE A DETOUR ALL THE WAY FROM KEYSTONE.
SORRY, SIR.
LET ME GET THOSE FOR YOU.
BE RIGHT BACK.
I WONDER IF HE'D REMEMBER ME.
OR WOULD MR. CARSON BE LIKE THE REST OF THE WORLD...
...WHERE I'M JUST A LOST MEMORY?
I CAN'T THINK ABOUT THAT NOW...
...NOT WHEN CENTRAL CITY IS IN DANGER.

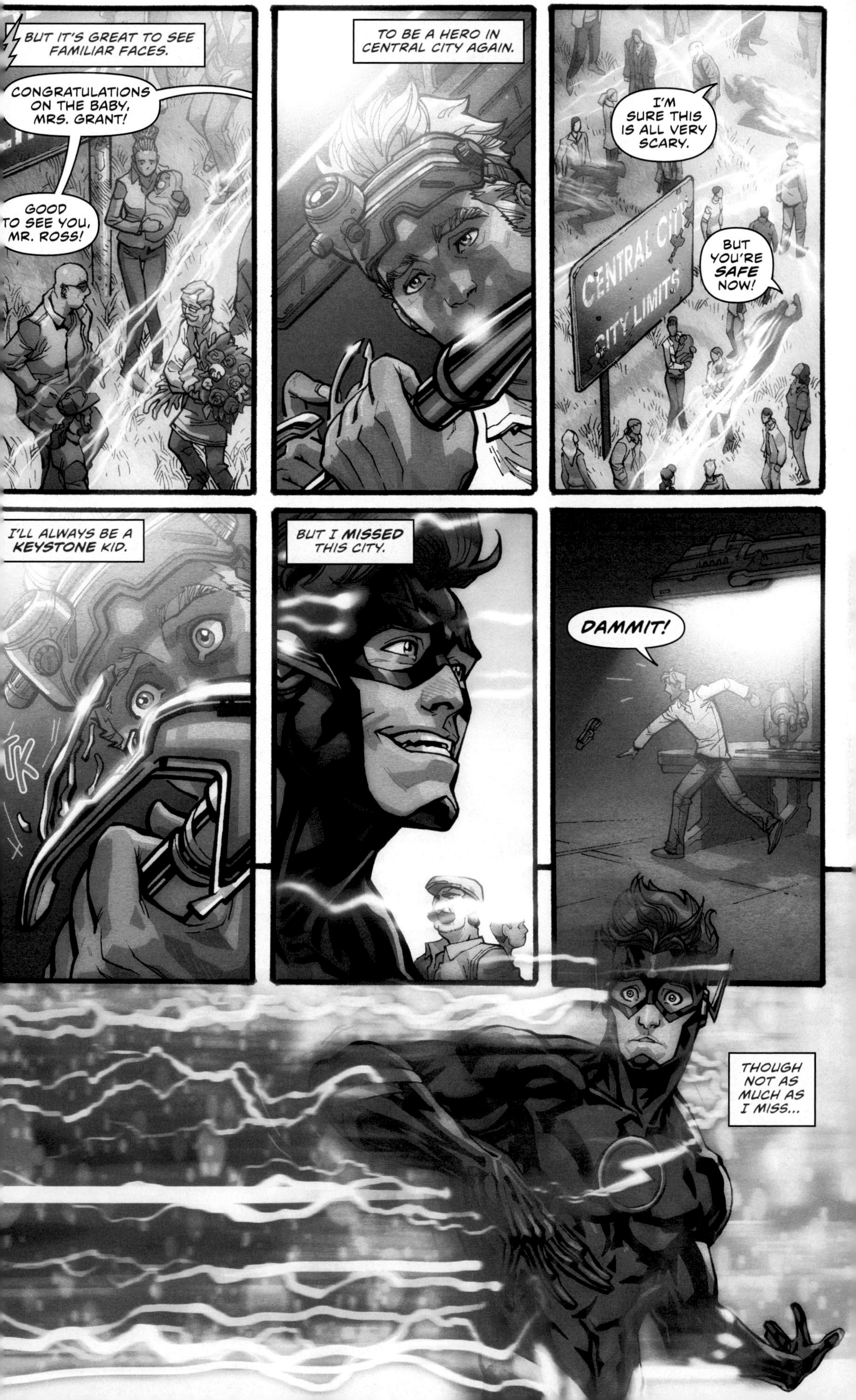
BUT IT'S GREAT TO SEE FAMILIAR FACES.
CONGRATULATIONS ON THE BABY, MRS. GRANT!
GOOD TO SEE YOU, MR. ROSS!
TO BE A HERO IN CENTRAL CITY AGAIN.
I'M SURE THIS IS ALL VERY SCARY.
CENTRAL CITY
CITY LIMITS
BUT YOU'RE SAFE NOW!
I'LL ALWAYS BE A KEYSTONE KID.
BUT I MISSED THIS CITY.
DAMMIT!
THOUGH NOT AS MUCH AS I MISS...

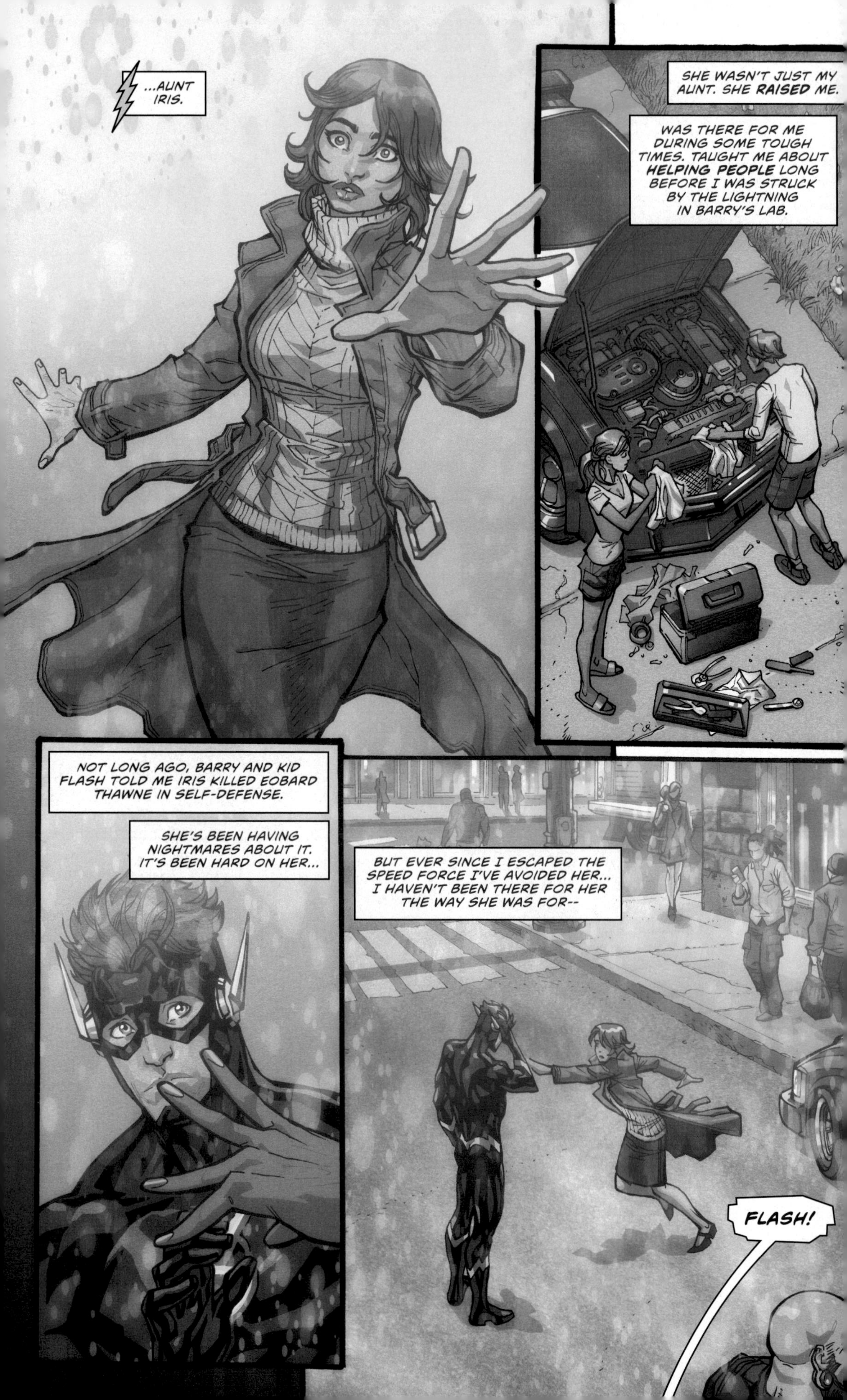
...AUNT IRIS.
SHE WASN'T JUST MY AUNT. SHE RAISED ME.
WAS THERE FOR ME DURING SOME TOUGH TIMES. TAUGHT ME ABOUT HELPING PEOPLE LONG BEFORE I WAS STRUCK BY THE LIGHTNING IN BARRY'S LAB.
NOT LONG AGO, BARRY AND KID FLASH TOLD ME IRIS KILLED EOBARD THAWNE IN SELF-DEFENSE.
SHE'S BEEN HAVING NIGHTMARES ABOUT IT. IT'S BEEN HARD ON HER...
BUT EVER SINCE I ESCAPED THE SPEED FORCE I'VE AVOIDED HER... I HAVEN'T BEEN THERE FOR HER THE WAY SHE WAS FOR--
FLASH!

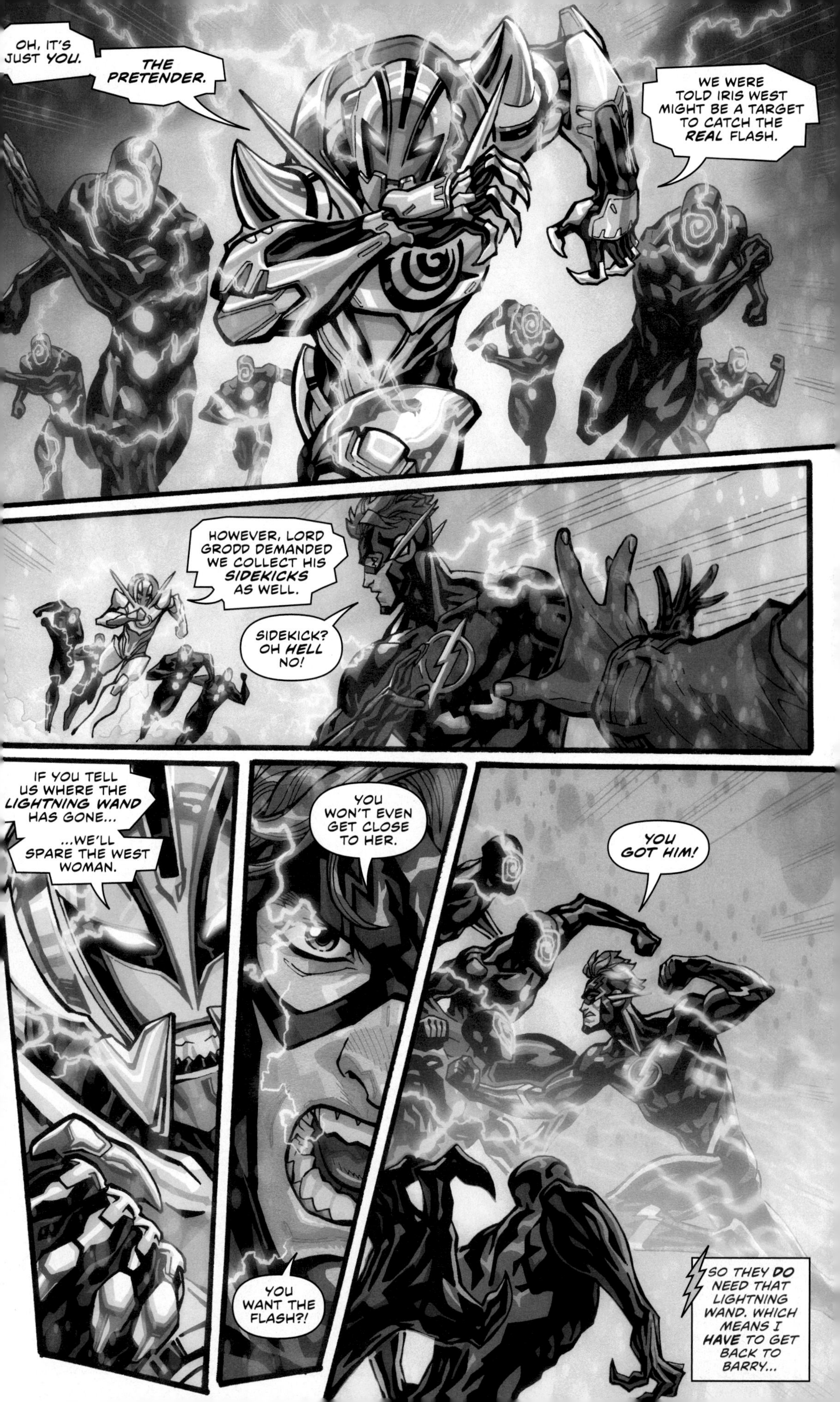
OH, IT'S JUST YOU.
THE PRETENDER.
WE WERE TOLD IRIS WEST MIGHT BE A TARGET TO CATCH THE REAL FLASH.
HOWEVER, LORD GRODD DEMANDED WE COLLECT HIS SIDEKICKS AS WELL.
SIDEKICK? OH HELL NO!
IF YOU TELL US WHERE THE LIGHTNING WAND HAS GONE...
...WE'LL SPARE THE WEST WOMAN.
YOU WON'T EVEN GET CLOSE TO HER.
YOU WANT THE FLASH?!
YOU GOT HIM!
SO THEY DO NEED THAT LIGHTNING WAND. WHICH MEANS I HAVE TO GET BACK TO BARRY...

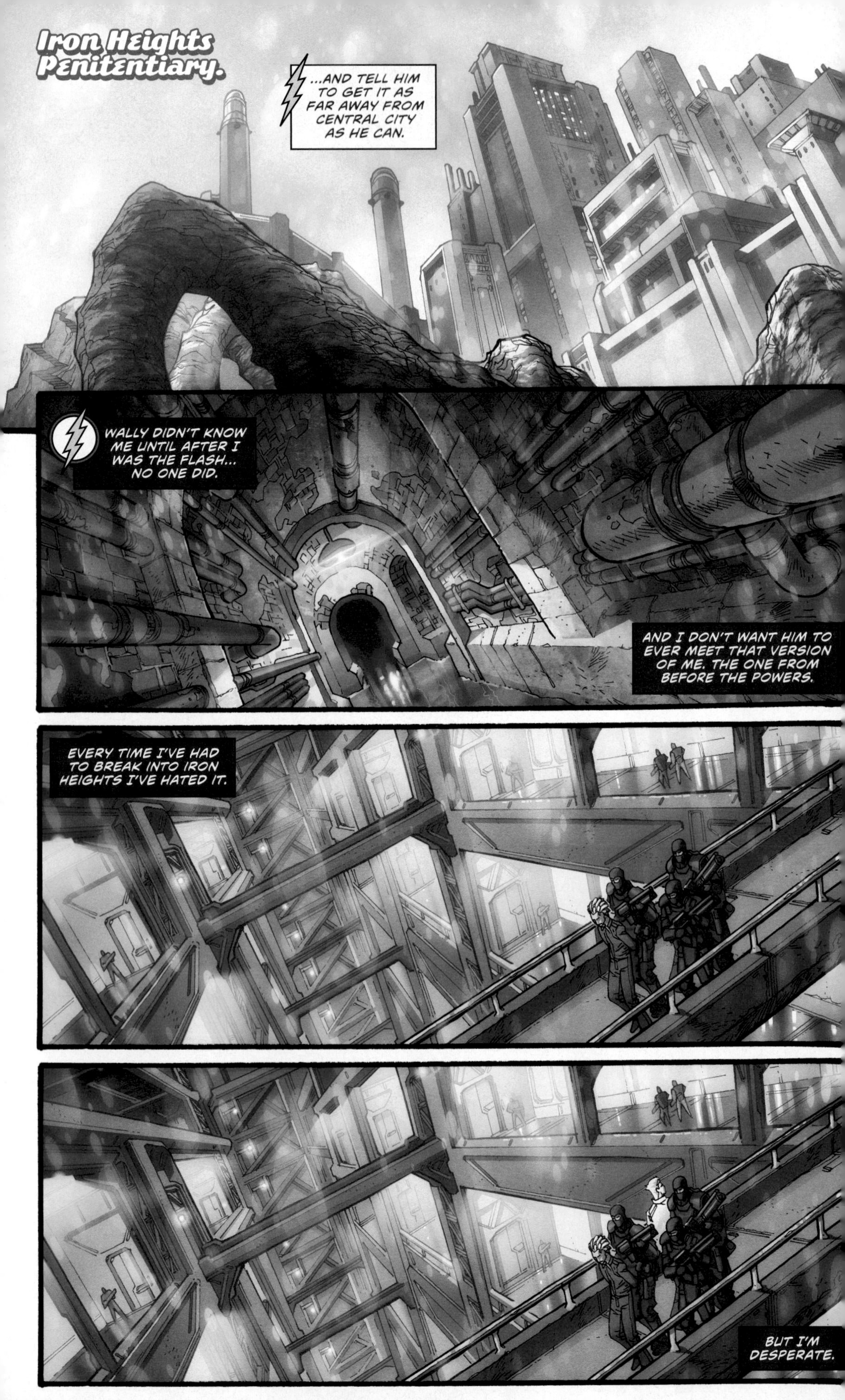
Iron Heights Penitentiary.
...AND TELL HIM TO GET IT AS FAR AWAY FROM CENTRAL CITY AS HE CAN.
WALLY DIDN'T KNOW ME UNTIL AFTER I WAS THE FLASH... NO ONE DID.
AND I DON'T WANT HIM TO EVER MEET THAT VERSION OF ME. THE ONE FROM BEFORE THE POWERS.
EVERY TIME I'VE HAD TO BREAK INTO IRON HEIGHTS I'VE HATED IT.
BUT I'M DESPERATE.

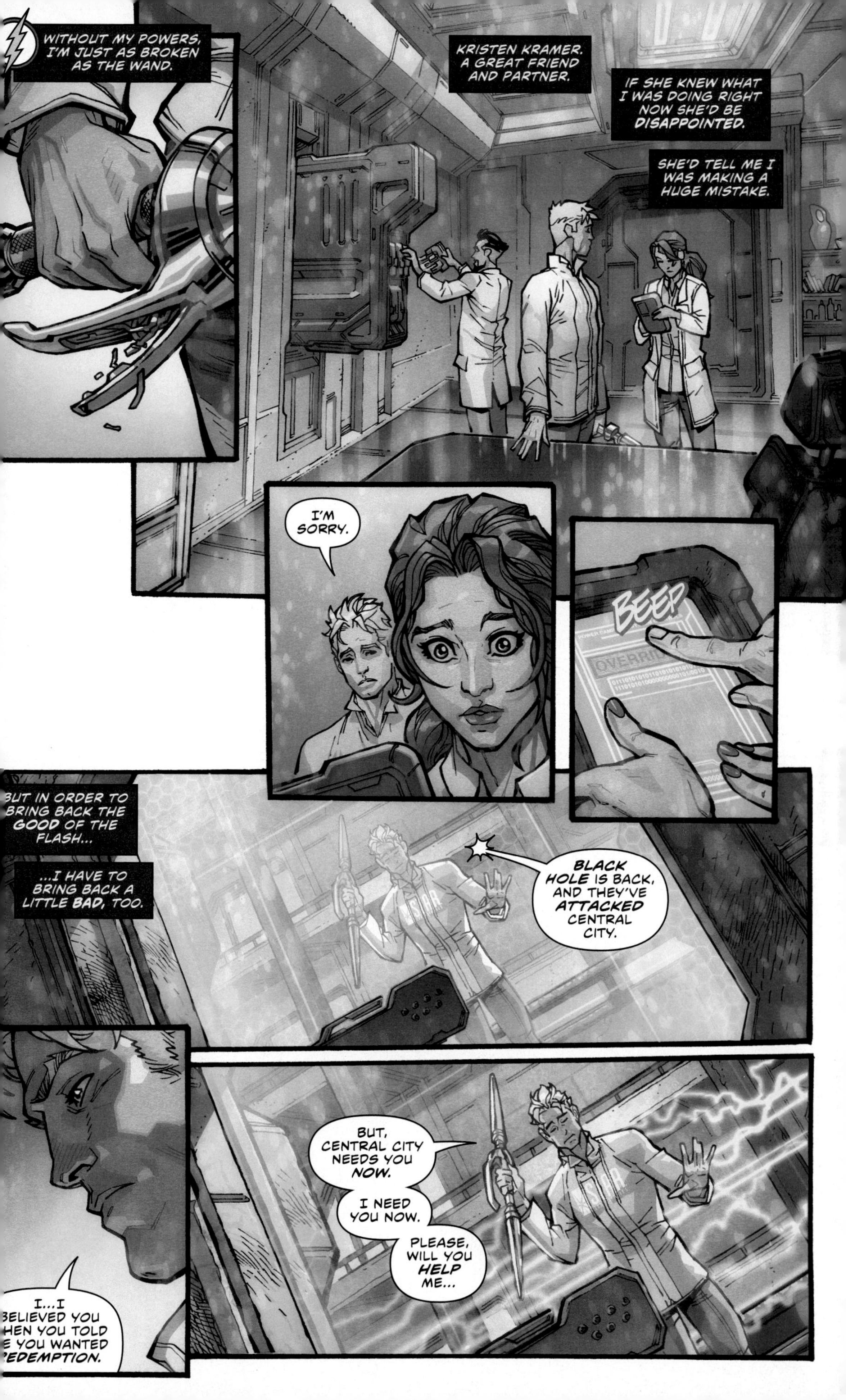

WITHOUT MY POWERS, I'M JUST AS BROKEN AS THE WAND.
KRISTEN KRAMER. A GREAT FRIEND AND PARTNER.
IF SHE KNEW WHAT I WAS DOING RIGHT NOW SHE'D BE DISAPPOINTED.
SHE'D TELL ME I WAS MAKING A HUGE MISTAKE.
I'M SORRY.
BEEP
BUT IN ORDER TO BRING BACK THE GOOD OF THE FLASH...
...I HAVE TO BRING BACK A LITTLE BAD, TOO.
BLACK HOLE IS BACK, AND THEY'VE ATTACKED CENTRAL CITY.
BUT, CENTRAL CITY NEEDS YOU NOW.
I NEED YOU NOW.
PLEASE, WILL YOU HELP ME...
I...I
BELIEVED YOU
HEN YOU TOLD
E YOU WANTED
EDEMPTION.

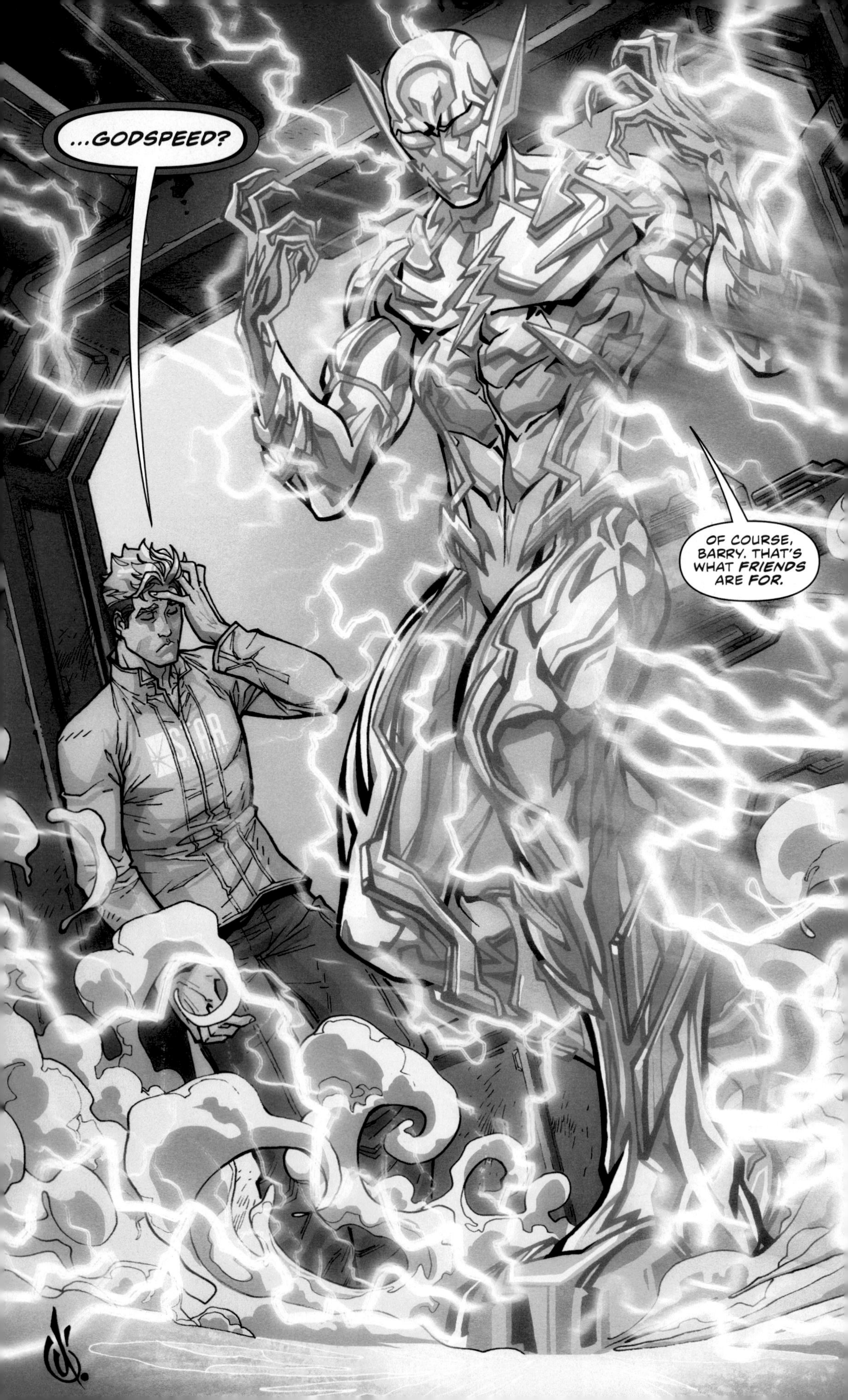
...GODSPEED?
OF COURSE, BARRY. THAT'S WHAT FRIENDS ARE FOR.

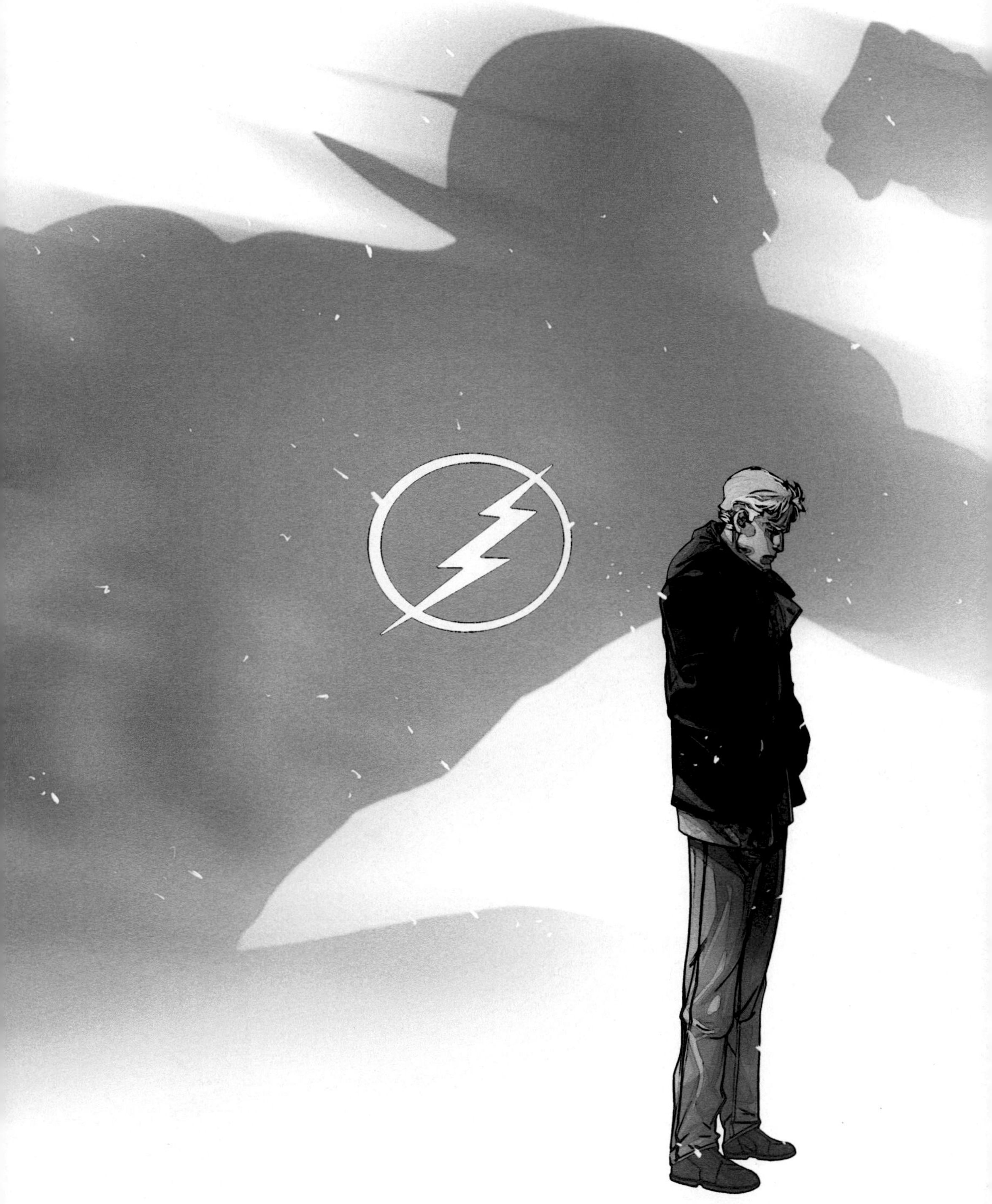

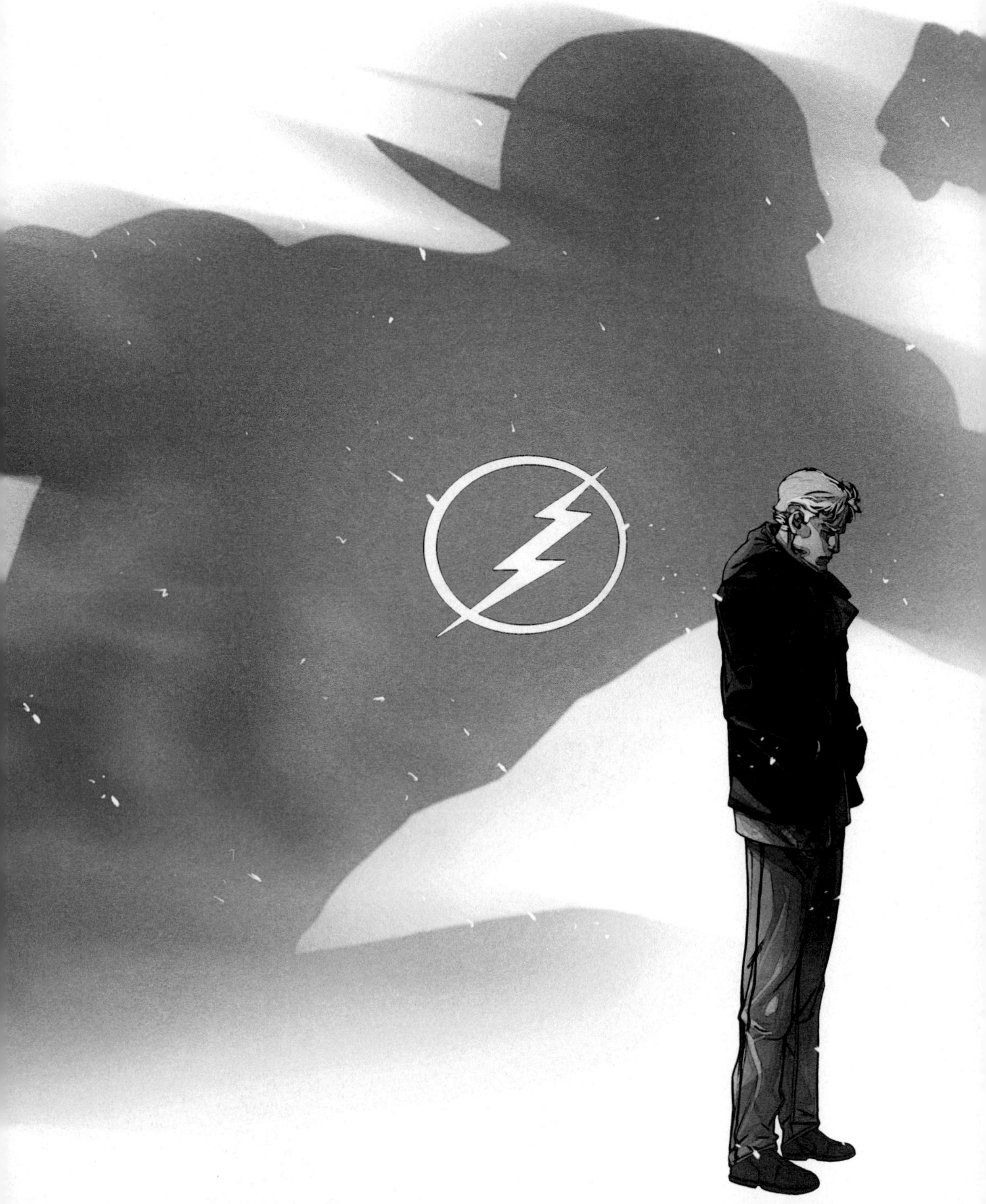

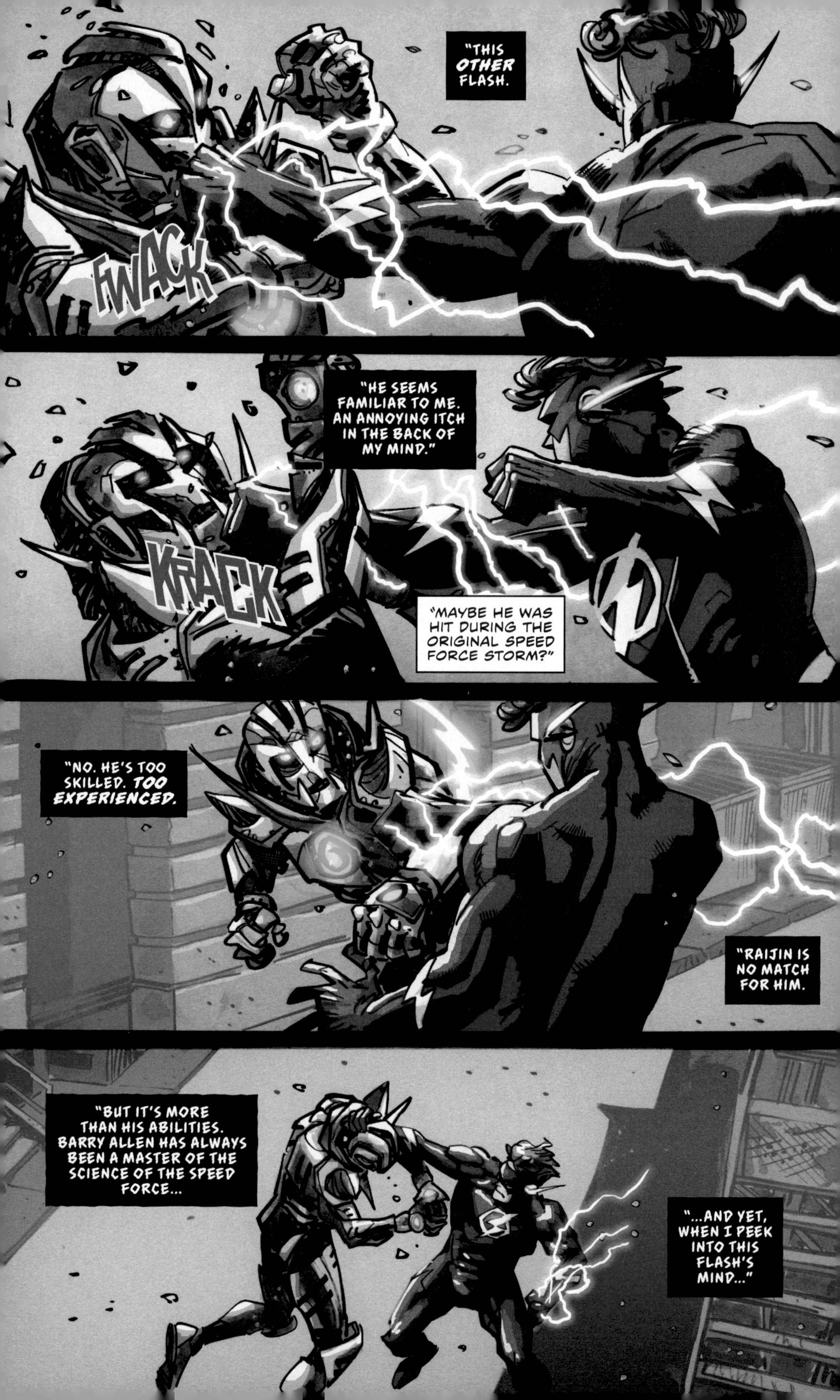
"THIS *OTHER* FLASH.
FWACK
"HE SEEMS FAMILIAR TO ME. AN ANNOYING ITCH IN THE BACK OF MY MIND."
KRACK
"MAYBE HE WAS HIT DURING THE ORIGINAL SPEED FORCE STORM?"
"NO. HE'S TOO SKILLED. *TOO EXPERIENCED.*
"RAIJIN IS NO MATCH FOR HIM.
"BUT IT'S MORE THAN HIS ABILITIES. BARRY ALLEN HAS ALWAYS BEEN A MASTER OF THE SCIENCE OF THE SPEED FORCE...
"...AND YET, WHEN I PEEK INTO THIS FLASH'S MIND..."

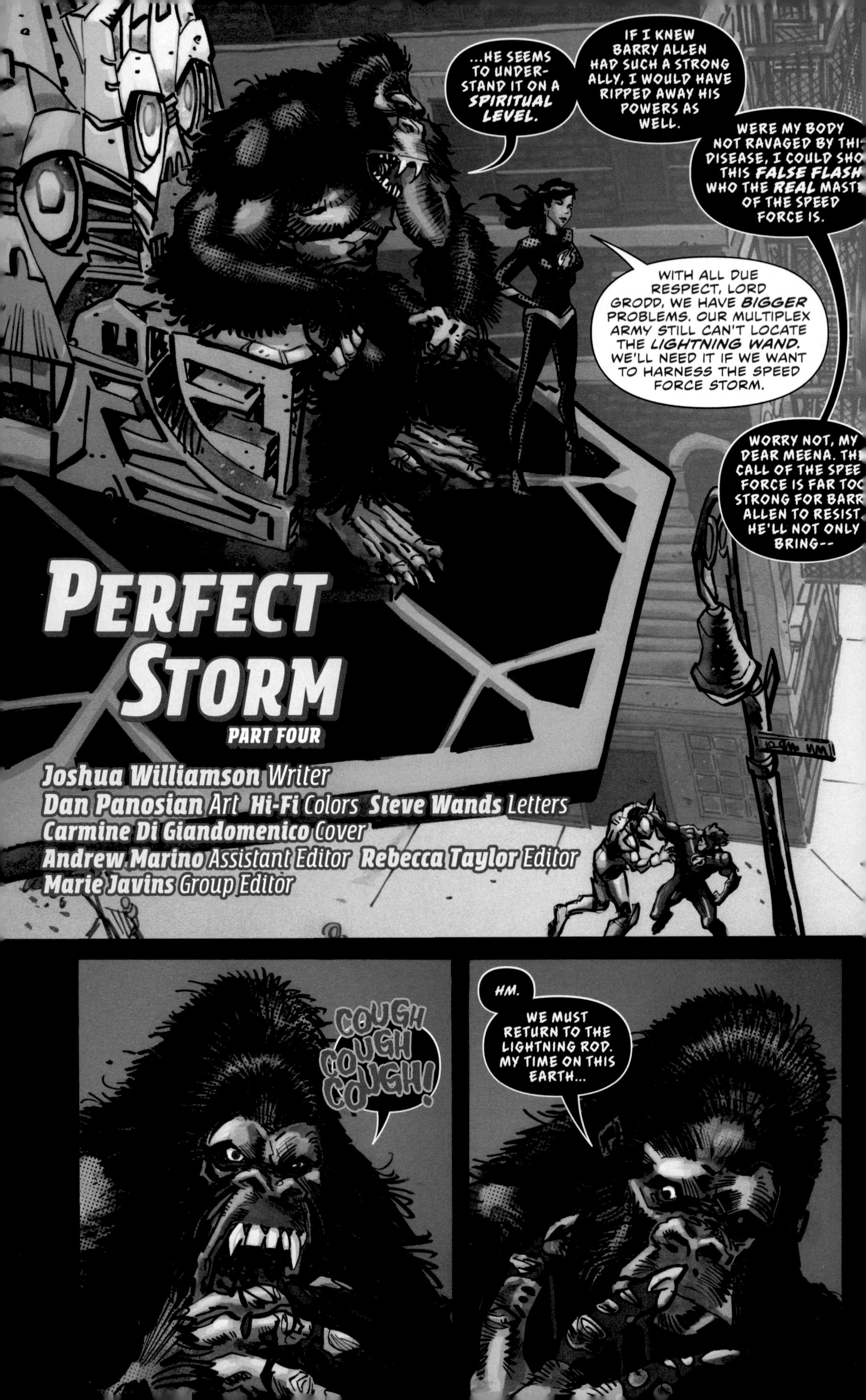
...HE SEEMS TO UNDERSTAND IT ON A SPIRITUAL LEVEL.
IF I KNEW BARRY ALLEN HAD SUCH A STRONG ALLY, I WOULD HAVE RIPPED AWAY HIS POWERS AS WELL.
WERE MY BODY NOT RAVAGED BY THI DISEASE, I COULD SHO THIS FALSE FLASH WHO THE REAL MAST OF THE SPEED FORCE IS.
WITH ALL DUE RESPECT, LORD GRODD, WE HAVE BIGGER PROBLEMS. OUR MULTIPLEX ARMY STILL CAN'T LOCATE THE LIGHTNING WAND. WE'LL NEED IT IF WE WANT TO HARNESS THE SPEED FORCE STORM.
WORRY NOT, MY DEAR MEENA. TH CALL OF THE SPEE FORCE IS FAR TOO STRONG FOR BARR ALLEN TO RESIST. HE'LL NOT ONLY BRING--
PERFECT STORM
PART FOUR
Joshua Williamson Writer
Dan Panosian Art Hi-Fi Colors Steve Wands Letters
Carmine Di Giandomenico Cover
Andrew Marino Assistant Editor Rebecca Taylor Editor
Marie Javins Group Editor
COUGH COUGH COUGH!
HM.
WE MUST RETURN TO THE LIGHTNING ROD. MY TIME ON THIS EARTH...

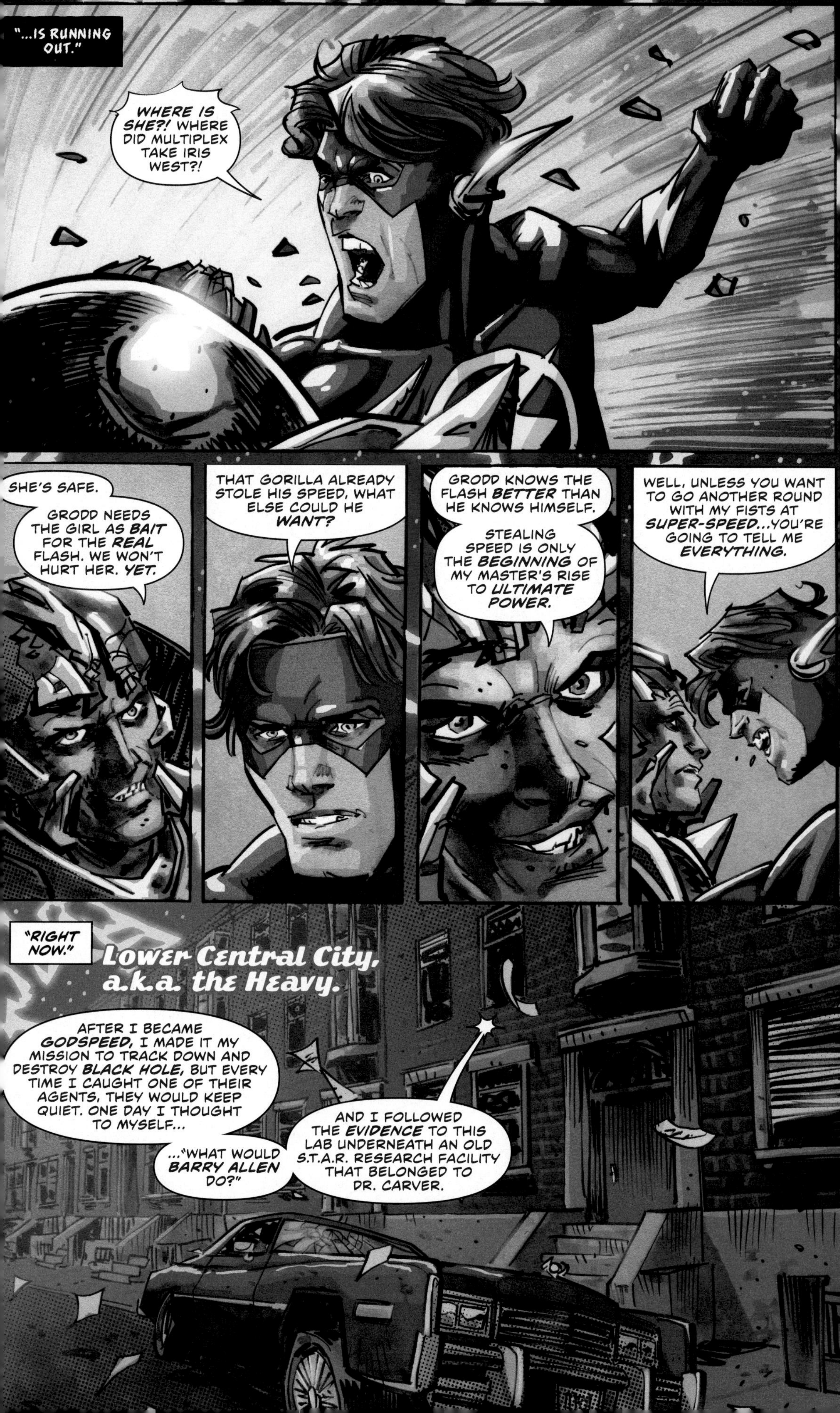
"...IS RUNNING OUT."
WHERE IS SHE?! WHERE DID MULTIPLEX TAKE IRIS WEST?!
SHE'S SAFE.
GRODD NEEDS THE GIRL AS BAIT FOR THE REAL FLASH. WE WON'T HURT HER. YET.
THAT GORILLA ALREADY STOLE HIS SPEED. WHAT ELSE COULD HE WANT?
GRODD KNOWS THE FLASH BETTER THAN HE KNOWS HIMSELF.
STEALING SPEED IS ONLY THE BEGINNING OF MY MASTER'S RISE TO ULTIMATE POWER.
WELL, UNLESS YOU WANT TO GO ANOTHER ROUND WITH MY FISTS AT SUPER-SPEED...YOU'RE GOING TO TELL ME EVERYTHING.
"RIGHT NOW."
Lower Central City, a.k.a. the Heavy.
AFTER I BECAME GODSPEED, I MADE IT MY MISSION TO TRACK DOWN AND DESTROY BLACK HOLE, BUT EVERY TIME I CAUGHT ONE OF THEIR AGENTS, THEY WOULD KEEP QUIET. ONE DAY I THOUGHT TO MYSELF...
..."WHAT WOULD BARRY ALLEN DO?"
AND I FOLLOWED THE EVIDENCE TO THIS LAB UNDERNEATH AN OLD S.T.A.R. RESEARCH FACILITY THAT BELONGED TO DR. CARVER.

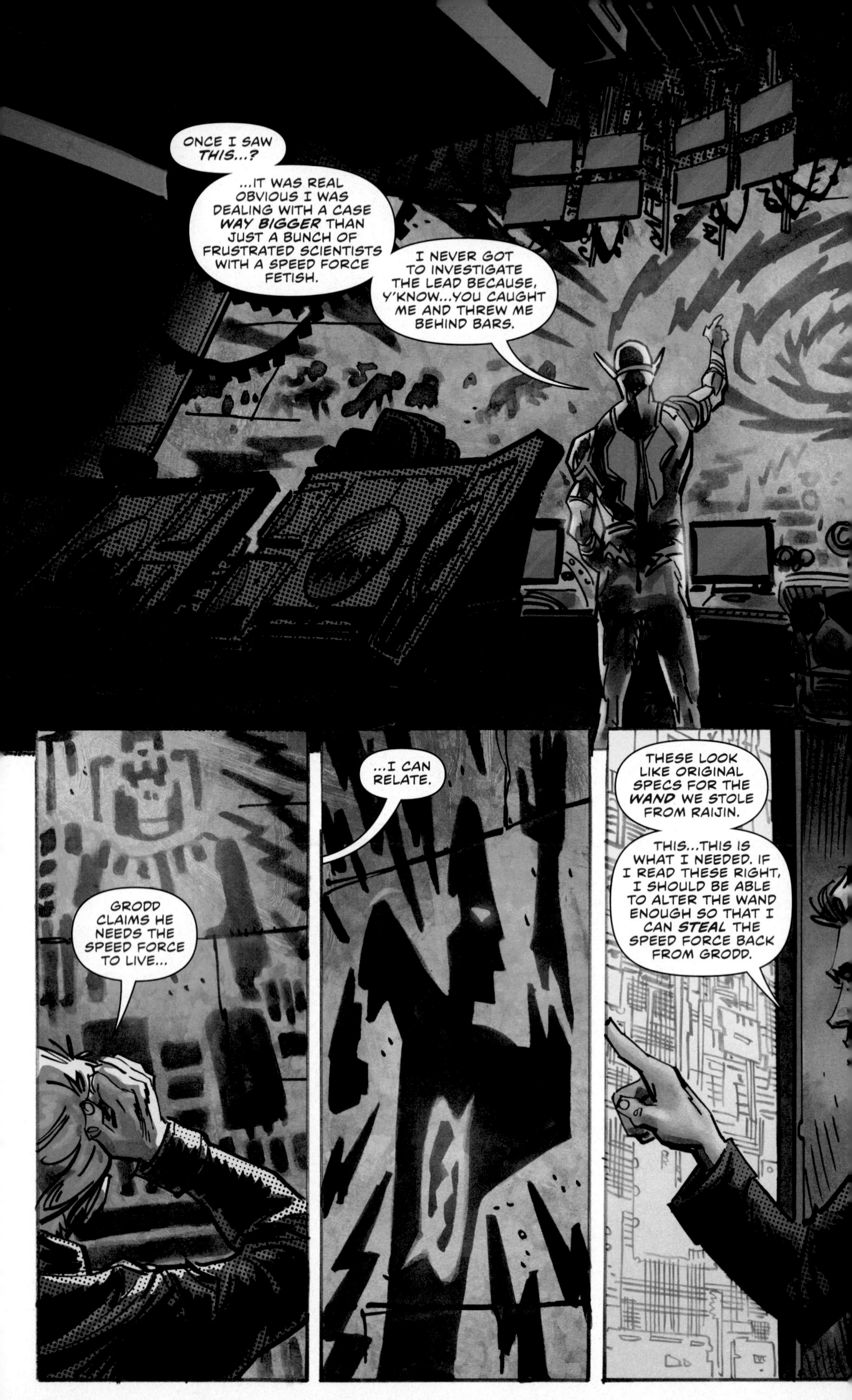

ONCE I SAW THIS...?
...IT WAS REAL OBVIOUS I WAS DEALING WITH A CASE WAY BIGGER THAN JUST A BUNCH OF FRUSTRATED SCIENTISTS WITH A SPEED FORCE FETISH.
I NEVER GOT TO INVESTIGATE THE LEAD BECAUSE, Y'KNOW...YOU CAUGHT ME AND THREW ME BEHIND BARS.
GRODD CLAIMS HE NEEDS THE SPEED FORCE TO LIVE...
...I CAN RELATE.
THESE LOOK LIKE ORIGINAL SPECS FOR THE WAND WE STOLE FROM RAIJIN.
THIS...THIS IS WHAT I NEEDED. IF I READ THESE RIGHT, I SHOULD BE ABLE TO ALTER THE WAND ENOUGH SO THAT I CAN STEAL THE SPEED FORCE BACK FROM GRODD.

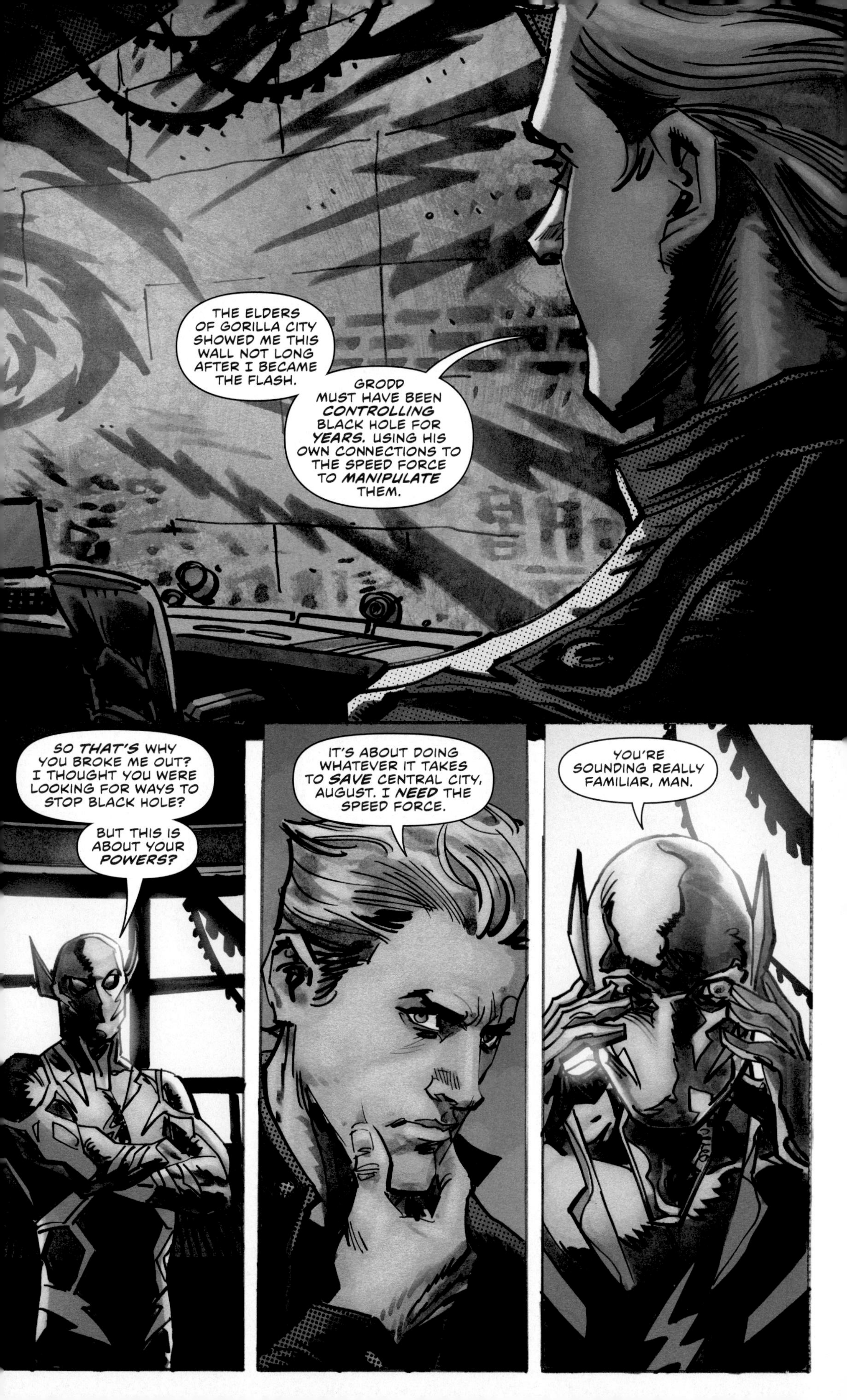
THE ELDERS OF GORILLA CITY SHOWED ME THIS WALL NOT LONG AFTER I BECAME THE FLASH.
GRODD MUST HAVE BEEN CONTROLLING BLACK HOLE FOR YEARS. USING HIS OWN CONNECTIONS TO THE SPEED FORCE TO MANIPULATE THEM.
SO THAT'S WHY YOU BROKE ME OUT? I THOUGHT YOU WERE LOOKING FOR WAYS TO STOP BLACK HOLE?
BUT THIS IS ABOUT YOUR POWERS?
IT'S ABOUT DOING WHATEVER IT TAKES TO SAVE CENTRAL CITY, AUGUST. I NEED THE SPEED FORCE.
YOU'RE SOUNDING REALLY FAMILIAR, MAN.

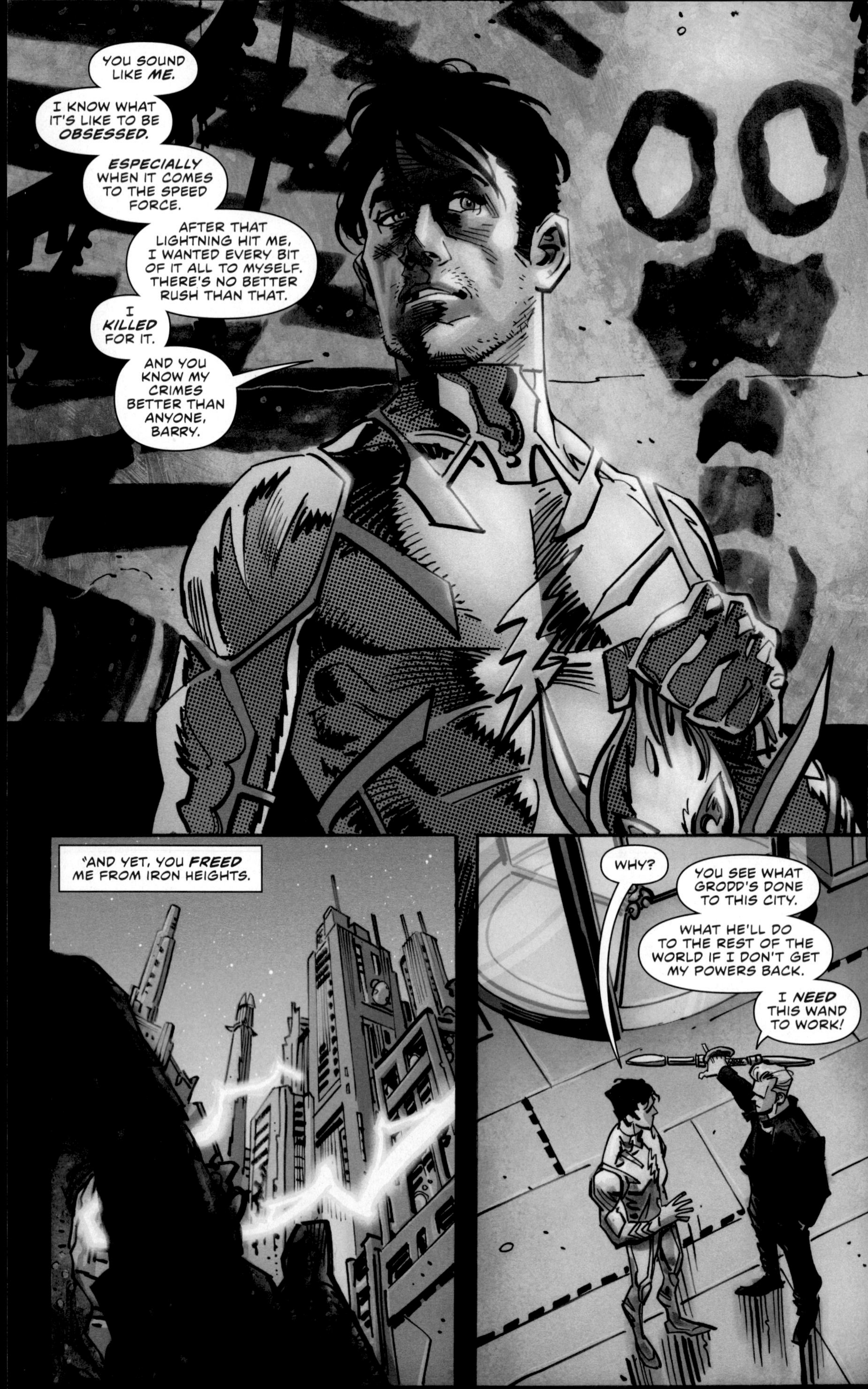
YOU SOUND LIKE *ME.*
I KNOW WHAT IT'S LIKE TO BE *OBSESSED.*
ESPECIALLY WHEN IT COMES TO THE SPEED FORCE.
AFTER THAT LIGHTNING HIT ME, I WANTED EVERY BIT OF IT ALL TO MYSELF. THERE'S NO BETTER RUSH THAN THAT.
I *KILLED* FOR IT.
AND YOU KNOW MY CRIMES BETTER THAN ANYONE, BARRY.
"AND YET, YOU *FREED* ME FROM IRON HEIGHTS.
WHY?
YOU SEE WHAT GRODD'S DONE TO THIS CITY.
WHAT HE'LL DO TO THE REST OF THE WORLD IF I DON'T GET MY POWERS BACK.
I *NEED* THIS WAND TO WORK!

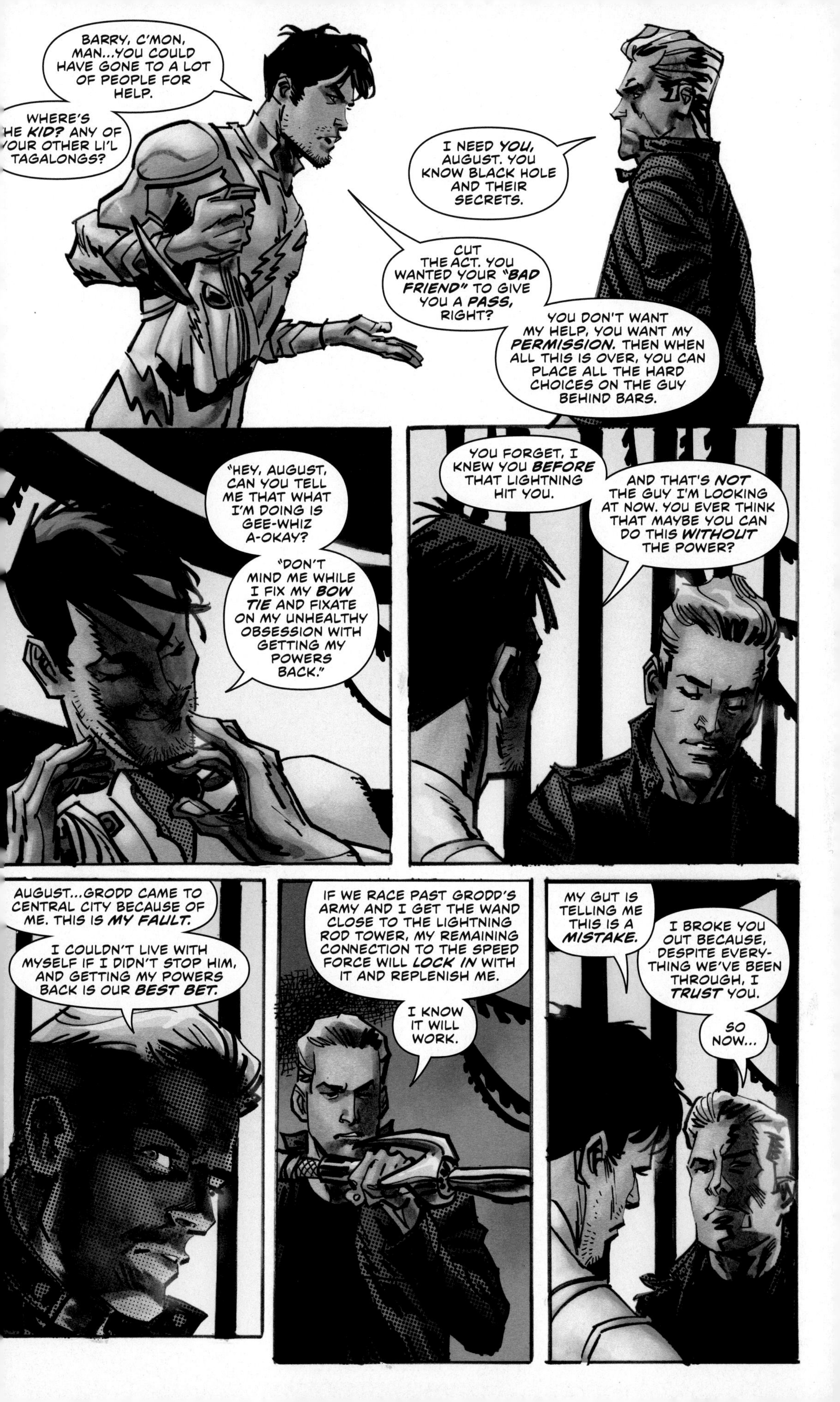
BARRY, C'MON, MAN...YOU COULD HAVE GONE TO A LOT OF PEOPLE FOR HELP.
WHERE'S THE KID? ANY OF YOUR OTHER LI'L TAGALONGS?
I NEED YOU, AUGUST. YOU KNOW BLACK HOLE AND THEIR SECRETS.
CUT THE ACT. YOU WANTED YOUR "BAD FRIEND" TO GIVE YOU A PASS, RIGHT?
YOU DON'T WANT MY HELP, YOU WANT MY PERMISSION. THEN WHEN ALL THIS IS OVER, YOU CAN PLACE ALL THE HARD CHOICES ON THE GUY BEHIND BARS.
"HEY, AUGUST, CAN YOU TELL ME THAT WHAT I'M DOING IS GEE-WHIZ A-OKAY?
"DON'T MIND ME WHILE I FIX MY BOW TIE AND FIXATE ON MY UNHEALTHY OBSESSION WITH GETTING MY POWERS BACK."
YOU FORGET, I KNEW YOU BEFORE THAT LIGHTNING HIT YOU.
AND THAT'S NOT THE GUY I'M LOOKING AT NOW. YOU EVER THINK THAT MAYBE YOU CAN DO THIS WITHOUT THE POWER?
AUGUST...GRODD CAME TO CENTRAL CITY BECAUSE OF ME. THIS IS MY FAULT.
I COULDN'T LIVE WITH MYSELF IF I DIDN'T STOP HIM, AND GETTING MY POWERS BACK IS OUR BEST BET.
IF WE RACE PAST GRODD'S ARMY AND I GET THE WAND CLOSE TO THE LIGHTNING ROD TOWER, MY REMAINING CONNECTION TO THE SPEED FORCE WILL LOCK IN WITH IT AND REPLENISH ME.
I KNOW IT WILL WORK.
MY GUT IS TELLING ME THIS IS A MISTAKE.
I BROKE YOU OUT BECAUSE, DESPITE EVERY-THING WE'VE BEEN THROUGH, I TRUST YOU.
SO NOW...

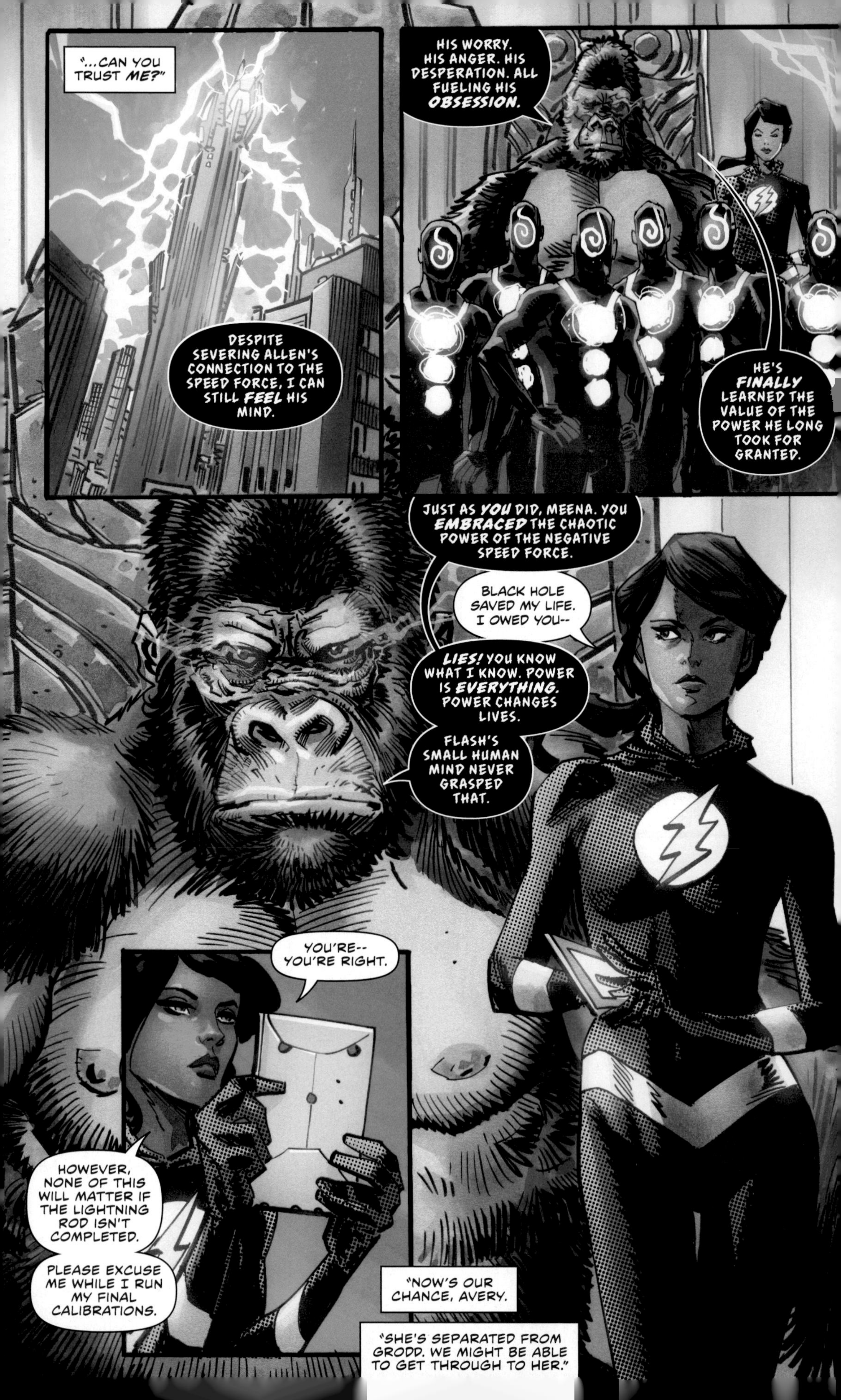
"...CAN YOU TRUST ME?"
DESPITE SEVERING ALLEN'S CONNECTION TO THE SPEED FORCE, I CAN STILL FEEL HIS MIND.
HIS WORRY. HIS ANGER. HIS DESPERATION. ALL FUELING HIS OBSESSION.
HE'S FINALLY LEARNED THE VALUE OF THE POWER HE LONG TOOK FOR GRANTED.
JUST AS YOU DID, MEENA. YOU EMBRACED THE CHAOTIC POWER OF THE NEGATIVE SPEED FORCE.
BLACK HOLE SAVED MY LIFE. I OWED YOU--
LIES! YOU KNOW WHAT I KNOW. POWER IS EVERYTHING. POWER CHANGES LIVES.
FLASH'S SMALL HUMAN MIND NEVER GRASPED THAT.
YOU'RE-- YOU'RE RIGHT.
HOWEVER, NONE OF THIS WILL MATTER IF THE LIGHTNING ROD ISN'T COMPLETED.
PLEASE EXCUSE ME WHILE I RUN MY FINAL CALIBRATIONS.
"NOW'S OUR CHANCE, AVERY.
"SHE'S SEPARATED FROM GRODD. WE MIGHT BE ABLE TO GET THROUGH TO HER."

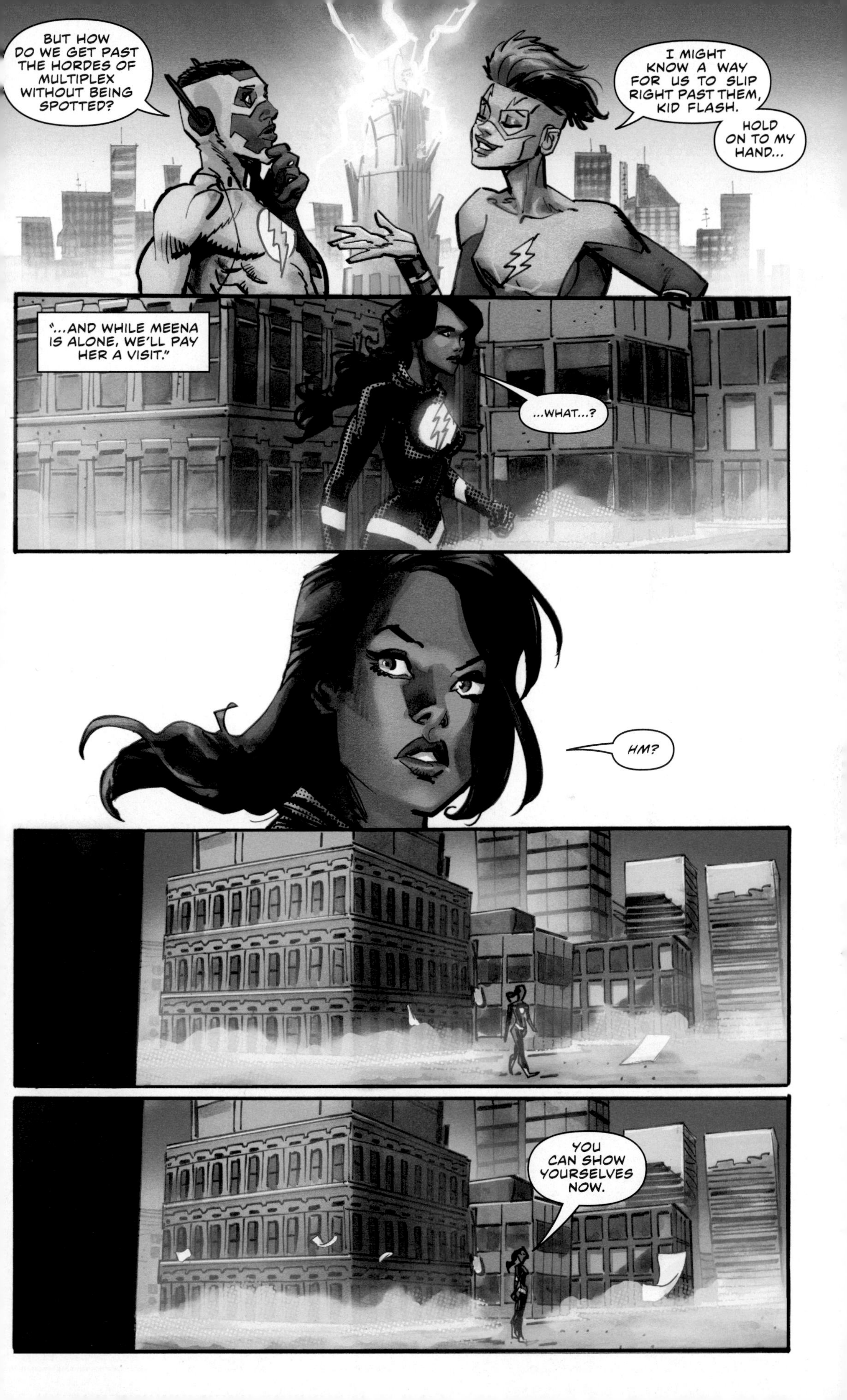
BUT HOW DO WE GET PAST THE HORDES OF MULTIPLEX WITHOUT BEING SPOTTED?
I MIGHT KNOW A WAY FOR US TO SLIP RIGHT PAST THEM, KID FLASH.
HOLD ON TO MY HAND...
"...AND WHILE MEENA IS ALONE, WE'LL PAY HER A VISIT."
...WHAT...?
HM?
YOU CAN SHOW YOURSELVES NOW.

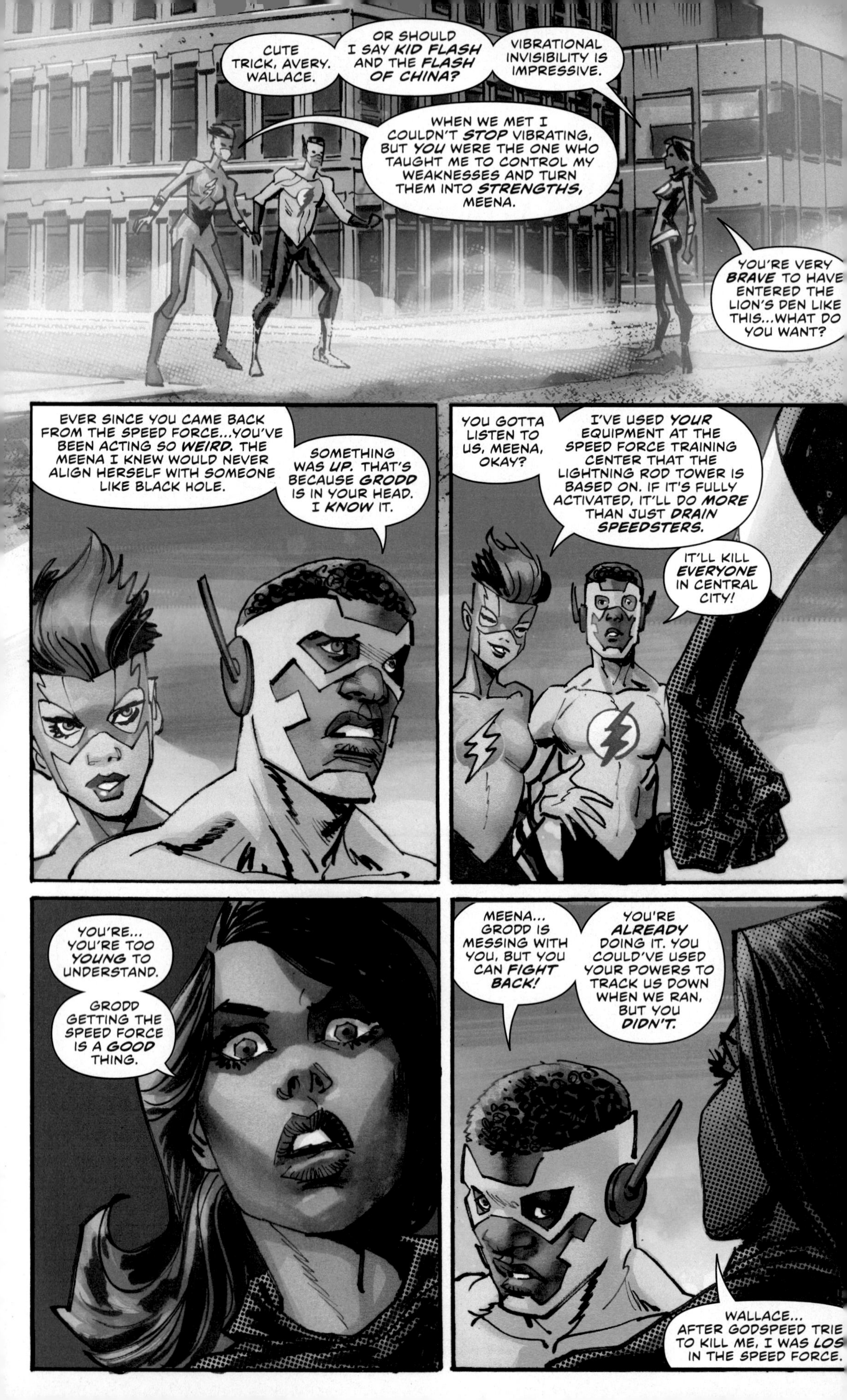
CUTE TRICK, AVERY. WALLACE.
OR SHOULD I SAY KID FLASH AND THE FLASH OF CHINA?
VIBRATIONAL INVISIBILITY IS IMPRESSIVE.
WHEN WE MET I COULDN'T STOP VIBRATING, BUT YOU WERE THE ONE WHO TAUGHT ME TO CONTROL MY WEAKNESSES AND TURN THEM INTO STRENGTHS, MEENA.
YOU'RE VERY BRAVE TO HAVE ENTERED THE LION'S DEN LIKE THIS...WHAT DO YOU WANT?
EVER SINCE YOU CAME BACK FROM THE SPEED FORCE...YOU'VE BEEN ACTING SO WEIRD. THE MEENA I KNEW WOULD NEVER ALIGN HERSELF WITH SOMEONE LIKE BLACK HOLE.
SOMETHING WAS UP. THAT'S BECAUSE GRODD IS IN YOUR HEAD. I KNOW IT.
YOU GOTTA LISTEN TO US, MEENA, OKAY?
I'VE USED YOUR EQUIPMENT AT THE SPEED FORCE TRAINING CENTER THAT THE LIGHTNING ROD TOWER IS BASED ON. IF IT'S FULLY ACTIVATED, IT'LL DO MORE THAN JUST DRAIN SPEEDSTERS.
IT'LL KILL EVERYONE IN CENTRAL CITY!
YOU'RE... YOU'RE TOO YOUNG TO UNDERSTAND.
GRODD GETTING THE SPEED FORCE IS A GOOD THING.
MEENA... GRODD IS MESSING WITH YOU, BUT YOU CAN FIGHT BACK!
YOU'RE ALREADY DOING IT. YOU COULD'VE USED YOUR POWERS TO TRACK US DOWN WHEN WE RAN, BUT YOU DIDN'T.
WALLACE... AFTER GODSPEED TRIE TO KILL ME, I WAS LOS IN THE SPEED FORCE.

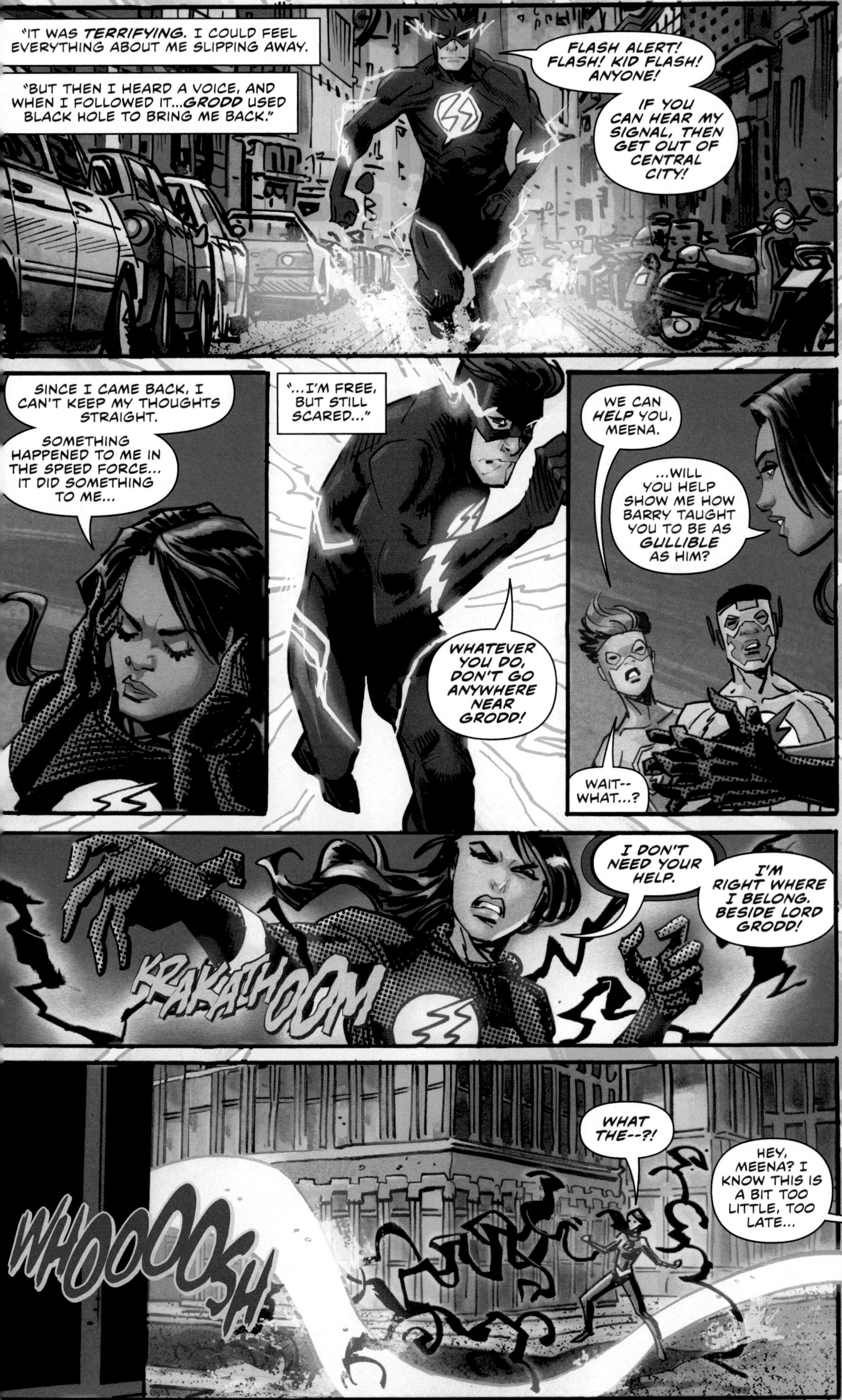
"IT WAS TERRIFYING. I COULD FEEL EVERYTHING ABOUT ME SLIPPING AWAY.
"BUT THEN I HEARD A VOICE, AND WHEN I FOLLOWED IT...GRODD USED BLACK HOLE TO BRING ME BACK."
FLASH ALERT! FLASH! KID FLASH! ANYONE!
IF YOU CAN HEAR MY SIGNAL, THEN GET OUT OF CENTRAL CITY!
SINCE I CAME BACK, I CAN'T KEEP MY THOUGHTS STRAIGHT.
SOMETHING HAPPENED TO ME IN THE SPEED FORCE... IT DID SOMETHING TO ME...
"...I'M FREE, BUT STILL SCARED..."
WHATEVER YOU DO, DON'T GO ANYWHERE NEAR GRODD!
WE CAN HELP YOU, MEENA.
...WILL YOU HELP SHOW ME HOW BARRY TAUGHT YOU TO BE AS GULLIBLE AS HIM?
WAIT-- WHAT...?
KRAKATHOOM
I DON'T NEED YOUR HELP.
I'M RIGHT WHERE I BELONG. BESIDE LORD GRODD!
WHOOOOSH
WHAT THE--?!
HEY, MEENA? I KNOW THIS IS A BIT TOO LITTLE, TOO LATE...

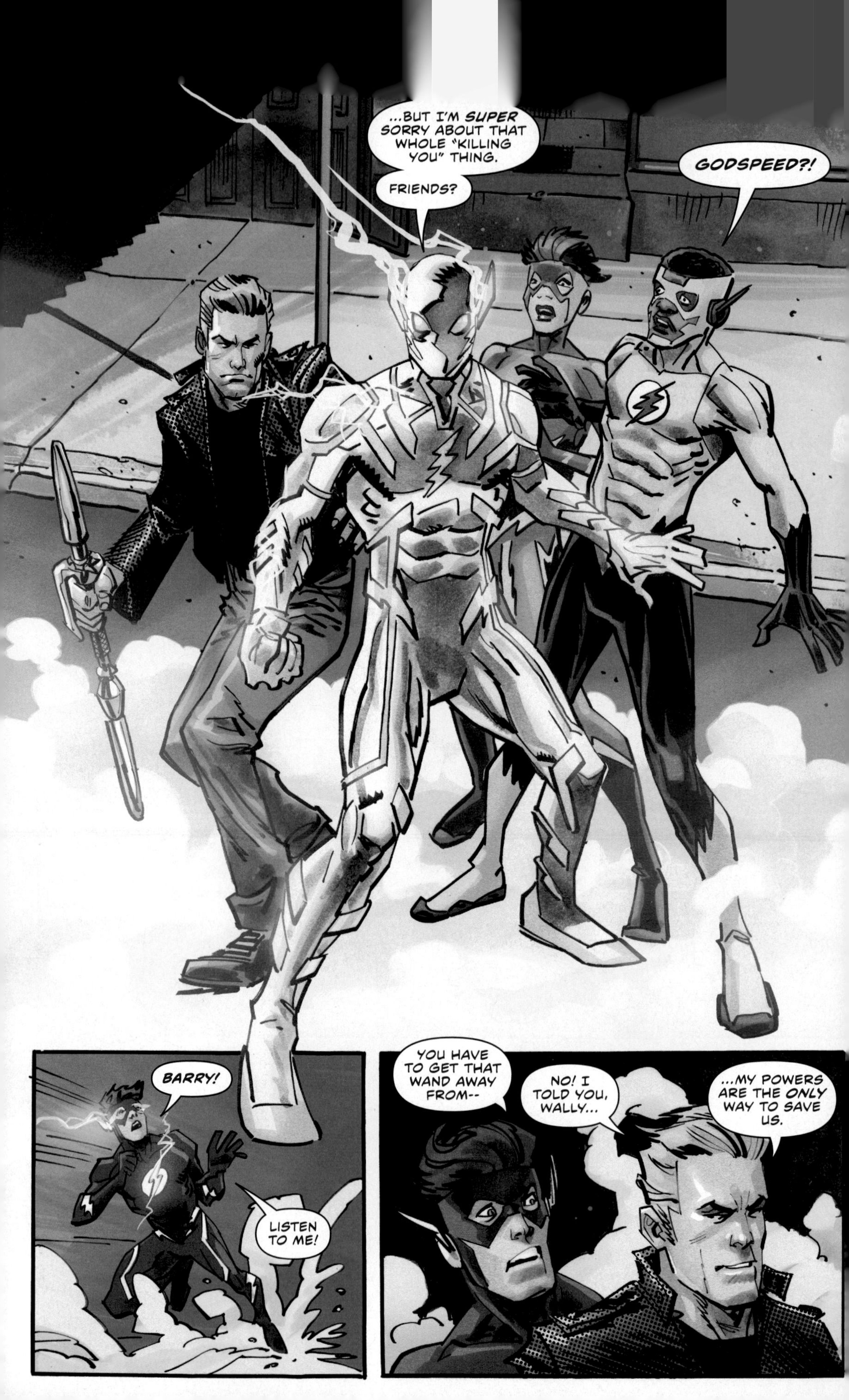
...BUT I'M SUPER SORRY ABOUT THAT WHOLE "KILLING YOU" THING.
FRIENDS?
GODSPEED?!
BARRY!
LISTEN TO ME!
YOU HAVE TO GET THAT WAND AWAY FROM--
NO! I TOLD YOU, WALLY...
...MY POWERS ARE THE ONLY WAY TO SAVE US.

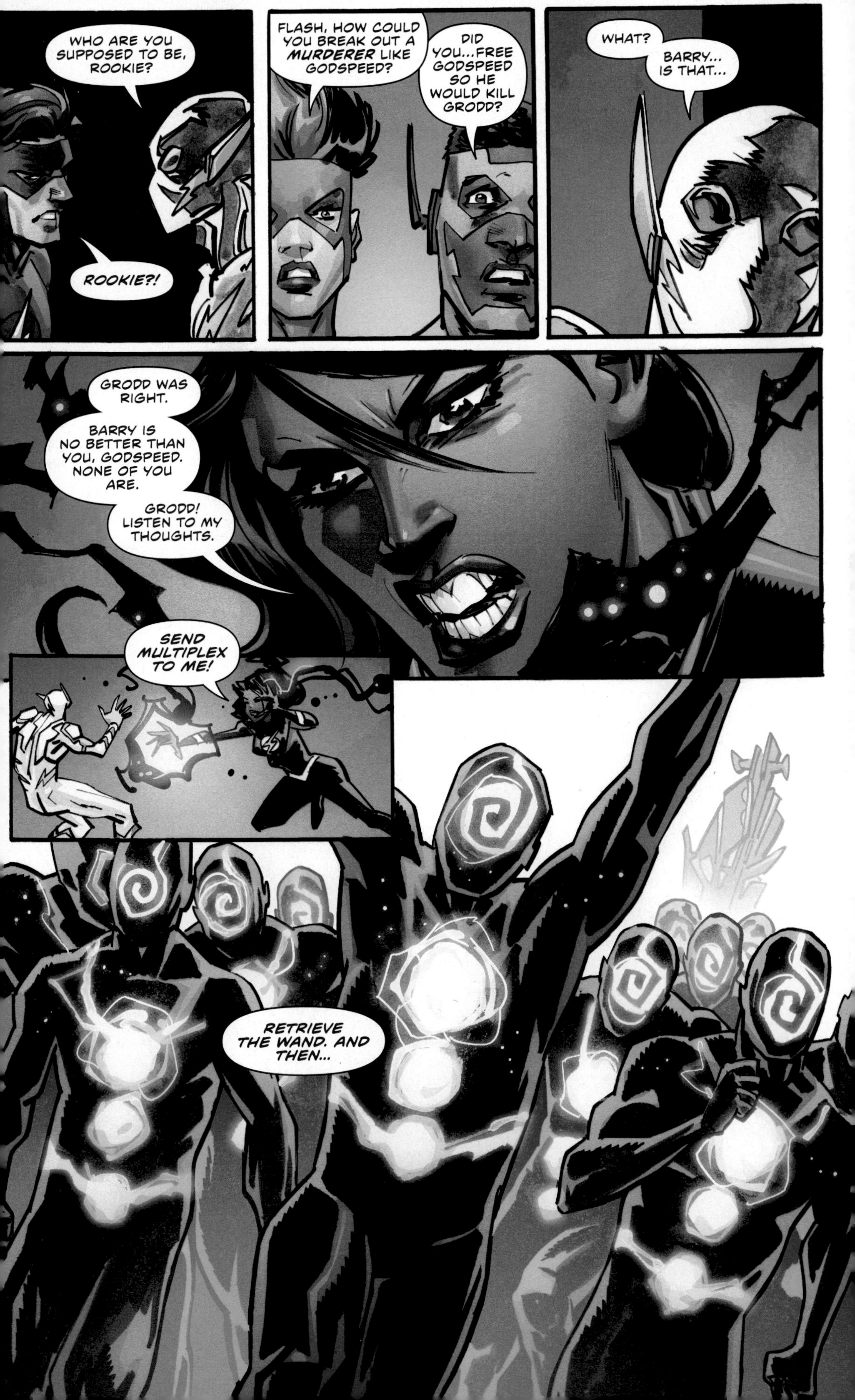
WHO ARE YOU SUPPOSED TO BE, ROOKIE?
ROOKIE?!
FLASH, HOW COULD YOU BREAK OUT A *MURDERER* LIKE GODSPEED?
DID YOU...FREE GODSPEED SO HE WOULD KILL GRODD?
WHAT?
BARRY... IS THAT...
GRODD WAS RIGHT.
BARRY IS NO BETTER THAN YOU, GODSPEED. NONE OF YOU ARE.
GRODD! LISTEN TO MY THOUGHTS.
SEND MULTIPLEX TO ME!
RETRIEVE THE WAND. AND THEN...

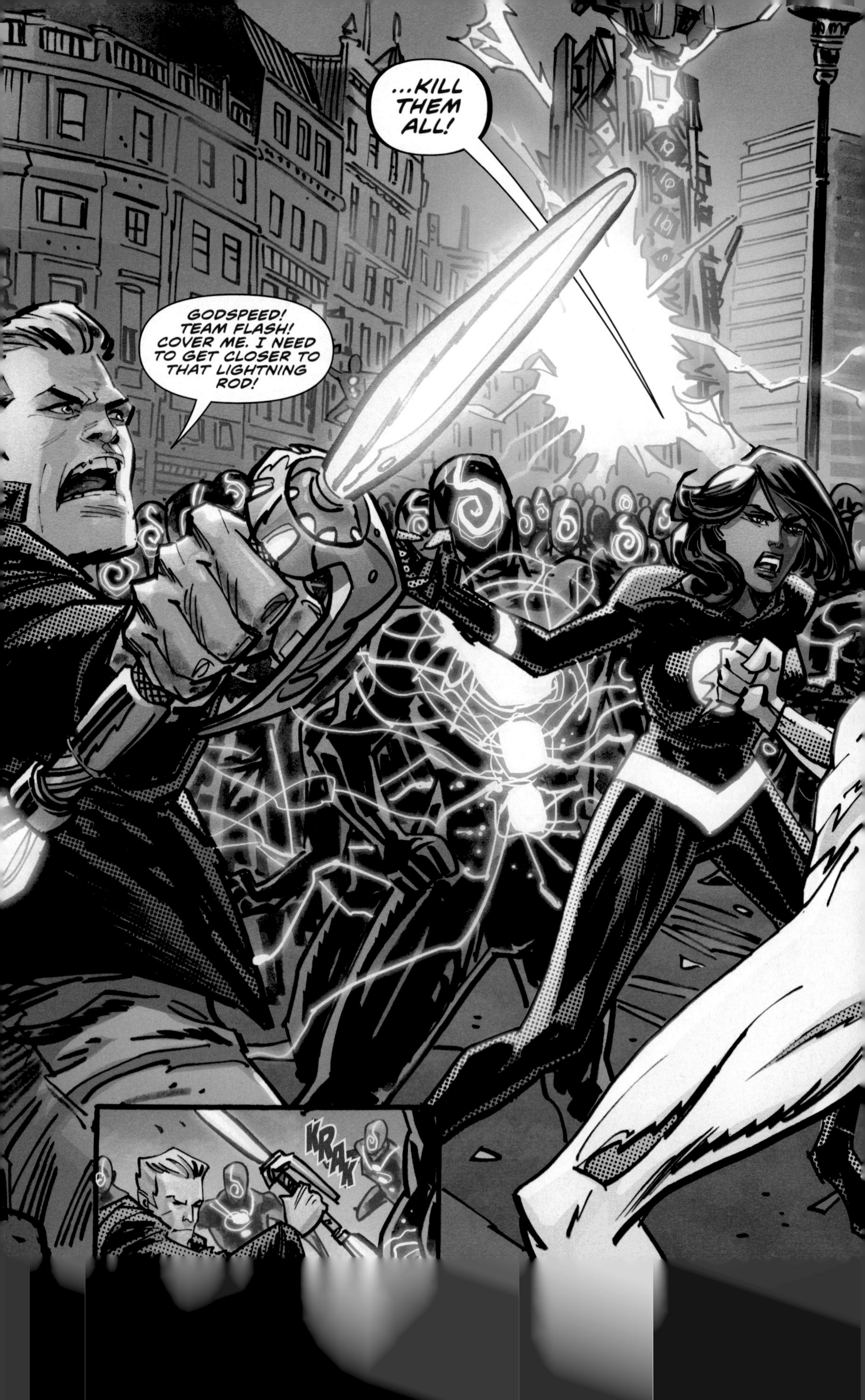
...KILL THEM ALL!
GODSPEED! TEAM FLASH! COVER ME. I NEED TO GET CLOSER TO THAT LIGHTNING ROD!
KRAK

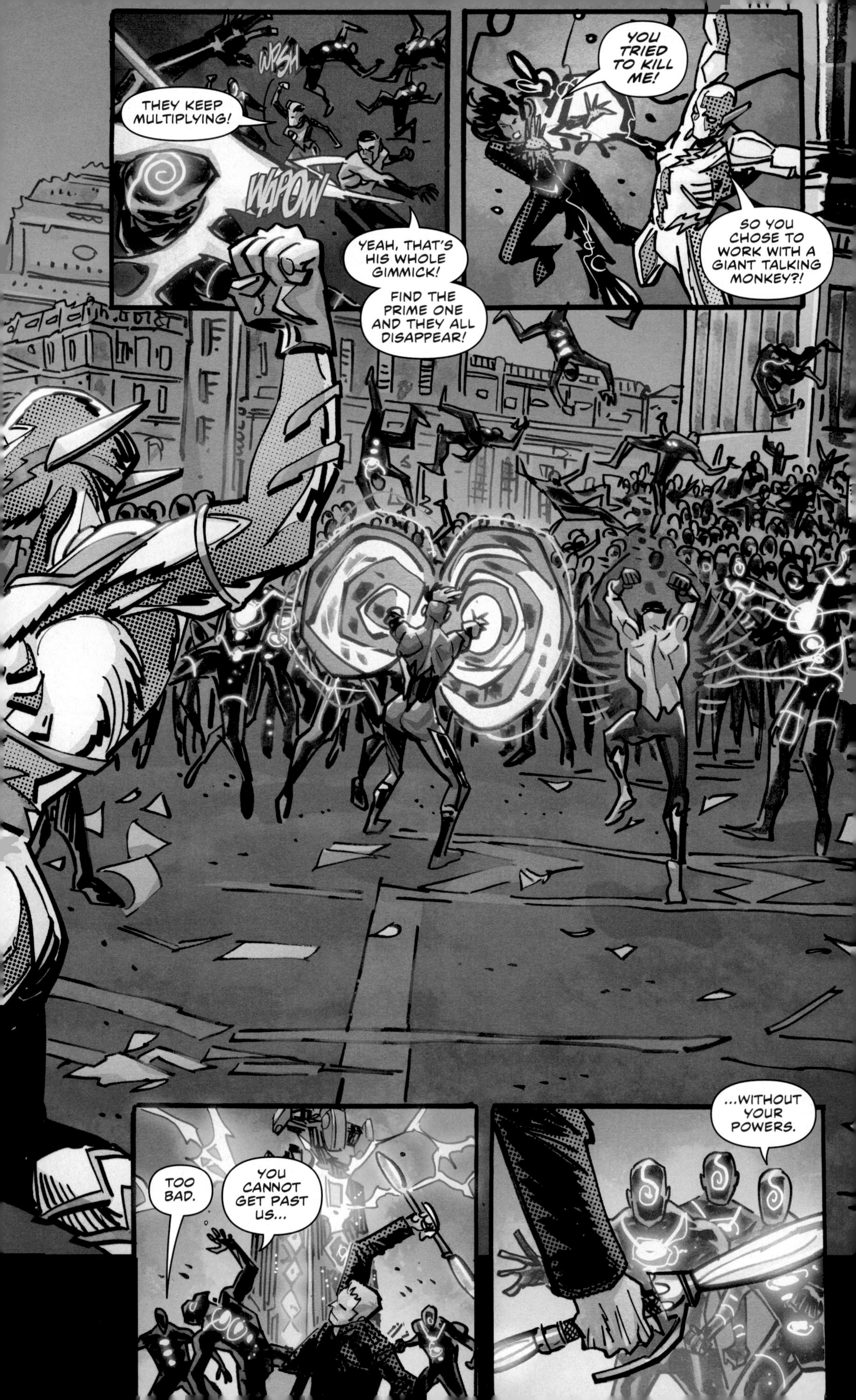
WPSH
THEY KEEP MULTIPLYING!
WAPOW
YOU TRIED TO KILL ME!
SO YOU CHOSE TO WORK WITH A GIANT TALKING MONKEY?!
YEAH, THAT'S HIS WHOLE GIMMICK!
FIND THE PRIME ONE AND THEY ALL DISAPPEAR!
TOO BAD.
YOU CANNOT GET PAST US...
...WITHOUT YOUR POWERS.

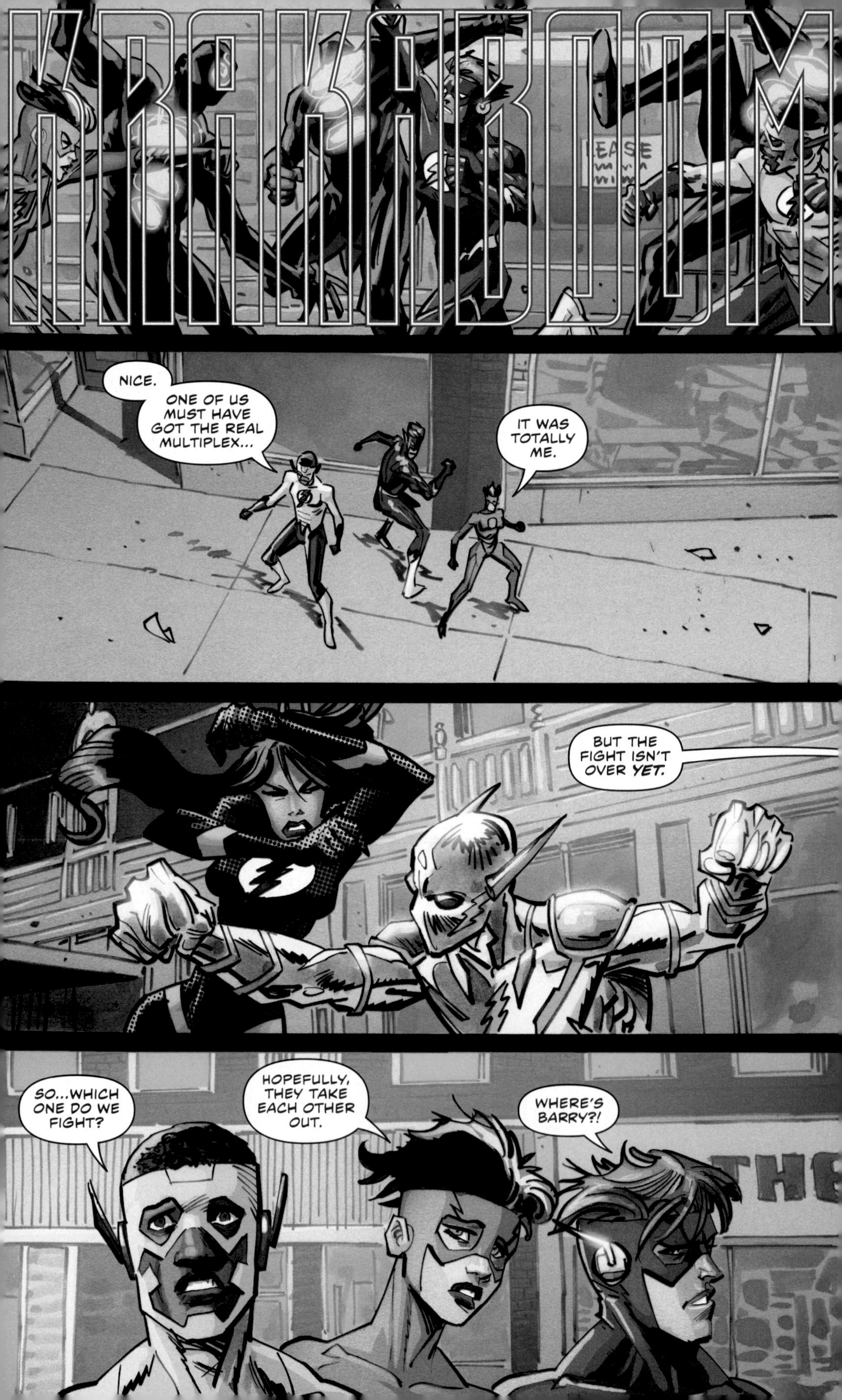
KRAKABOOM
NICE.
ONE OF US MUST HAVE GOT THE REAL MULTIPLEX...
IT WAS TOTALLY ME.
BUT THE FIGHT ISN'T OVER YET.
SO...WHICH ONE DO WE FIGHT?
HOPEFULLY, THEY TAKE EACH OTHER OUT.
WHERE'S BARRY?!

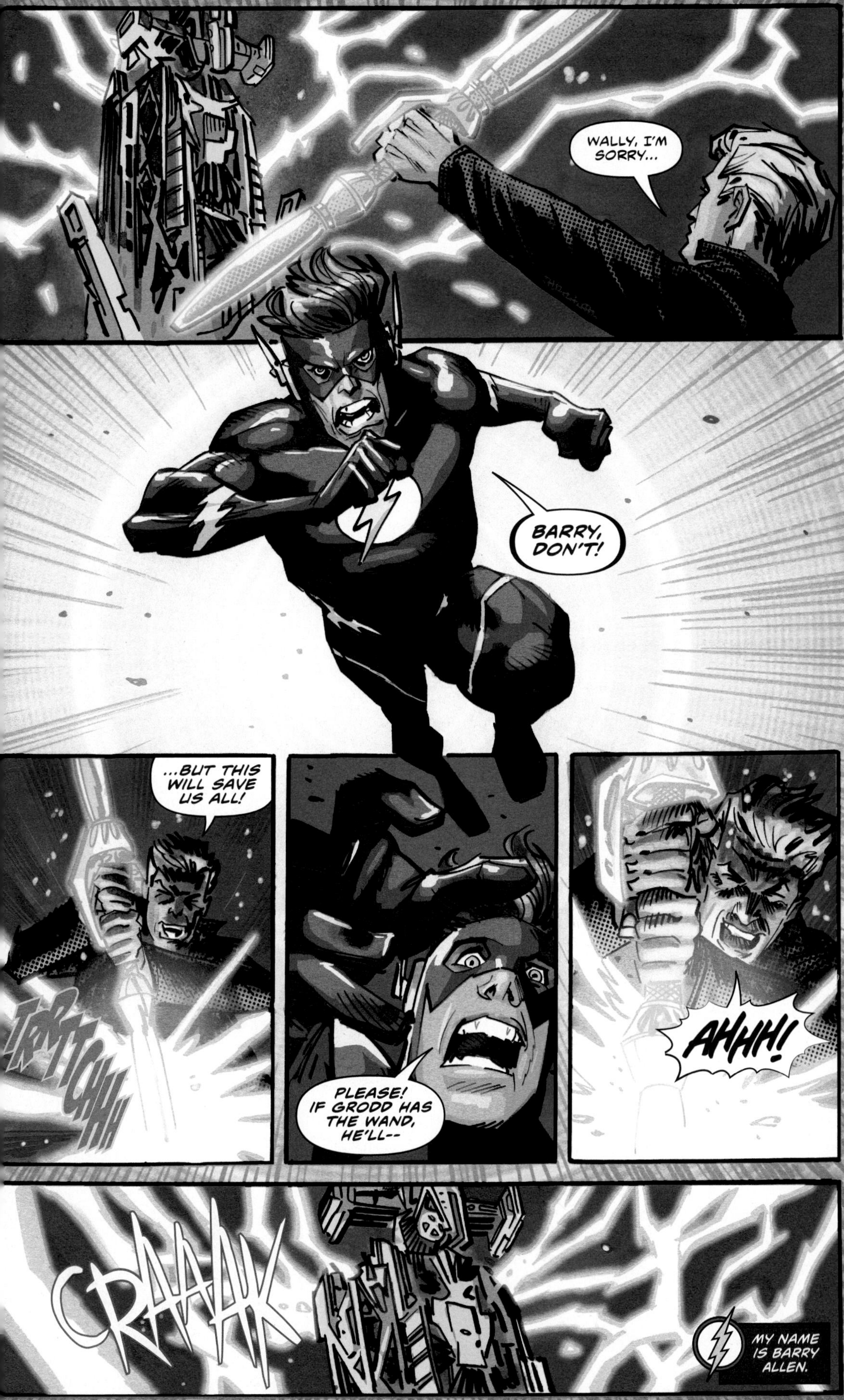
WALLY, I'M SORRY...
BARRY, DON'T!
...BUT THIS WILL SAVE US ALL!
TRRTCHHH
PLEASE! IF GRODD HAS THE WAND, HE'LL--
AHHH!
CRAAAK
MY NAME IS BARRY ALLEN.

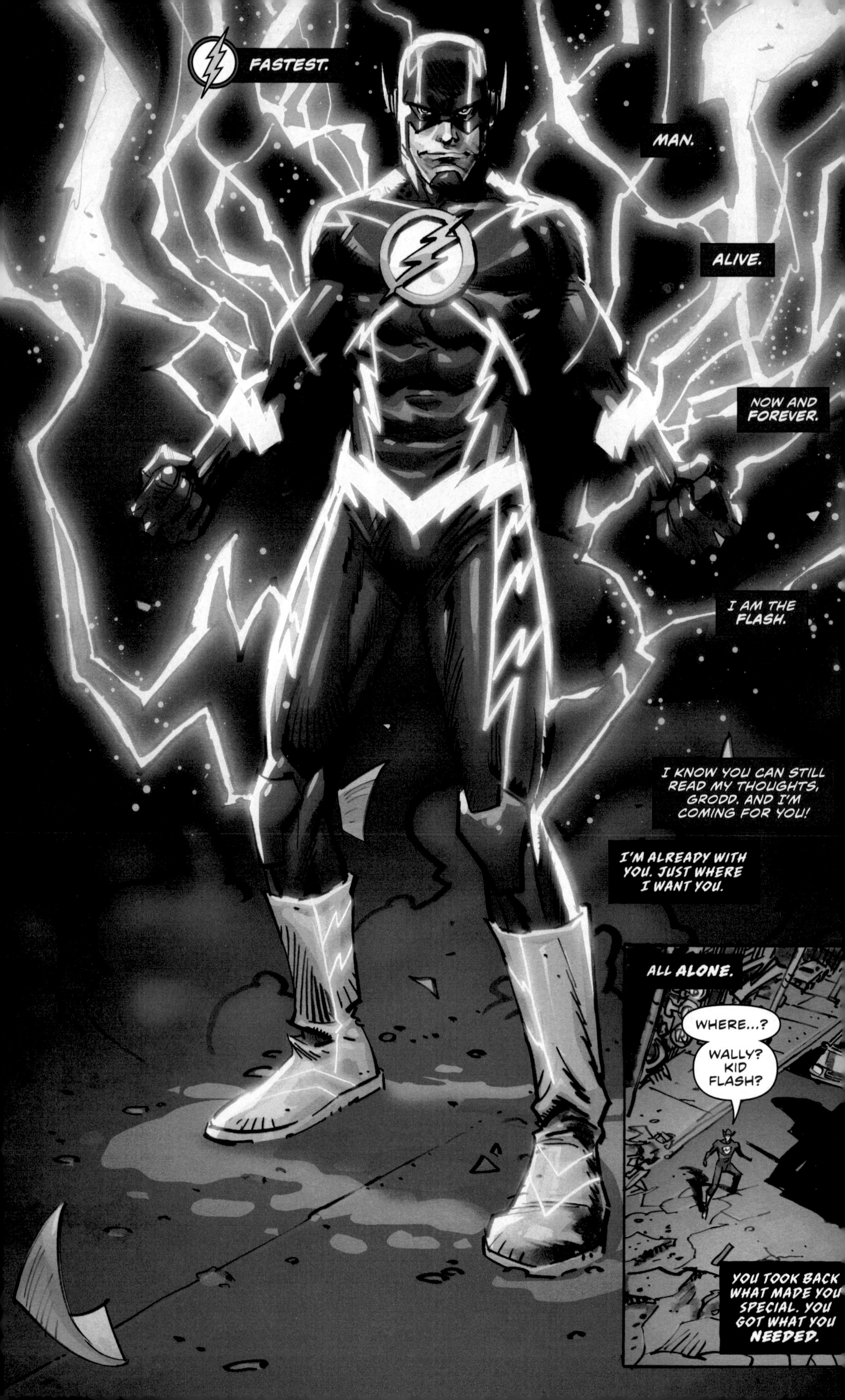
FASTEST.
MAN.
ALIVE.
NOW AND FOREVER.
I AM THE FLASH.
I KNOW YOU CAN STILL READ MY THOUGHTS, GRODD. AND I'M COMING FOR YOU!
I'M ALREADY WITH YOU. JUST WHERE I WANT YOU.
ALL ALONE.
WHERE...?
WALLY? KID FLASH?
YOU TOOK BACK WHAT MADE YOU SPECIAL. YOU GOT WHAT YOU NEEDED.

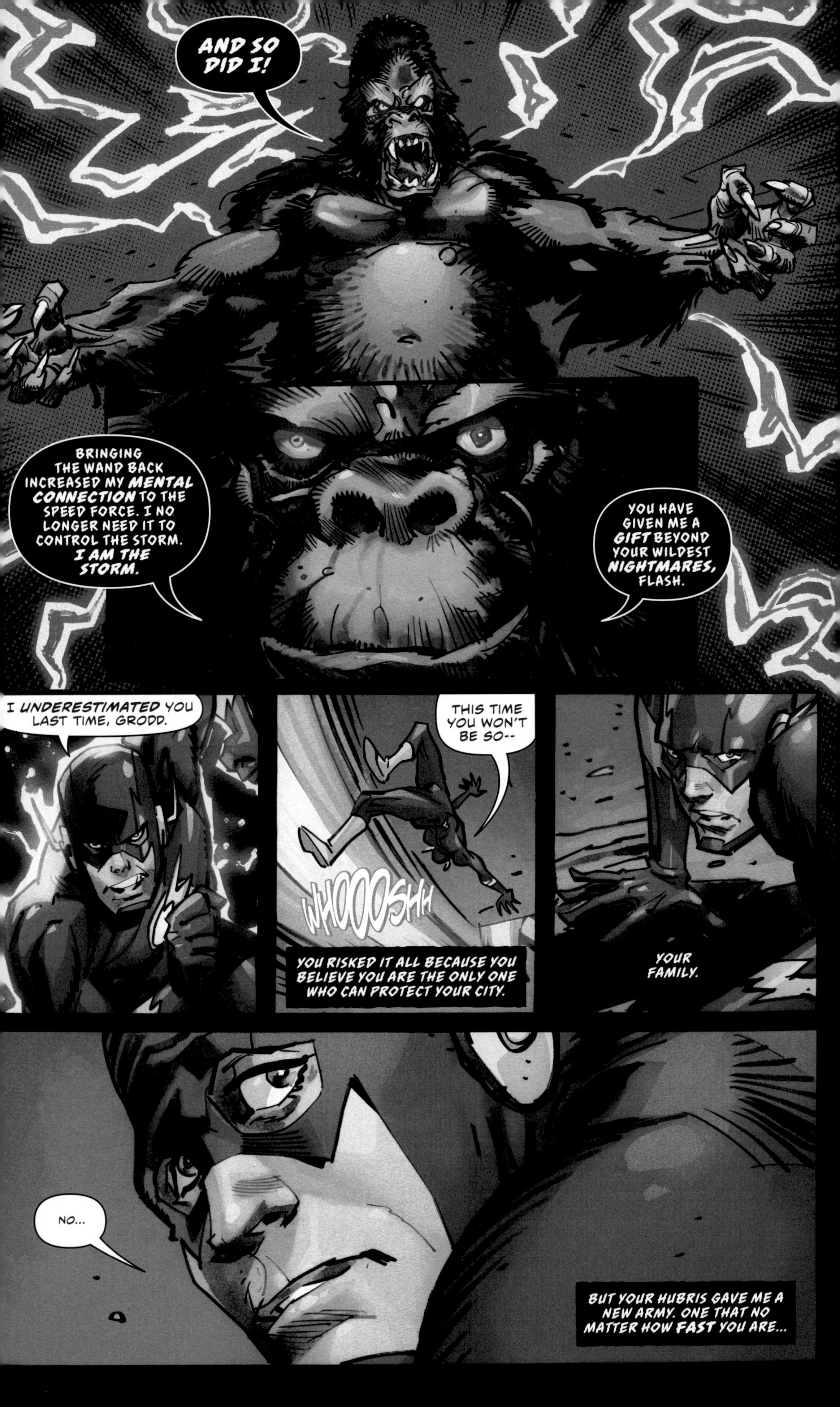
AND SO DID I!
BRINGING THE WAND BACK INCREASED MY MENTAL CONNECTION TO THE SPEED FORCE. I NO LONGER NEED IT TO CONTROL THE STORM. I AM THE STORM.
YOU HAVE GIVEN ME A GIFT BEYOND YOUR WILDEST NIGHTMARES, FLASH.
I UNDERESTIMATED YOU LAST TIME, GRODD.
THIS TIME YOU WON'T BE SO--
WHOOOSHH
YOU RISKED IT ALL BECAUSE YOU BELIEVE YOU ARE THE ONLY ONE WHO CAN PROTECT YOUR CITY.
YOUR FAMILY.
NO...
BUT YOUR HUBRIS GAVE ME A NEW ARMY. ONE THAT NO MATTER HOW FAST YOU ARE...

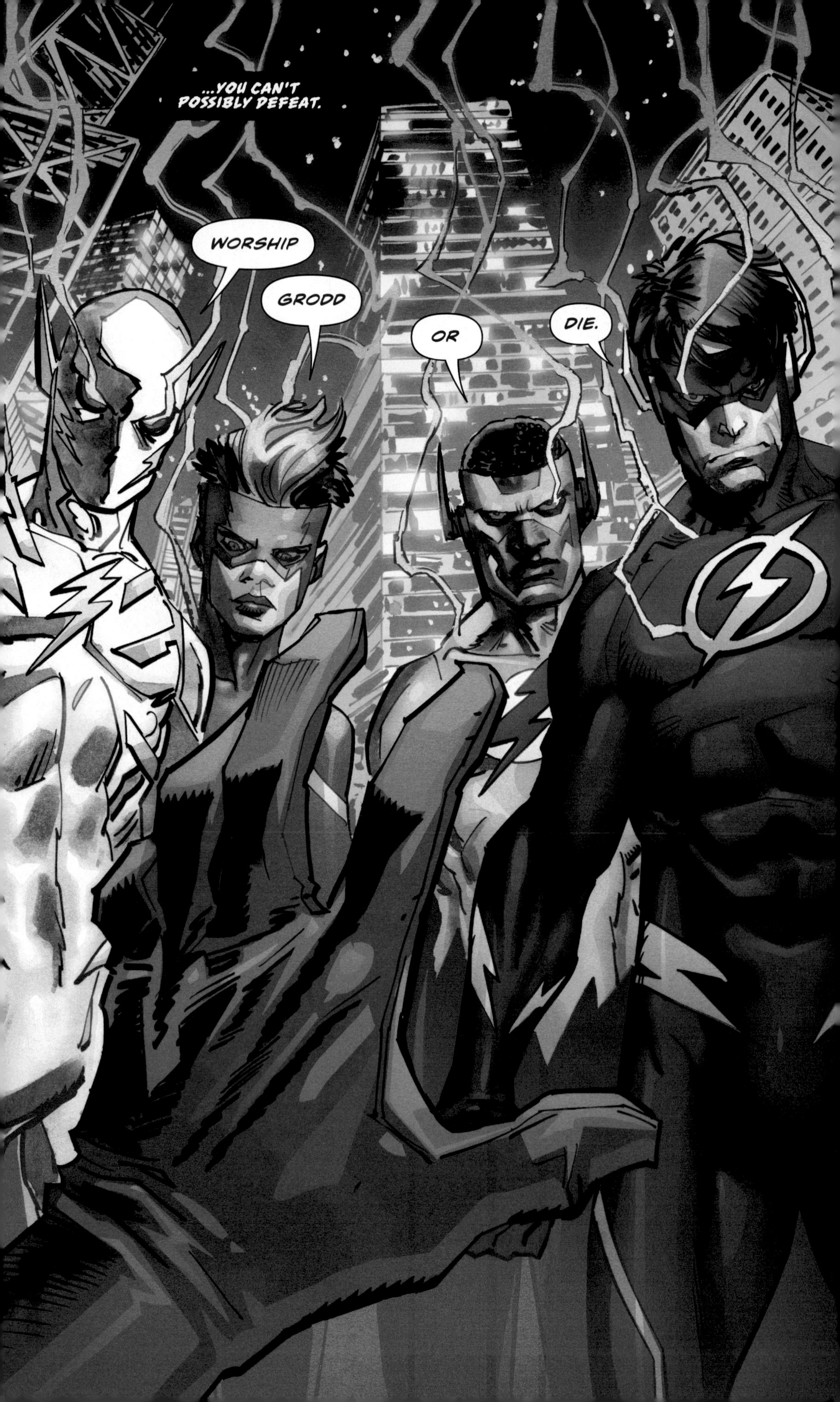
...YOU CAN'T
POSSIBLY DEFEAT.
WORSHIP
GRODD
OR
DIE.

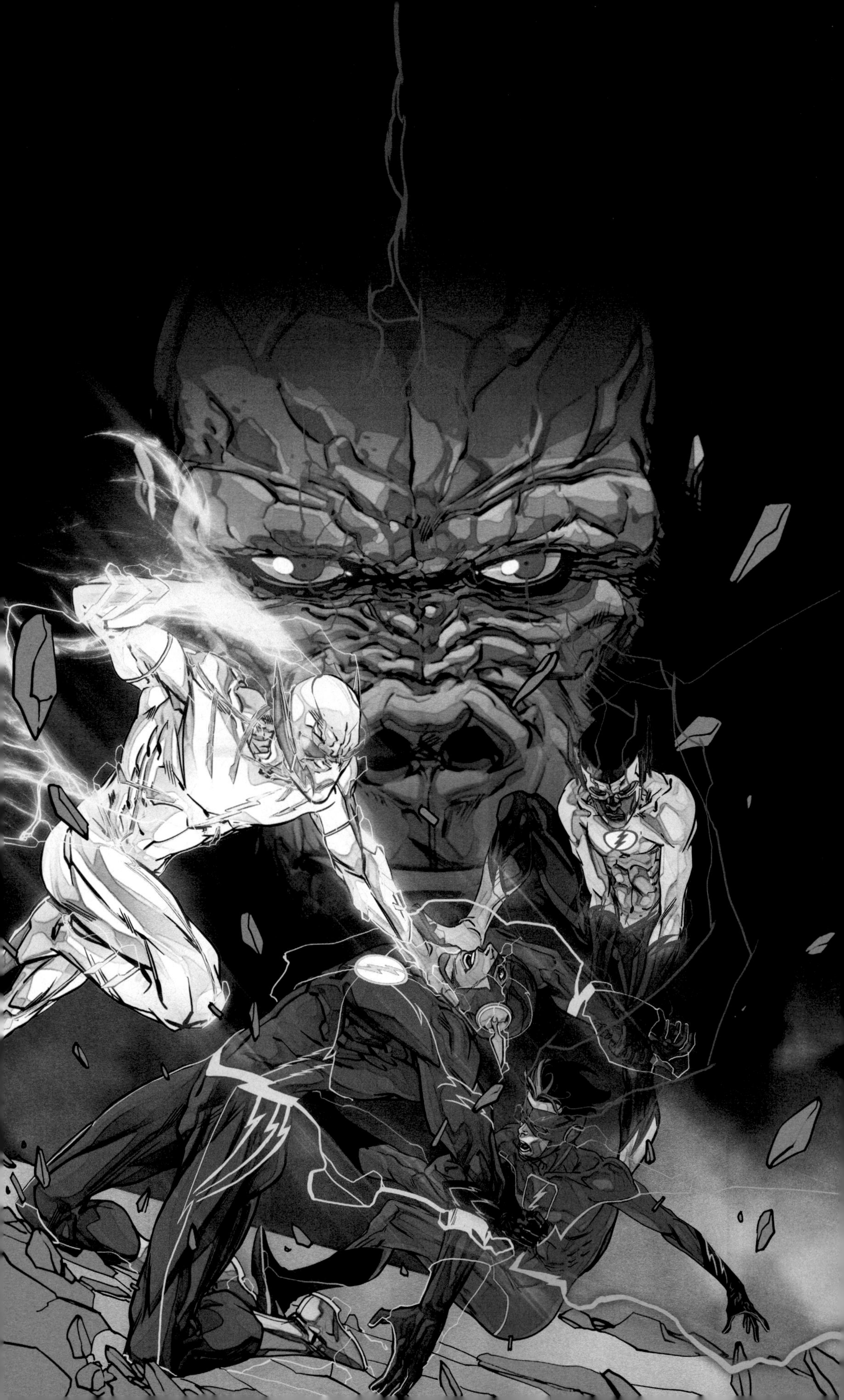

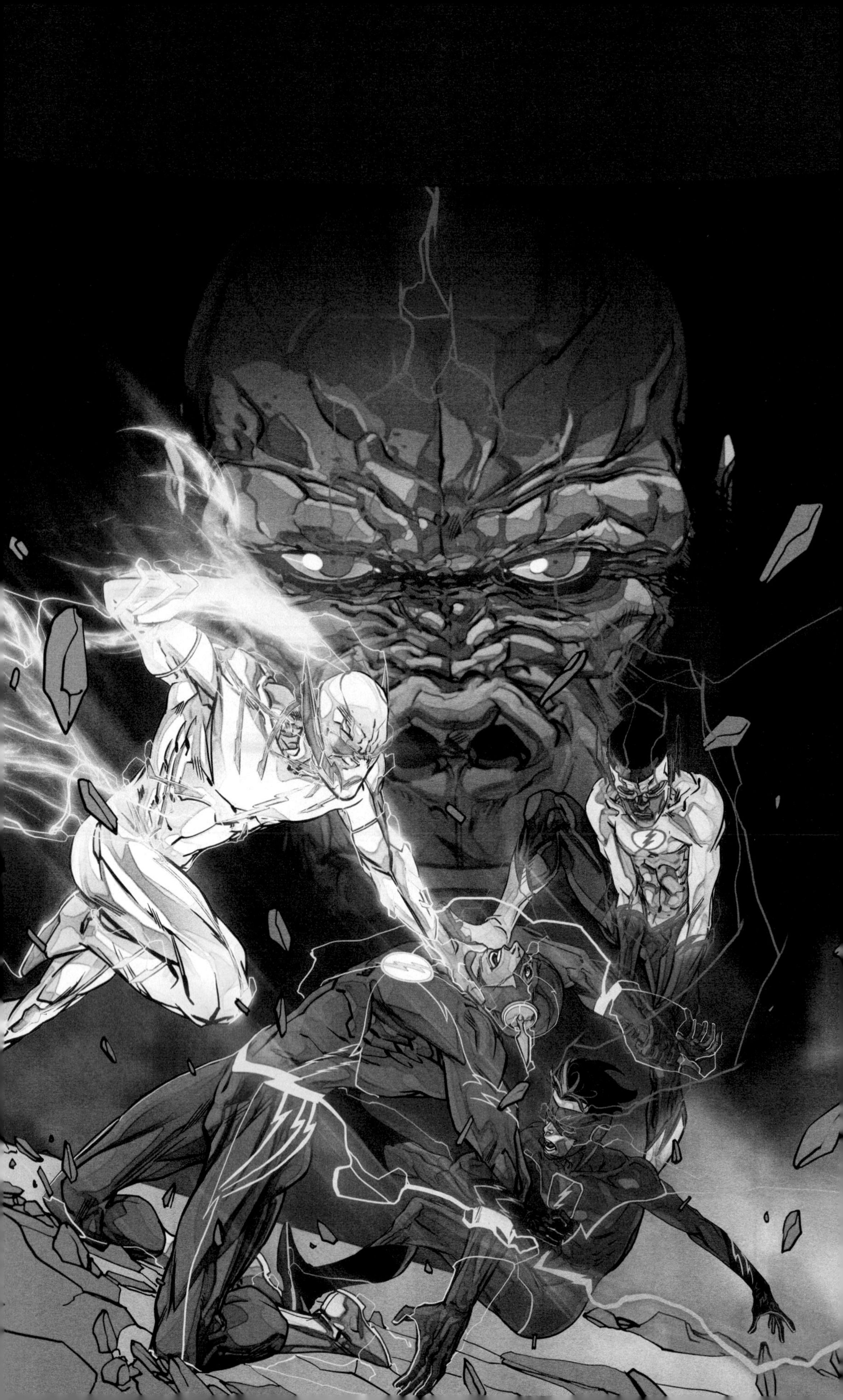

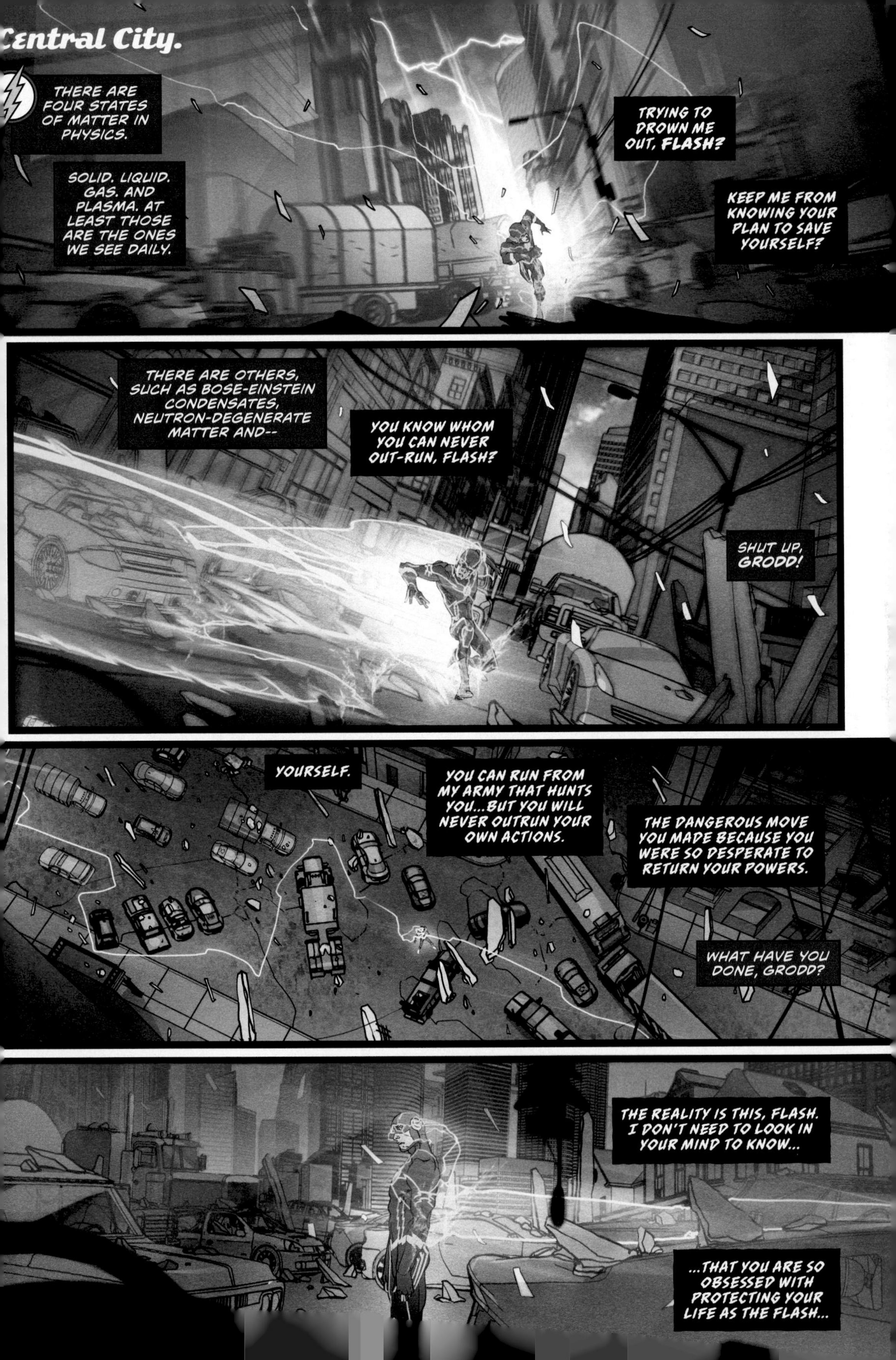
Central City.
THERE ARE FOUR STATES OF MATTER IN PHYSICS.
SOLID. LIQUID. GAS. AND PLASMA. AT LEAST THOSE ARE THE ONES WE SEE DAILY.
TRYING TO DROWN ME OUT, FLASH?
KEEP ME FROM KNOWING YOUR PLAN TO SAVE YOURSELF?
THERE ARE OTHERS, SUCH AS BOSE-EINSTEIN CONDENSATES, NEUTRON-DEGENERATE MATTER AND--
YOU KNOW WHOM YOU CAN NEVER OUT-RUN, FLASH?
SHUT UP, GRODD!
YOURSELF.
YOU CAN RUN FROM MY ARMY THAT HUNTS YOU...BUT YOU WILL NEVER OUTRUN YOUR OWN ACTIONS.
THE DANGEROUS MOVE YOU MADE BECAUSE YOU WERE SO DESPERATE TO RETURN YOUR POWERS.
WHAT HAVE YOU DONE, GRODD?
THE REALITY IS THIS, FLASH. I DON'T NEED TO LOOK IN YOUR MIND TO KNOW...
...THAT YOU ARE SO OBSESSED WITH PROTECTING YOUR LIFE AS THE FLASH...

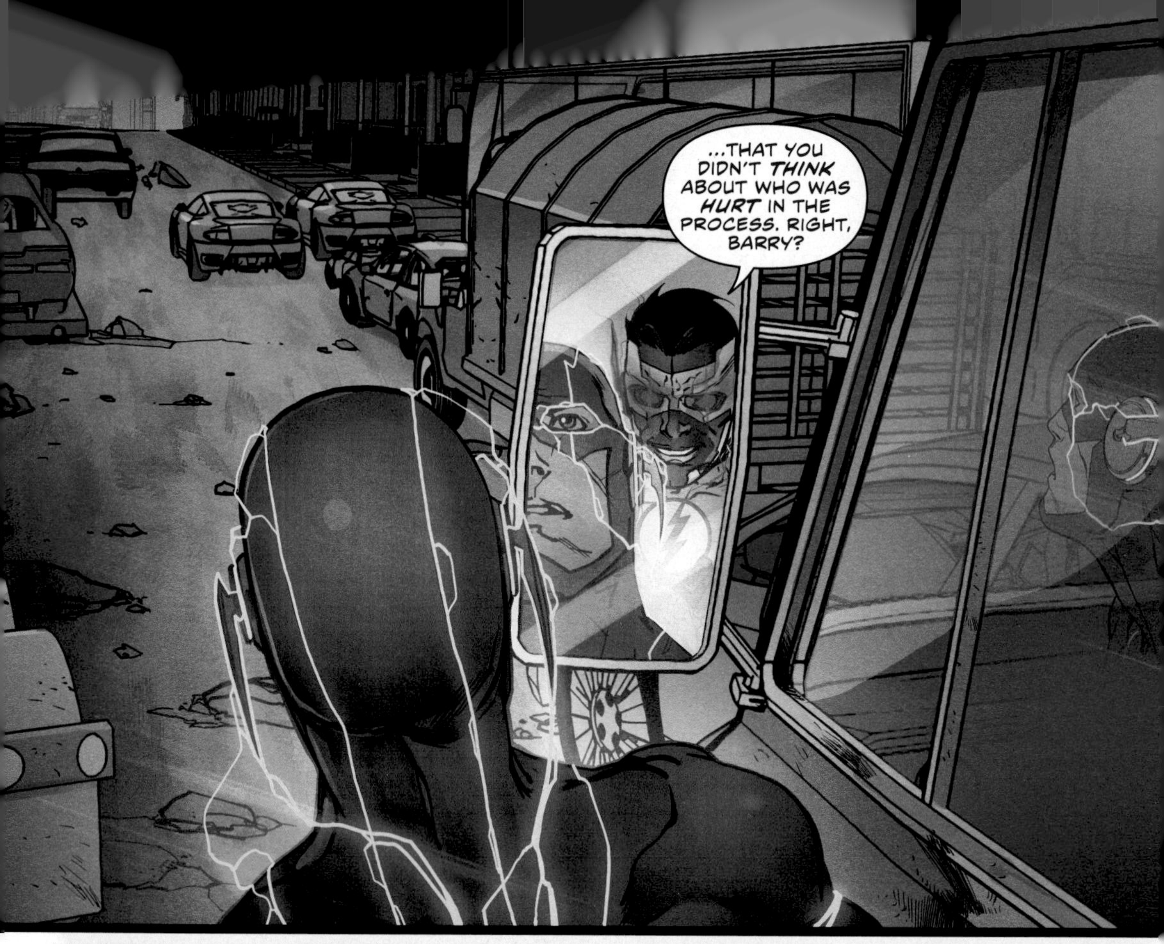
...THAT YOU DIDN'T *THINK* ABOUT WHO WAS *HURT* IN THE PROCESS. RIGHT, BARRY?

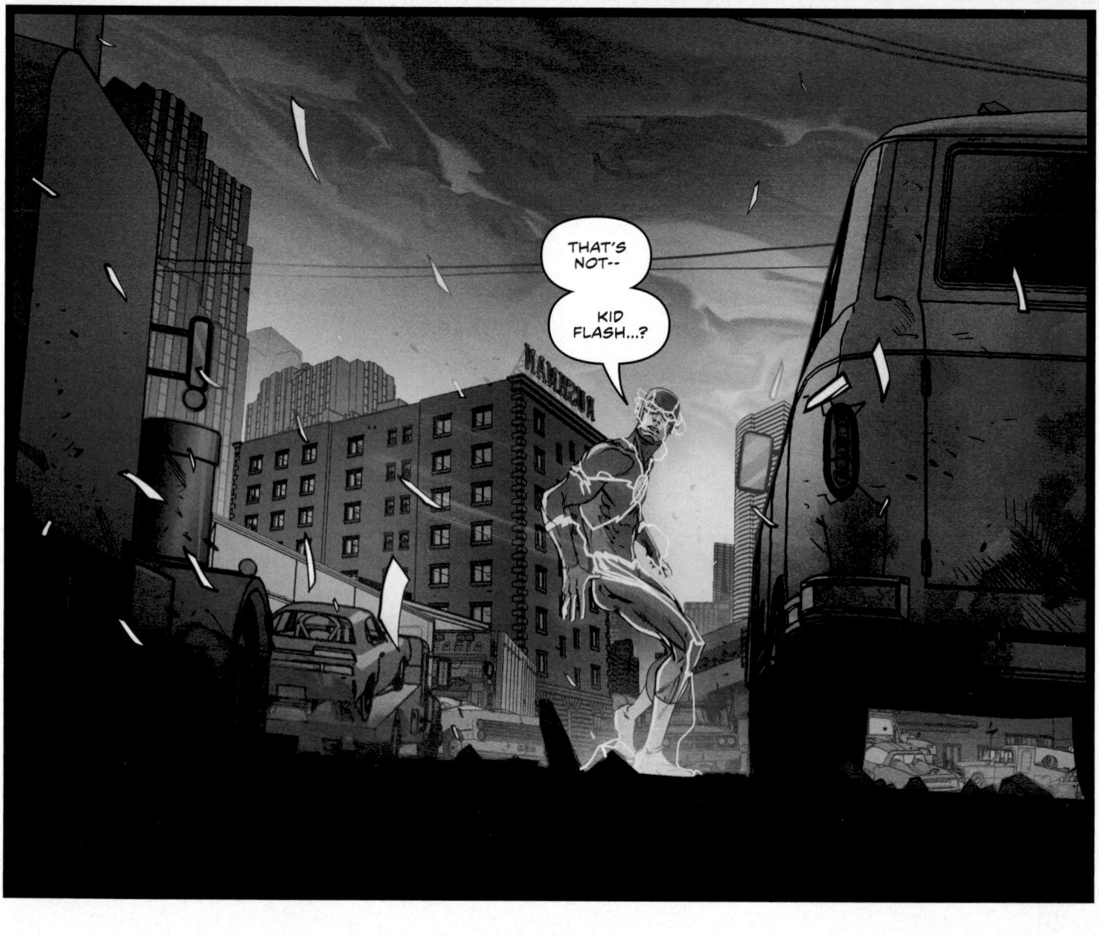
THAT'S NOT--
KID FLASH...?

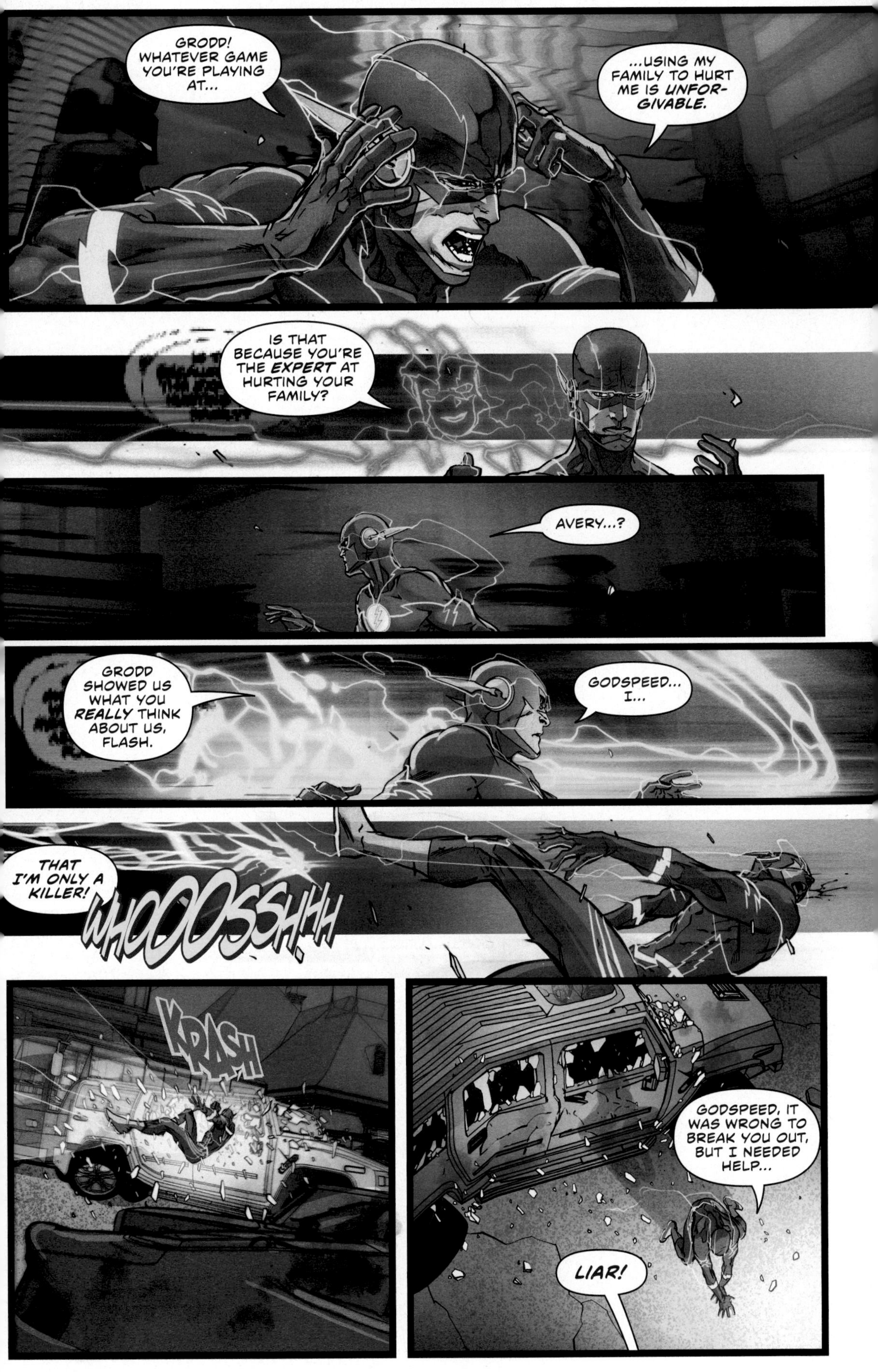
GRODD! WHATEVER GAME YOU'RE PLAYING AT...
...USING MY FAMILY TO HURT ME IS UNFORGIVABLE.
IS THAT BECAUSE YOU'RE THE EXPERT AT HURTING YOUR FAMILY?
AVERY...?
GRODD SHOWED US WHAT YOU REALLY THINK ABOUT US, FLASH.
GODSPEED... I...
THAT I'M ONLY A KILLER!
WHOOOSSHHH
KRASH
GODSPEED, IT WAS WRONG TO BREAK YOU OUT, BUT I NEEDED HELP...
LIAR!

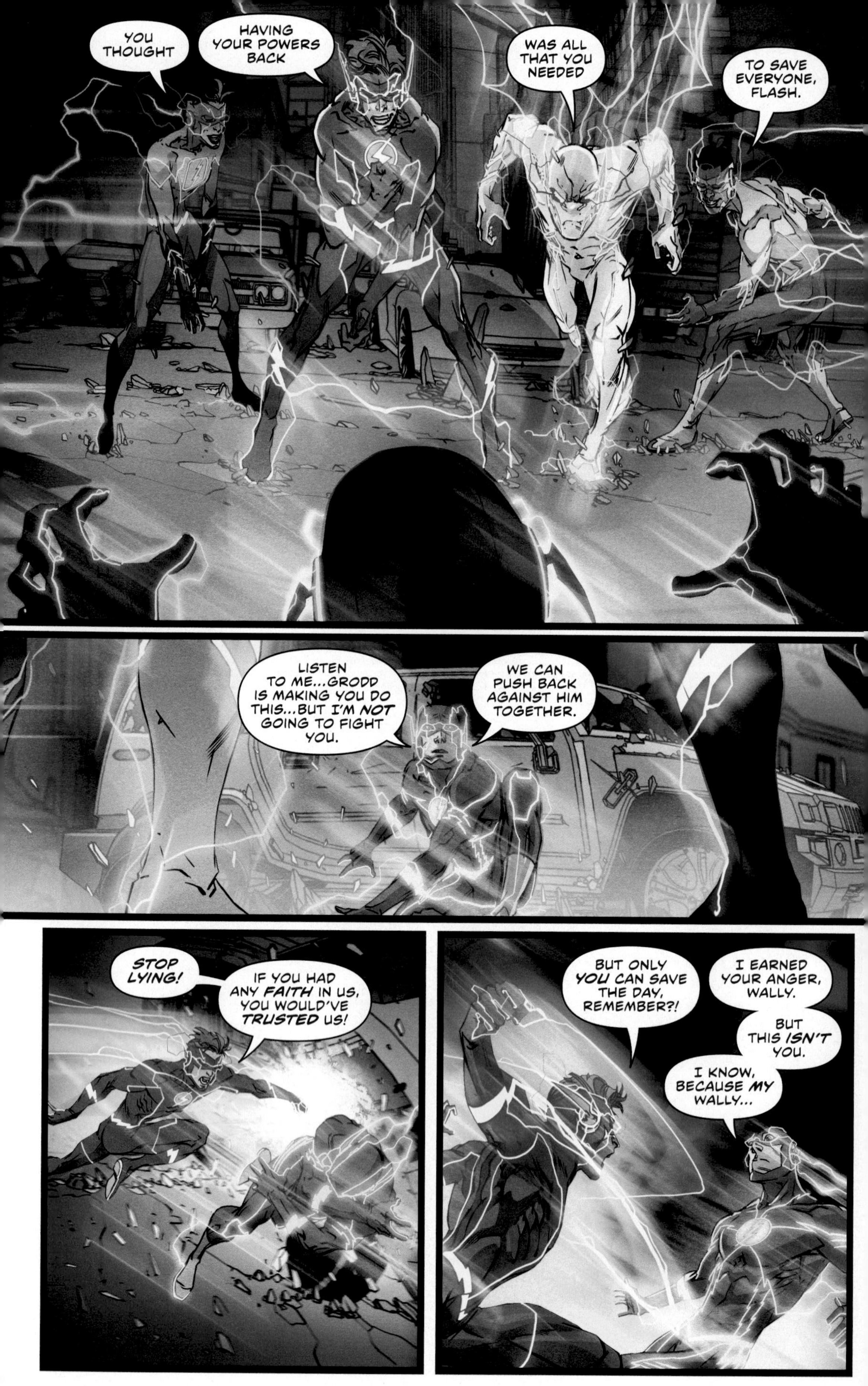
YOU THOUGHT
HAVING YOUR POWERS BACK
WAS ALL THAT YOU NEEDED
TO SAVE EVERYONE, FLASH.
LISTEN TO ME...GRODD IS MAKING YOU DO THIS...BUT I'M NOT GOING TO FIGHT YOU.
WE CAN PUSH BACK AGAINST HIM TOGETHER.
STOP LYING!
IF YOU HAD ANY FAITH IN US, YOU WOULD'VE TRUSTED US!
BUT ONLY YOU CAN SAVE THE DAY, REMEMBER?!
I EARNED YOUR ANGER, WALLY.
BUT THIS ISN'T YOU.
I KNOW, BECAUSE MY WALLY...

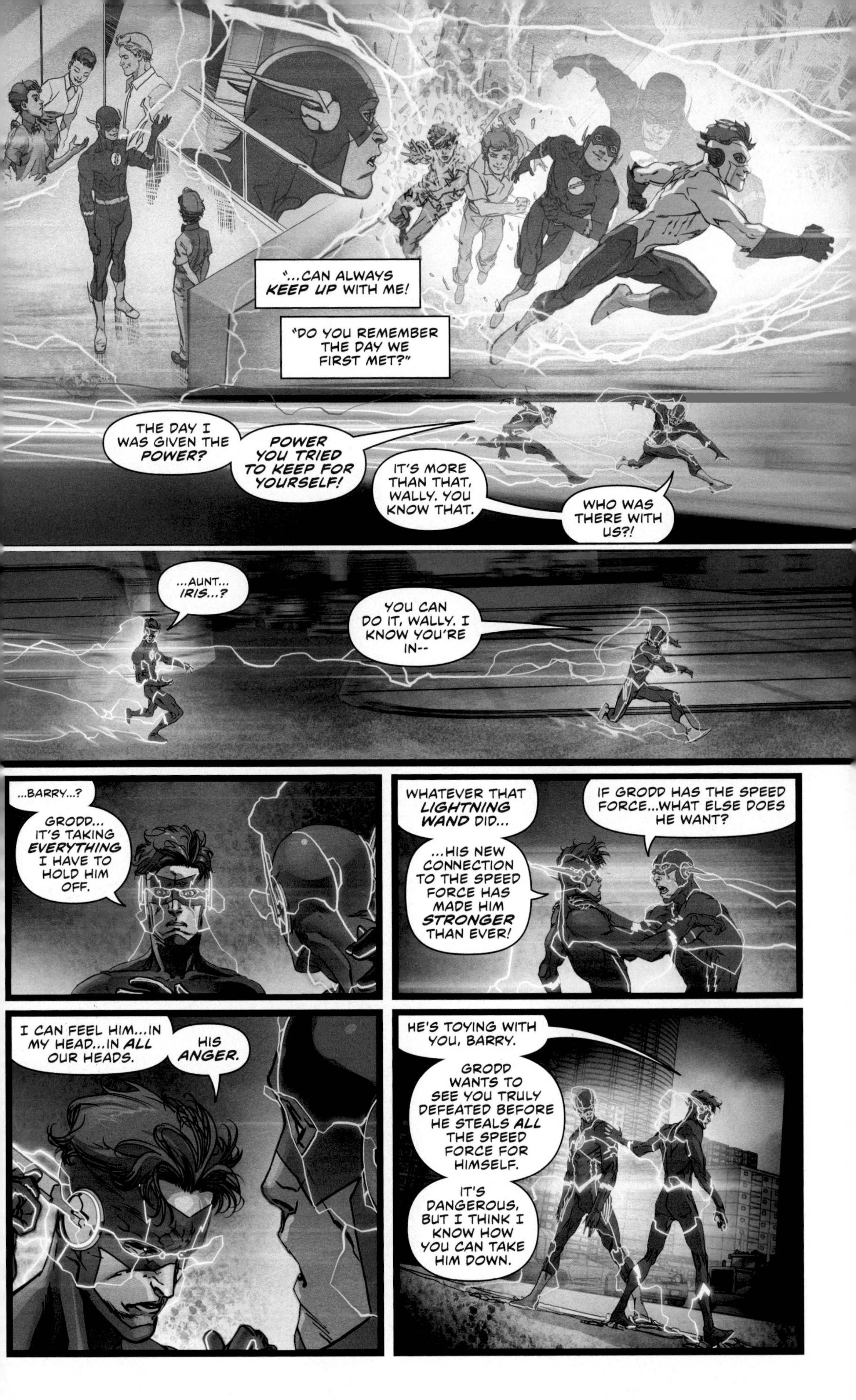

"...CAN ALWAYS KEEP UP WITH ME!
"DO YOU REMEMBER THE DAY WE FIRST MET?"
THE DAY I WAS GIVEN THE POWER?
POWER YOU TRIED TO KEEP FOR YOURSELF!
IT'S MORE THAN THAT, WALLY. YOU KNOW THAT.
WHO WAS THERE WITH US?!
...AUNT... IRIS...?
YOU CAN DO IT, WALLY. I KNOW YOU'RE IN--
...BARRY...?
GRODD... IT'S TAKING EVERYTHING I HAVE TO HOLD HIM OFF.
WHATEVER THAT LIGHTNING WAND DID...
...HIS NEW CONNECTION TO THE SPEED FORCE HAS MADE HIM STRONGER THAN EVER!
IF GRODD HAS THE SPEED FORCE...WHAT ELSE DOES HE WANT?
I CAN FEEL HIM...IN MY HEAD...IN ALL OUR HEADS.
HIS ANGER.
HE'S TOYING WITH YOU, BARRY.
GRODD WANTS TO SEE YOU TRULY DEFEATED BEFORE HE STEALS ALL THE SPEED FORCE FOR HIMSELF.
IT'S DANGEROUS, BUT I THINK I KNOW HOW YOU CAN TAKE HIM DOWN.

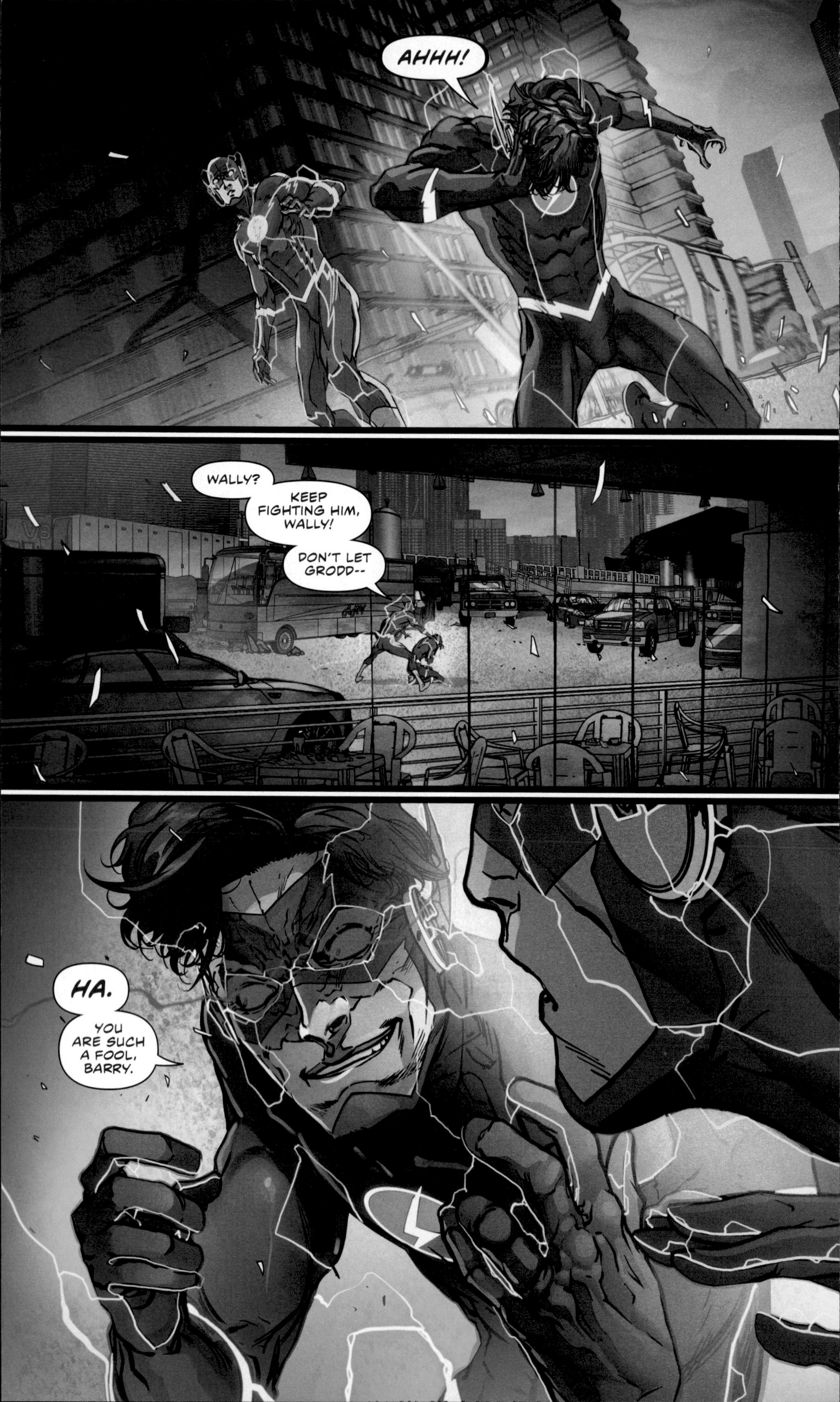
AHHH!
WALLY?
KEEP FIGHTING HIM, WALLY!
DON'T LET GRODD--
HA.
YOU ARE SUCH A FOOL, BARRY.

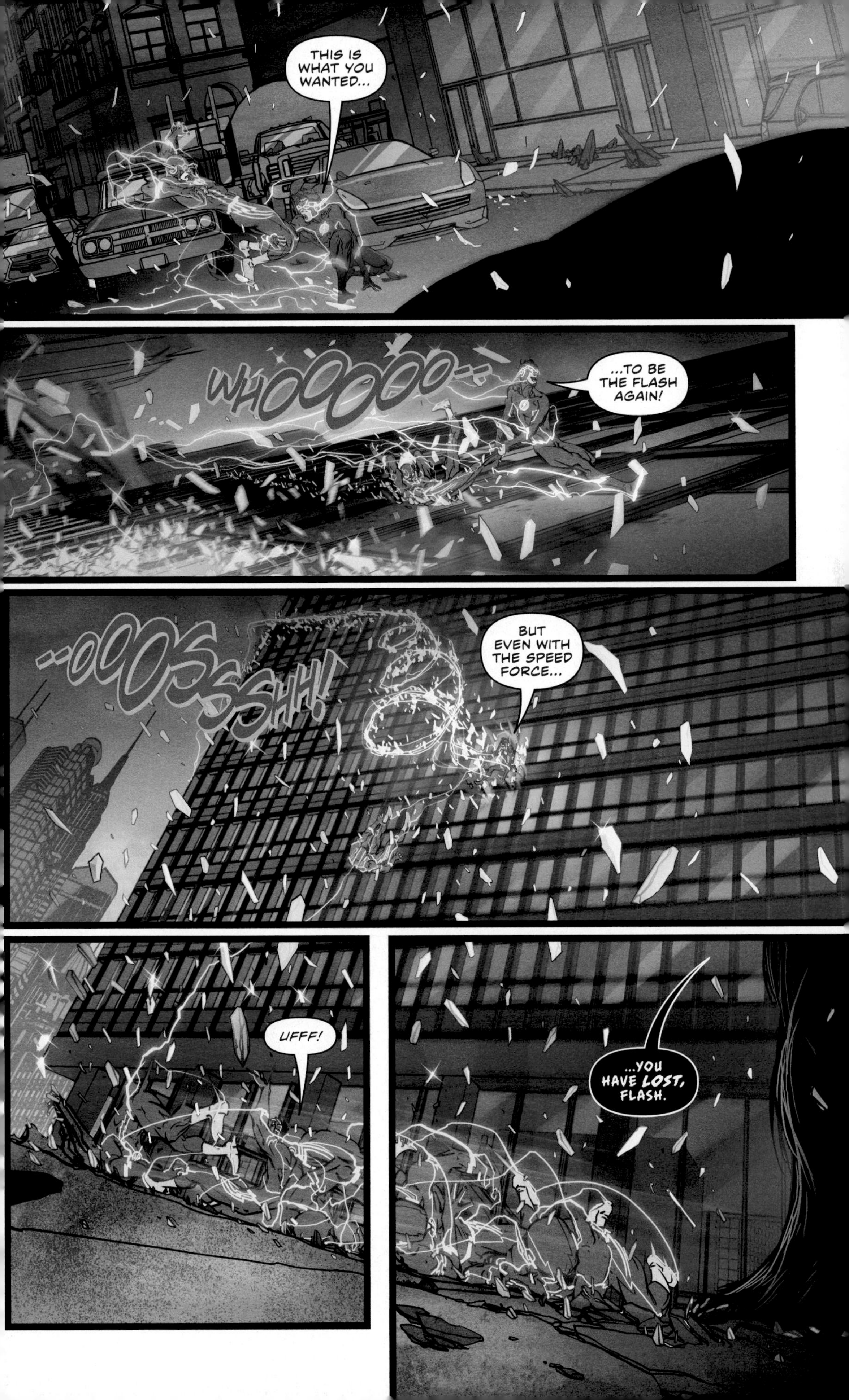
THIS IS WHAT YOU WANTED...
WHOOOOOO--
...TO BE THE FLASH AGAIN!
--OOOSSSHH!
BUT EVEN WITH THE SPEED FORCE...
UFFF!
...YOU HAVE LOST, FLASH.

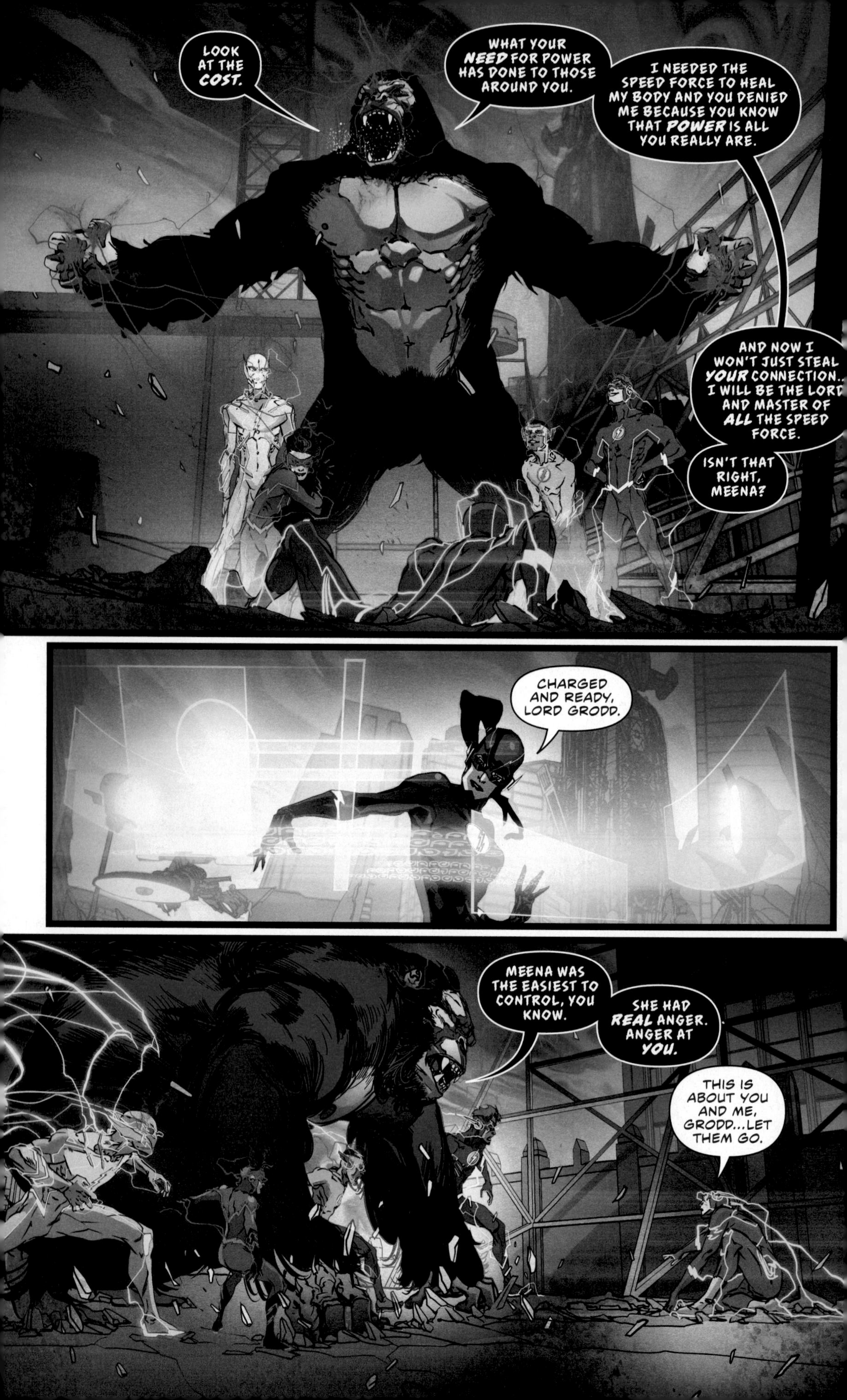
LOOK AT THE COST.
WHAT YOUR NEED FOR POWER HAS DONE TO THOSE AROUND YOU.
I NEEDED THE SPEED FORCE TO HEAL MY BODY AND YOU DENIED ME BECAUSE YOU KNOW THAT POWER IS ALL YOU REALLY ARE.
AND NOW I WON'T JUST STEAL YOUR CONNECTION.. I WILL BE THE LORD AND MASTER OF ALL THE SPEED FORCE.
ISN'T THAT RIGHT, MEENA?
CHARGED AND READY, LORD GRODD.
MEENA WAS THE EASIEST TO CONTROL, YOU KNOW.
SHE HAD REAL ANGER. ANGER AT YOU.
THIS IS ABOUT YOU AND ME, GRODD...LET THEM GO.

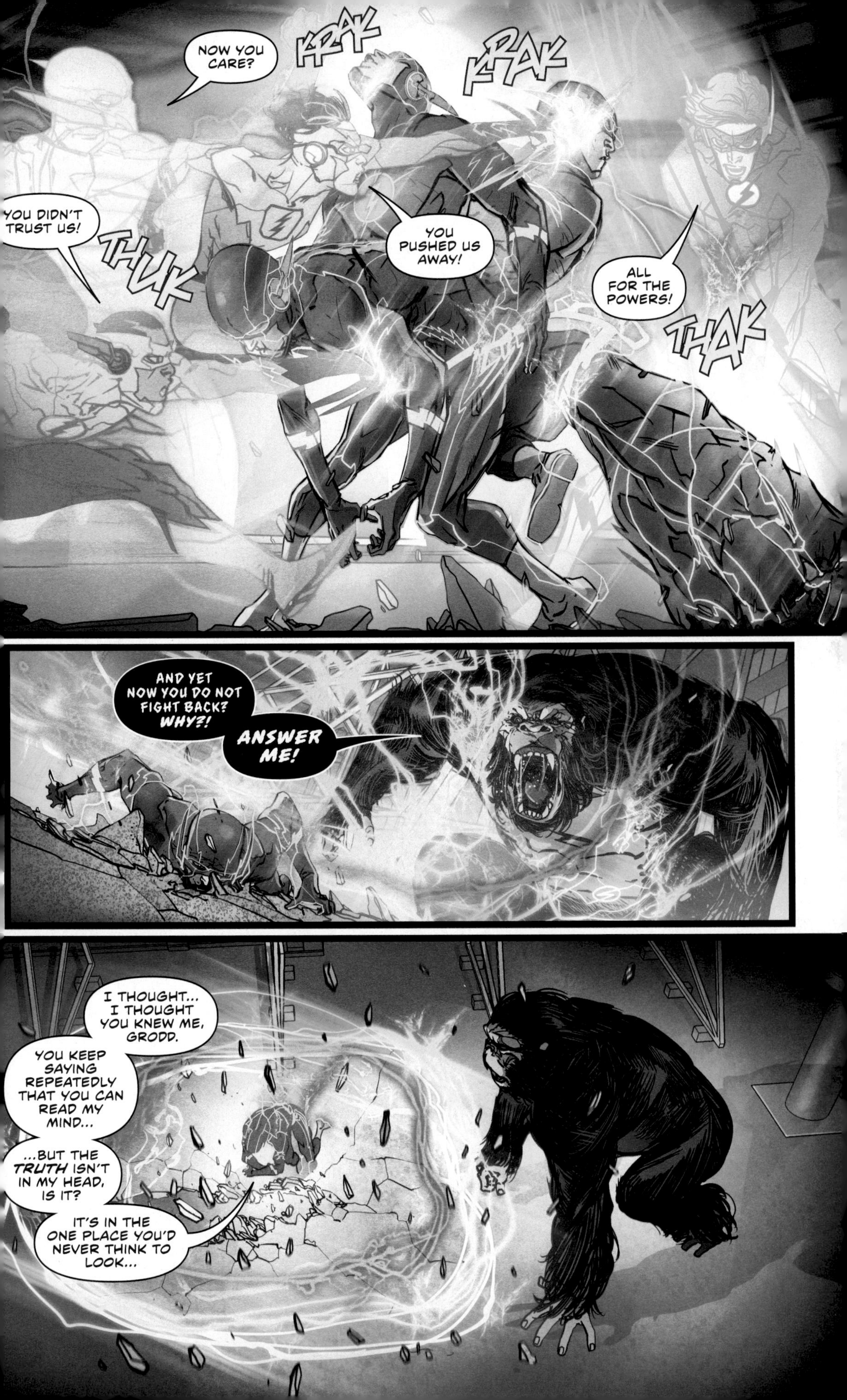
NOW YOU CARE?
KRAK
KRAK
YOU DIDN'T TRUST US!
THUK
YOU PUSHED US AWAY!
ALL FOR THE POWERS!
THAK
AND YET NOW YOU DO NOT FIGHT BACK? *WHY?!*
ANSWER ME!
I THOUGHT... I THOUGHT YOU KNEW ME, GRODD.
YOU KEEP SAYING REPEATEDLY THAT YOU CAN READ MY MIND...
...BUT THE *TRUTH* ISN'T IN MY HEAD, IS IT?
IT'S IN THE ONE PLACE YOU'D NEVER THINK TO LOOK...

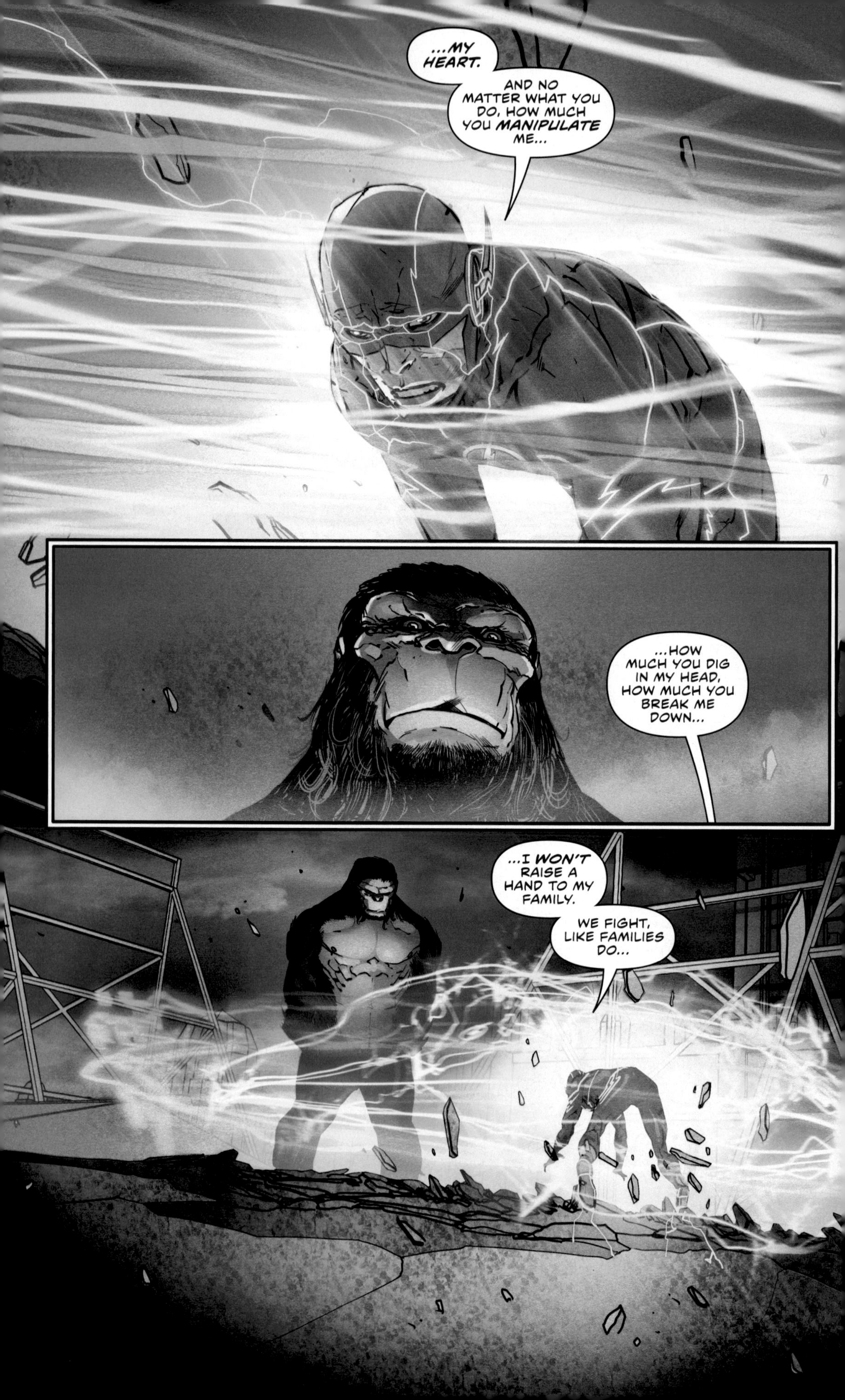
...MY HEART.
AND NO MATTER WHAT YOU DO, HOW MUCH YOU MANIPULATE ME...
...HOW MUCH YOU DIG IN MY HEAD, HOW MUCH YOU BREAK ME DOWN...
...I WON'T RAISE A HAND TO MY FAMILY.
WE FIGHT, LIKE FAMILIES DO...

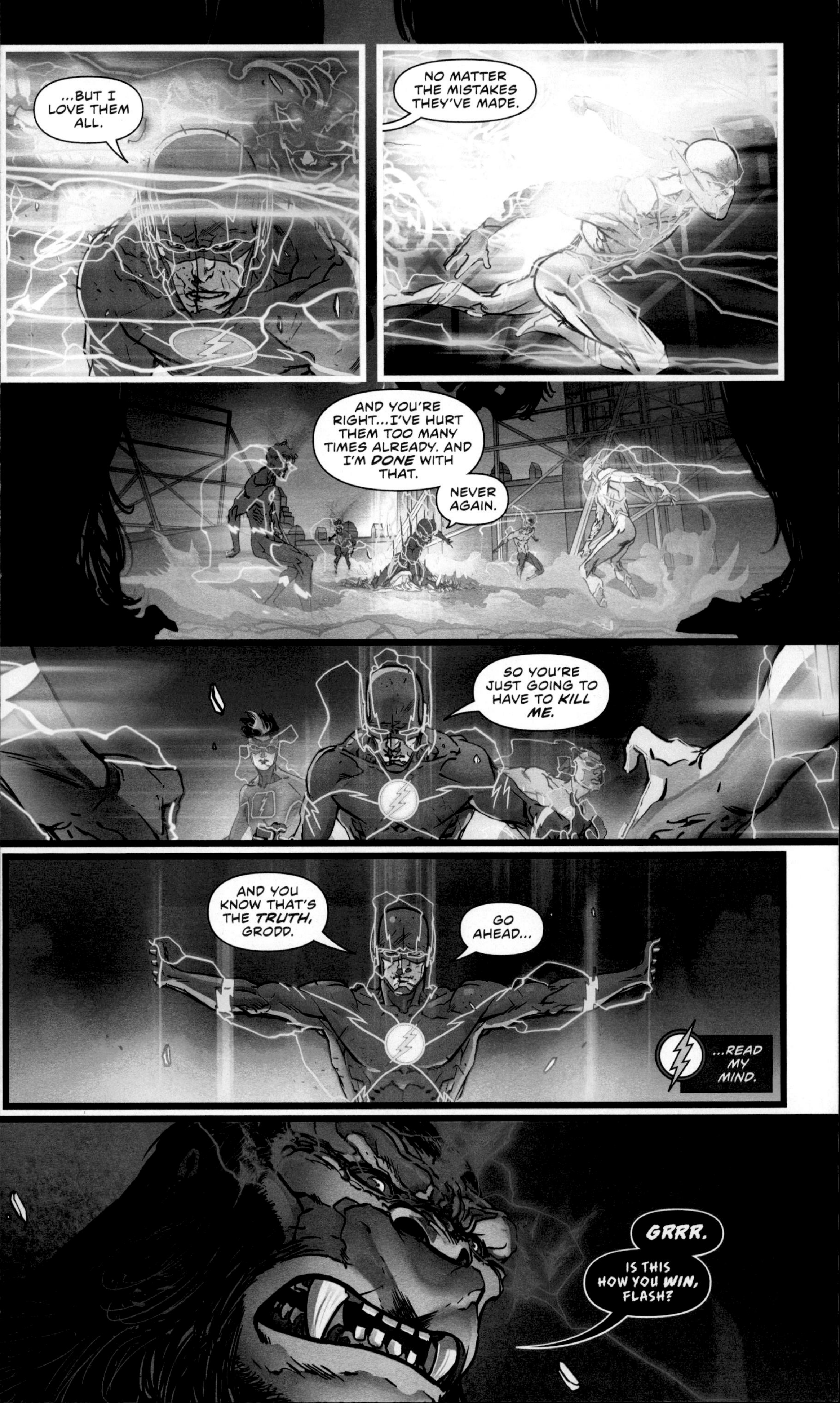

...BUT I LOVE THEM ALL.
NO MATTER THE MISTAKES THEY'VE MADE.
AND YOU'RE RIGHT...I'VE HURT THEM TOO MANY TIMES ALREADY. AND I'M *DONE* WITH THAT.
NEVER AGAIN.
SO YOU'RE JUST GOING TO HAVE TO *KILL ME.*
AND YOU KNOW THAT'S THE *TRUTH,* GRODD.
GO AHEAD...
...READ MY MIND.
GRRR.
IS THIS HOW YOU *WIN,* FLASH?

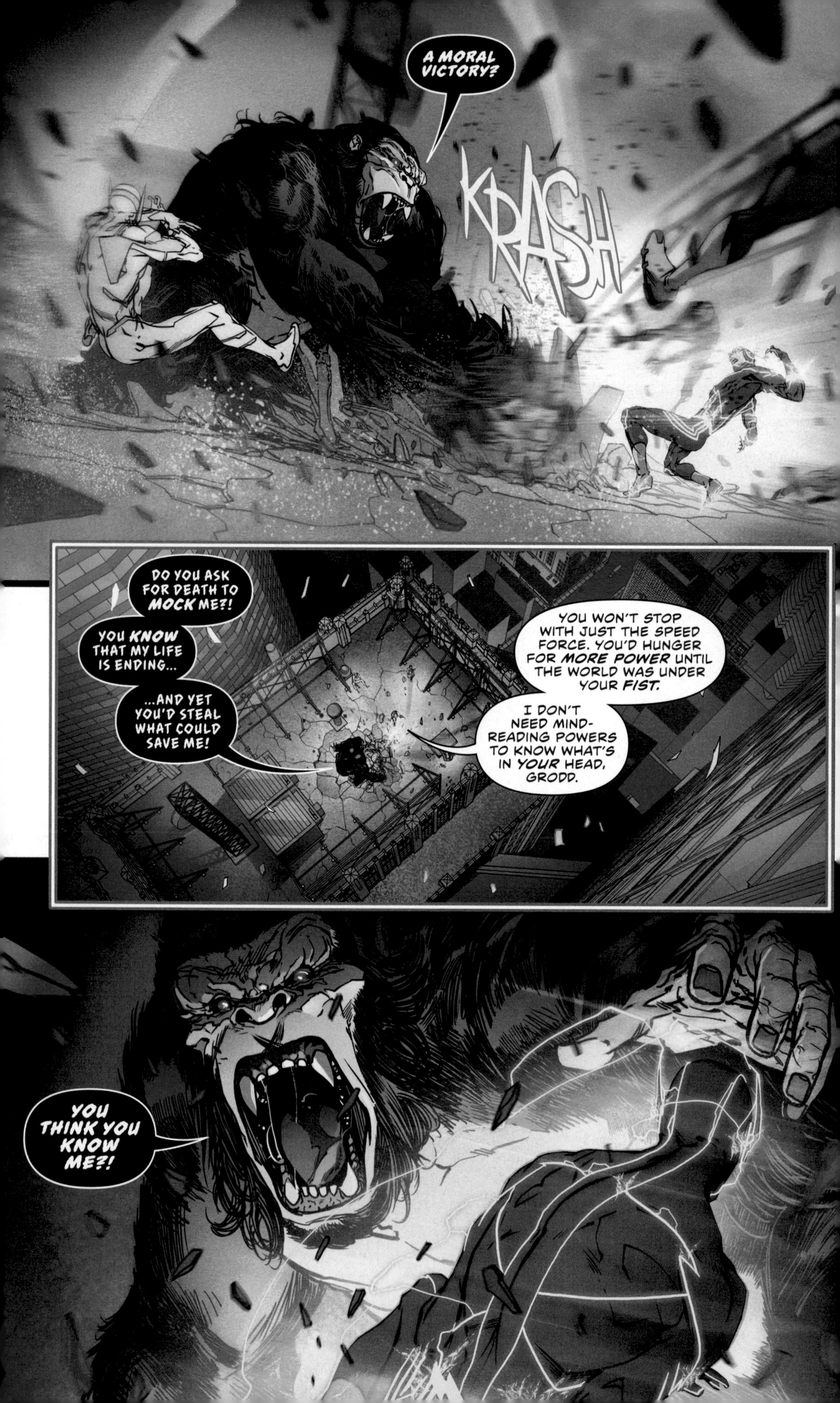
A MORAL VICTORY?
KRASH
DO YOU ASK FOR DEATH TO MOCK ME?!
YOU KNOW THAT MY LIFE IS ENDING...
...AND YET YOU'D STEAL WHAT COULD SAVE ME!
YOU WON'T STOP WITH JUST THE SPEED FORCE. YOU'D HUNGER FOR MORE POWER UNTIL THE WORLD WAS UNDER YOUR FIST.
I DON'T NEED MIND-READING POWERS TO KNOW WHAT'S IN YOUR HEAD, GRODD.
YOU THINK YOU KNOW ME?!

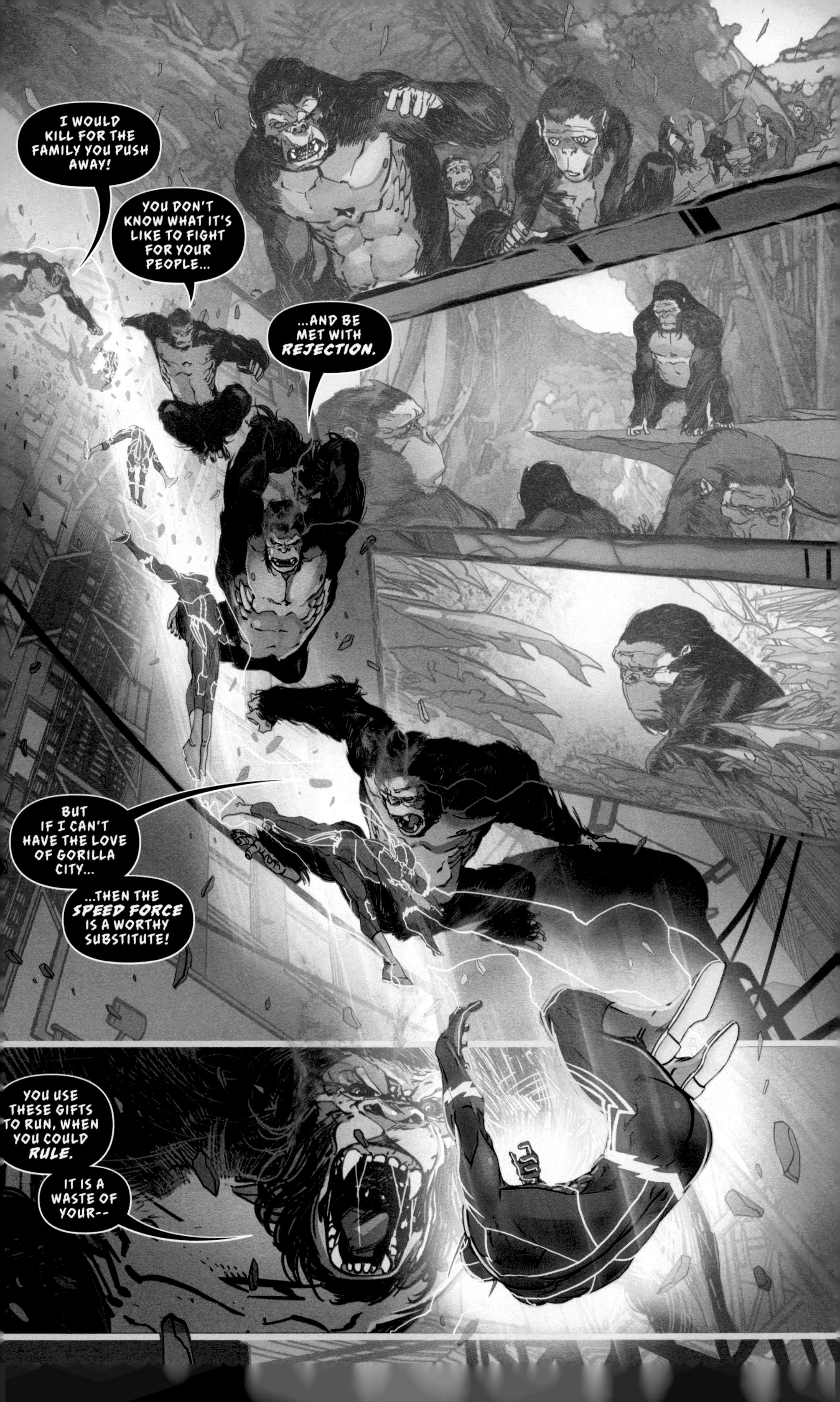
I WOULD KILL FOR THE FAMILY YOU PUSH AWAY!
YOU DON'T KNOW WHAT IT'S LIKE TO FIGHT FOR YOUR PEOPLE...
...AND BE MET WITH REJECTION.
BUT IF I CAN'T HAVE THE LOVE OF GORILLA CITY...
...THEN THE SPEED FORCE IS A WORTHY SUBSTITUTE!
YOU USE THESE GIFTS TO RUN, WHEN YOU COULD RULE.
IT IS A WASTE OF YOUR--

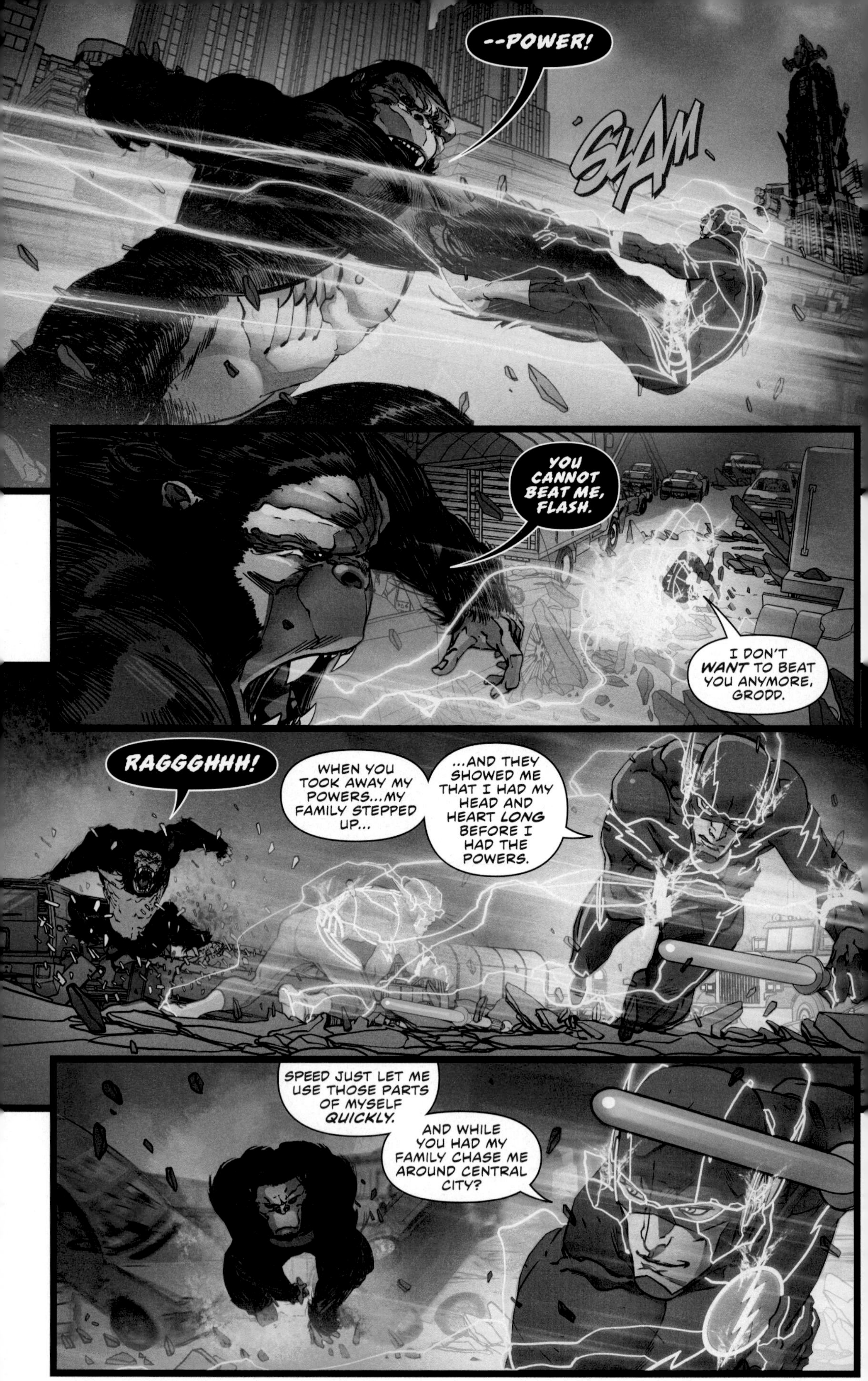
--POWER!
SLAM
YOU CANNOT BEAT ME, FLASH.
I DON'T *WANT* TO BEAT YOU ANYMORE, GRODD.
RAGGGHHH!
WHEN YOU TOOK AWAY MY POWERS...MY FAMILY STEPPED UP...
...AND THEY SHOWED ME THAT I HAD MY HEAD AND HEART *LONG* BEFORE I HAD THE POWERS.
SPEED JUST LET ME USE THOSE PARTS OF MYSELF *QUICKLY.*
AND WHILE YOU HAD MY FAMILY CHASE ME AROUND CENTRAL CITY?

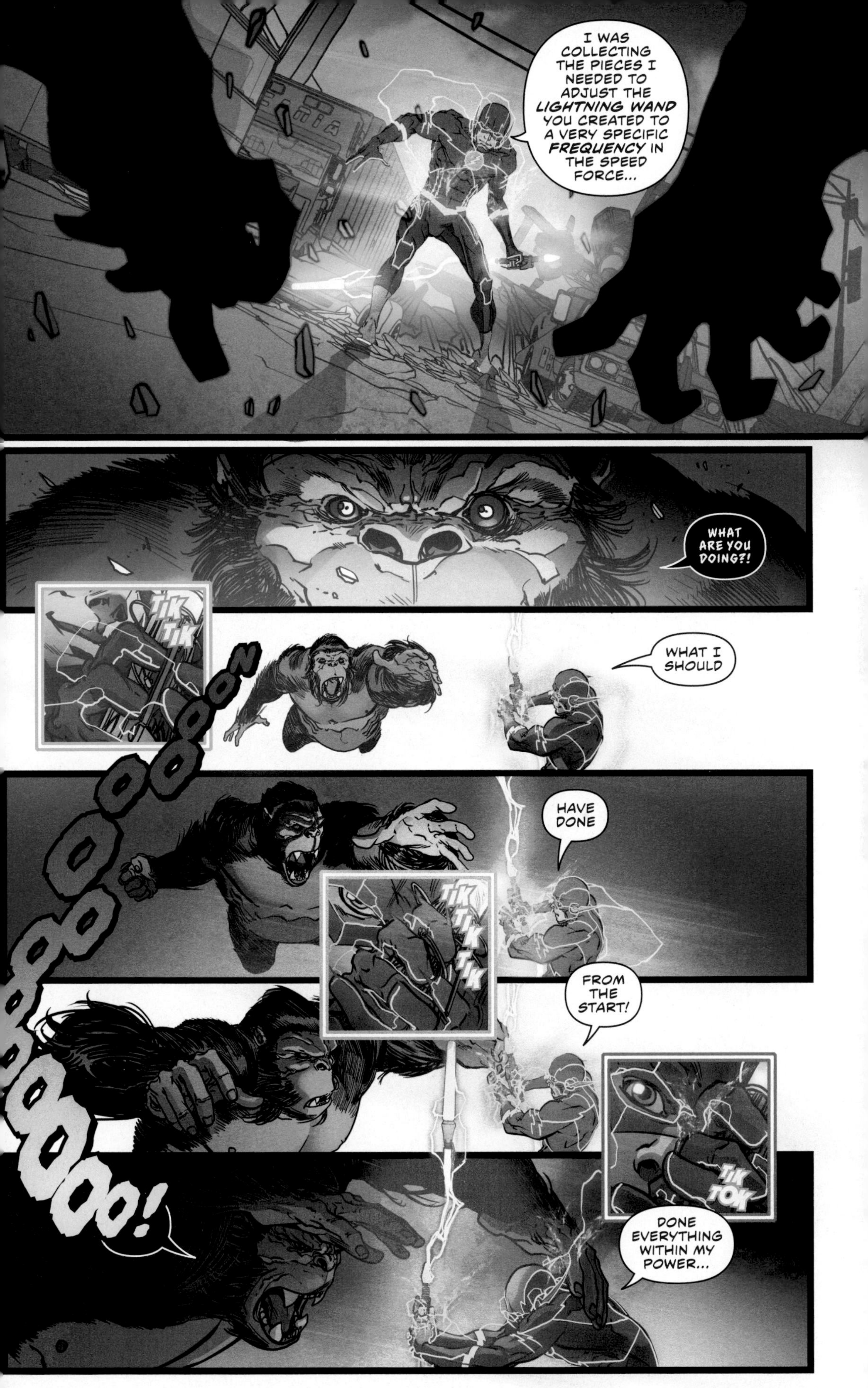
I WAS COLLECTING THE PIECES I NEEDED TO ADJUST THE LIGHTNING WAND YOU CREATED TO A VERY SPECIFIC FREQUENCY IN THE SPEED FORCE...
WHAT ARE YOU DOING?!
TIK TIK
WHAT I SHOULD
HAVE DONE
TIK TIK TIK
FROM THE START!
NOOOOOOOOOOOOOO!
TIK TOK
DONE EVERYTHING WITHIN MY POWER...

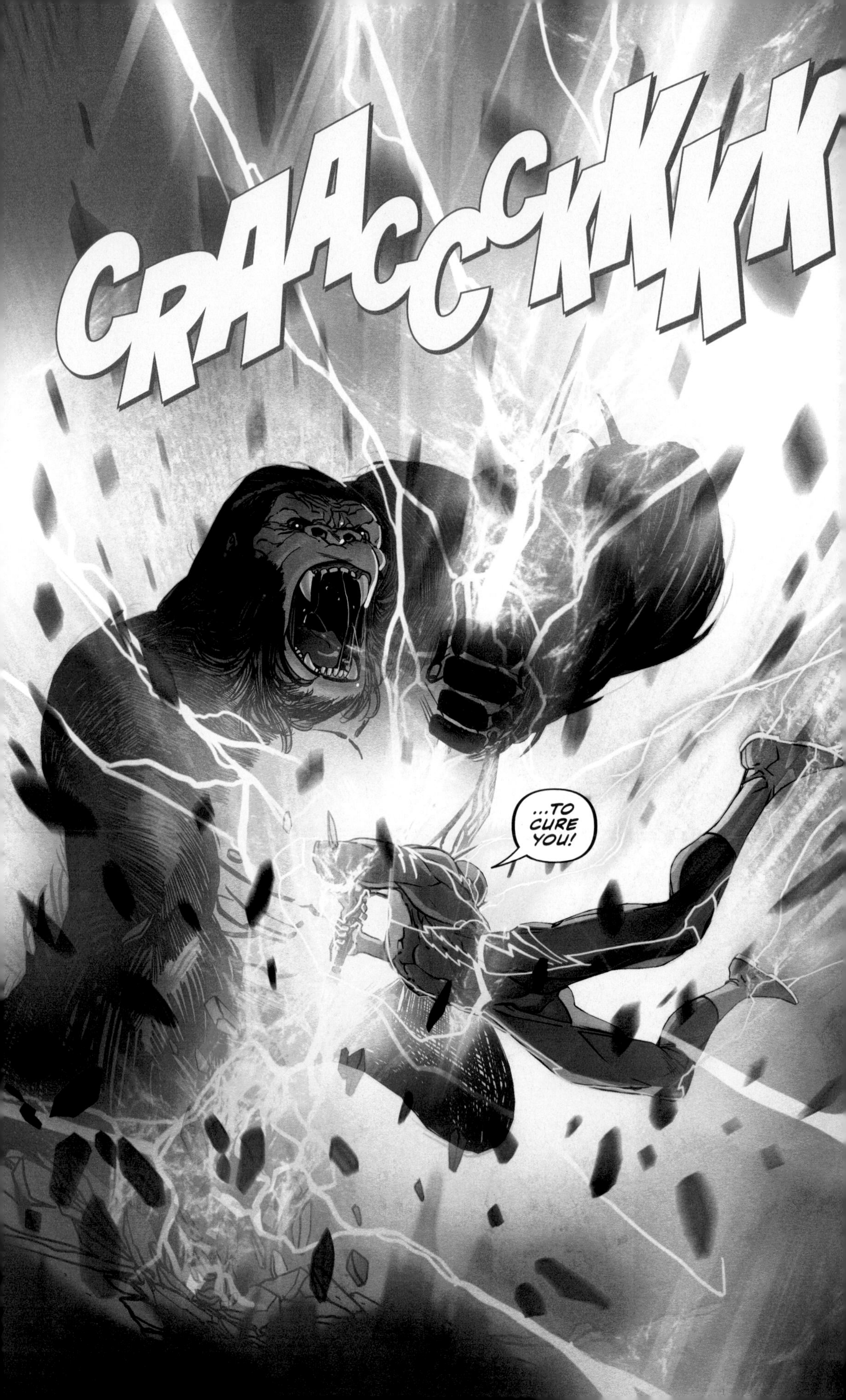
CRAACCCKKKK
...TO CURE YOU!

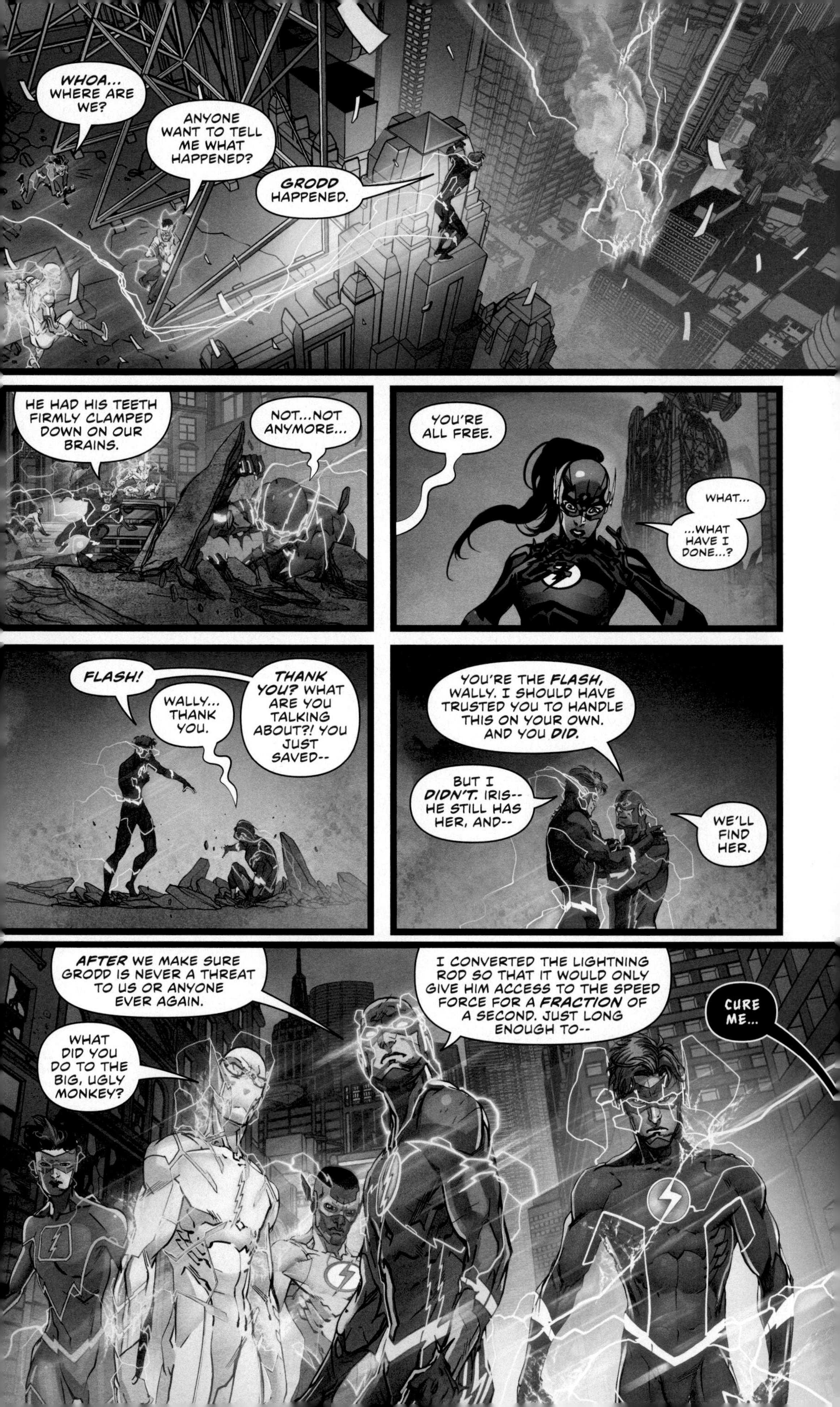
WHOA... WHERE ARE WE?
ANYONE WANT TO TELL ME WHAT HAPPENED?
GRODD HAPPENED.
HE HAD HIS TEETH FIRMLY CLAMPED DOWN ON OUR BRAINS.
NOT...NOT ANYMORE...
YOU'RE ALL FREE.
WHAT...
...WHAT HAVE I DONE...?
FLASH!
WALLY... THANK YOU.
THANK YOU? WHAT ARE YOU TALKING ABOUT?! YOU JUST SAVED--
YOU'RE THE FLASH, WALLY. I SHOULD HAVE TRUSTED YOU TO HANDLE THIS ON YOUR OWN. AND YOU DID.
BUT I DIDN'T. IRIS-- HE STILL HAS HER, AND--
WE'LL FIND HER.
AFTER WE MAKE SURE GRODD IS NEVER A THREAT TO US OR ANYONE EVER AGAIN.
WHAT DID YOU DO TO THE BIG, UGLY MONKEY?
I CONVERTED THE LIGHTNING ROD SO THAT IT WOULD ONLY GIVE HIM ACCESS TO THE SPEED FORCE FOR A FRACTION OF A SECOND. JUST LONG ENOUGH TO--
CURE ME...

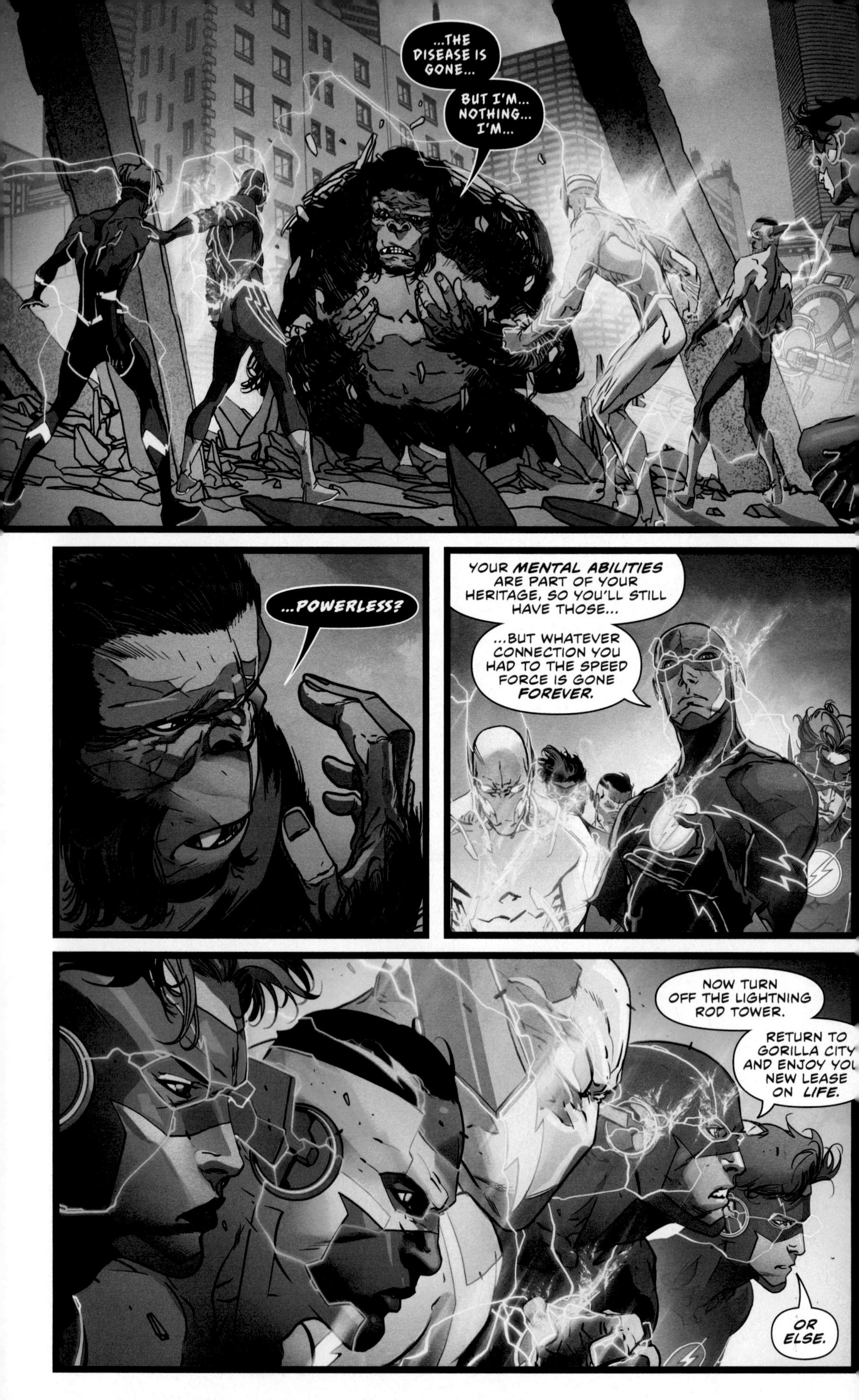
...THE DISEASE IS GONE...
BUT I'M... NOTHING... I'M...
...POWERLESS?
YOUR MENTAL ABILITIES ARE PART OF YOUR HERITAGE, SO YOU'LL STILL HAVE THOSE...
...BUT WHATEVER CONNECTION YOU HAD TO THE SPEED FORCE IS GONE FOREVER.
NOW TURN OFF THE LIGHTNING ROD TOWER.
RETURN TO GORILLA CITY AND ENJOY YOU NEW LEASE ON LIFE.
OR ELSE.

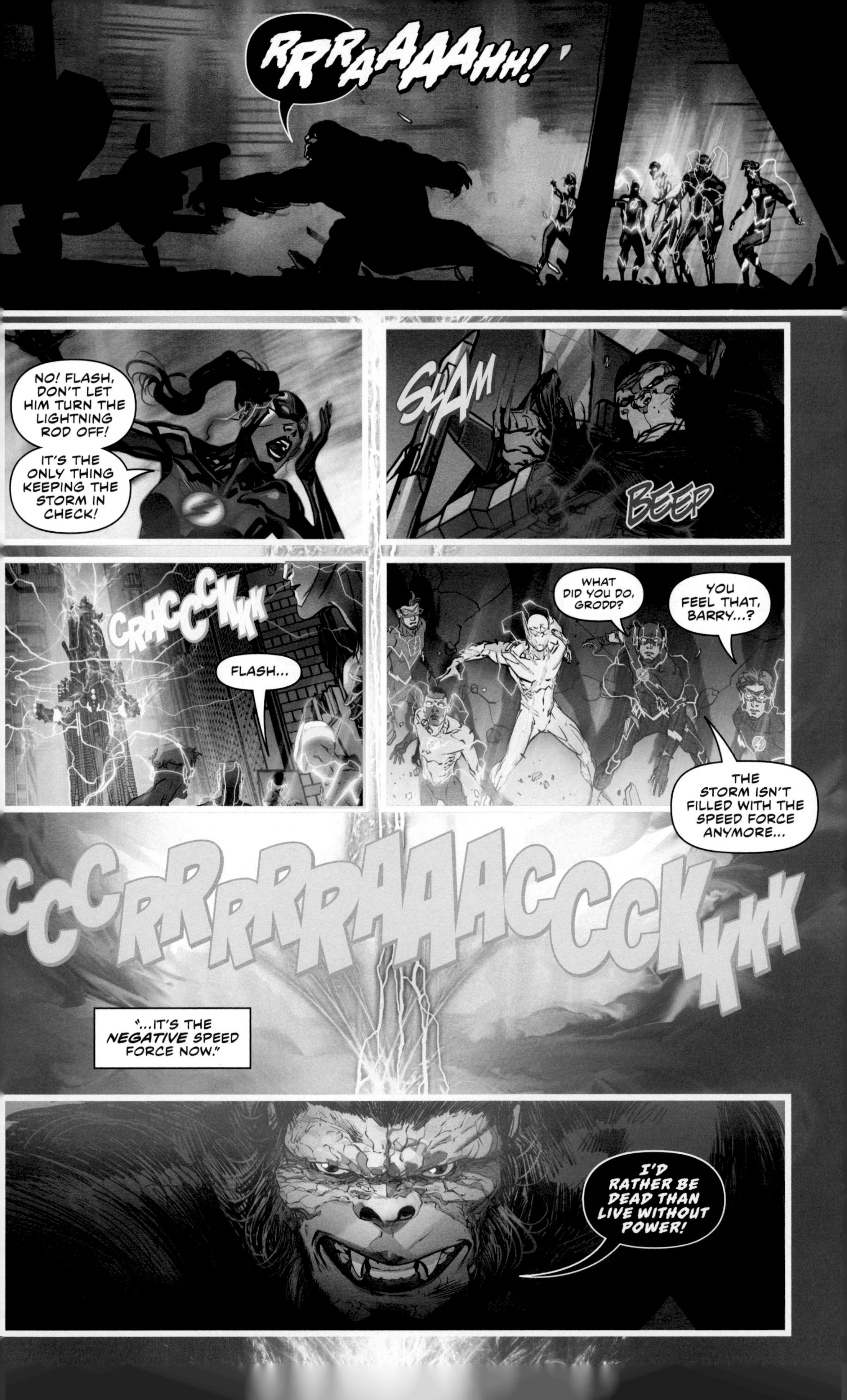
RRRAAAAHH!
NO! FLASH, DON'T LET HIM TURN THE LIGHTNING ROD OFF!
IT'S THE ONLY THING KEEPING THE STORM IN CHECK!
SLAM
BEEP
CRACCCKKK
FLASH...
WHAT DID YOU DO, GRODD?
YOU FEEL THAT, BARRY...?
THE STORM ISN'T FILLED WITH THE SPEED FORCE ANYMORE...
CCCRRRRRAAACCCKKKK
"...IT'S THE NEGATIVE SPEED FORCE NOW."
I'D RATHER BE DEAD THAN LIVE WITHOUT POWER!

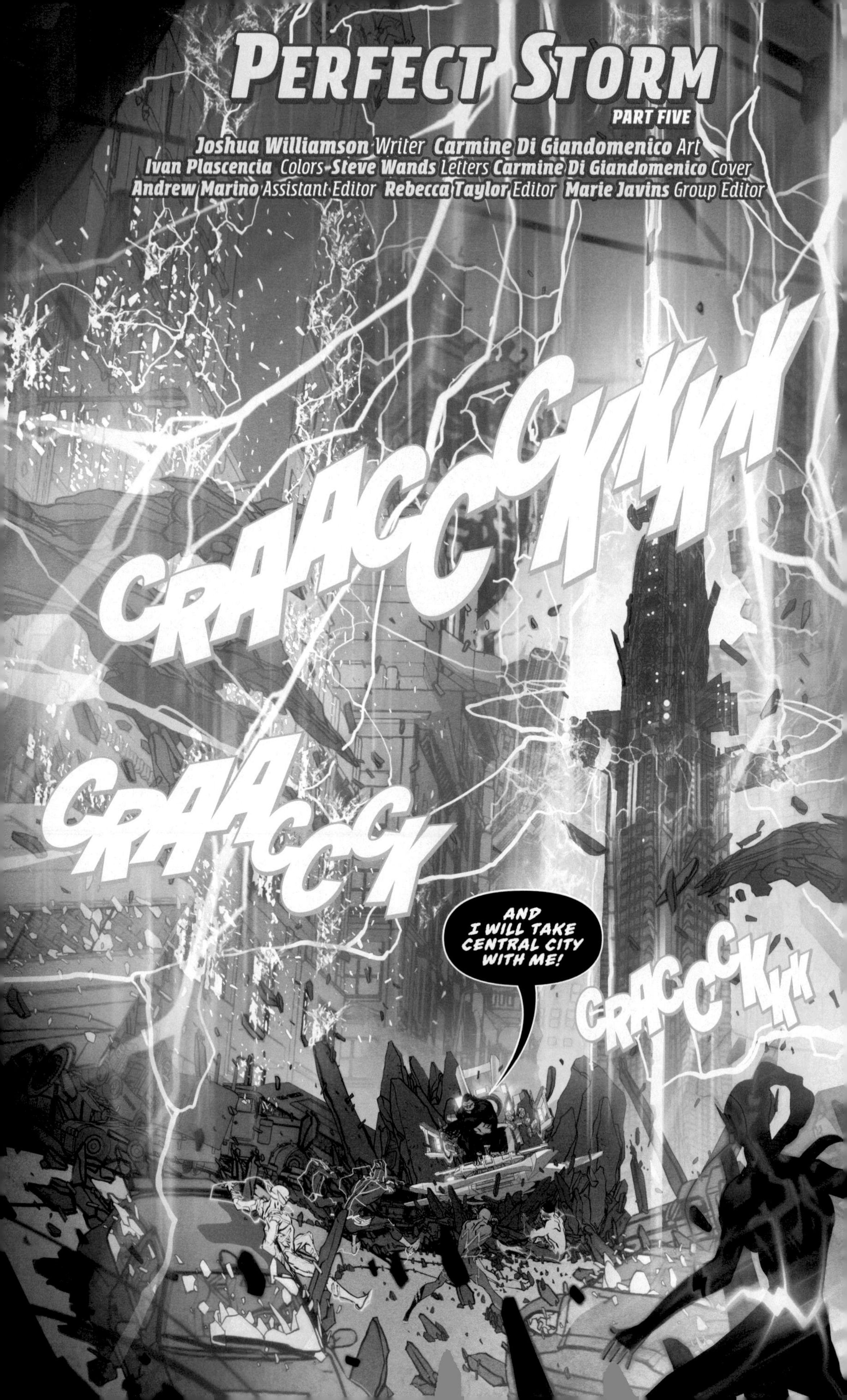
PERFECT STORM
PART FIVE
Joshua Williamson Writer Carmine Di Giandomenico Art
Ivan Plascencia Colors Steve Wands Letters Carmine Di Giandomenico Cover
Andrew Marino Assistant Editor Rebecca Taylor Editor Marie Javins Group Editor
CRAACCKKK
CRAACCCK
AND I WILL TAKE CENTRAL CITY WITH ME!
CRACCCKKK

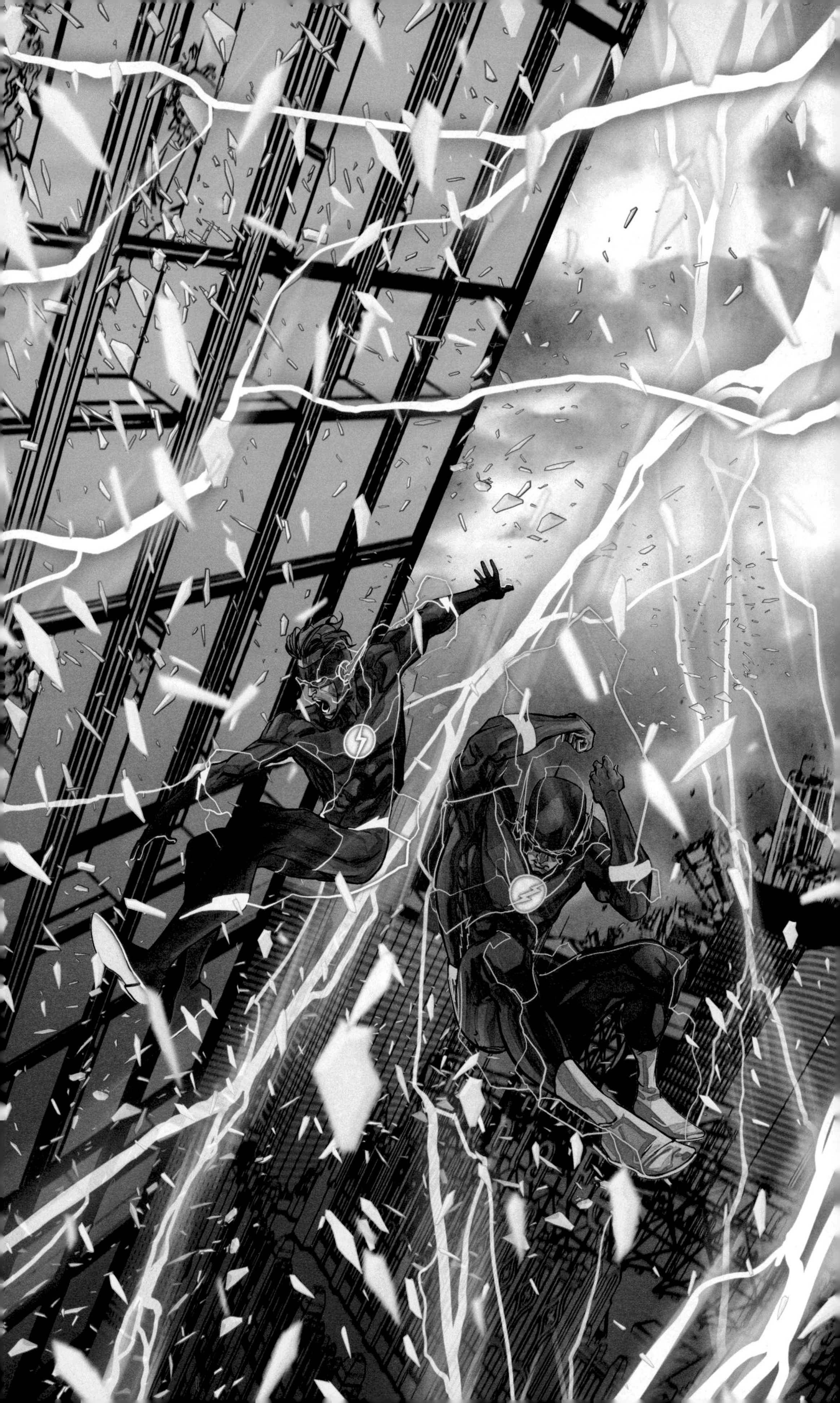

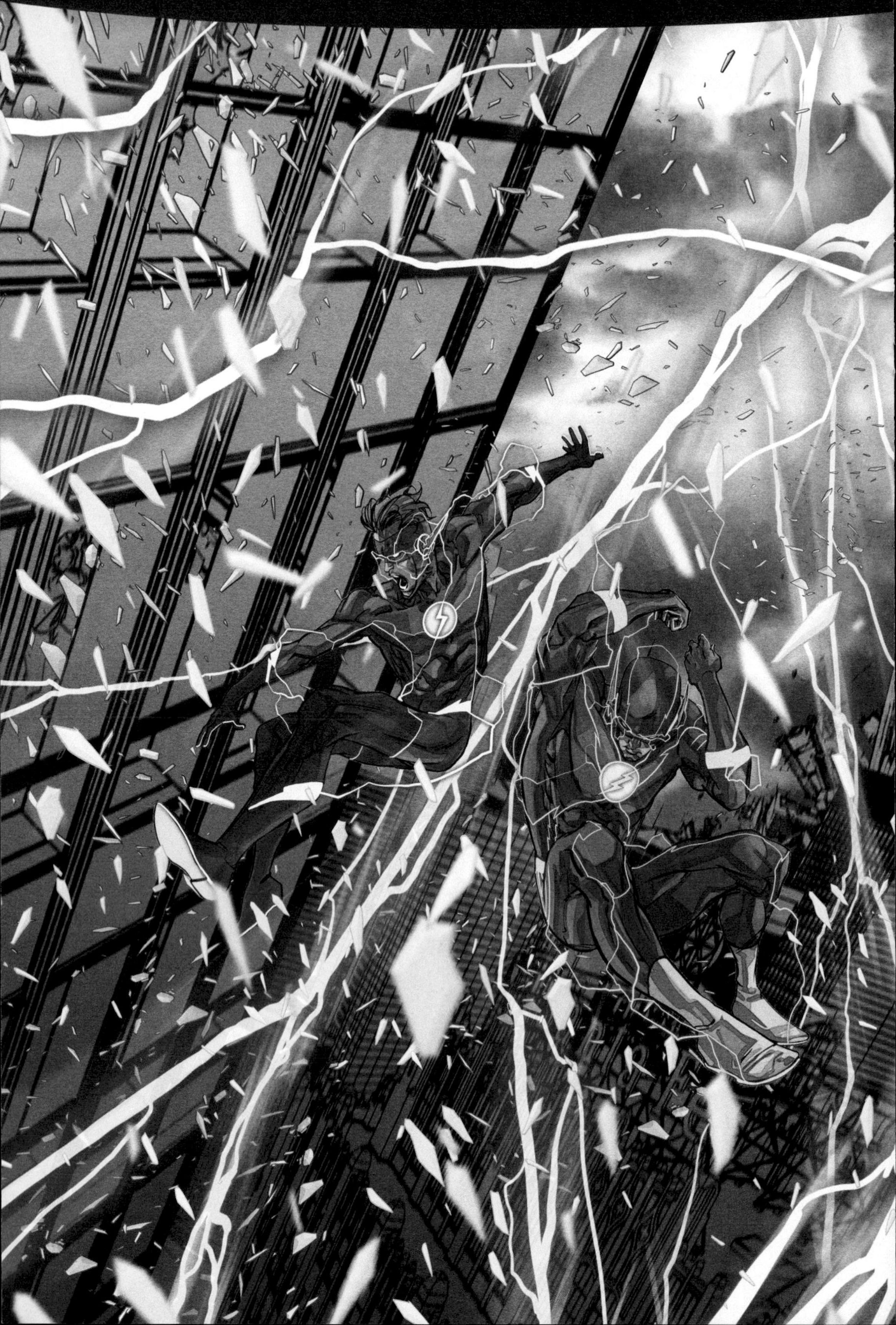

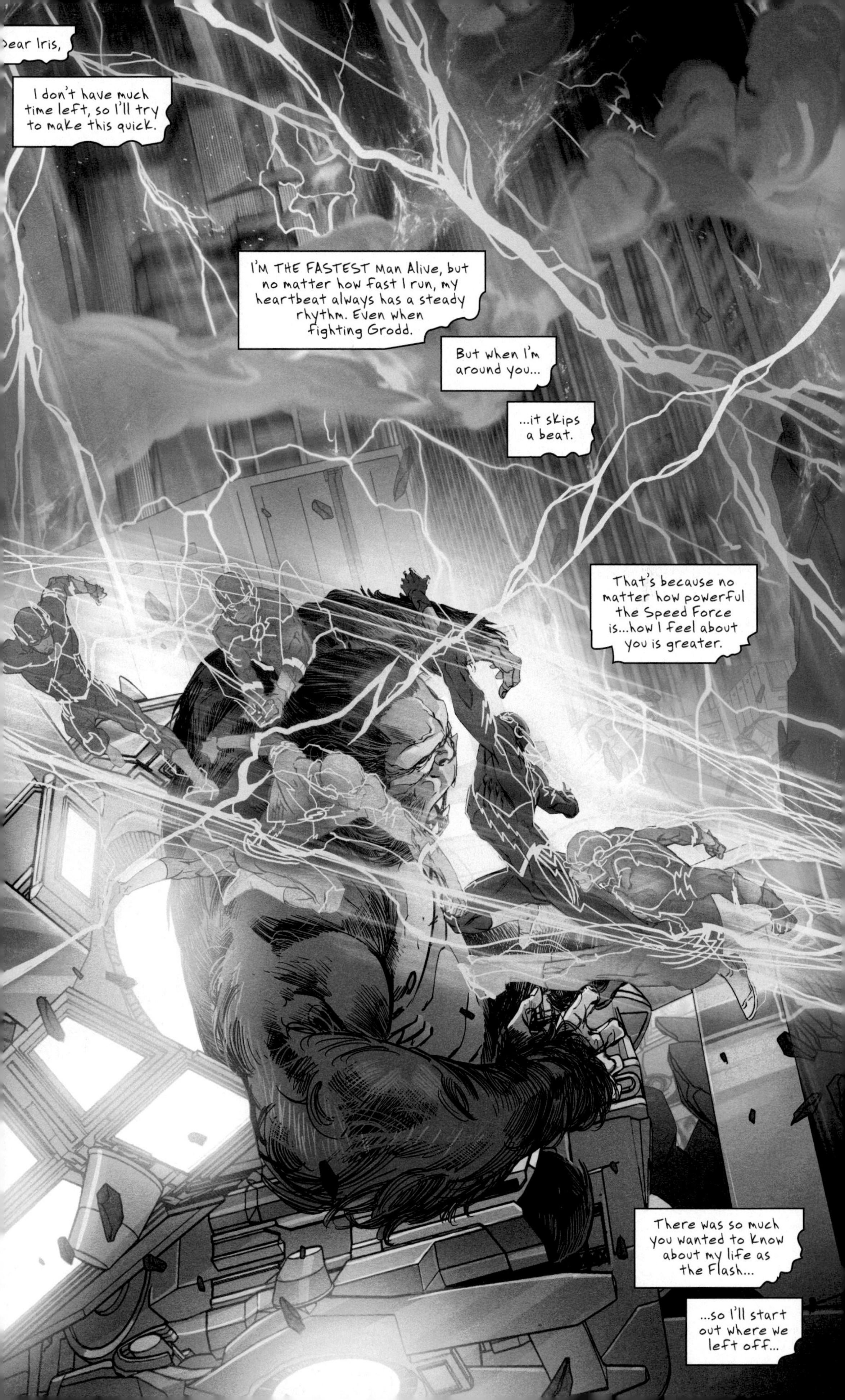
Dear Iris,
I don't have much time left, so I'll try to make this quick.
I'M THE FASTEST Man Alive, but no matter how fast I run, my heartbeat always has a steady rhythm. Even when fighting Grodd.
But when I'm around you...
...it skips a beat.
That's because no matter how powerful the Speed Force is...how I feel about you is greater.
There was so much you wanted to know about my life as the Flash...
...so I'll start out where we left off...

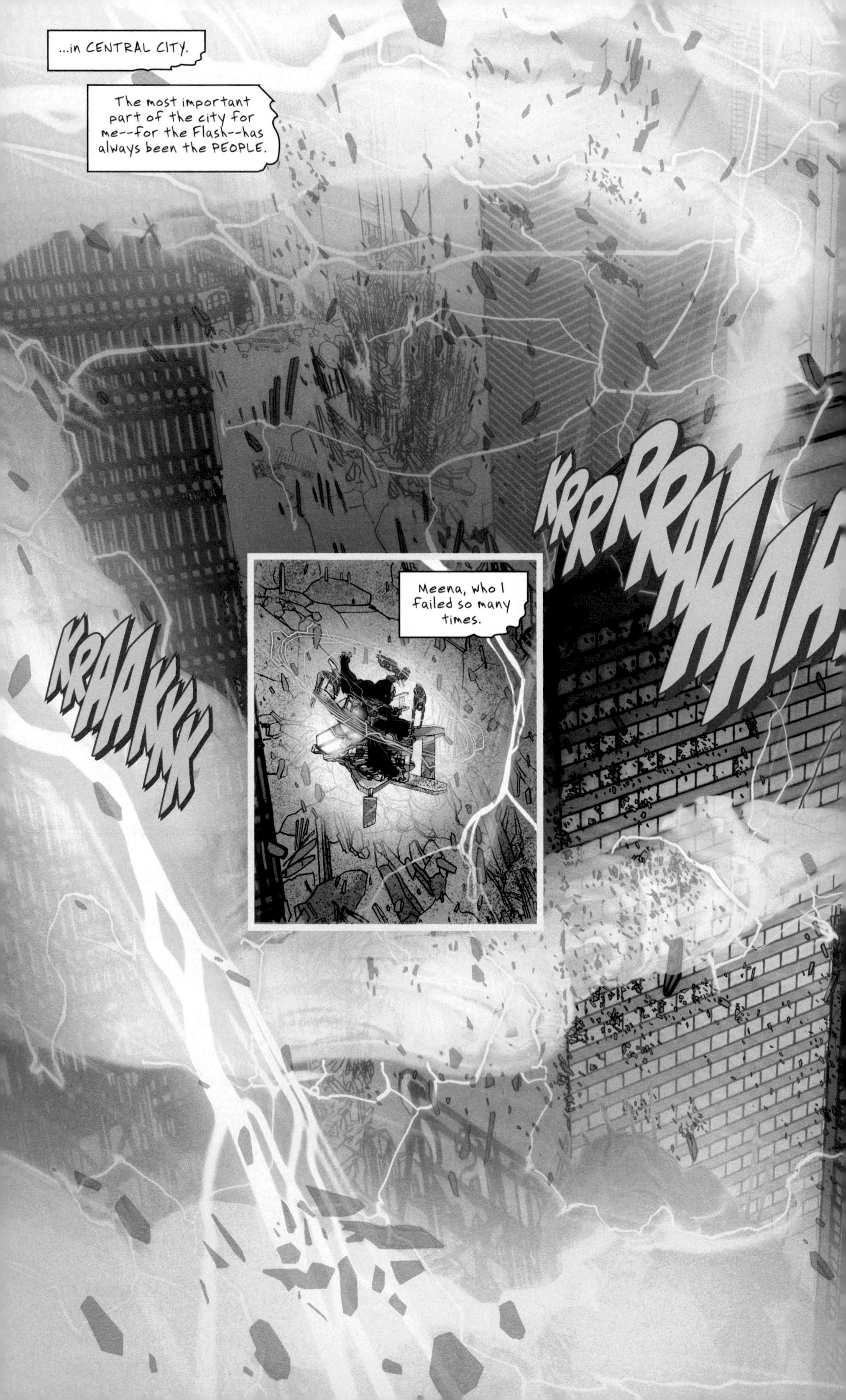
...in CENTRAL CITY.
The most important part of the city for me--for the Flash--has always been the PEOPLE.
KRRRRAAAAH
KRAAKKK
Meena, who I failed so many times.

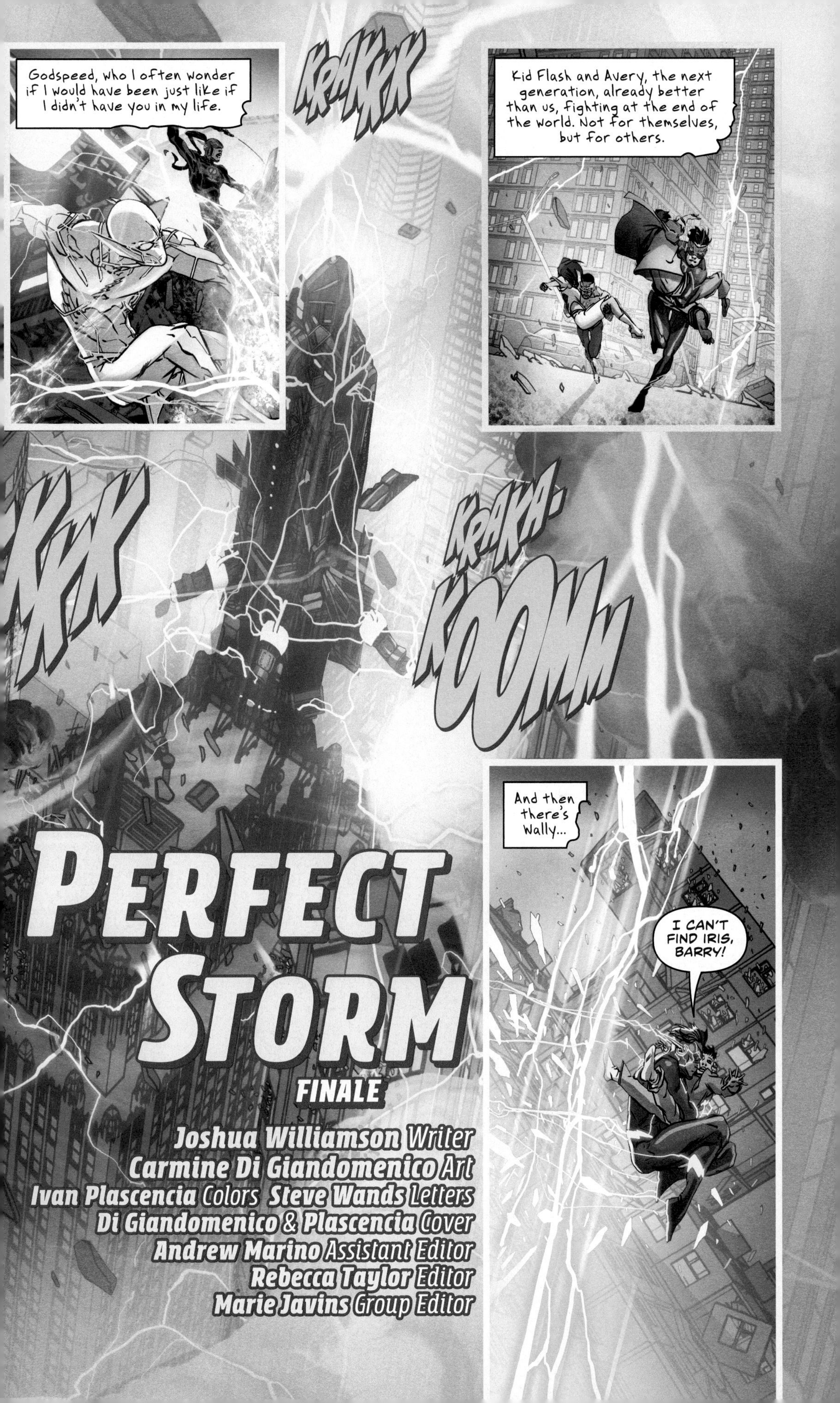

Godspeed, who I often wonder if I would have been just like if I didn't have you in my life.
KRAKKKK
Kid Flash and Avery, the next generation, already better than us, fighting at the end of the world. Not for themselves, but for others.
KKK
KRAKA-KOOMM
And then there's Wally...
I CAN'T FIND IRIS, BARRY!
PERFECT STORM
FINALE
Joshua Williamson Writer
Carmine Di Giandomenico Art
Ivan Plascencia Colors Steve Wands Letters
Di Giandomenico & Plascencia Cover
Andrew Marino Assistant Editor
Rebecca Taylor Editor
Marie Javins Group Editor

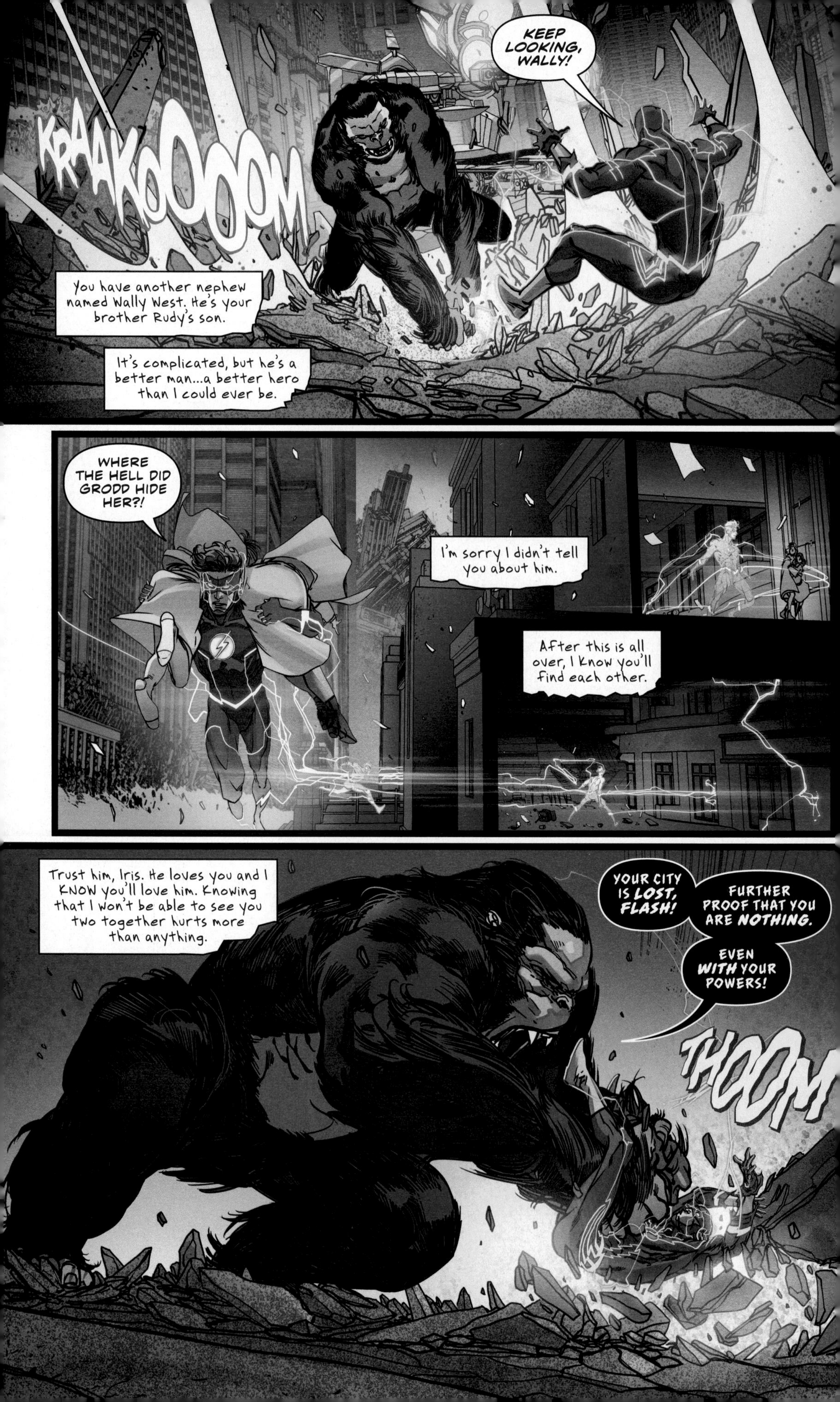
KEEP LOOKING, WALLY!
KRAAKOOOOM
You have another nephew named Wally West. He's your brother Rudy's son.
It's complicated, but he's a better man...a better hero than I could ever be.
WHERE THE HELL DID GRODD HIDE HER?!
I'm sorry I didn't tell you about him.
After this is all over, I know you'll find each other.
Trust him, Iris. He loves you and I KNOW you'll love him. Knowing that I won't be able to see you two together hurts more than anything.
YOUR CITY IS LOST, FLASH!
FURTHER PROOF THAT YOU ARE NOTHING.
EVEN WITH YOUR POWERS!
THOOM

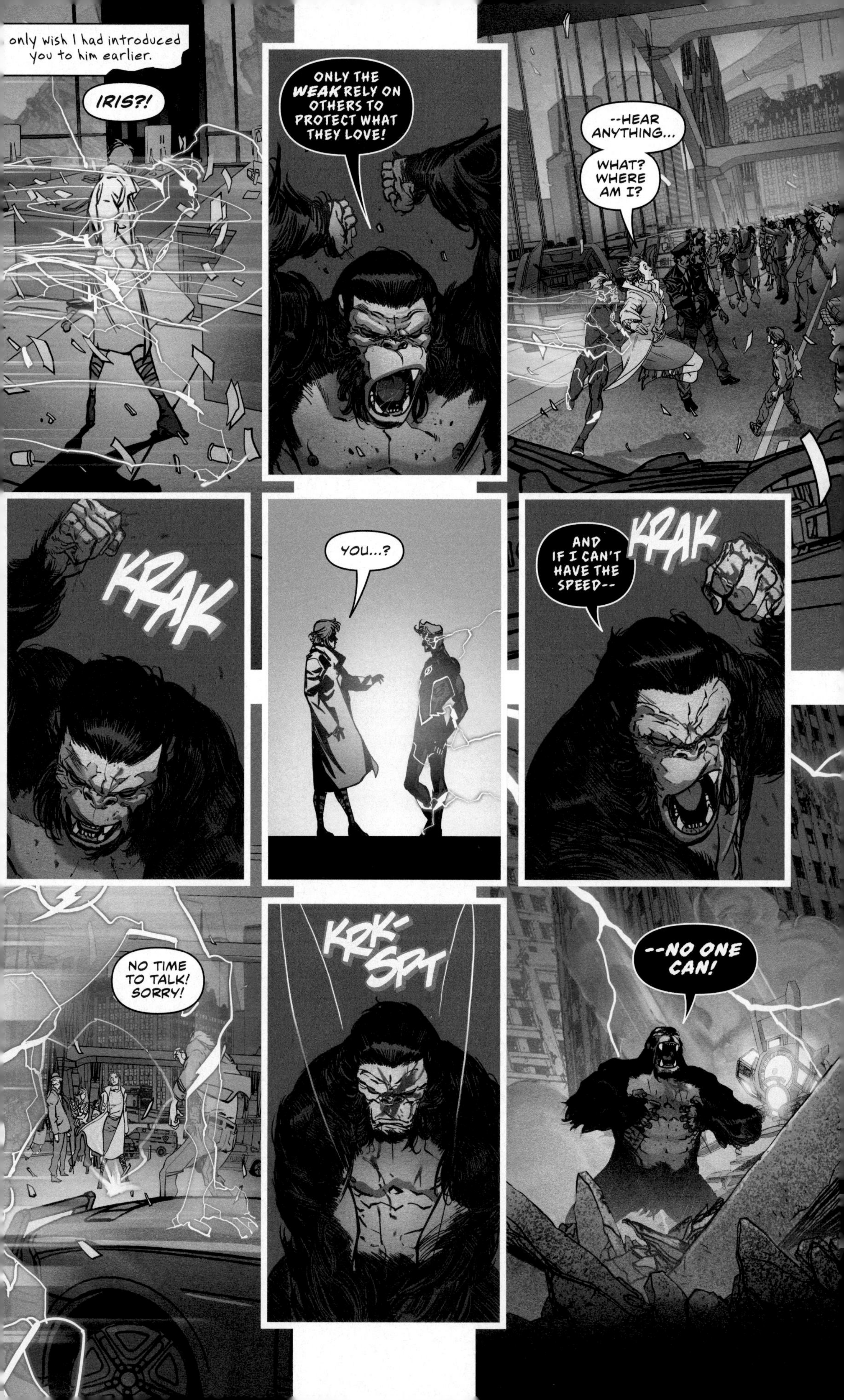
only wish I had introduced you to him earlier.
IRIS?!
ONLY THE WEAK RELY ON OTHERS TO PROTECT WHAT THEY LOVE!
--HEAR ANYTHING...
WHAT? WHERE AM I?
KRAK
YOU...?
AND IF I CAN'T HAVE THE SPEED--
KRAK
NO TIME TO TALK! SORRY!
KRK-SPT
--NO ONE CAN!

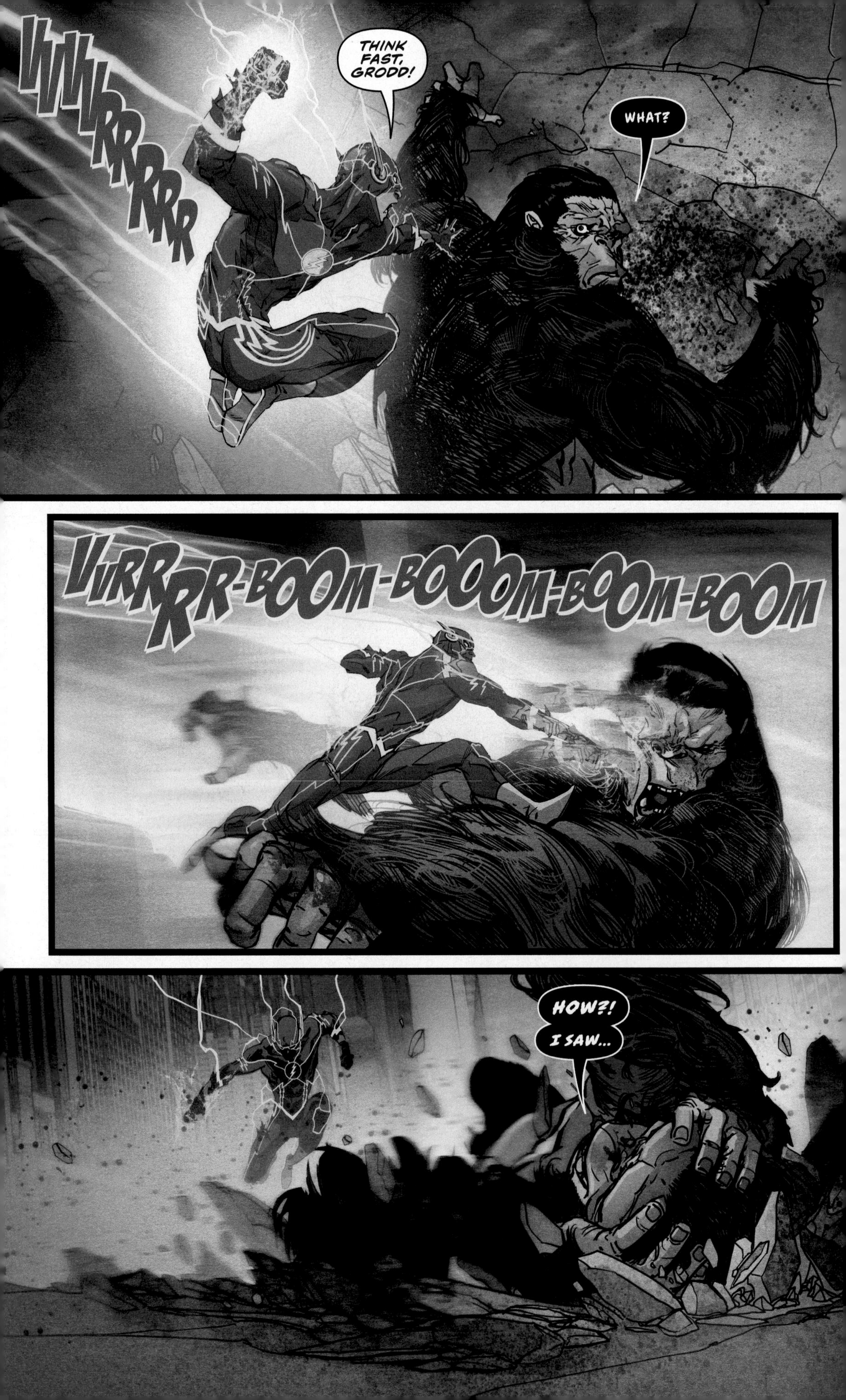
VVVVVRRRRRRR
THINK FAST, GRODD!
WHAT?
VVRRRR-BOOM-BOOOM-BOOM-BOOM
HOW?!
I SAW...

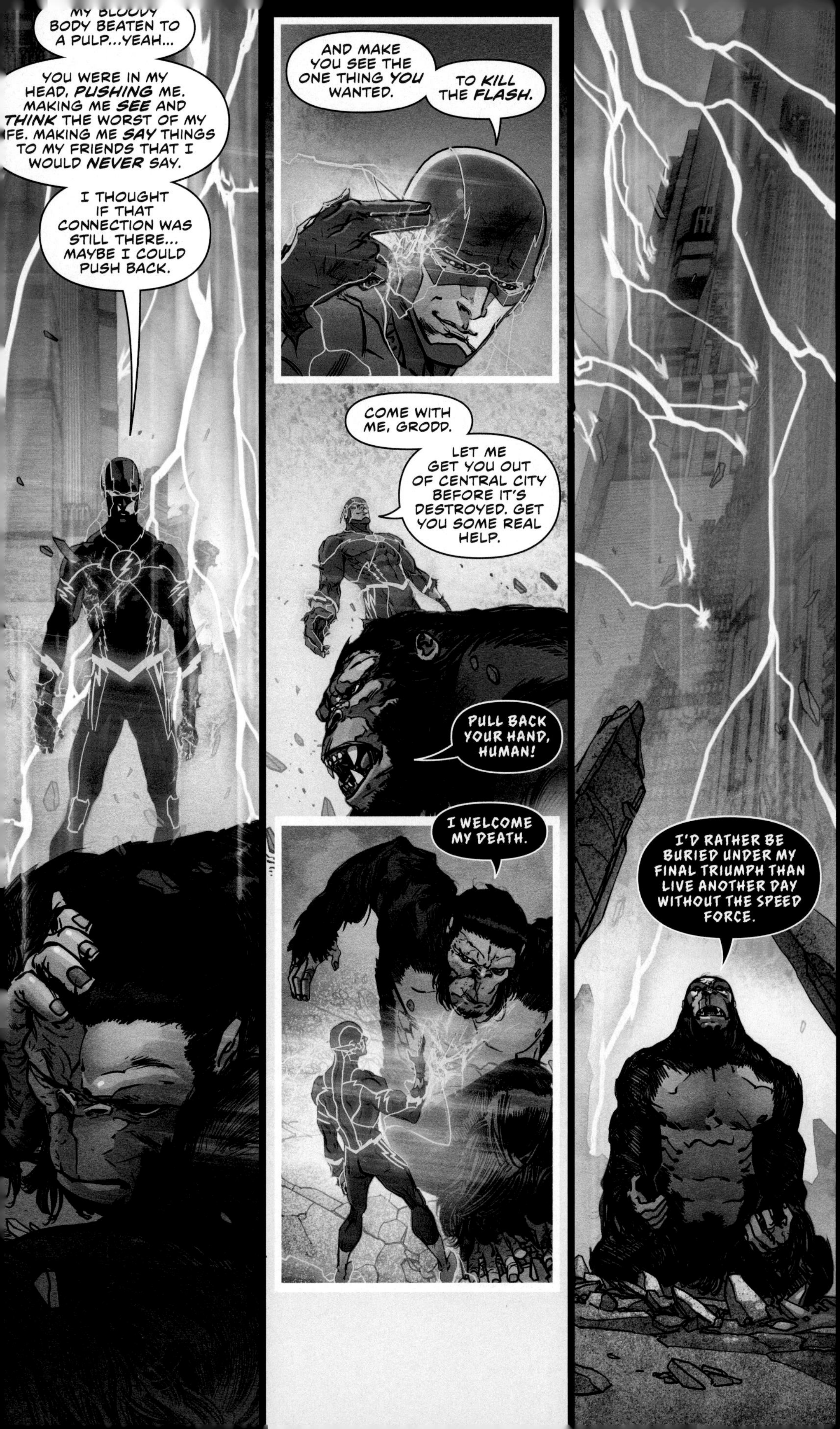
MY BLOODY BODY BEATEN TO A PULP...YEAH...
YOU WERE IN MY HEAD, PUSHING ME. MAKING ME SEE AND THINK THE WORST OF MY FE. MAKING ME SAY THINGS TO MY FRIENDS THAT I WOULD NEVER SAY.
I THOUGHT IF THAT CONNECTION WAS STILL THERE... MAYBE I COULD PUSH BACK.
AND MAKE YOU SEE THE ONE THING YOU WANTED.
TO KILL THE FLASH.
COME WITH ME, GRODD.
LET ME GET YOU OUT OF CENTRAL CITY BEFORE IT'S DESTROYED. GET YOU SOME REAL HELP.
PULL BACK YOUR HAND, HUMAN!
I WELCOME MY DEATH.
I'D RATHER BE BURIED UNDER MY FINAL TRIUMPH THAN LIVE ANOTHER DAY WITHOUT THE SPEED FORCE.

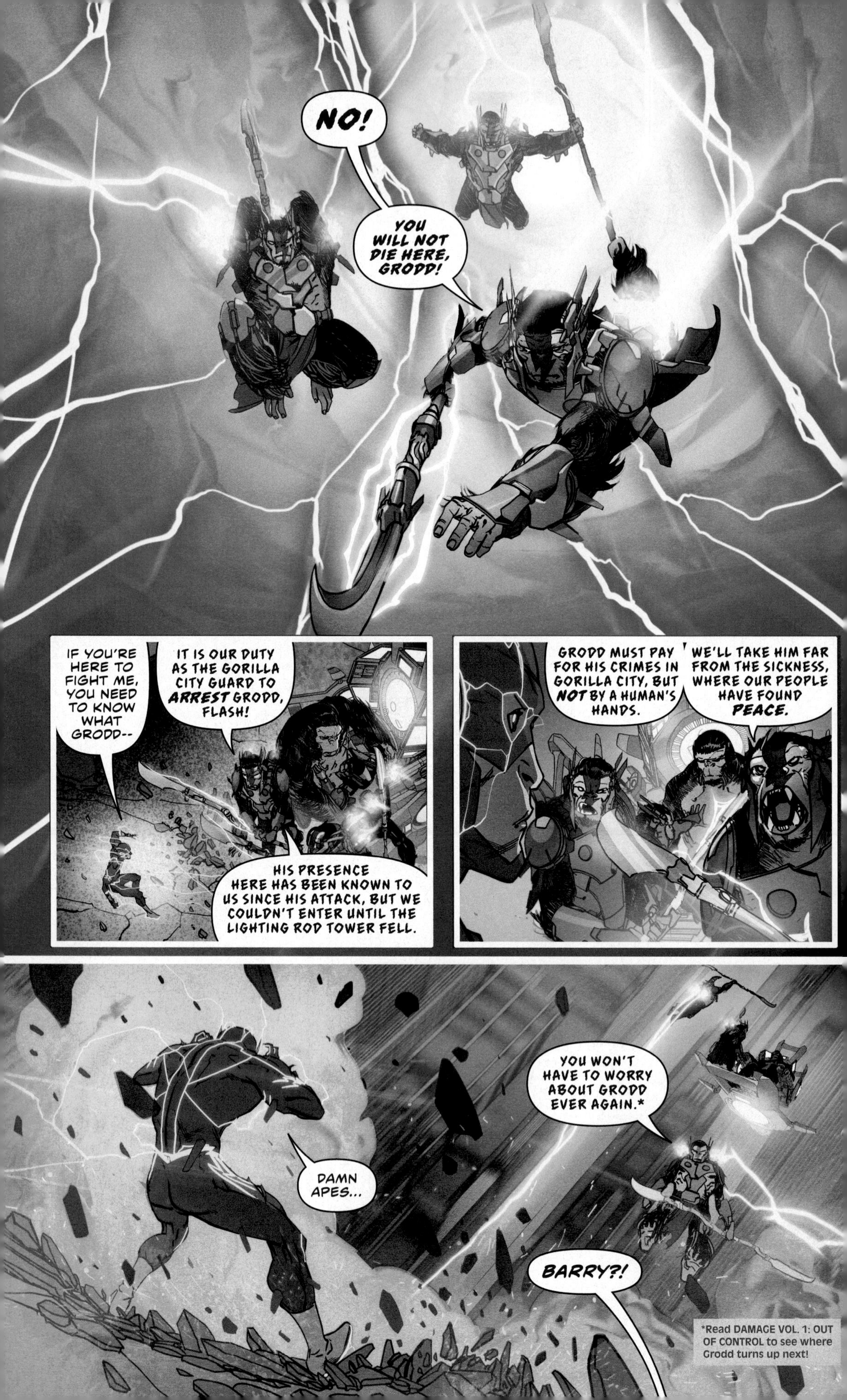
NO!
YOU WILL NOT DIE HERE, GRODD!
IF YOU'RE HERE TO FIGHT ME, YOU NEED TO KNOW WHAT GRODD--
IT IS OUR DUTY AS THE GORILLA CITY GUARD TO ARREST GRODD, FLASH!
HIS PRESENCE HERE HAS BEEN KNOWN TO US SINCE HIS ATTACK, BUT WE COULDN'T ENTER UNTIL THE LIGHTING ROD TOWER FELL.
GRODD MUST PAY FOR HIS CRIMES IN GORILLA CITY, BUT NOT BY A HUMAN'S HANDS.
WE'LL TAKE HIM FAR FROM THE SICKNESS, WHERE OUR PEOPLE HAVE FOUND PEACE.
YOU WON'T HAVE TO WORRY ABOUT GRODD EVER AGAIN.*
DAMN APES...
BARRY?!
*Read DAMAGE VOL. 1: OUT OF CONTROL to see where Grodd turns up next!

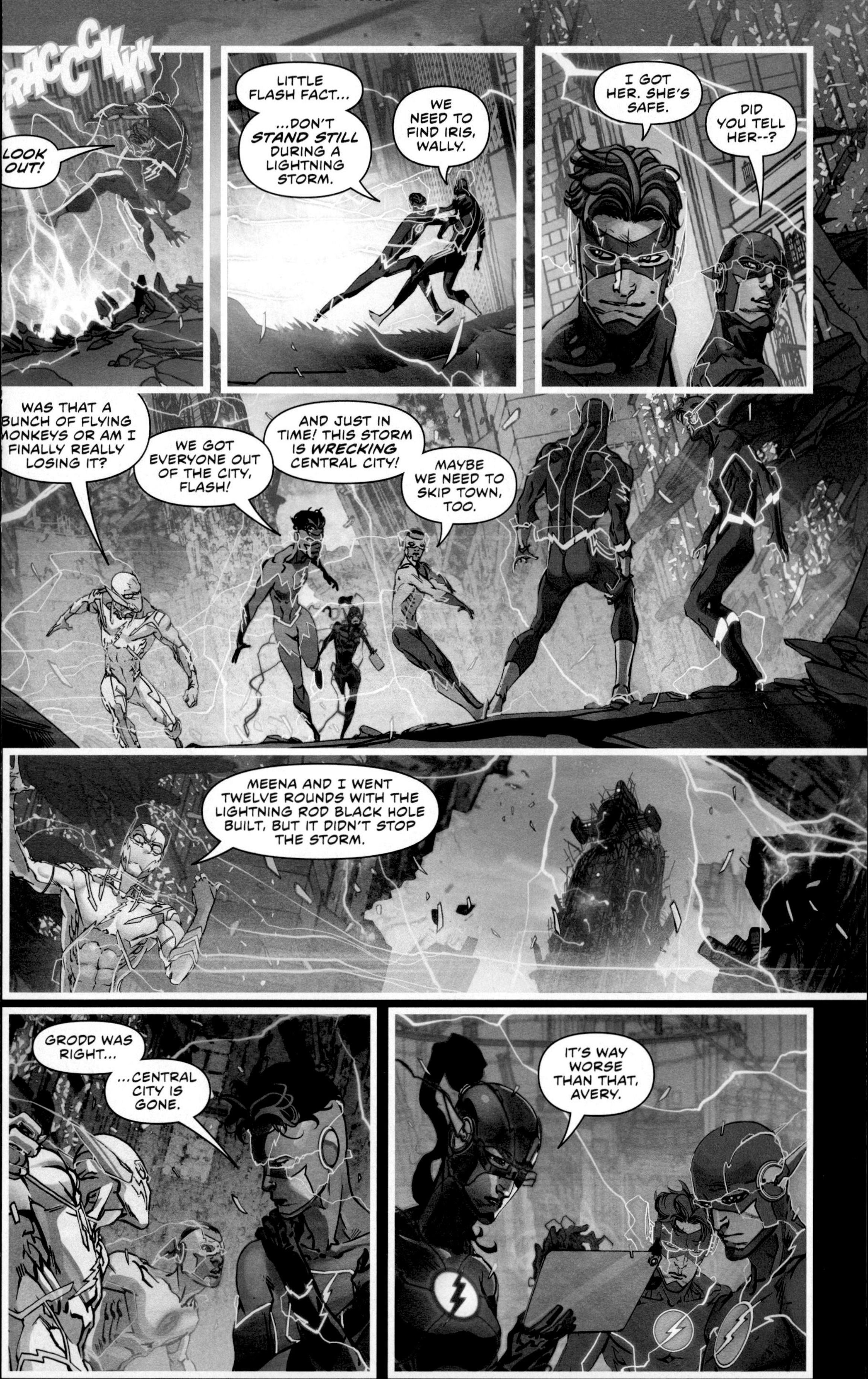
KRRACCCKKK
LOOK OUT!
LITTLE FLASH FACT...
...DON'T STAND STILL DURING A LIGHTNING STORM.
WE NEED TO FIND IRIS, WALLY.
I GOT HER. SHE'S SAFE.
DID YOU TELL HER--?
WAS THAT A BUNCH OF FLYING MONKEYS OR AM I FINALLY REALLY LOSING IT?
WE GOT EVERYONE OUT OF THE CITY, FLASH!
AND JUST IN TIME! THIS STORM IS WRECKING CENTRAL CITY!
MAYBE WE NEED TO SKIP TOWN, TOO.
MEENA AND I WENT TWELVE ROUNDS WITH THE LIGHTNING ROD BLACK HOLE BUILT, BUT IT DIDN'T STOP THE STORM.
GRODD WAS RIGHT...
...CENTRAL CITY IS GONE.
IT'S WAY WORSE THAN THAT, AVERY.

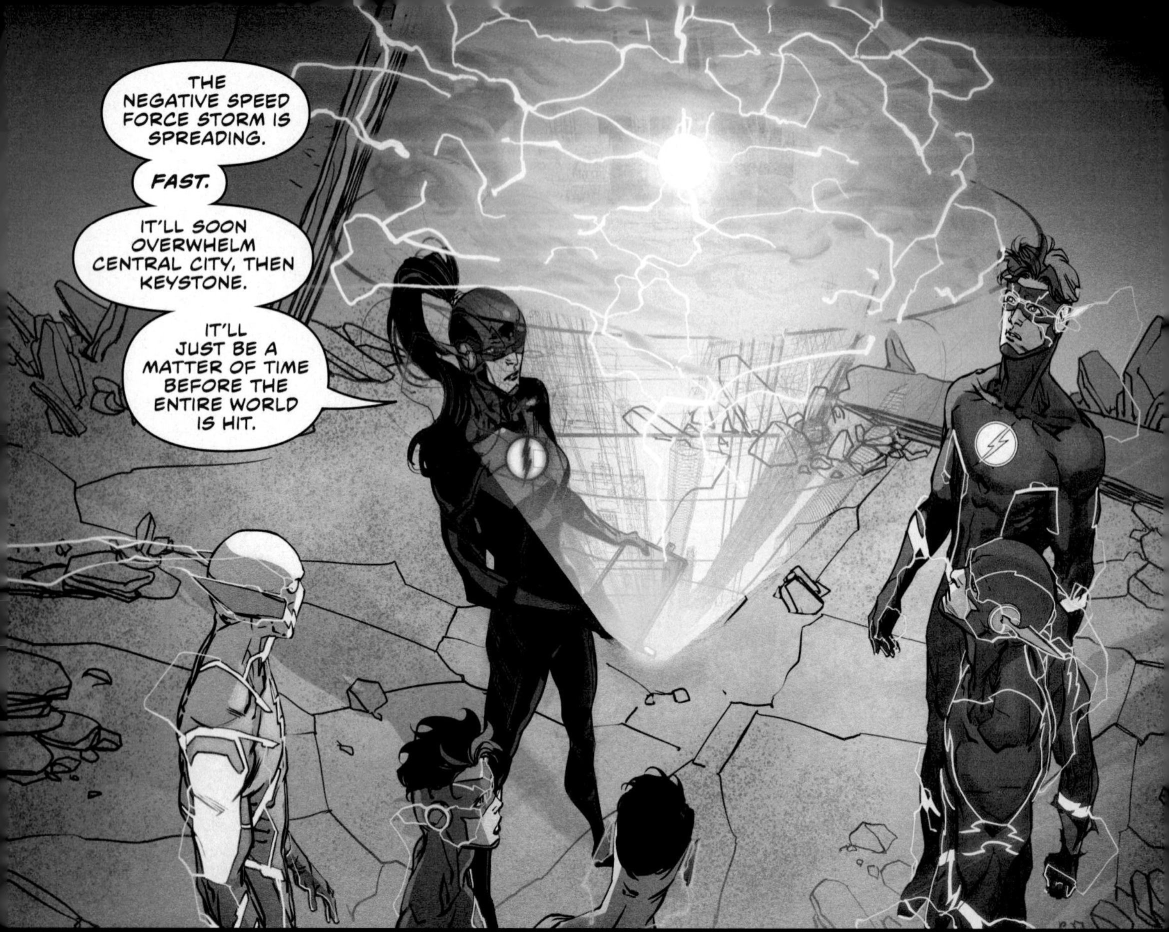
THE NEGATIVE SPEED FORCE STORM IS SPREADING.
FAST.
IT'LL SOON OVERWHELM CENTRAL CITY, THEN KEYSTONE.
IT'LL JUST BE A MATTER OF TIME BEFORE THE ENTIRE WORLD IS HIT.

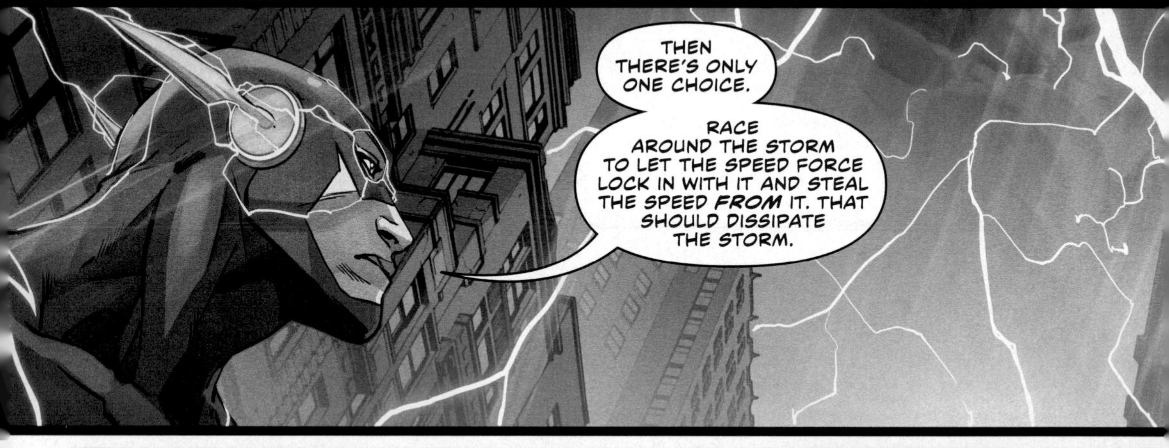
THEN THERE'S ONLY ONE CHOICE.
RACE AROUND THE STORM TO LET THE SPEED FORCE LOCK IN WITH IT AND STEAL THE SPEED FROM IT. THAT SHOULD DISSIPATE THE STORM.

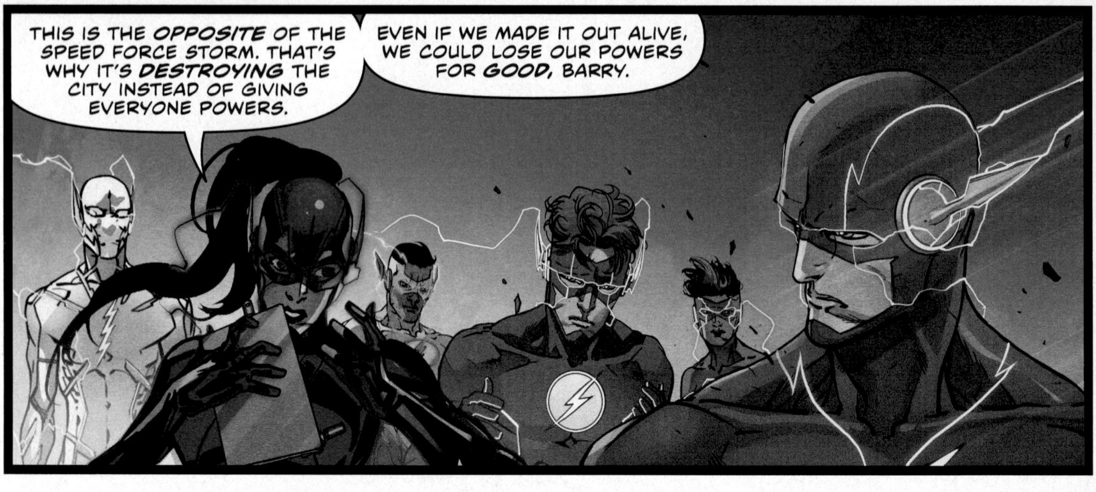
THIS IS THE OPPOSITE OF THE SPEED FORCE STORM. THAT'S WHY IT'S DESTROYING THE CITY INSTEAD OF GIVING EVERYONE POWERS.
EVEN IF WE MADE IT OUT ALIVE, WE COULD LOSE OUR POWERS FOR GOOD, BARRY.

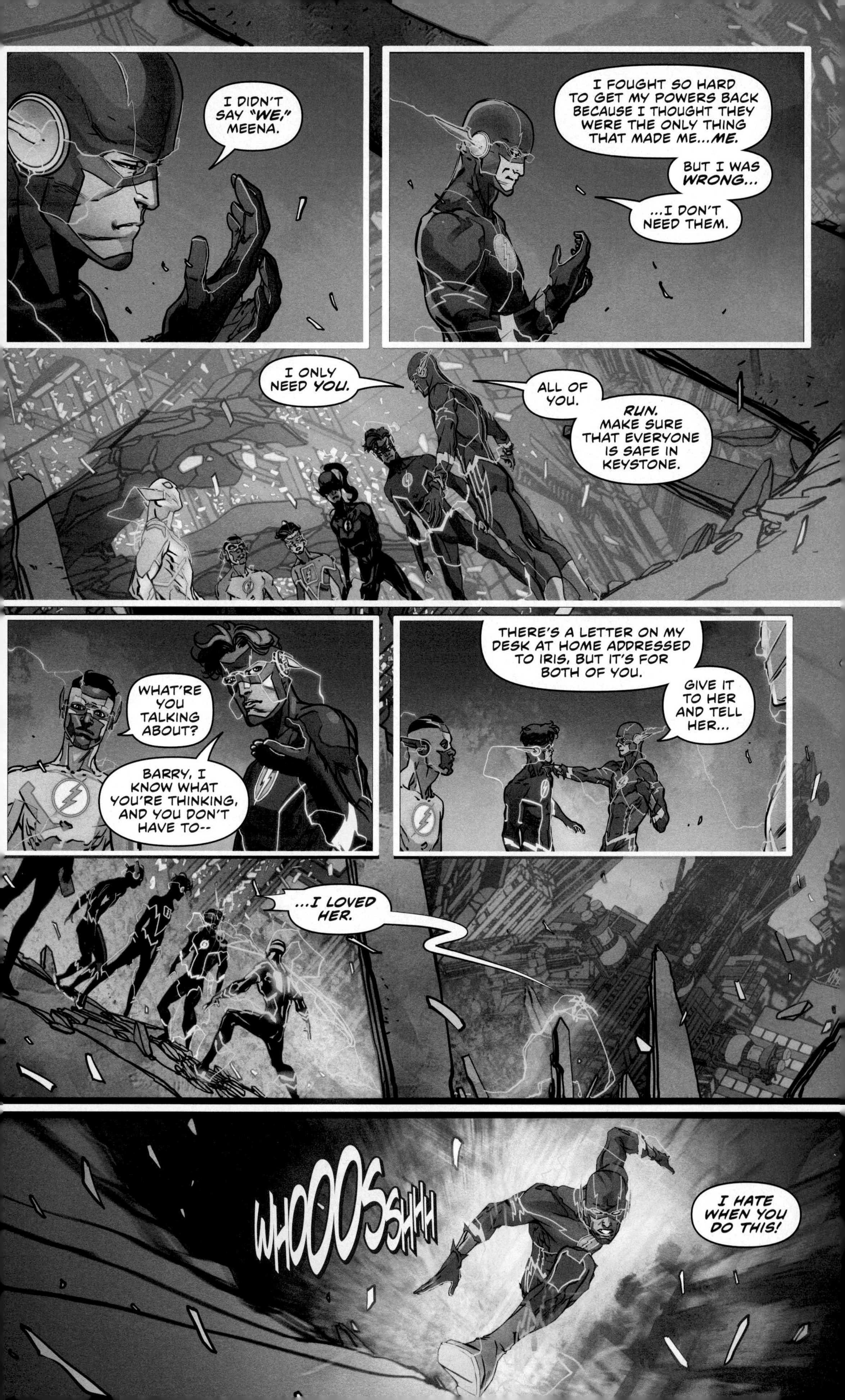
I DIDN'T SAY "WE," MEENA.
I FOUGHT SO HARD TO GET MY POWERS BACK BECAUSE I THOUGHT THEY WERE THE ONLY THING THAT MADE ME...ME.
BUT I WAS WRONG...
...I DON'T NEED THEM.
I ONLY NEED YOU.
ALL OF YOU.
RUN. MAKE SURE THAT EVERYONE IS SAFE IN KEYSTONE.
WHAT'RE YOU TALKING ABOUT?
BARRY, I KNOW WHAT YOU'RE THINKING, AND YOU DON'T HAVE TO--
THERE'S A LETTER ON MY DESK AT HOME ADDRESSED TO IRIS, BUT IT'S FOR BOTH OF YOU.
GIVE IT TO HER AND TELL HER...
...I LOVED HER.
WHOOOSSHHH
I HATE WHEN YOU DO THIS!

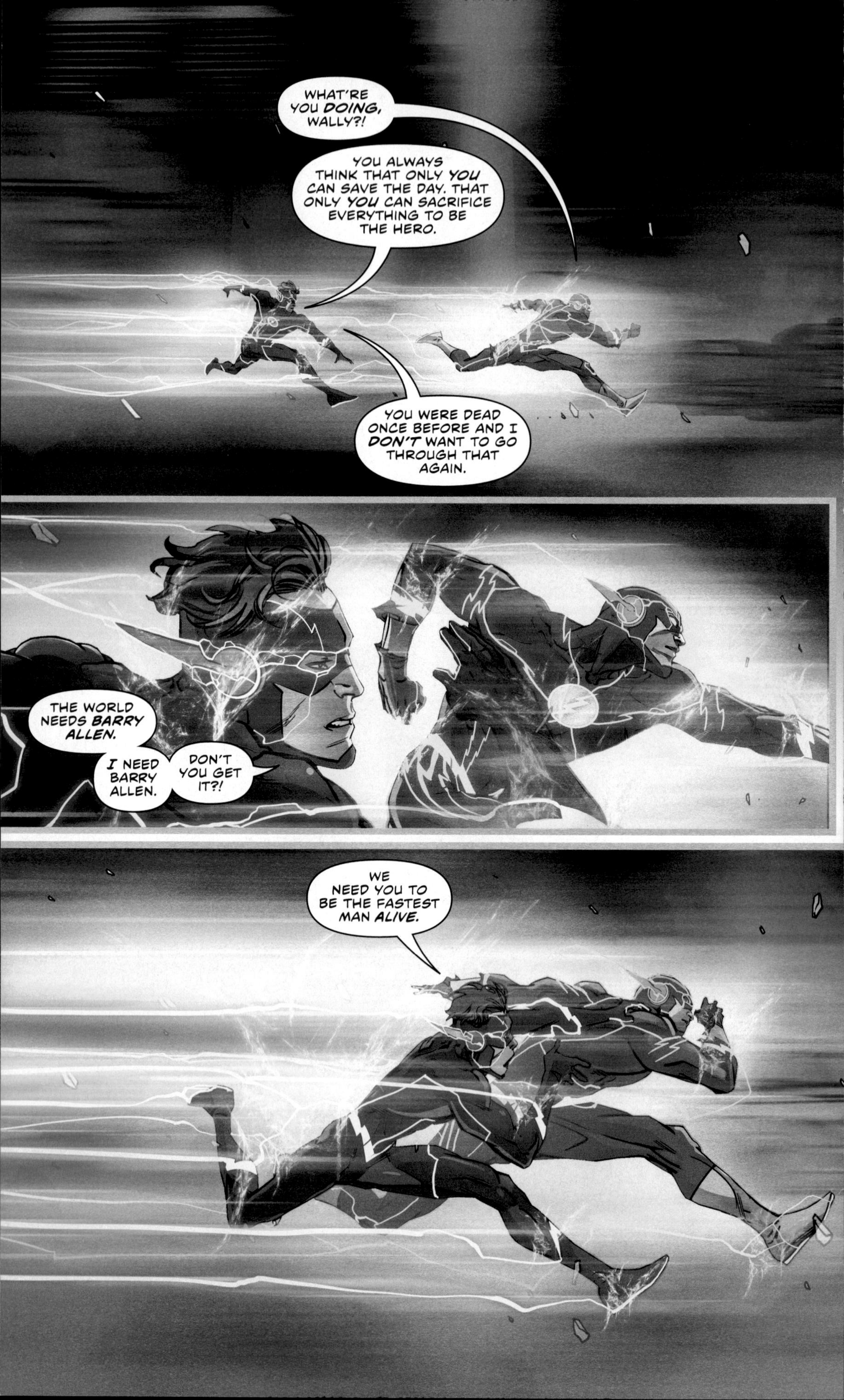
WHAT'RE YOU DOING, WALLY?!
YOU ALWAYS THINK THAT ONLY YOU CAN SAVE THE DAY. THAT ONLY YOU CAN SACRIFICE EVERYTHING TO BE THE HERO.
YOU WERE DEAD ONCE BEFORE AND I DON'T WANT TO GO THROUGH THAT AGAIN.
THE WORLD NEEDS BARRY ALLEN.
I NEED BARRY ALLEN.
DON'T YOU GET IT?!
WE NEED YOU TO BE THE FASTEST MAN ALIVE.

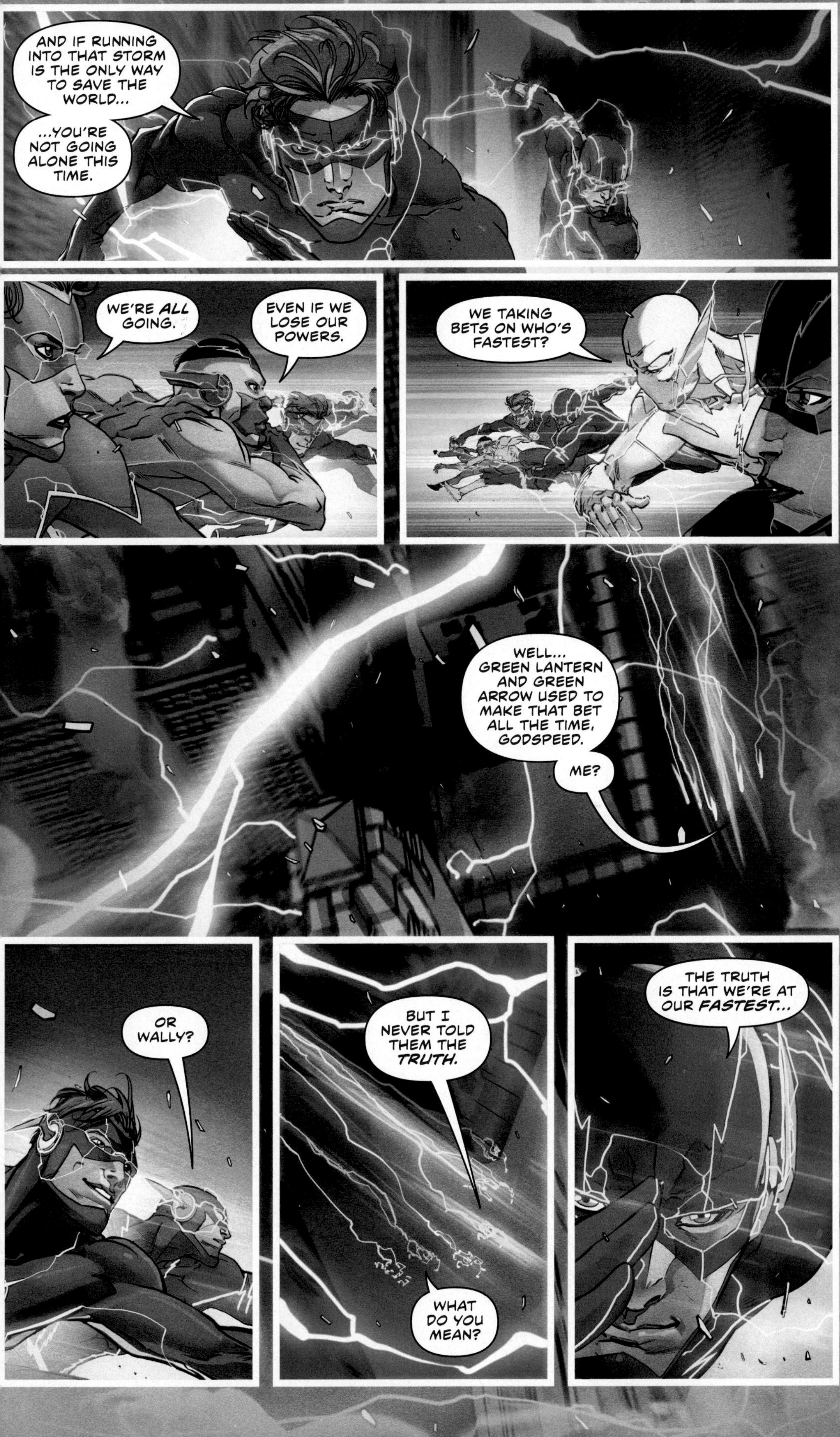
AND IF RUNNING INTO THAT STORM IS THE ONLY WAY TO SAVE THE WORLD...
...YOU'RE NOT GOING ALONE THIS TIME.
WE'RE *ALL* GOING.
EVEN IF WE LOSE OUR POWERS.
WE TAKING BETS ON WHO'S FASTEST?
WELL... GREEN LANTERN AND GREEN ARROW USED TO MAKE THAT BET ALL THE TIME, GODSPEED.
ME?
OR WALLY?
BUT I NEVER TOLD THEM THE *TRUTH.*
WHAT DO YOU MEAN?
THE TRUTH IS THAT WE'RE AT OUR *FASTEST...*

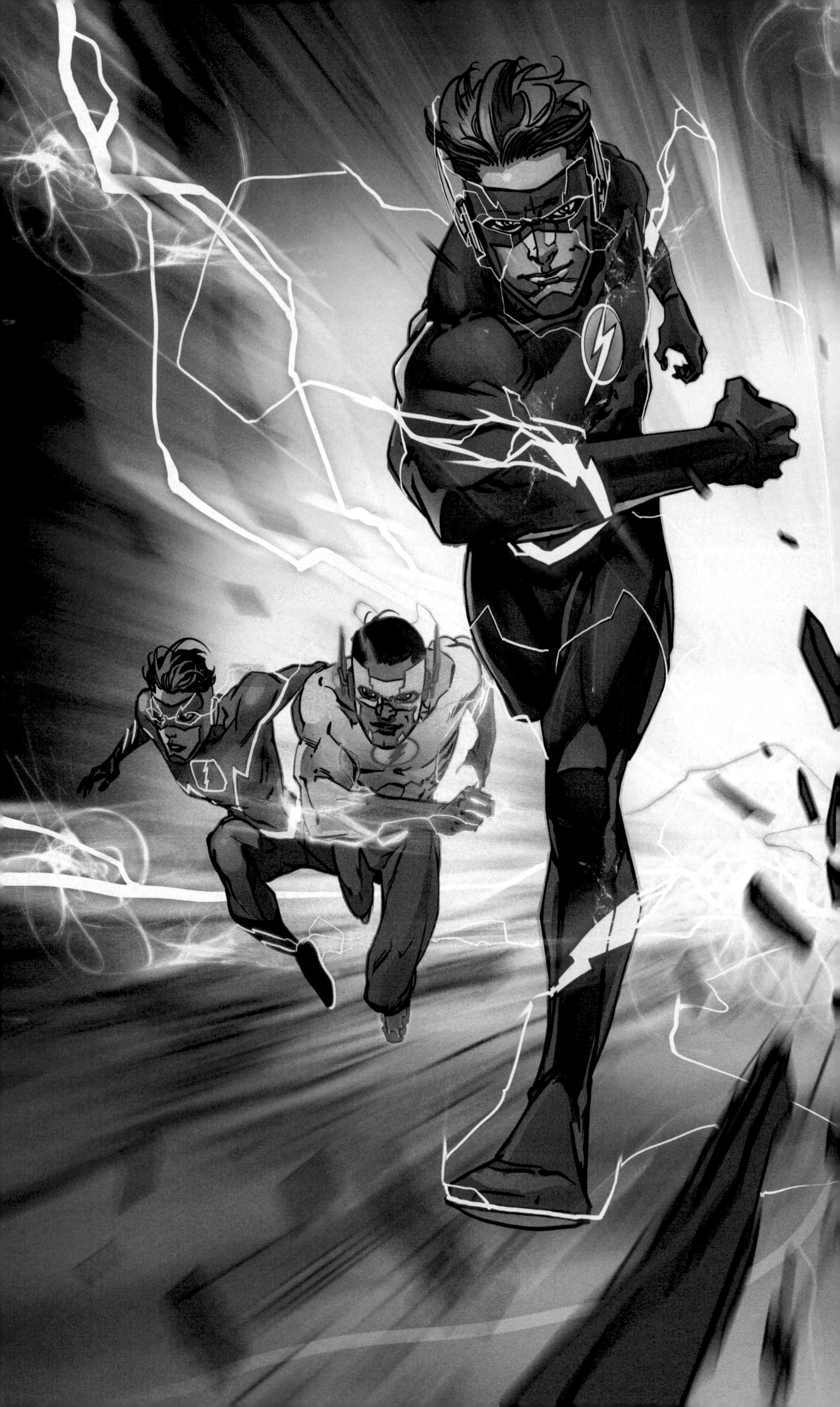

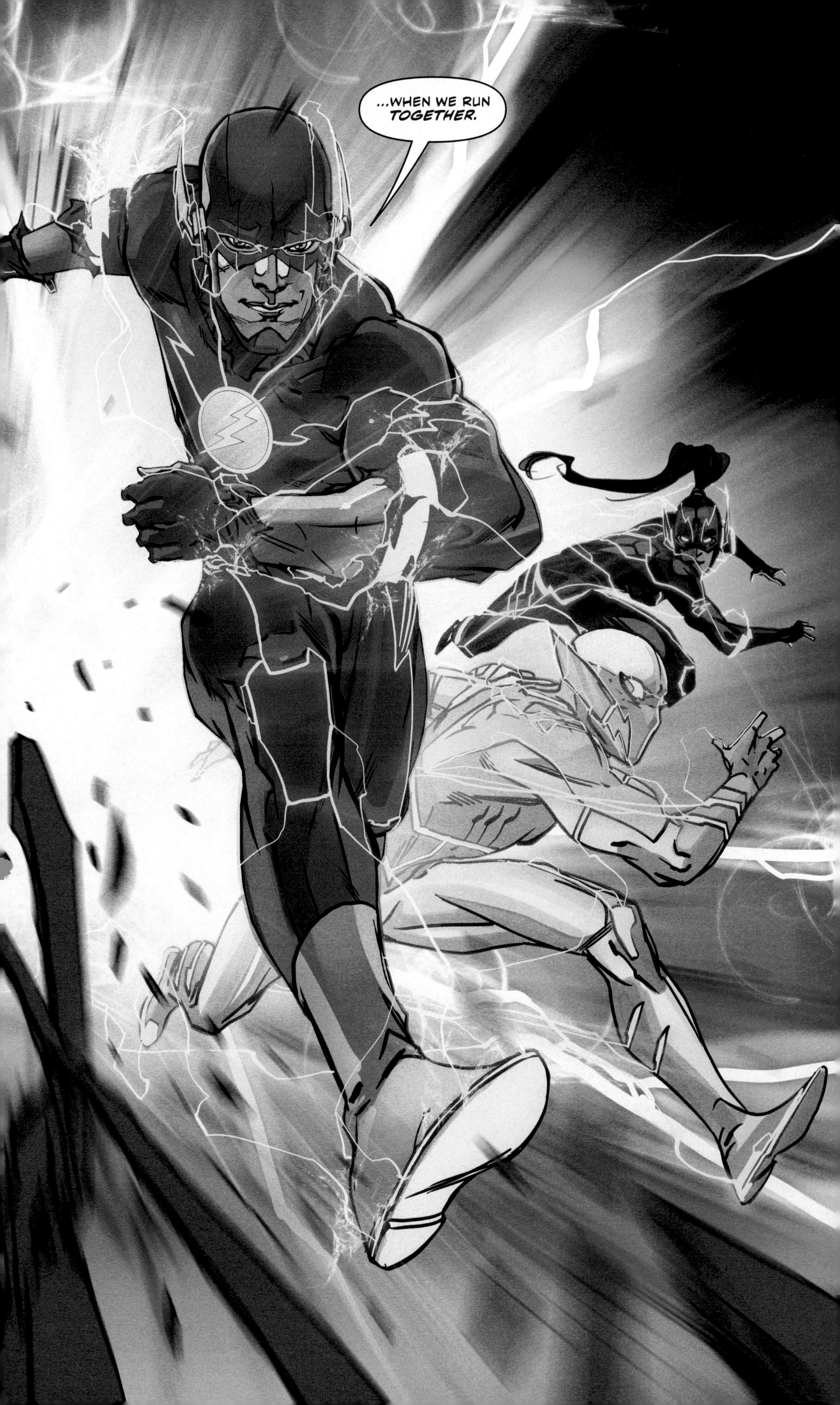
...WHEN WE RUN TOGETHER.

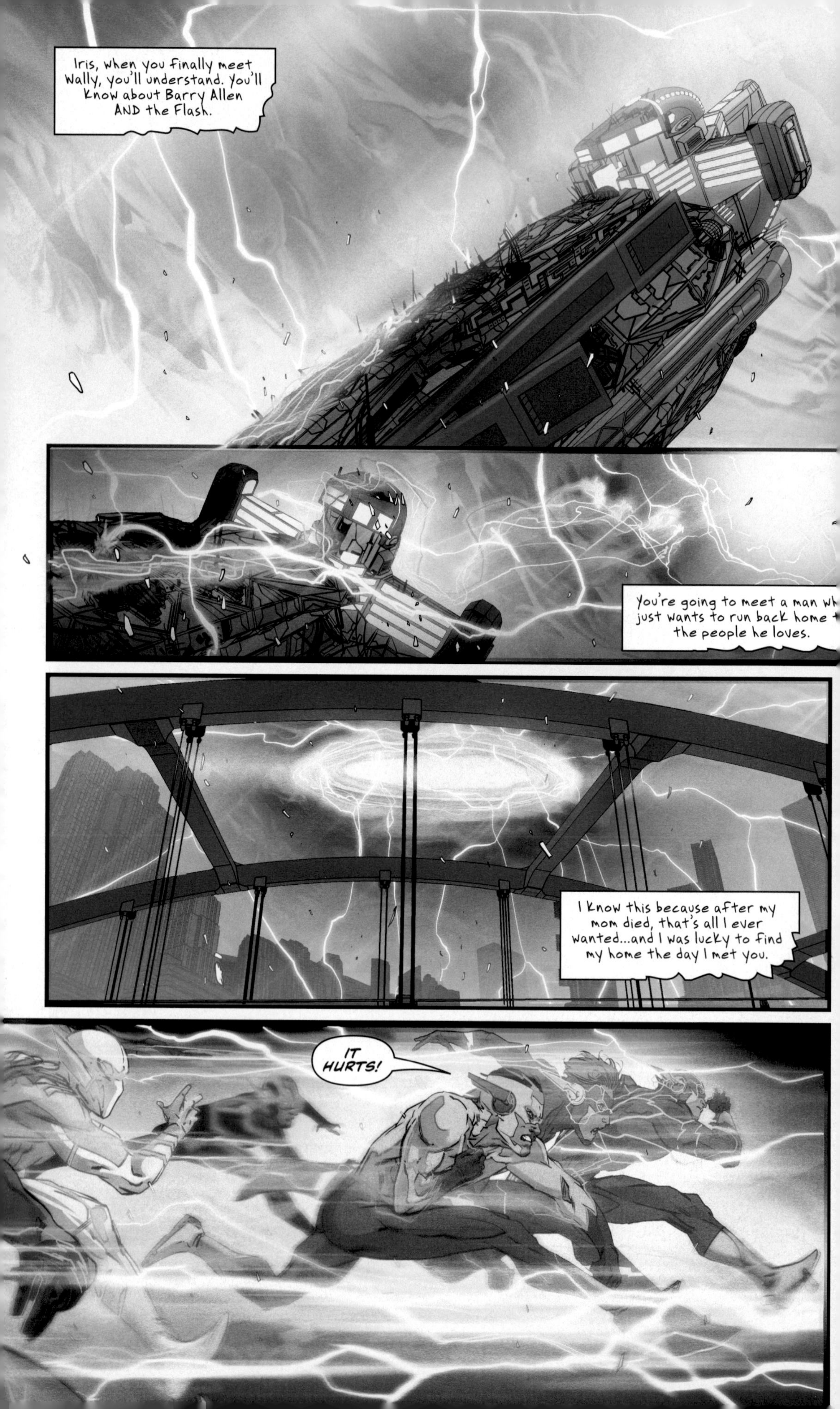
Iris, when you finally meet Wally, you'll understand. You'll know about Barry Allen AND the Flash.
You're going to meet a man wh
just wants to run back home t
the people he loves.
I know this because after my mom died, that's all I ever wanted...and I was lucky to find my home the day I met you.
IT HURTS!

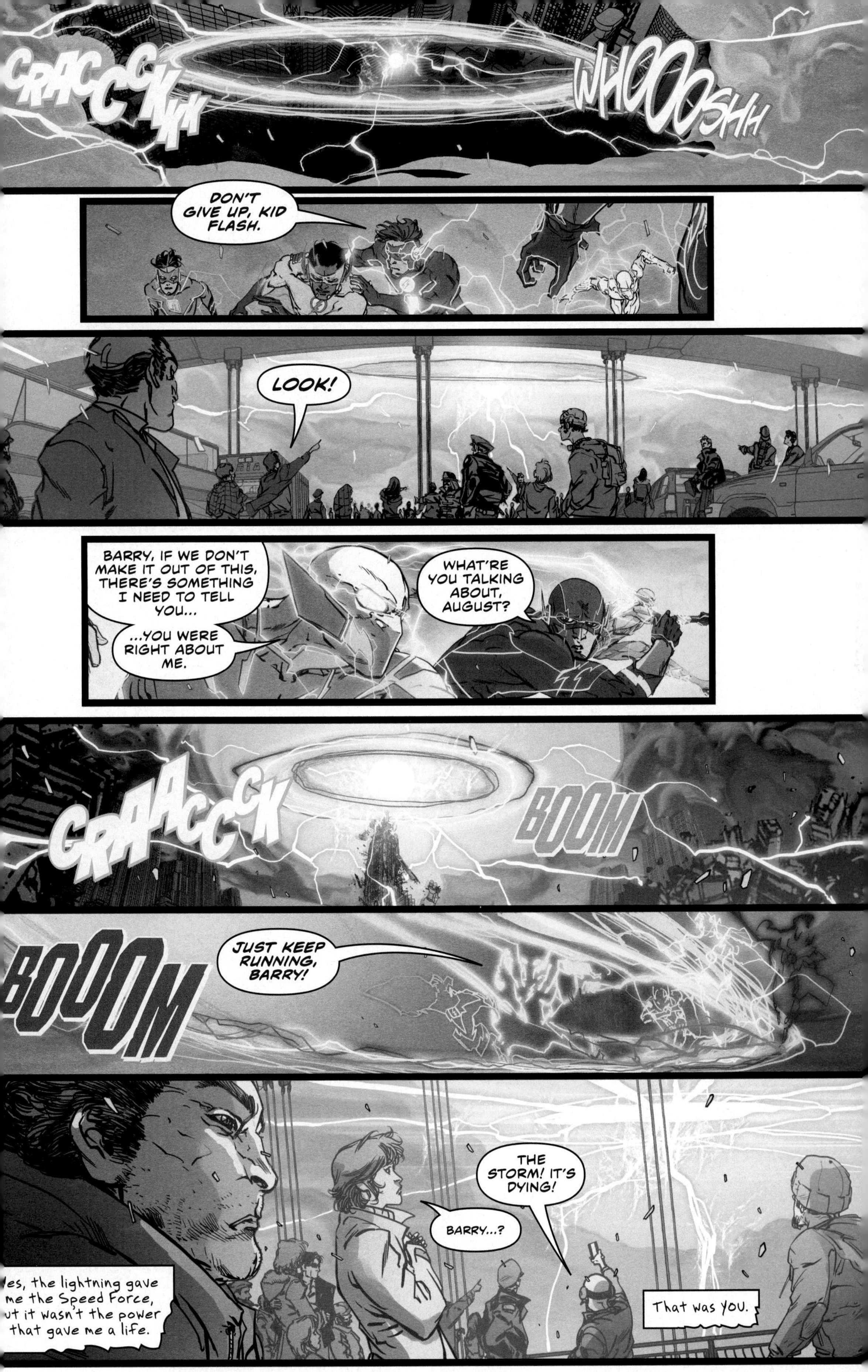
CRACCCKKK
WHOOOSHH
DON'T GIVE UP, KID FLASH.
LOOK!
BARRY, IF WE DON'T MAKE IT OUT OF THIS, THERE'S SOMETHING I NEED TO TELL YOU...
...YOU WERE RIGHT ABOUT ME.
WHAT'RE YOU TALKING ABOUT, AUGUST?
CRAAACCCK
BOOM
BOOOM
JUST KEEP RUNNING, BARRY!
BARRY...?
THE STORM! IT'S DYING!
es, the lightning gave me the Speed Force, ut it wasn't the power that gave me a life.
That was YOU.

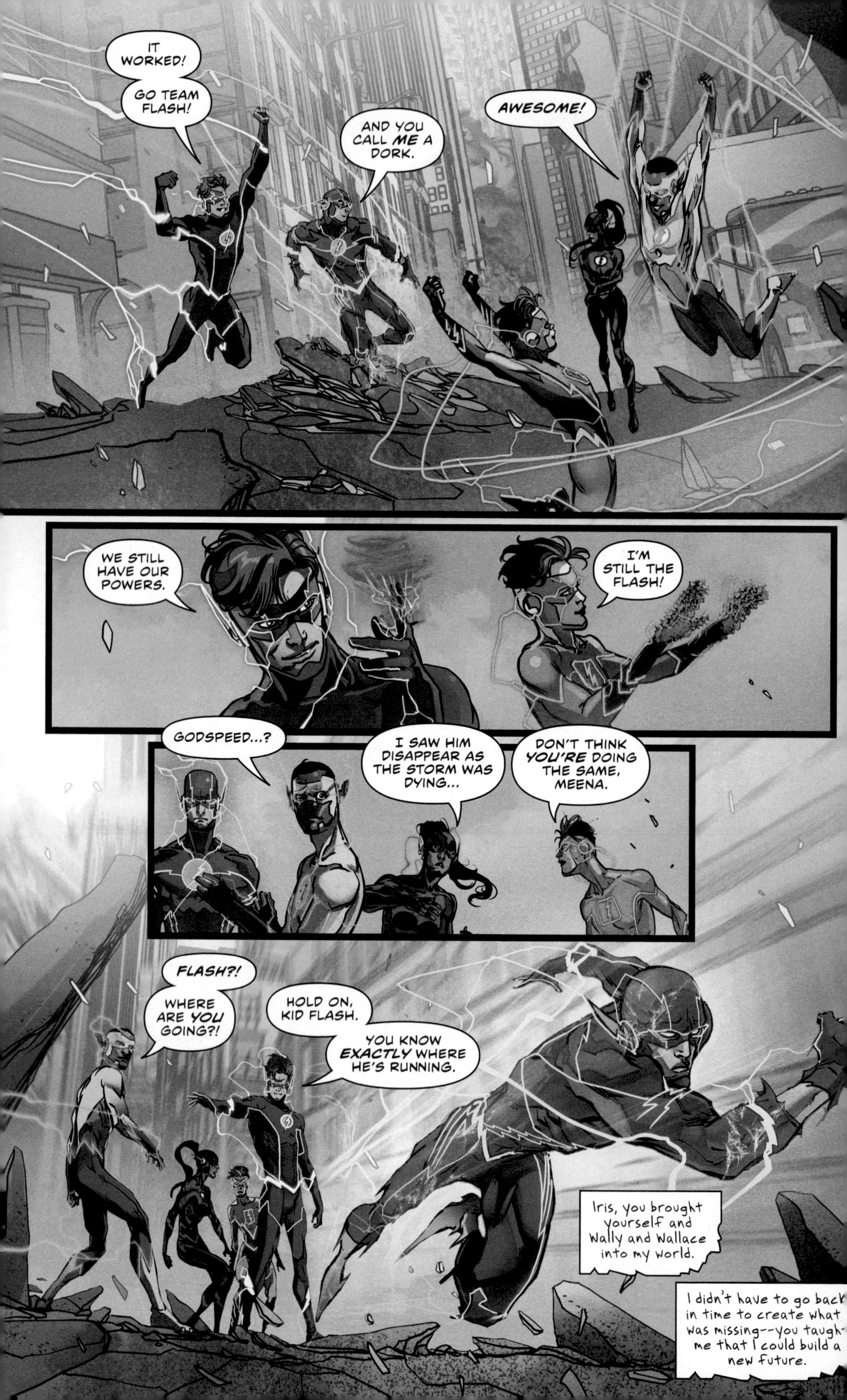
IT WORKED!
GO TEAM FLASH!
AND YOU CALL ME A DORK.
AWESOME!
WE STILL HAVE OUR POWERS.
I'M STILL THE FLASH!
GODSPEED...?
I SAW HIM DISAPPEAR AS THE STORM WAS DYING...
DON'T THINK YOU'RE DOING THE SAME, MEENA.
FLASH?!
WHERE ARE YOU GOING?!
HOLD ON, KID FLASH.
YOU KNOW EXACTLY WHERE HE'S RUNNING.
Iris, you brought yourself and Wally and Wallace into my world.
I didn't have to go back in time to create what was missing--you taught me that I could build a new future.

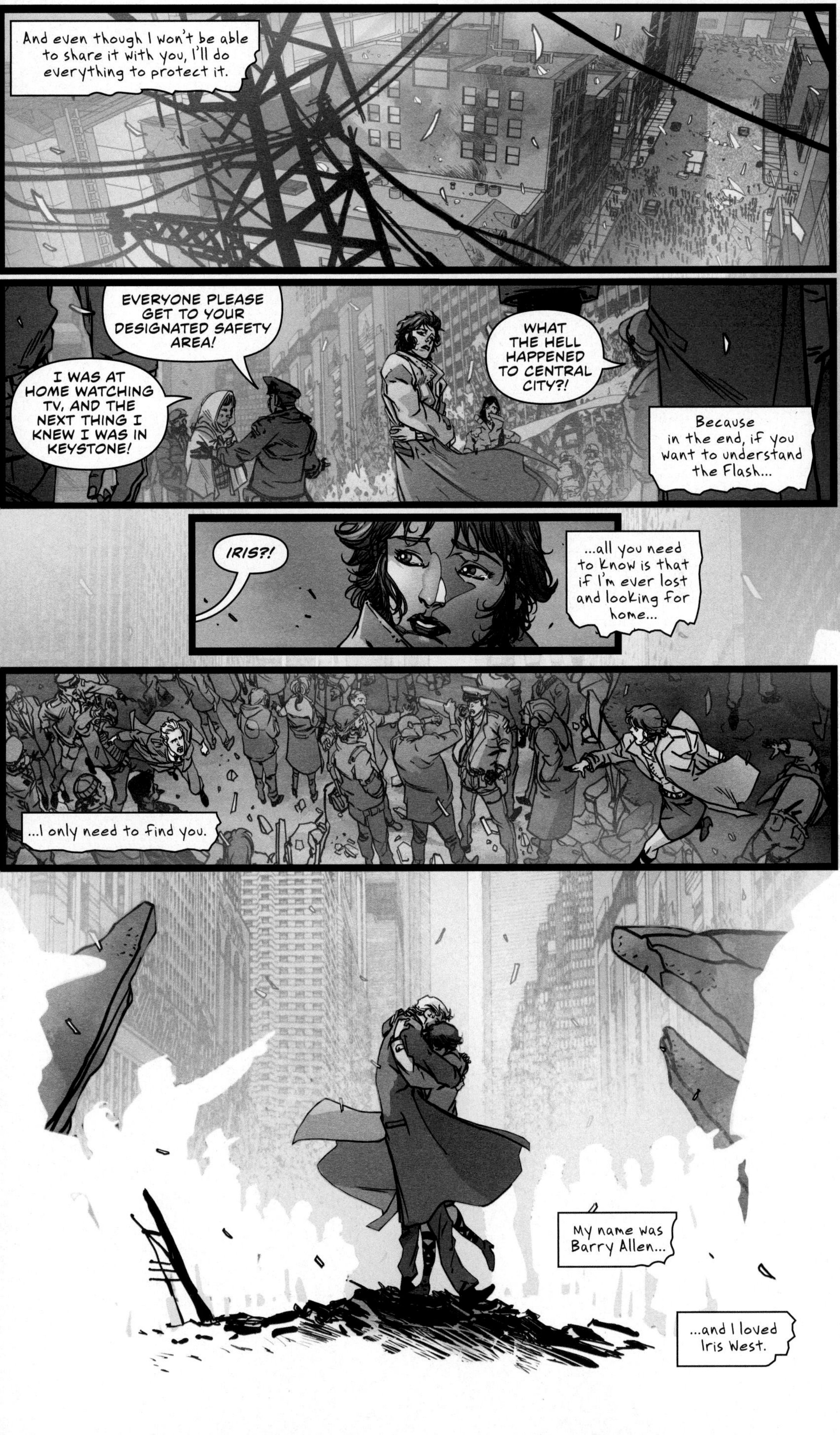

And even though I won't be able to share it with you, I'll do everything to protect it.
EVERYONE PLEASE GET TO YOUR DESIGNATED SAFETY AREA!
I WAS AT HOME WATCHING TV, AND THE NEXT THING I KNEW I WAS IN KEYSTONE!
WHAT THE HELL HAPPENED TO CENTRAL CITY?!
Because in the end, if you want to understand the Flash...
IRIS?!
...all you need to know is that if I'm ever lost and looking for home...
...I only need to find you.
My name was Barry Allen...
...and I loved Iris West.

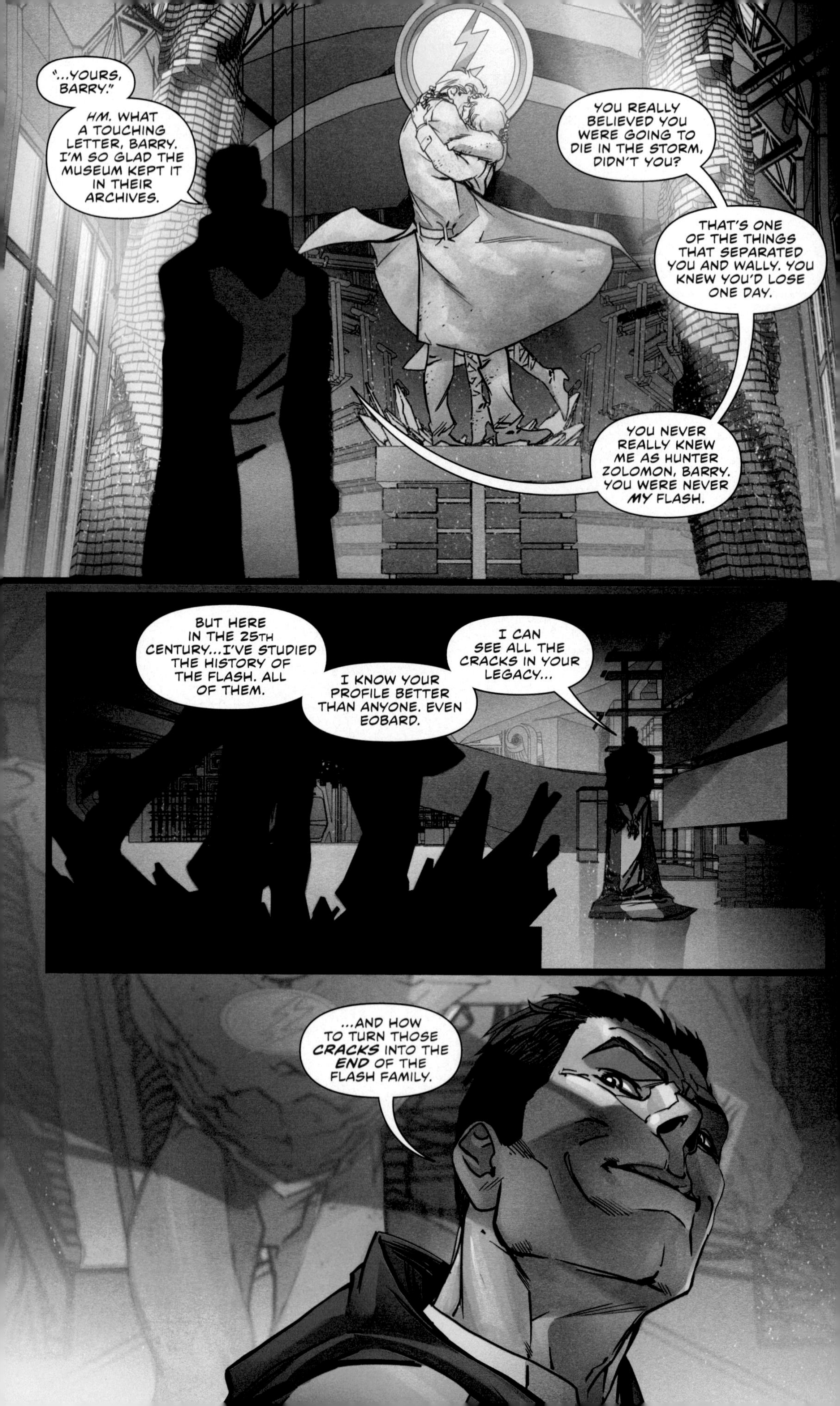
"...YOURS, BARRY."
HM. WHAT A TOUCHING LETTER, BARRY. I'M SO GLAD THE MUSEUM KEPT IT IN THEIR ARCHIVES.
YOU REALLY BELIEVED YOU WERE GOING TO DIE IN THE STORM, DIDN'T YOU?
THAT'S ONE OF THE THINGS THAT SEPARATED YOU AND WALLY. YOU KNEW YOU'D LOSE ONE DAY.
YOU NEVER REALLY KNEW ME AS HUNTER ZOLOMON, BARRY. YOU WERE NEVER *MY* FLASH.
BUT HERE IN THE 25TH CENTURY...I'VE STUDIED THE HISTORY OF THE FLASH. ALL OF THEM.
I KNOW YOUR PROFILE BETTER THAN ANYONE. EVEN EOBARD.
I CAN SEE ALL THE CRACKS IN YOUR LEGACY...
...AND HOW TO TURN THOSE *CRACKS* INTO THE *END* OF THE FLASH FAMILY.

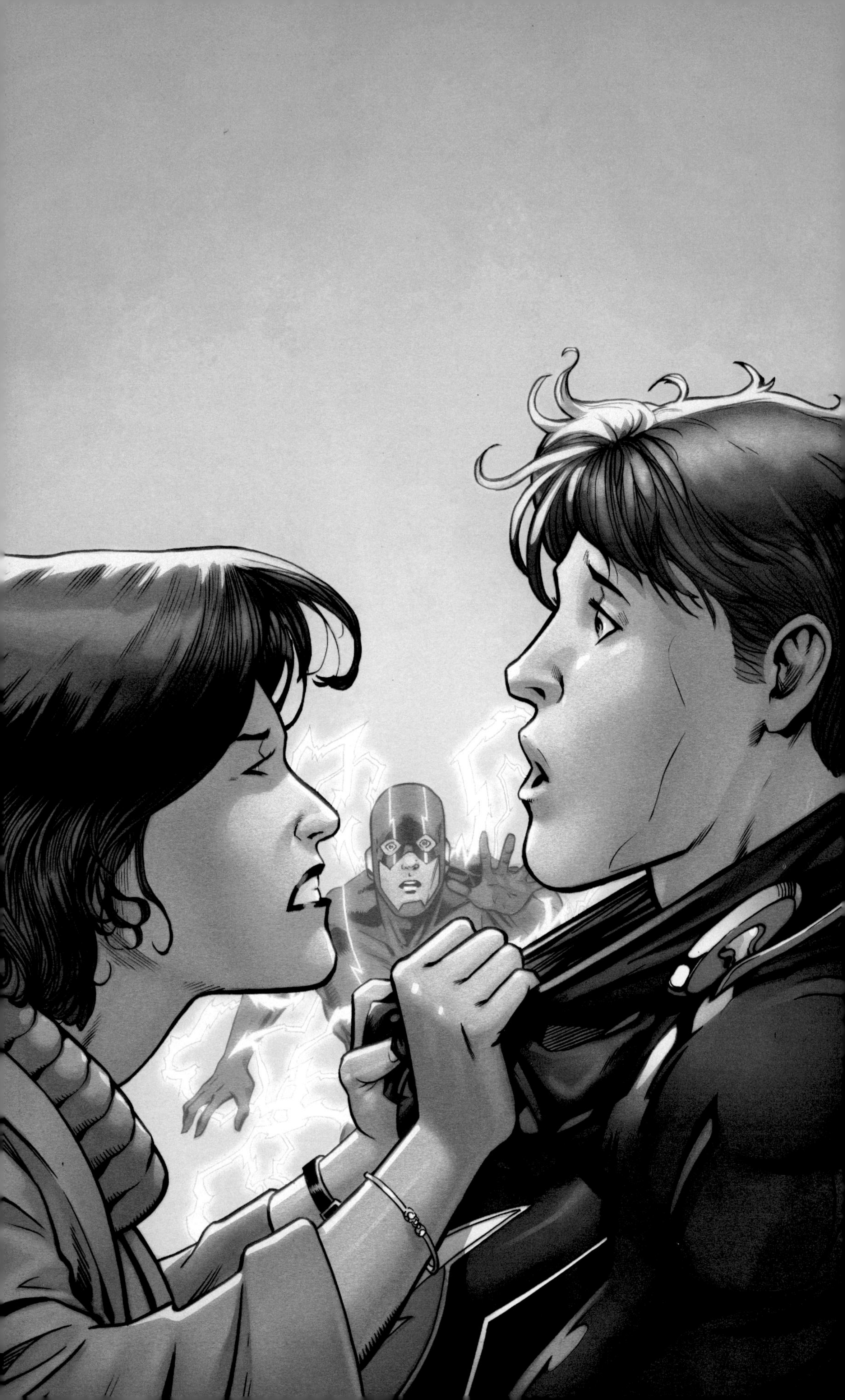

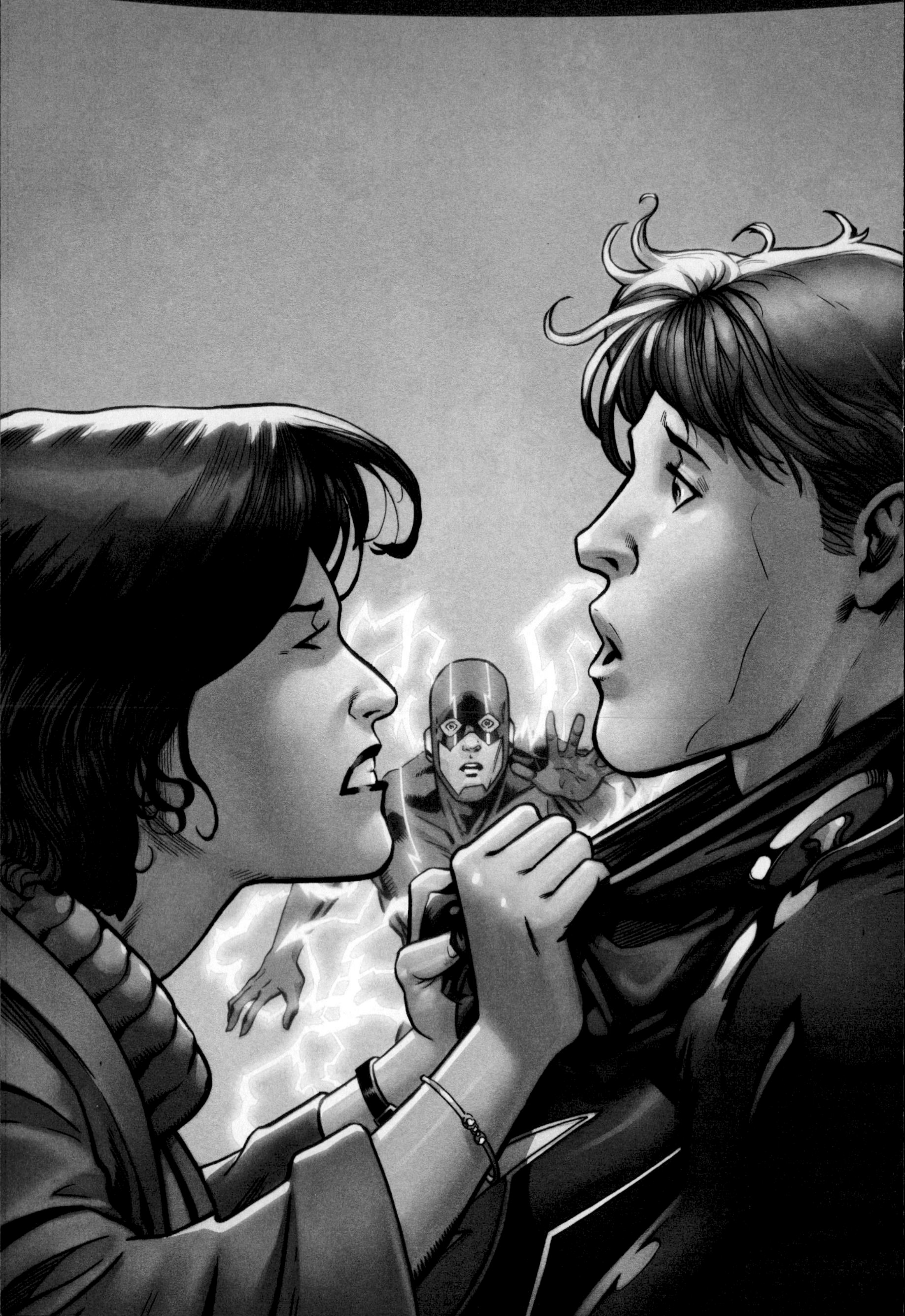

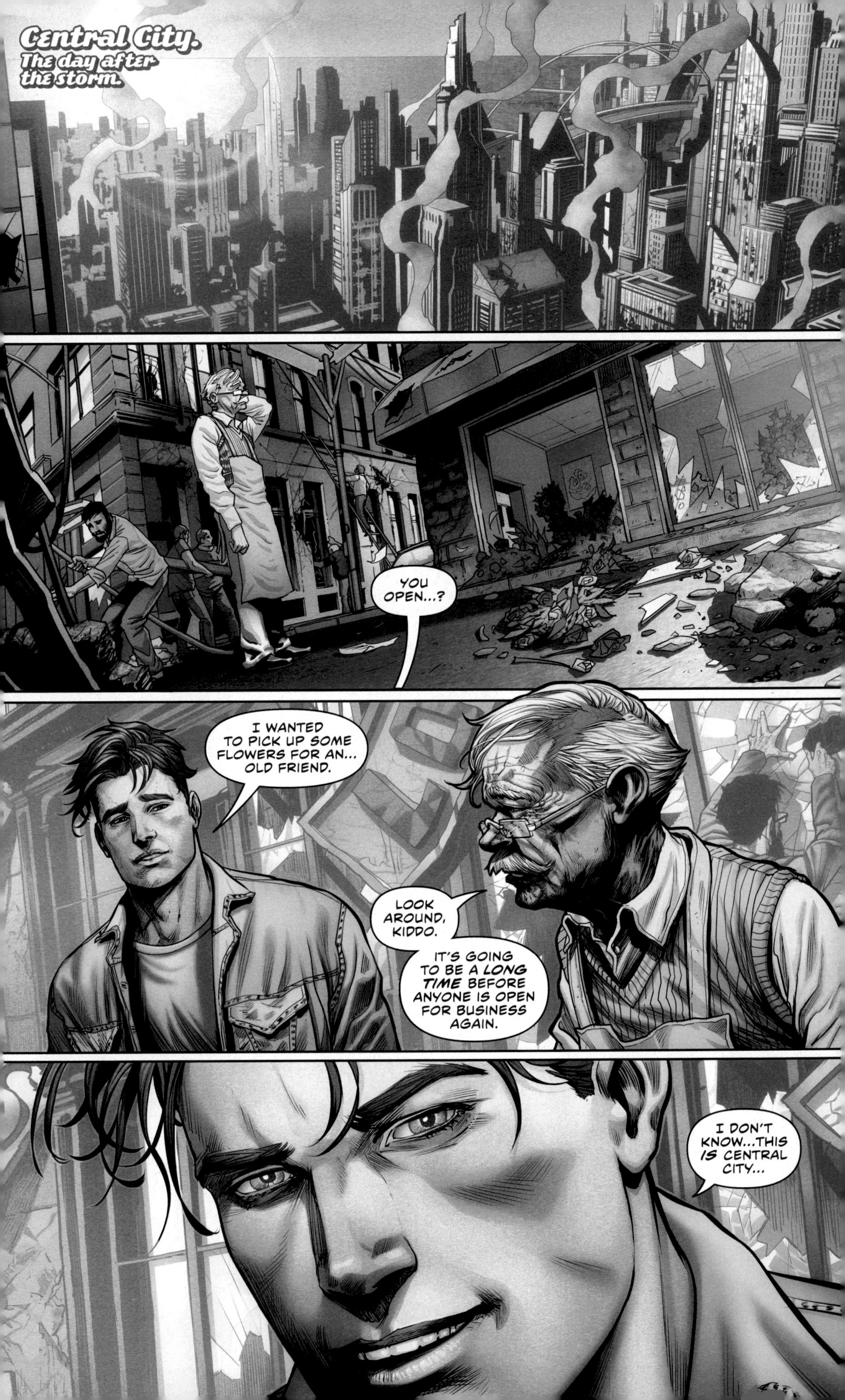
Central City.
The day after the storm.
YOU OPEN...?
I WANTED TO PICK UP SOME FLOWERS FOR AN... OLD FRIEND.
LOOK AROUND, KIDDO.
IT'S GOING TO BE A LONG TIME BEFORE ANYONE IS OPEN FOR BUSINESS AGAIN.
I DON'T KNOW...THIS IS CENTRAL CITY...

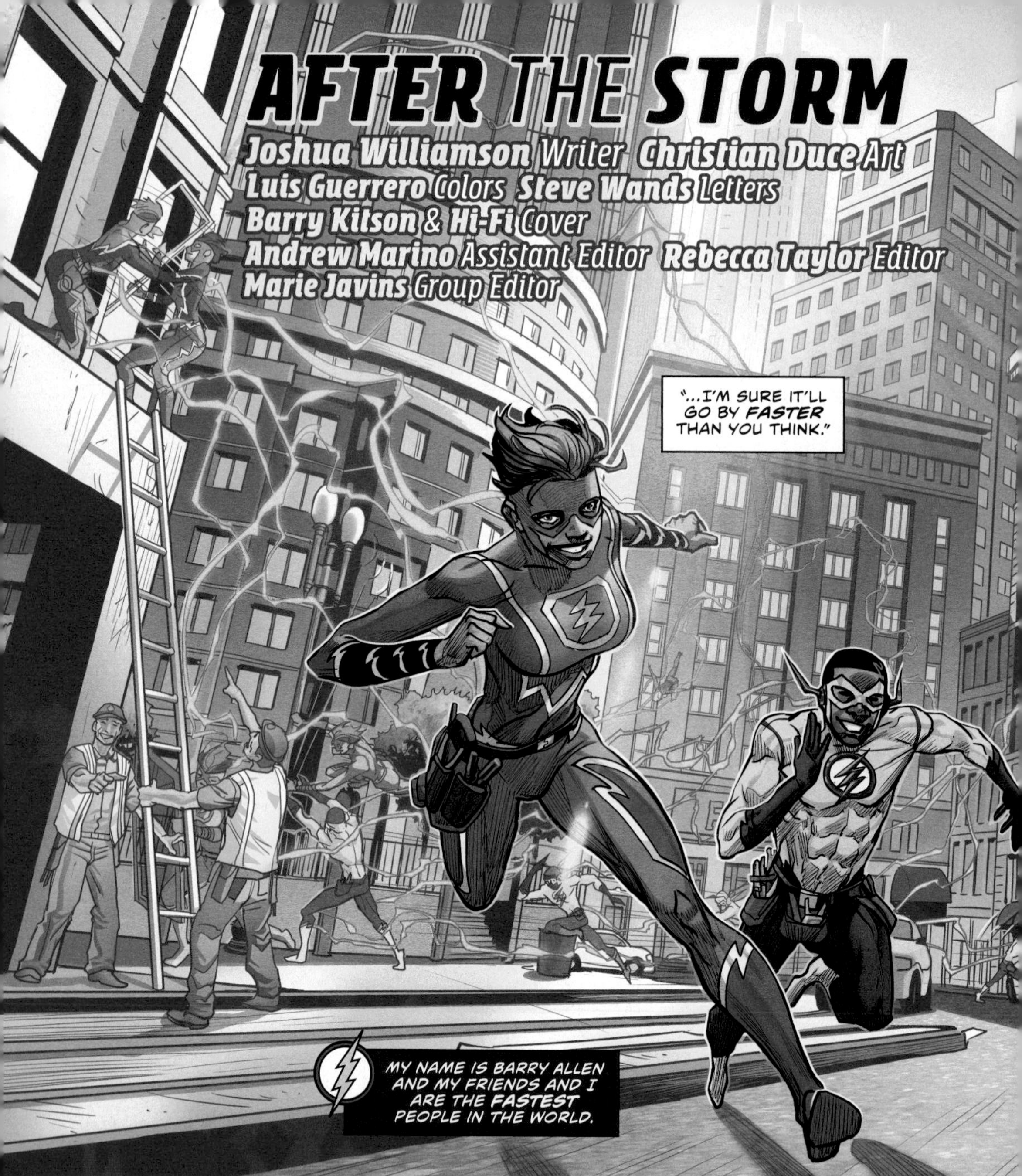
AFTER THE STORM
Joshua Williamson Writer Christian Duce Art
Luis Guerrero Colors Steve Wands Letters
Barry Kitson & Hi-Fi Cover
Andrew Marino Assistant Editor Rebecca Taylor Editor
Marie Javins Group Editor
"...I'M SURE IT'LL GO BY FASTER THAN YOU THINK."
MY NAME IS BARRY ALLEN AND MY FRIENDS AND I ARE THE FASTEST PEOPLE IN THE WORLD.

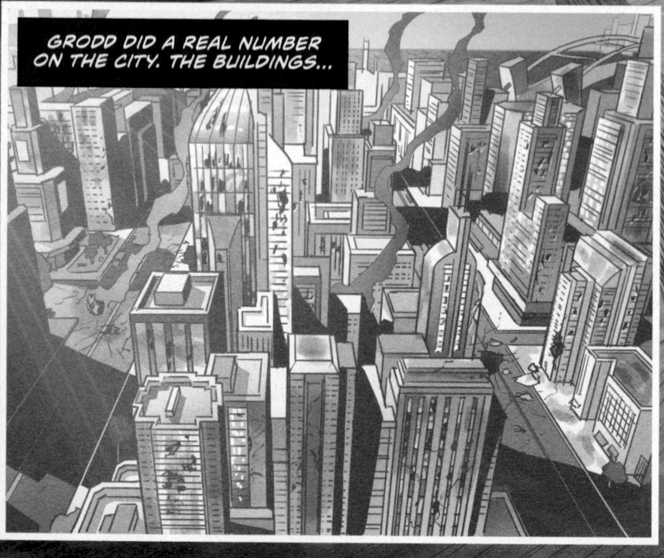
GRODD DID A REAL NUMBER ON THE CITY. THE BUILDINGS...

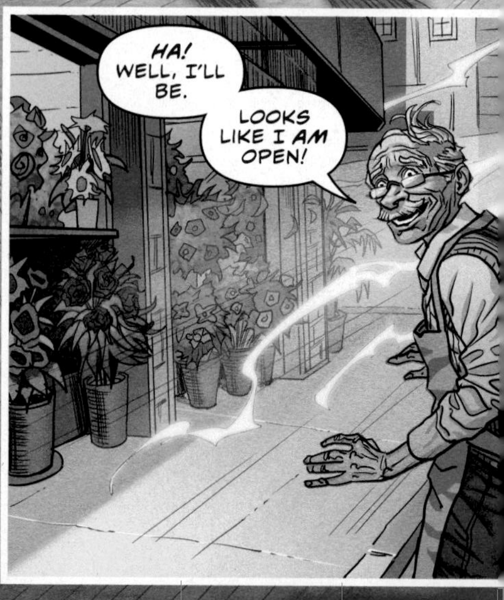
HA! WELL, I'LL BE.
LOOKS LIKE I AM OPEN!

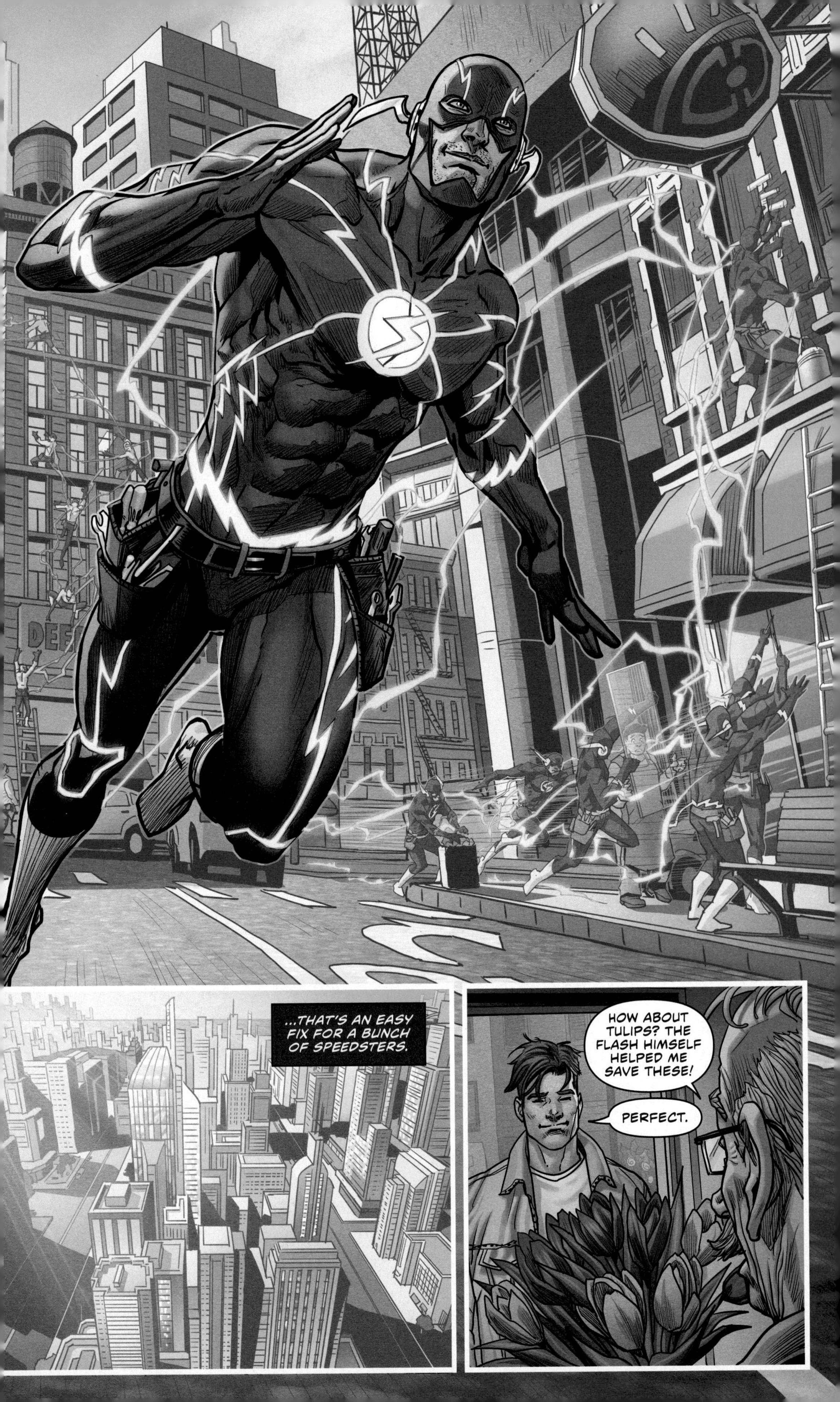
...THAT'S AN EASY FIX FOR A BUNCH OF SPEEDSTERS.
HOW ABOUT TULIPS? THE FLASH HIMSELF HELPED ME SAVE THESE!
PERFECT.

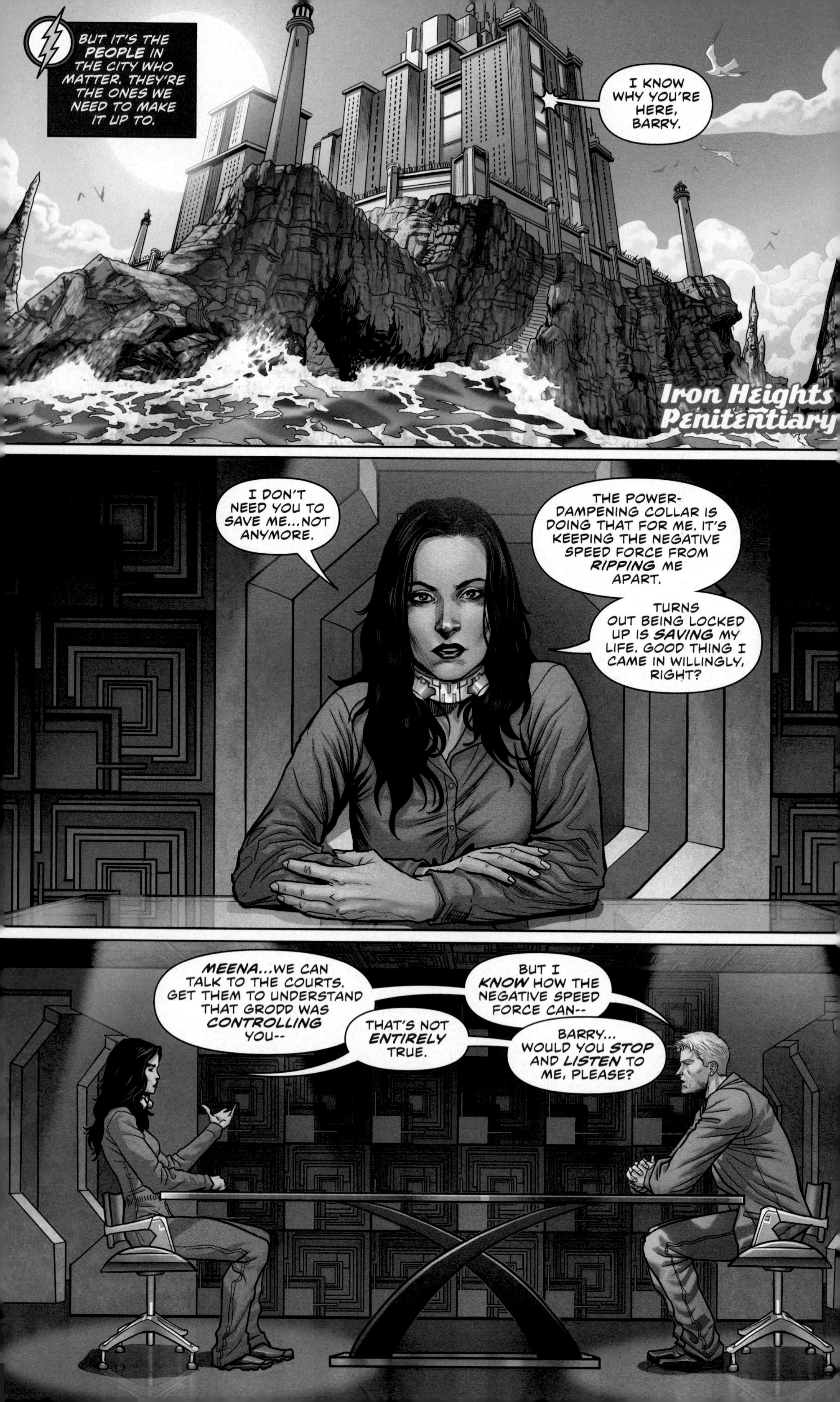

BUT IT'S THE PEOPLE IN THE CITY WHO MATTER. THEY'RE THE ONES WE NEED TO MAKE IT UP TO.
I KNOW WHY YOU'RE HERE, BARRY.
Iron Heights Penitentiary
I DON'T NEED YOU TO SAVE ME...NOT ANYMORE.
THE POWER-DAMPENING COLLAR IS DOING THAT FOR ME. IT'S KEEPING THE NEGATIVE SPEED FORCE FROM RIPPING ME APART.
TURNS OUT BEING LOCKED UP IS SAVING MY LIFE. GOOD THING I CAME IN WILLINGLY, RIGHT?
MEENA...WE CAN TALK TO THE COURTS. GET THEM TO UNDERSTAND THAT GRODD WAS CONTROLLING YOU--
THAT'S NOT ENTIRELY TRUE.
BUT I KNOW HOW THE NEGATIVE SPEED FORCE CAN--
BARRY... WOULD YOU STOP AND LISTEN TO ME, PLEASE?

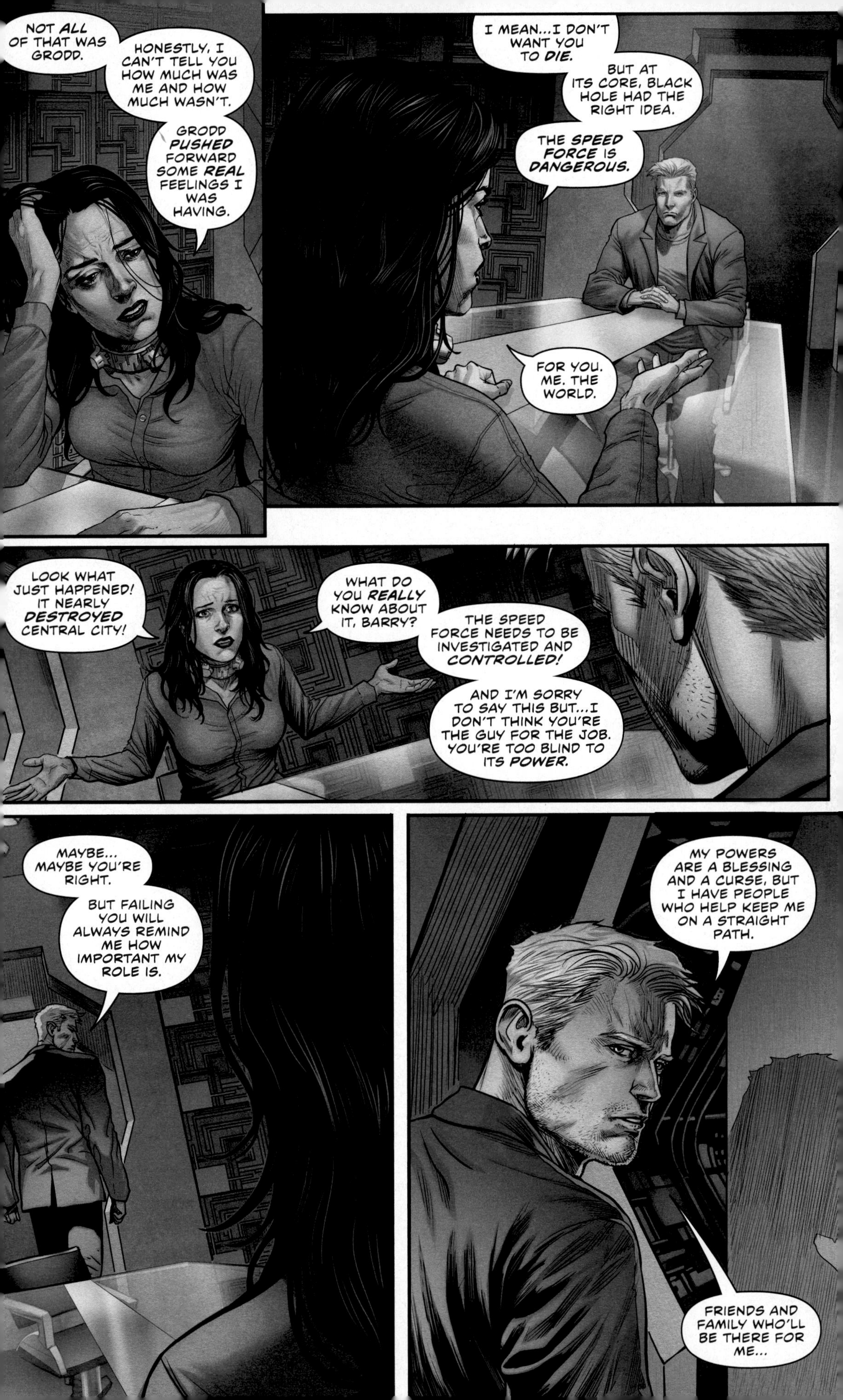
NOT ALL OF THAT WAS GRODD.
HONESTLY, I CAN'T TELL YOU HOW MUCH WAS ME AND HOW MUCH WASN'T.
GRODD PUSHED FORWARD SOME REAL FEELINGS I WAS HAVING.
I MEAN...I DON'T WANT YOU TO DIE.
BUT AT ITS CORE, BLACK HOLE HAD THE RIGHT IDEA.
THE SPEED FORCE IS DANGEROUS.
FOR YOU. ME. THE WORLD.
LOOK WHAT JUST HAPPENED! IT NEARLY DESTROYED CENTRAL CITY!
WHAT DO YOU REALLY KNOW ABOUT IT, BARRY?
THE SPEED FORCE NEEDS TO BE INVESTIGATED AND CONTROLLED!
AND I'M SORRY TO SAY THIS BUT...I DON'T THINK YOU'RE THE GUY FOR THE JOB. YOU'RE TOO BLIND TO ITS POWER.
MAYBE... MAYBE YOU'RE RIGHT.
BUT FAILING YOU WILL ALWAYS REMIND ME HOW IMPORTANT MY ROLE IS.
MY POWERS ARE A BLESSING AND A CURSE, BUT I HAVE PEOPLE WHO HELP KEEP ME ON A STRAIGHT PATH.
FRIENDS AND FAMILY WHO'LL BE THERE FOR ME...

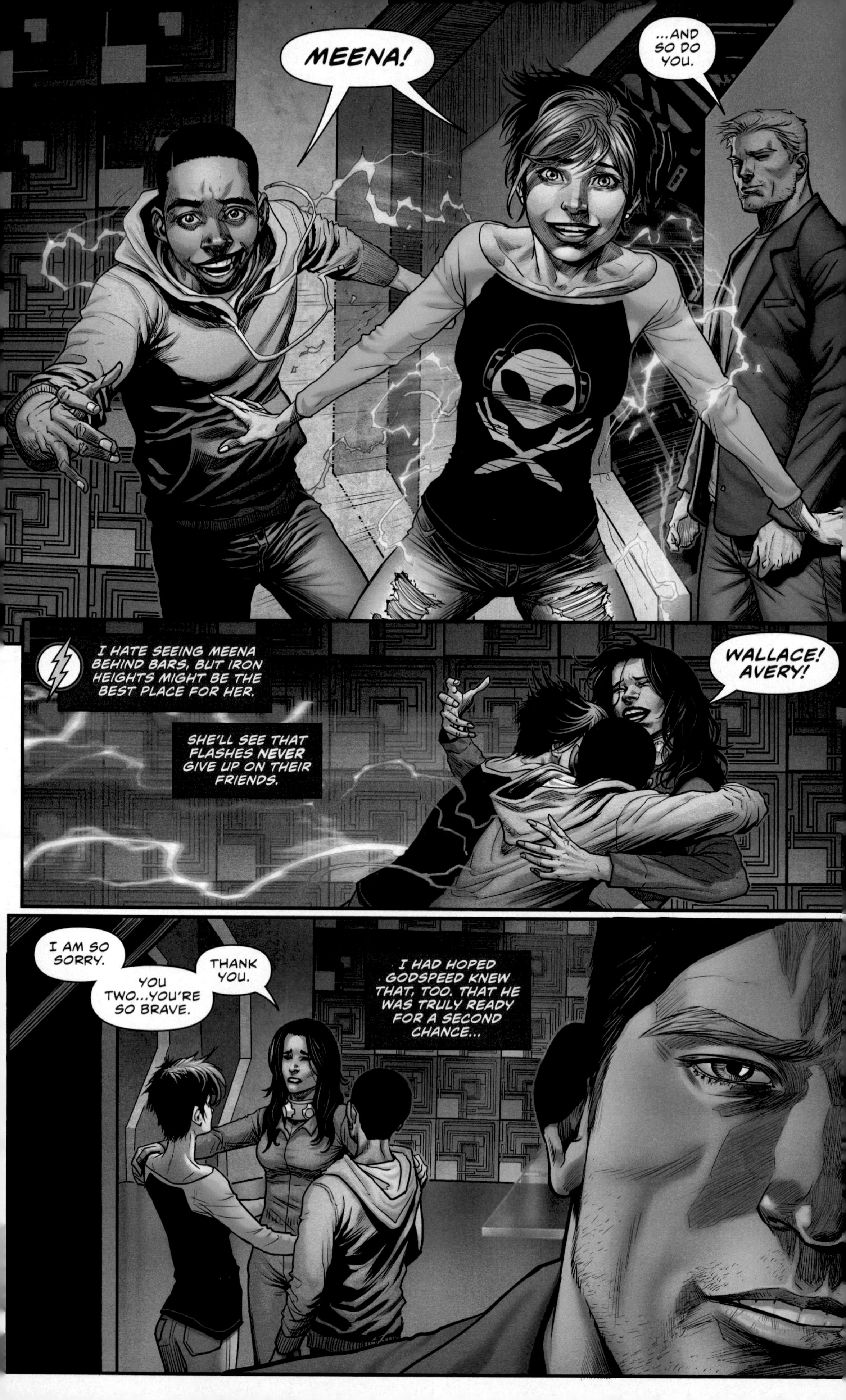
MEENA!
...AND SO DO YOU.
I HATE SEEING MEENA BEHIND BARS, BUT IRON HEIGHTS MIGHT BE THE BEST PLACE FOR HER.
SHE'LL SEE THAT FLASHES NEVER GIVE UP ON THEIR FRIENDS.
WALLACE! AVERY!
I AM SO SORRY.
YOU TWO...YOU'RE SO BRAVE.
THANK YOU.
I HAD HOPED GODSPEED KNEW THAT, TOO. THAT HE WAS TRULY READY FOR A SECOND CHANCE...

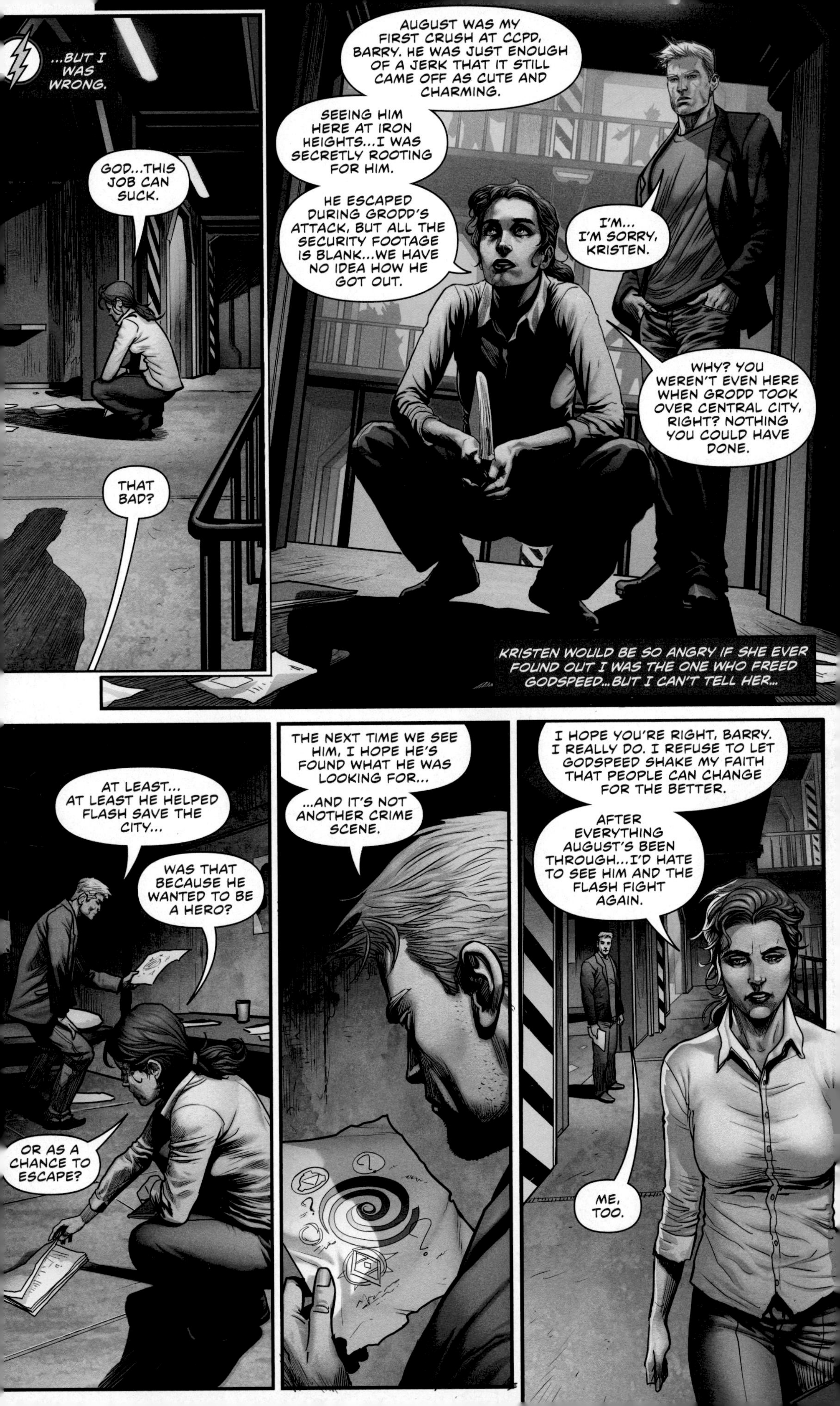

...BUT I WAS WRONG.
GOD...THIS JOB CAN SUCK.
THAT BAD?
AUGUST WAS MY FIRST CRUSH AT CCPD, BARRY. HE WAS JUST ENOUGH OF A JERK THAT IT STILL CAME OFF AS CUTE AND CHARMING.
SEEING HIM HERE AT IRON HEIGHTS...I WAS SECRETLY ROOTING FOR HIM.
HE ESCAPED DURING GRODD'S ATTACK, BUT ALL THE SECURITY FOOTAGE IS BLANK...WE HAVE NO IDEA HOW HE GOT OUT.
I'M... I'M SORRY, KRISTEN.
WHY? YOU WEREN'T EVEN HERE WHEN GRODD TOOK OVER CENTRAL CITY, RIGHT? NOTHING YOU COULD HAVE DONE.
KRISTEN WOULD BE SO ANGRY IF SHE EVER FOUND OUT I WAS THE ONE WHO FREED GODSPEED...BUT I CAN'T TELL HER...
AT LEAST... AT LEAST HE HELPED FLASH SAVE THE CITY...
WAS THAT BECAUSE HE WANTED TO BE A HERO?
OR AS A CHANCE TO ESCAPE?
THE NEXT TIME WE SEE HIM, I HOPE HE'S FOUND WHAT HE WAS LOOKING FOR...
...AND IT'S NOT ANOTHER CRIME SCENE.
I HOPE YOU'RE RIGHT, BARRY. I REALLY DO. I REFUSE TO LET GODSPEED SHAKE MY FAITH THAT PEOPLE CAN CHANGE FOR THE BETTER.
AFTER EVERYTHING AUGUST'S BEEN THROUGH...I'D HATE TO SEE HIM AND THE FLASH FIGHT AGAIN.
ME, TOO.

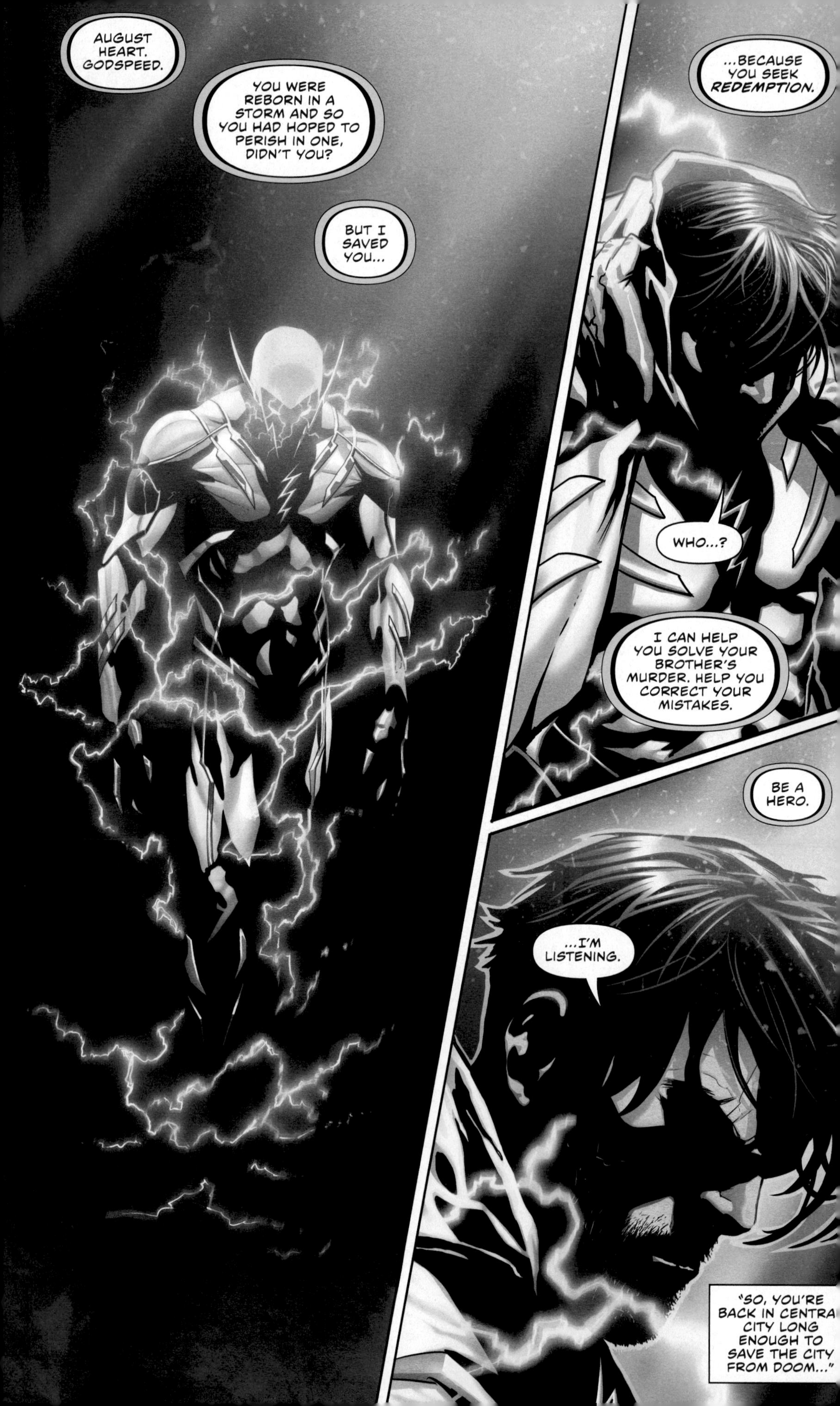
AUGUST HEART. GODSPEED.
YOU WERE REBORN IN A STORM AND SO YOU HAD HOPED TO PERISH IN ONE, DIDN'T YOU?
BUT I SAVED YOU...
...BECAUSE YOU SEEK *REDEMPTION*.
WHO...?
I CAN HELP YOU SOLVE YOUR BROTHER'S MURDER. HELP YOU CORRECT YOUR MISTAKES.
BE A HERO.
...I'M LISTENING.
"SO, YOU'RE BACK IN CENTRA CITY LONG ENOUGH TO SAVE THE CITY FROM DOOM..."

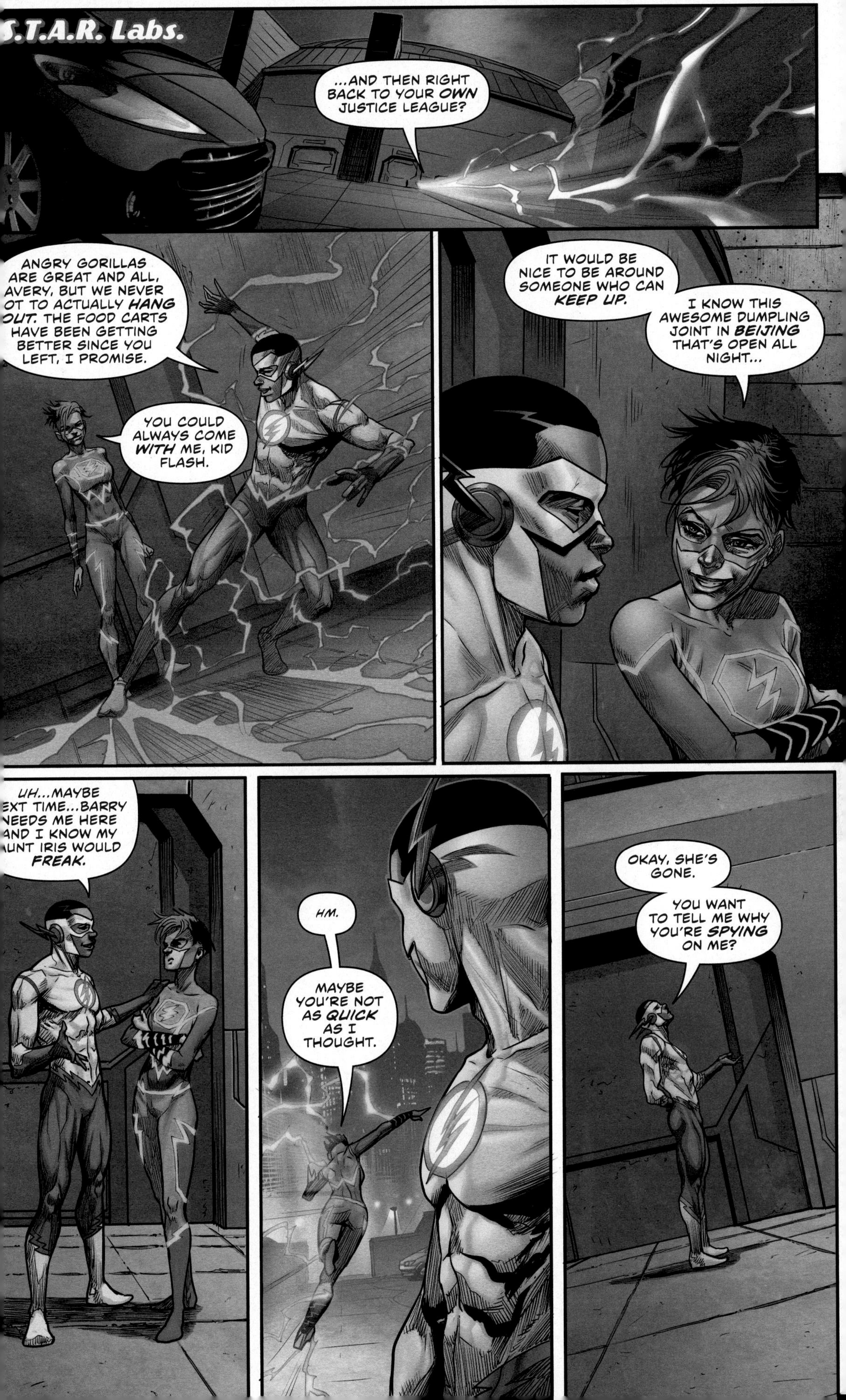
S.T.A.R. Labs.
...AND THEN RIGHT BACK TO YOUR OWN JUSTICE LEAGUE?
ANGRY GORILLAS ARE GREAT AND ALL, AVERY, BUT WE NEVER OT TO ACTUALLY HANG OUT. THE FOOD CARTS HAVE BEEN GETTING BETTER SINCE YOU LEFT, I PROMISE.
YOU COULD ALWAYS COME WITH ME, KID FLASH.
IT WOULD BE NICE TO BE AROUND SOMEONE WHO CAN KEEP UP.
I KNOW THIS AWESOME DUMPLING JOINT IN BEIJING THAT'S OPEN ALL NIGHT...
UH...MAYBE EXT TIME...BARRY NEEDS ME HERE AND I KNOW MY UNT IRIS WOULD FREAK.
HM.
MAYBE YOU'RE NOT AS QUICK AS I THOUGHT.
OKAY, SHE'S GONE.
YOU WANT TO TELL ME WHY YOU'RE SPYING ON ME?

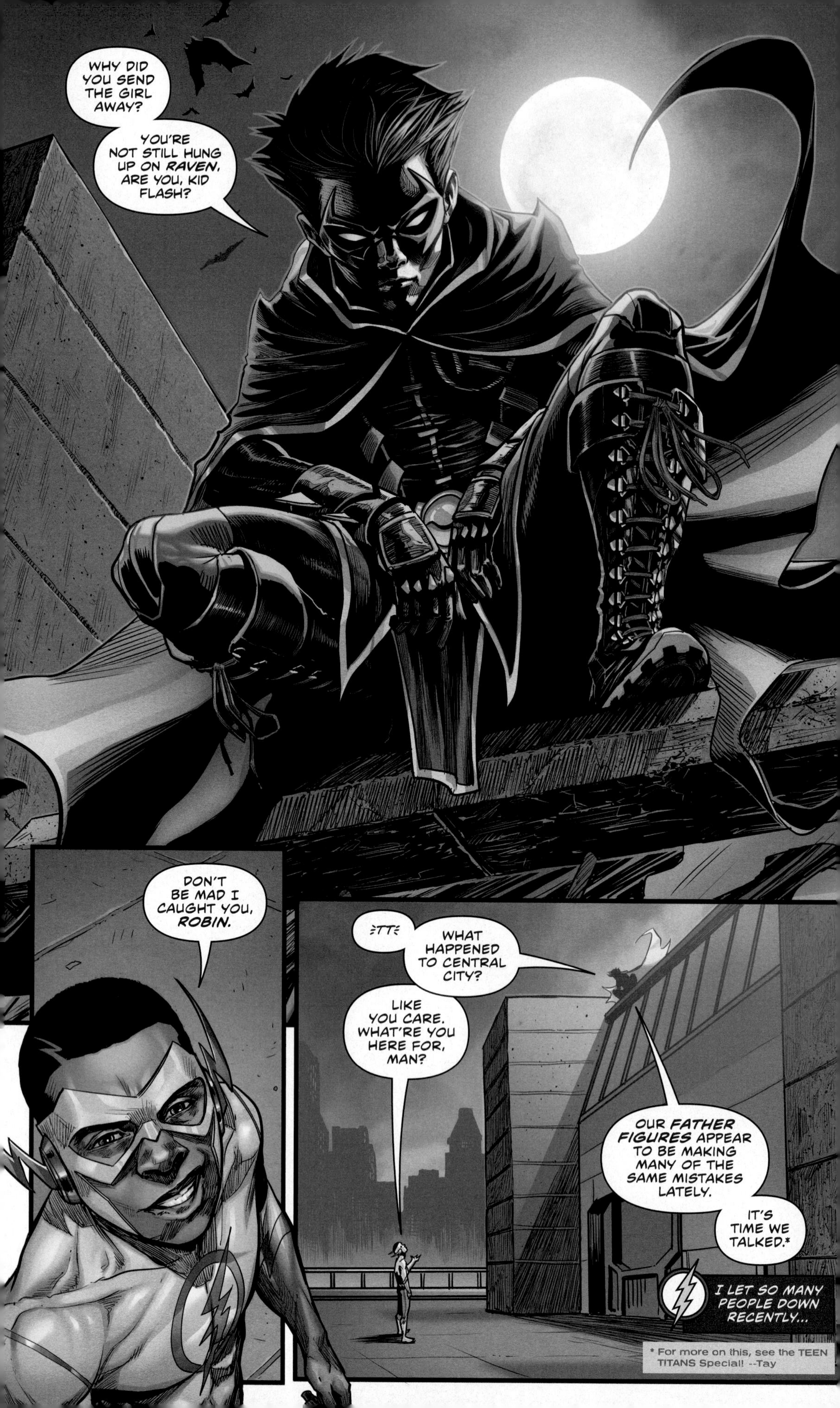
WHY DID YOU SEND THE GIRL AWAY?
YOU'RE NOT STILL HUNG UP ON *RAVEN*, ARE YOU, KID FLASH?
DON'T BE MAD I CAUGHT YOU, **ROBIN**.
TT
WHAT HAPPENED TO CENTRAL CITY?
LIKE YOU CARE. WHAT'RE YOU HERE FOR, MAN?
OUR ***FATHER FIGURES*** APPEAR TO BE MAKING MANY OF THE SAME MISTAKES LATELY.
IT'S TIME WE TALKED.*
I LET SO MANY PEOPLE DOWN RECENTLY...
* For more on this, see the TEEN TITANS Special! --Tay

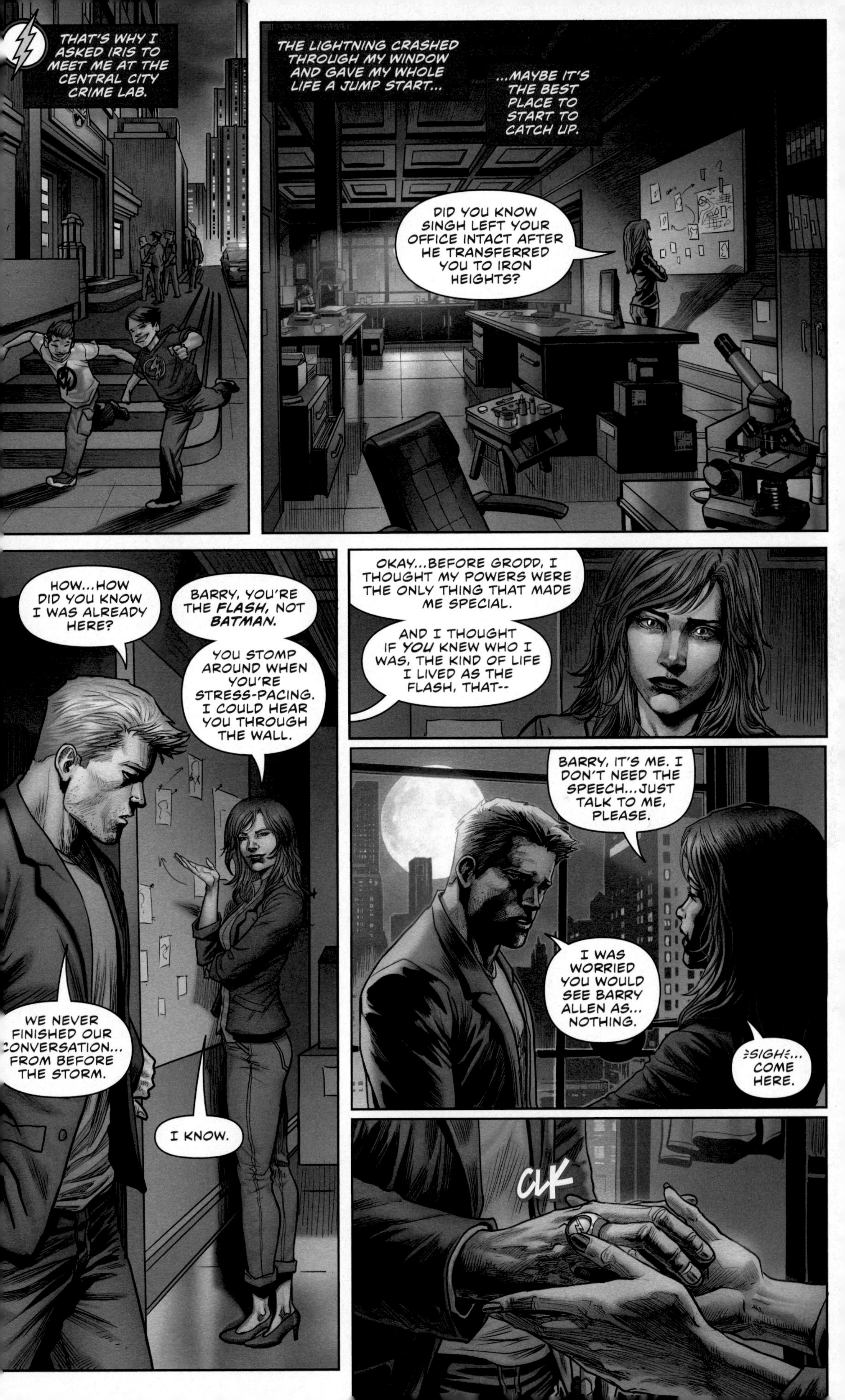
THAT'S WHY I ASKED IRIS TO MEET ME AT THE CENTRAL CITY CRIME LAB.
THE LIGHTNING CRASHED THROUGH MY WINDOW AND GAVE MY WHOLE LIFE A JUMP START...
...MAYBE IT'S THE BEST PLACE TO START TO CATCH UP.
DID YOU KNOW SINGH LEFT YOUR OFFICE INTACT AFTER HE TRANSFERRED YOU TO IRON HEIGHTS?
HOW...HOW DID YOU KNOW I WAS ALREADY HERE?
BARRY, YOU'RE THE FLASH, NOT BATMAN.
YOU STOMP AROUND WHEN YOU'RE STRESS-PACING. I COULD HEAR YOU THROUGH THE WALL.
WE NEVER FINISHED OUR CONVERSATION... FROM BEFORE THE STORM.
I KNOW.
OKAY...BEFORE GRODD, I THOUGHT MY POWERS WERE THE ONLY THING THAT MADE ME SPECIAL.
AND I THOUGHT IF YOU KNEW WHO I WAS, THE KIND OF LIFE I LIVED AS THE FLASH, THAT--
BARRY, IT'S ME. I DON'T NEED THE SPEECH...JUST TALK TO ME, PLEASE.
I WAS WORRIED YOU WOULD SEE BARRY ALLEN AS... NOTHING.
SIGH... COME HERE.
CLIK

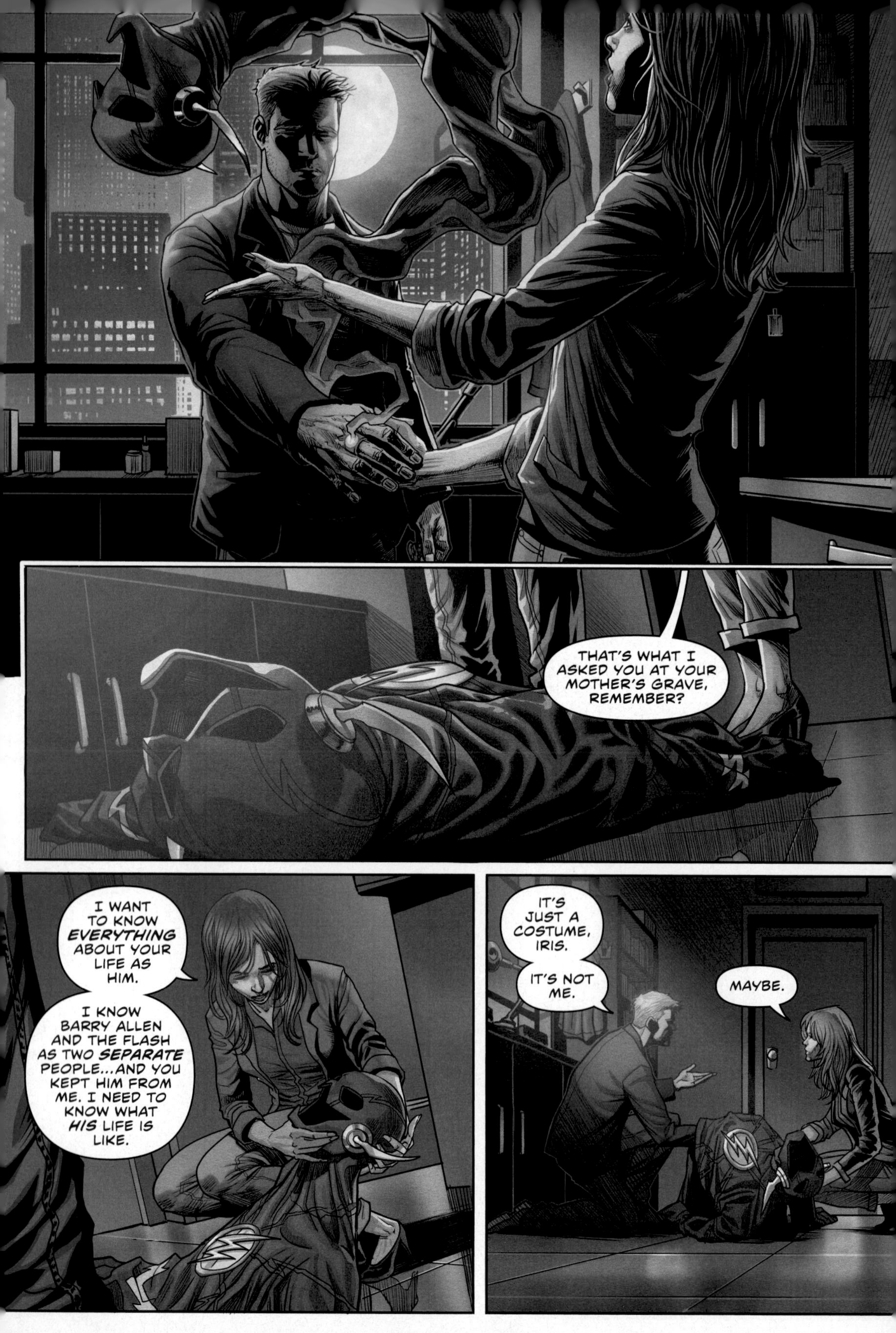
THAT'S WHAT I ASKED YOU AT YOUR MOTHER'S GRAVE, REMEMBER?
I WANT TO KNOW EVERYTHING ABOUT YOUR LIFE AS HIM.
I KNOW BARRY ALLEN AND THE FLASH AS TWO SEPARATE PEOPLE...AND YOU KEPT HIM FROM ME. I NEED TO KNOW WHAT HIS LIFE IS LIKE.
IT'S JUST A COSTUME, IRIS.
IT'S NOT ME.
MAYBE.

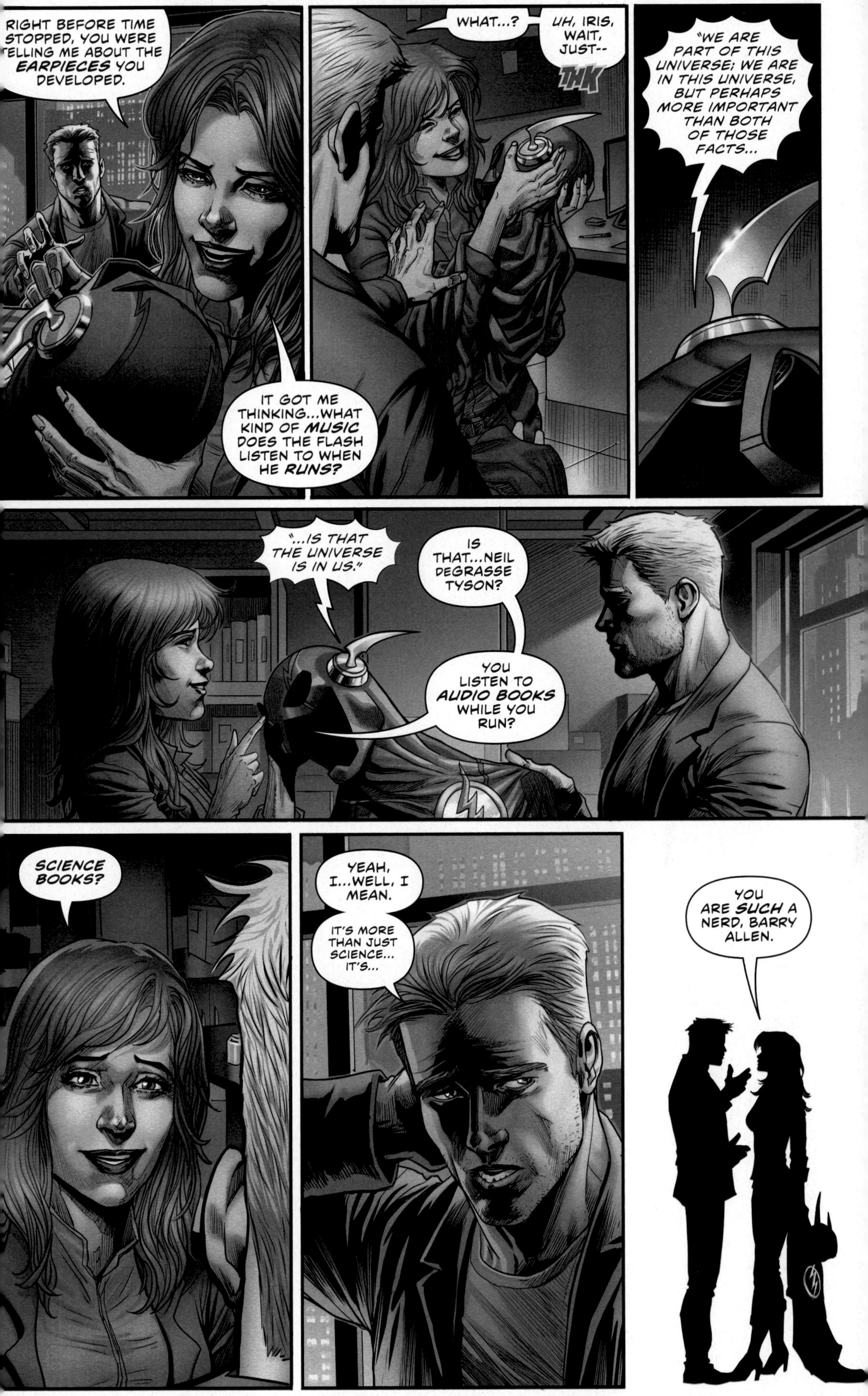
RIGHT BEFORE TIME STOPPED, YOU WERE TELLING ME ABOUT THE EARPIECES YOU DEVELOPED.
IT GOT ME THINKING...WHAT KIND OF MUSIC DOES THE FLASH LISTEN TO WHEN HE RUNS?
WHAT...?
UH, IRIS, WAIT, JUST--
THK
"WE ARE PART OF THIS UNIVERSE; WE ARE IN THIS UNIVERSE, BUT PERHAPS MORE IMPORTANT THAN BOTH OF THOSE FACTS...
"...IS THAT THE UNIVERSE IS IN US."
IS THAT...NEIL DEGRASSE TYSON?
YOU LISTEN TO AUDIO BOOKS WHILE YOU RUN?
SCIENCE BOOKS?
YEAH, I...WELL, I MEAN.
IT'S MORE THAN JUST SCIENCE... IT'S...
YOU ARE SUCH A NERD, BARRY ALLEN.

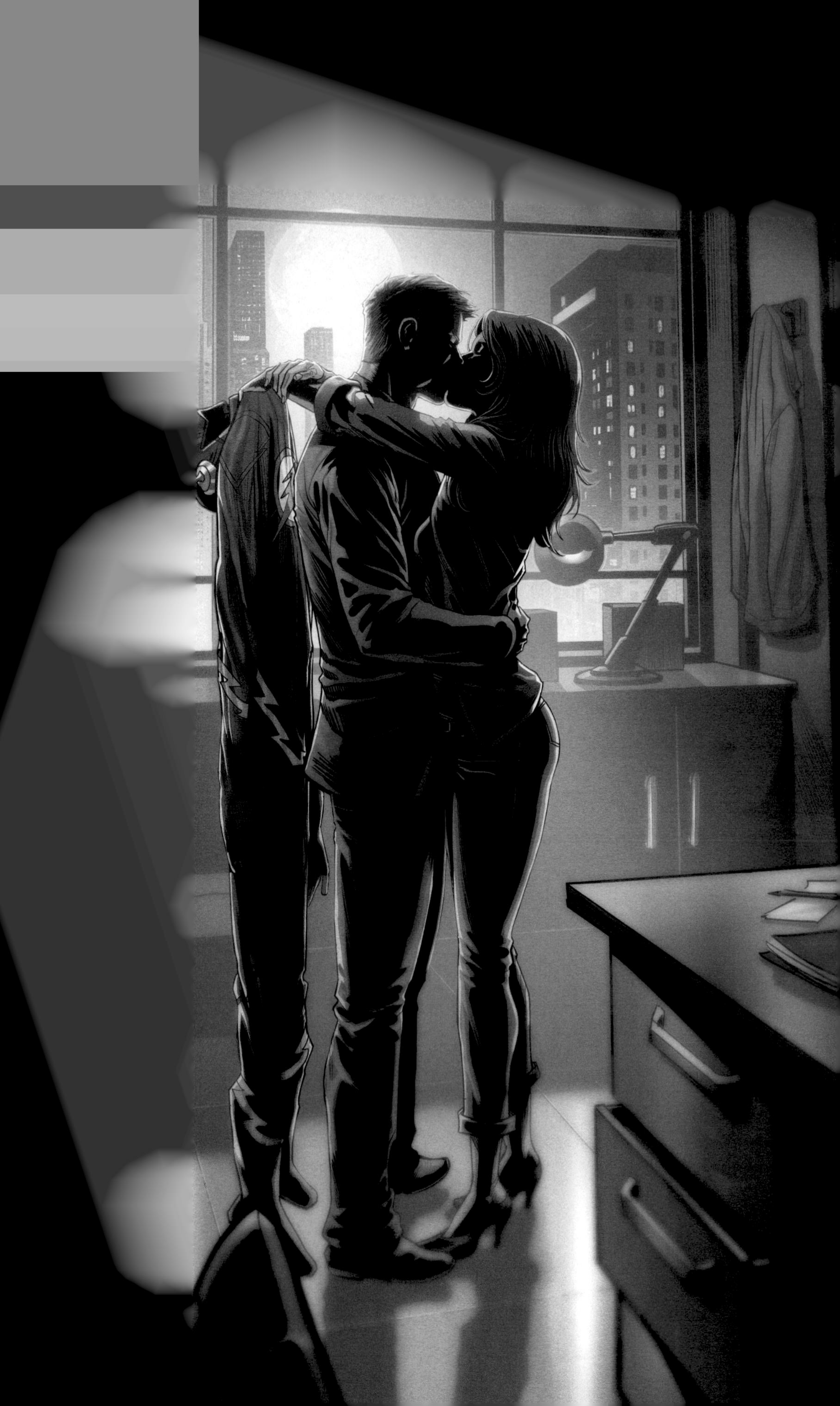

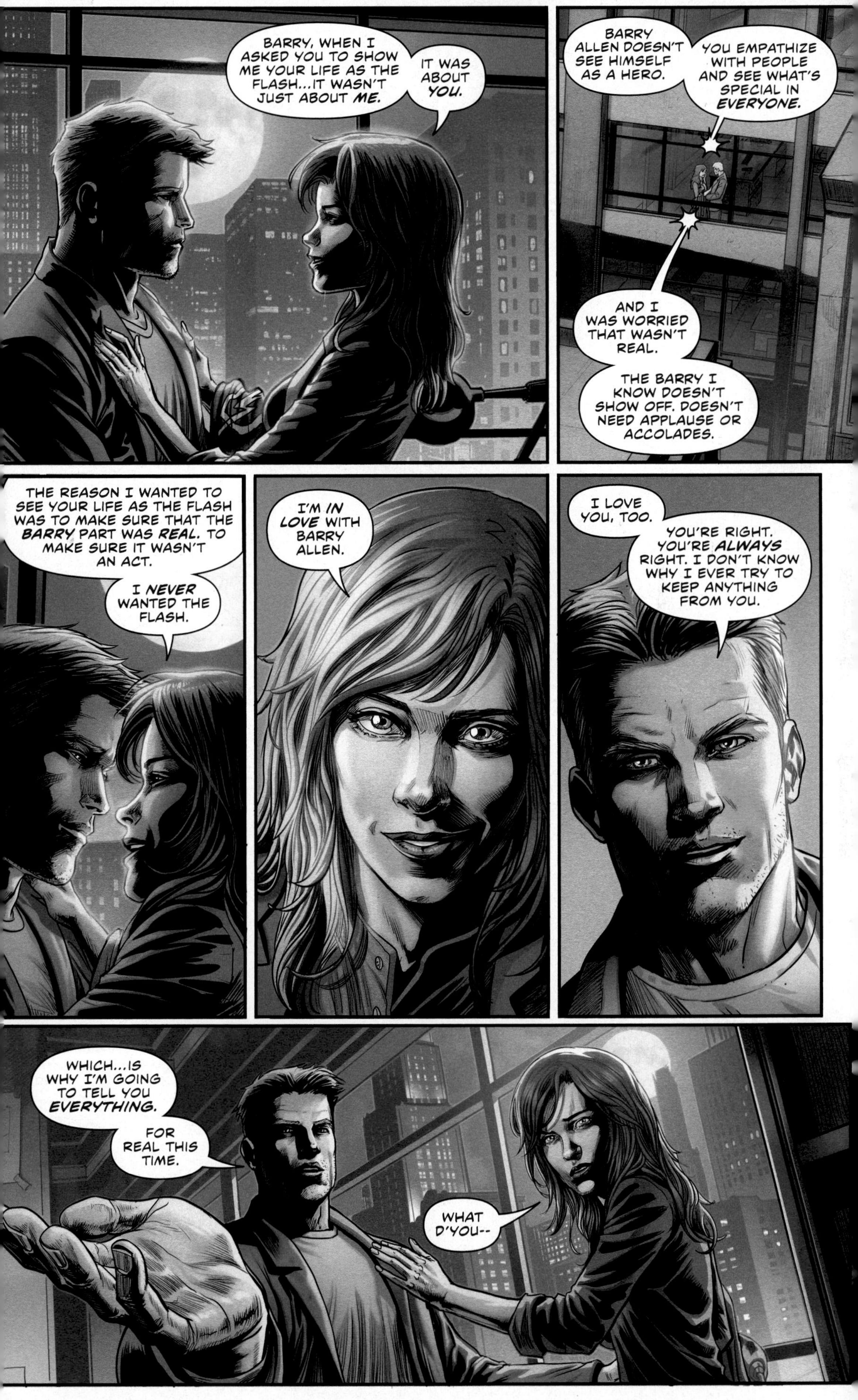

BARRY, WHEN I ASKED YOU TO SHOW ME YOUR LIFE AS THE FLASH...IT WASN'T JUST ABOUT ME.
IT WAS ABOUT YOU.
BARRY ALLEN DOESN'T SEE HIMSELF AS A HERO.
YOU EMPATHIZE WITH PEOPLE AND SEE WHAT'S SPECIAL IN EVERYONE.
AND I WAS WORRIED THAT WASN'T REAL.
THE BARRY I KNOW DOESN'T SHOW OFF. DOESN'T NEED APPLAUSE OR ACCOLADES.
THE REASON I WANTED TO SEE YOUR LIFE AS THE FLASH WAS TO MAKE SURE THAT THE BARRY PART WAS REAL. TO MAKE SURE IT WASN'T AN ACT.
I NEVER WANTED THE FLASH.
I'M IN LOVE WITH BARRY ALLEN.
I LOVE YOU, TOO.
YOU'RE RIGHT. YOU'RE ALWAYS RIGHT. I DON'T KNOW WHY I EVER TRY TO KEEP ANYTHING FROM YOU.
WHICH...IS WHY I'M GOING TO TELL YOU EVERYTHING.
FOR REAL THIS TIME.
WHAT D'YOU--

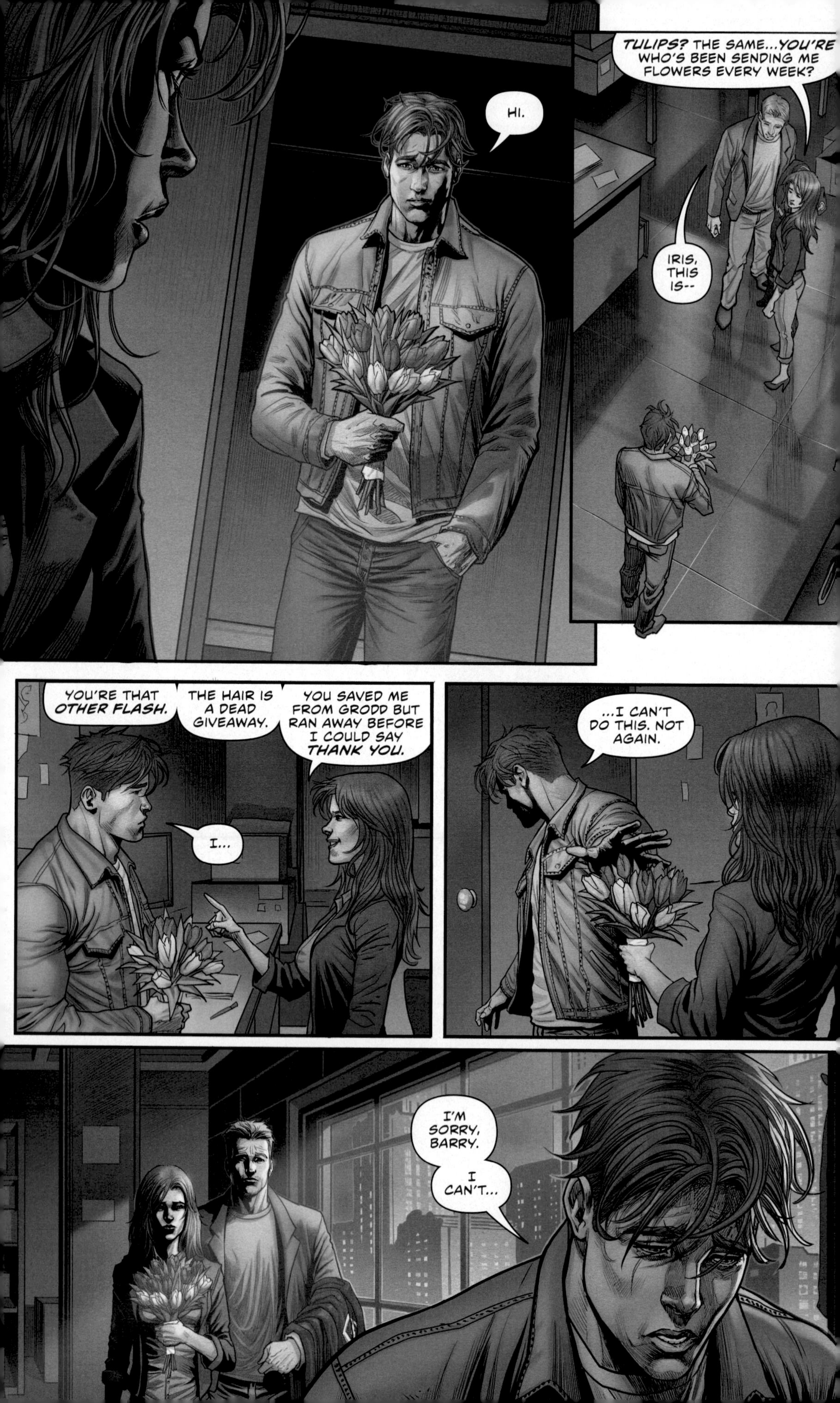
HI.
TULIPS? THE SAME...YOU'RE WHO'S BEEN SENDING ME FLOWERS EVERY WEEK?
IRIS, THIS IS--
YOU'RE THAT OTHER FLASH.
THE HAIR IS A DEAD GIVEAWAY.
YOU SAVED ME FROM GRODD BUT RAN AWAY BEFORE I COULD SAY THANK YOU.
I...
...I CAN'T DO THIS. NOT AGAIN.
I'M SORRY, BARRY.
I CAN'T...

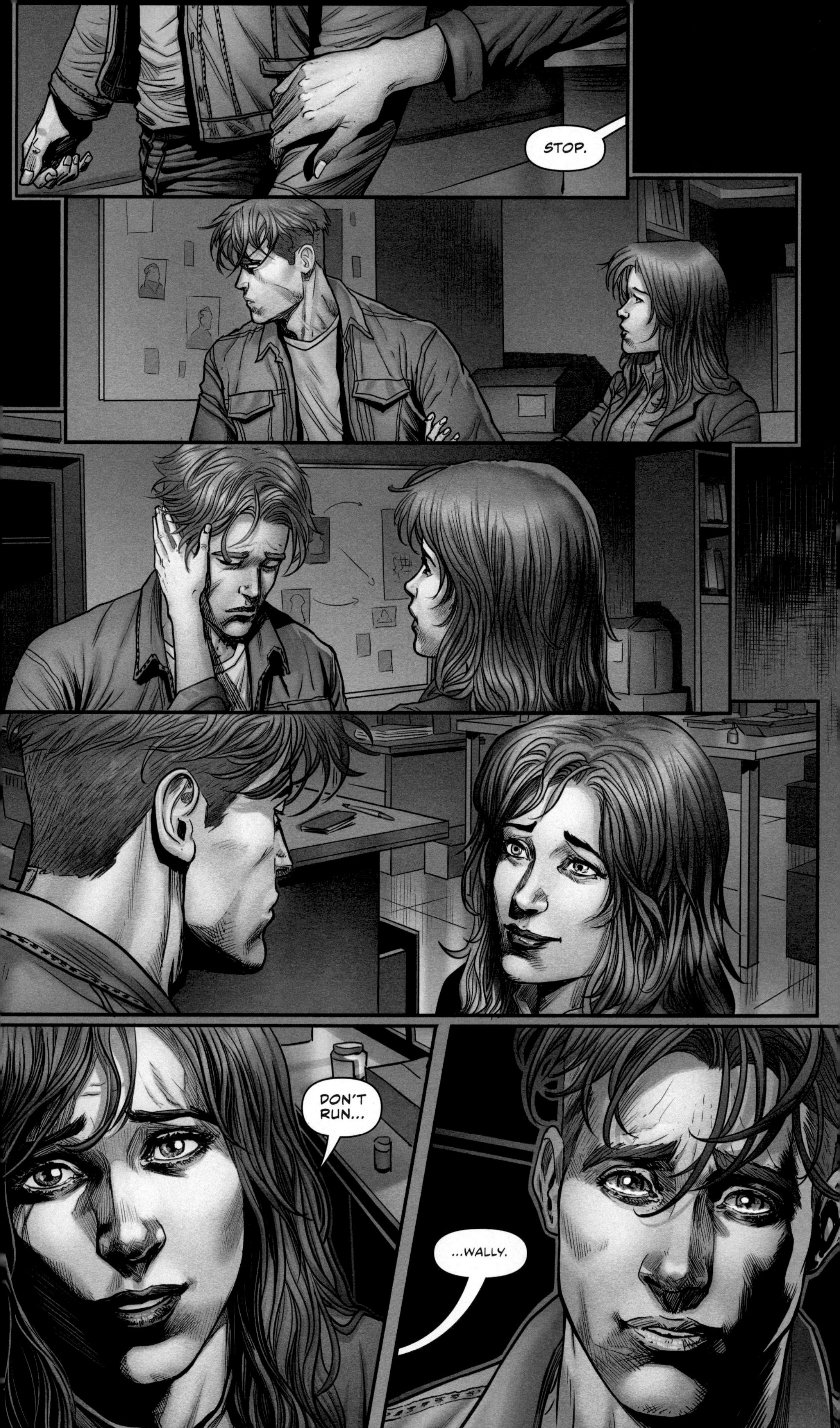
STOP.
DON'T RUN...
...WALLY.

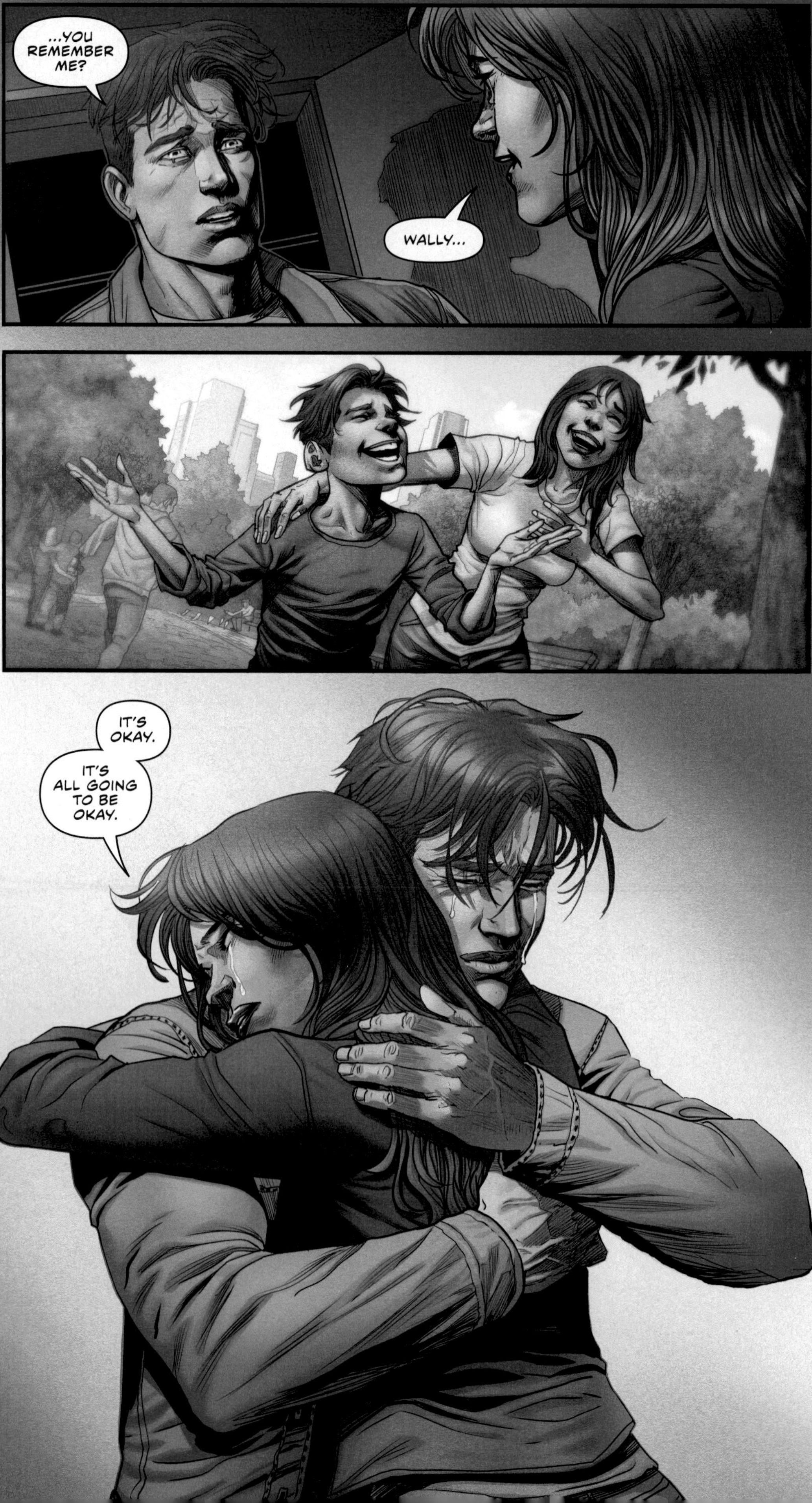
...YOU REMEMBER ME?
WALLY...
IT'S OKAY.
IT'S ALL GOING TO BE OKAY.

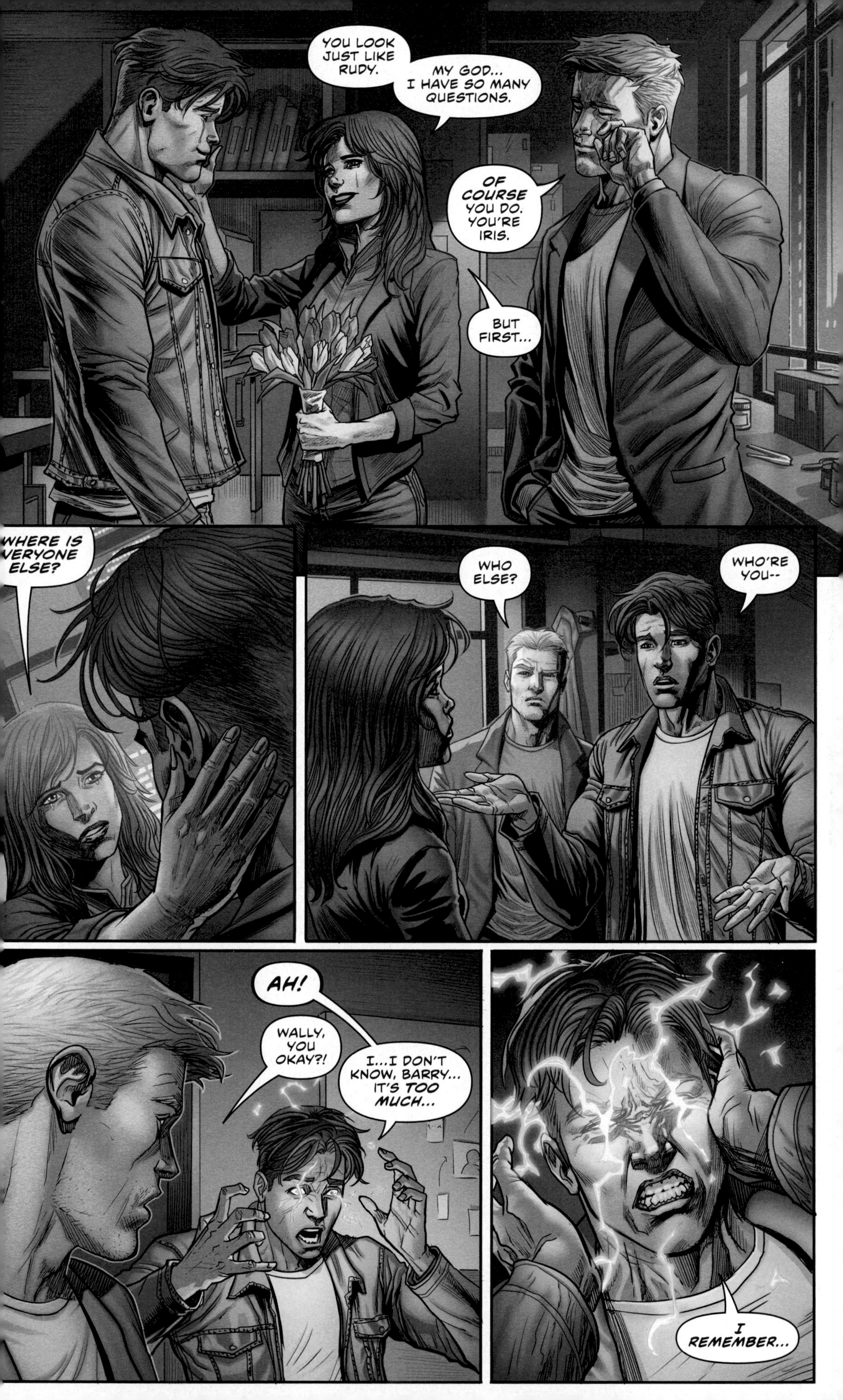
YOU LOOK JUST LIKE RUDY.
MY GOD... I HAVE SO MANY QUESTIONS.
OF COURSE YOU DO. YOU'RE IRIS.
BUT FIRST...
WHERE IS EVERYONE ELSE?
WHO ELSE?
WHO'RE YOU--
AH!
WALLY, YOU OKAY?!
I...I DON'T KNOW, BARRY... IT'S TOO MUCH...
I REMEMBER...

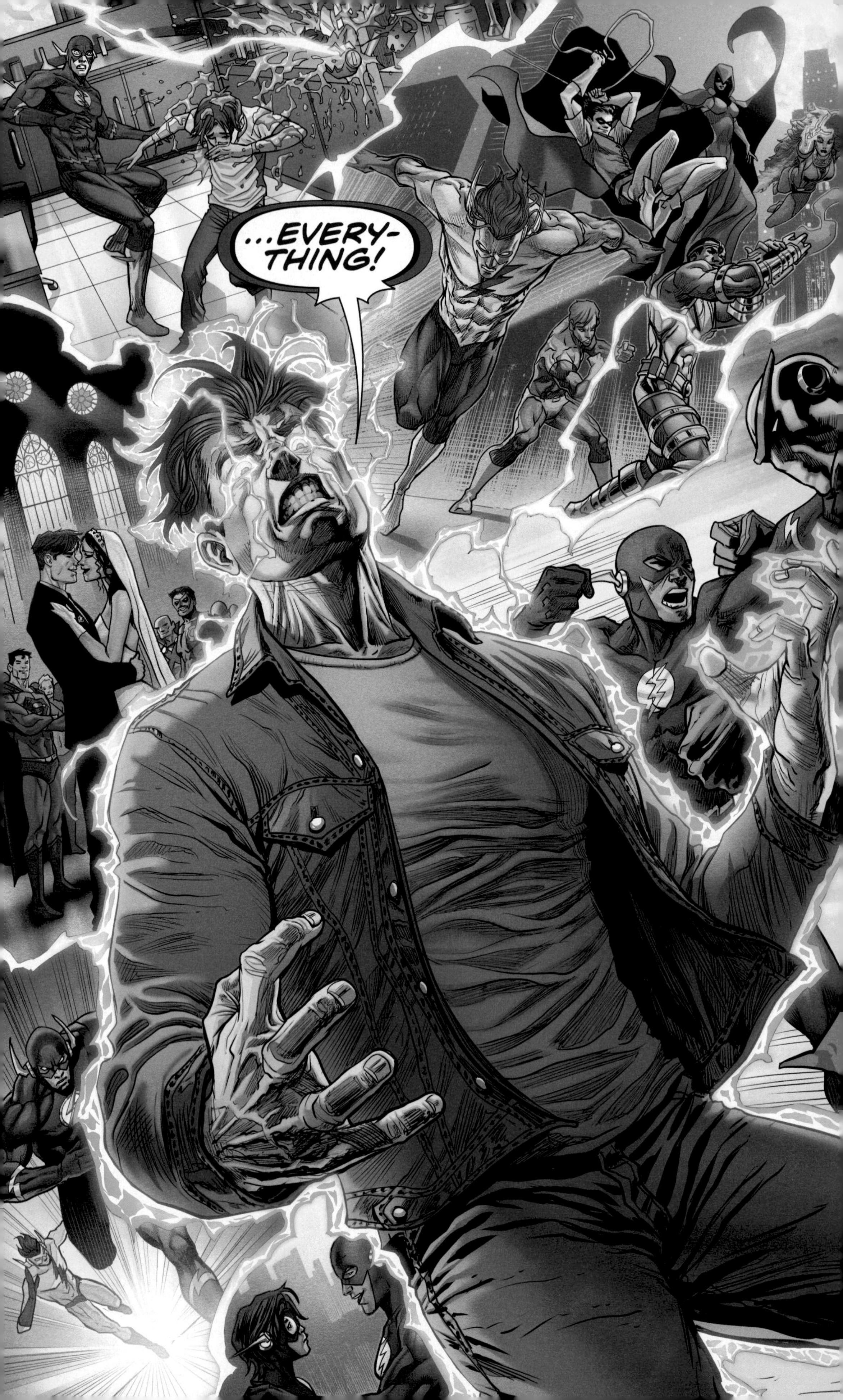
...EVERY-THING!

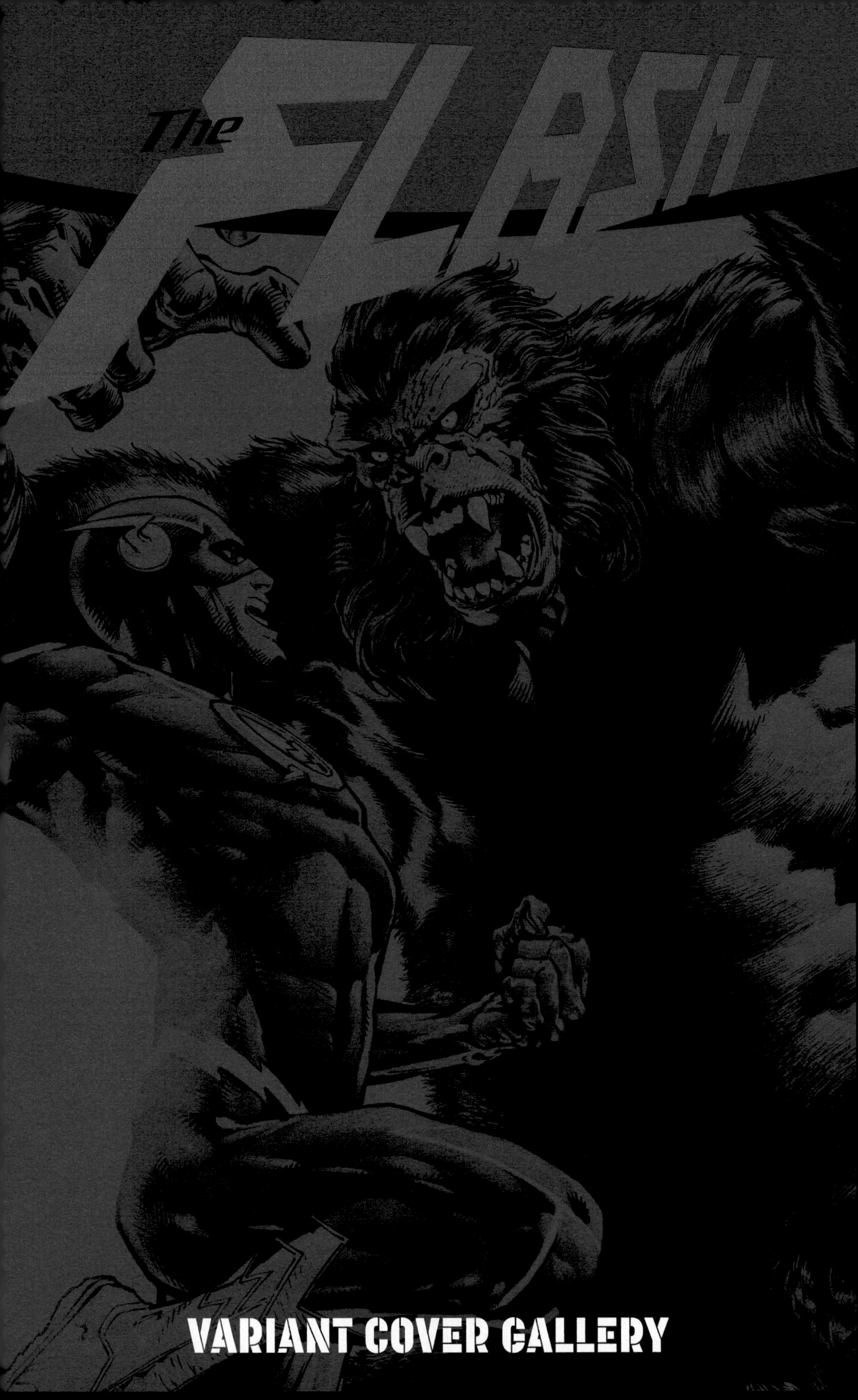
The FLASH

VARIANT COVER GALLERY

THE FLASH #39 variant cover
by TONY S. DANIEL and TOMEU MOREY

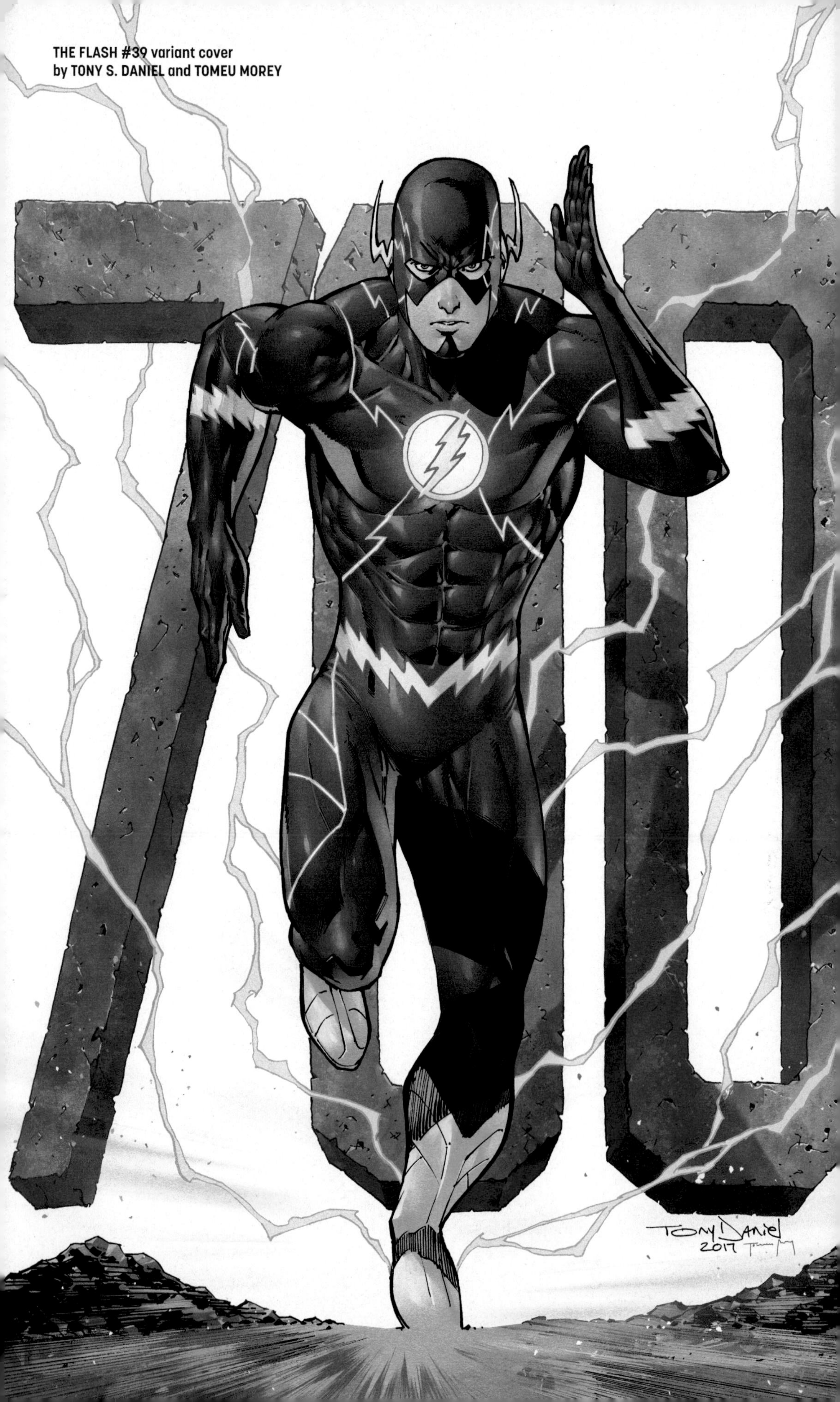
TONY DANIEL
2017

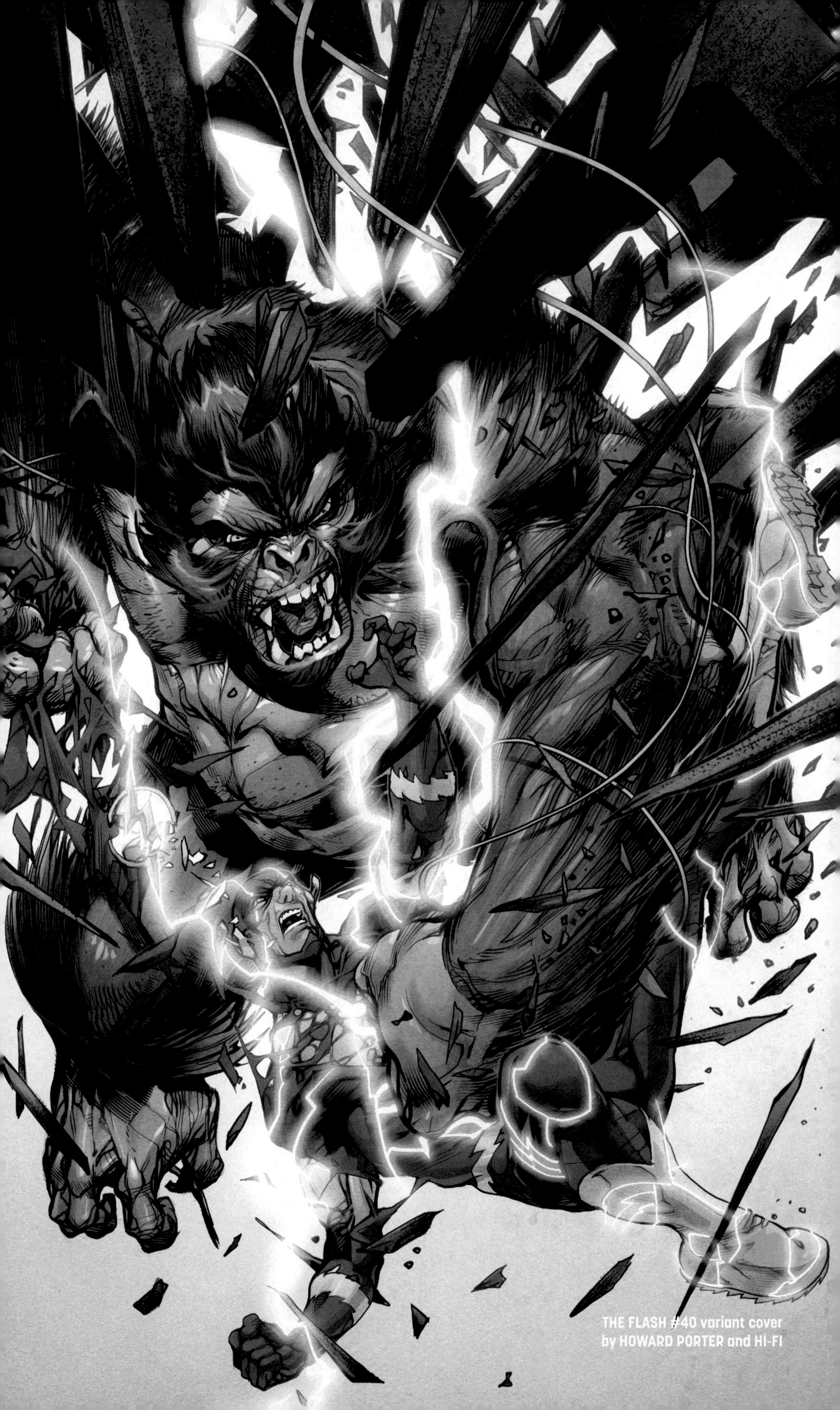

THE FLASH #40 variant cover
by HOWARD PORTER and HI-FI

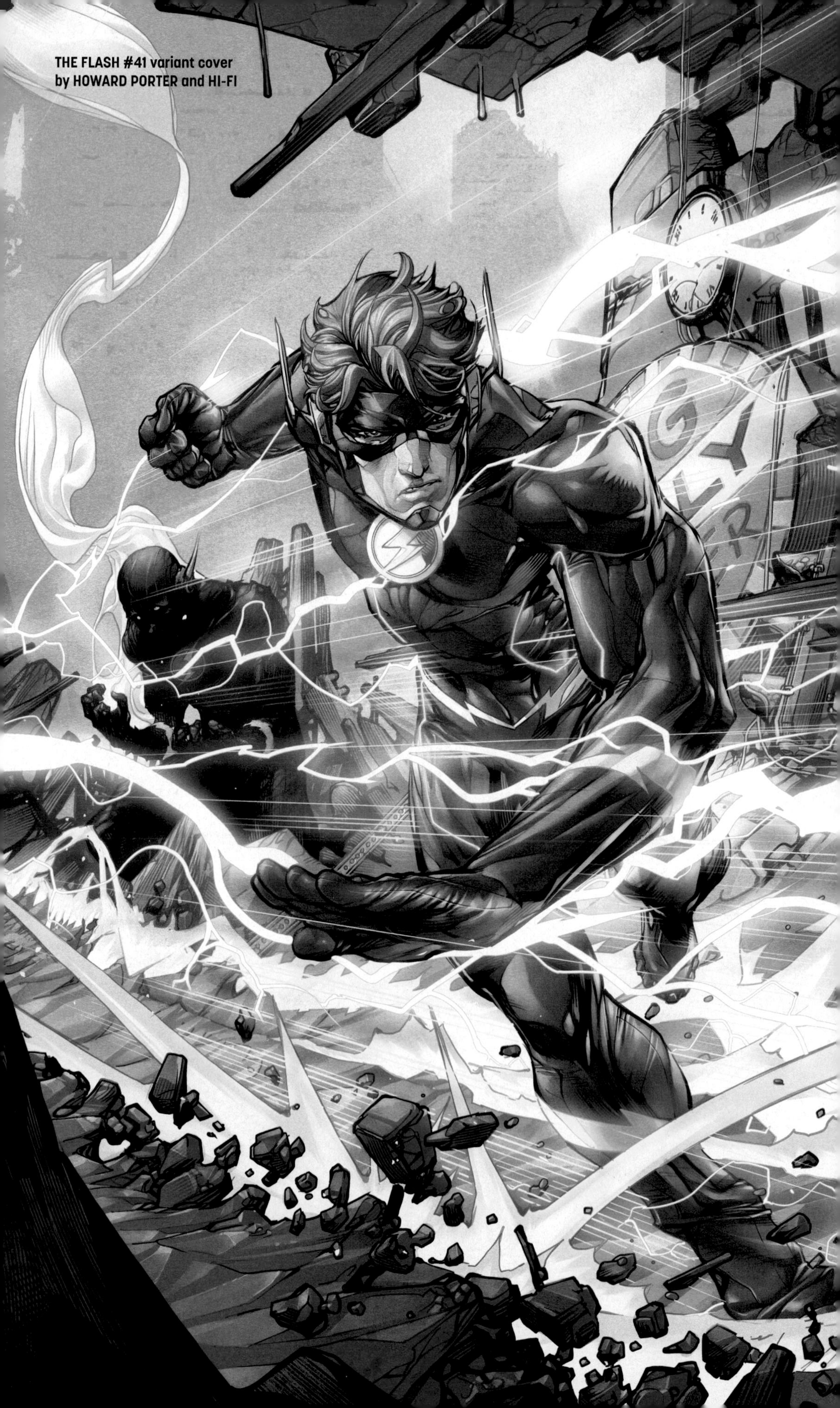

THE FLASH #41 variant cover
by HOWARD PORTER and HI-FI

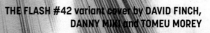

THE FLASH #42 variant cover by DAVID FINCH,
DANNY MIKI and TOMEU MOREY

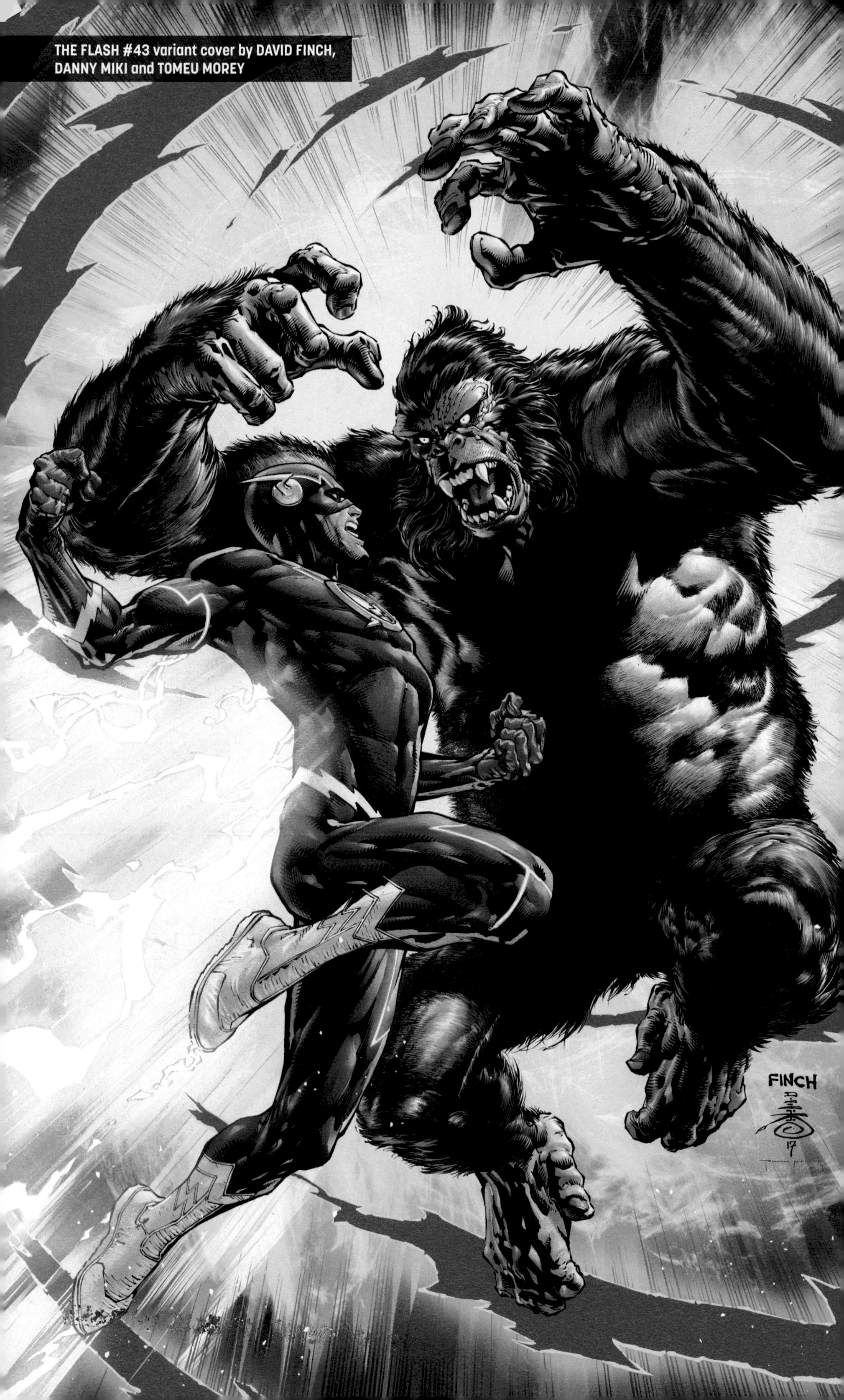

THE FLASH #43 variant cover by DAVID FINCH,
DANNY MIKI and TOMEU MOREY

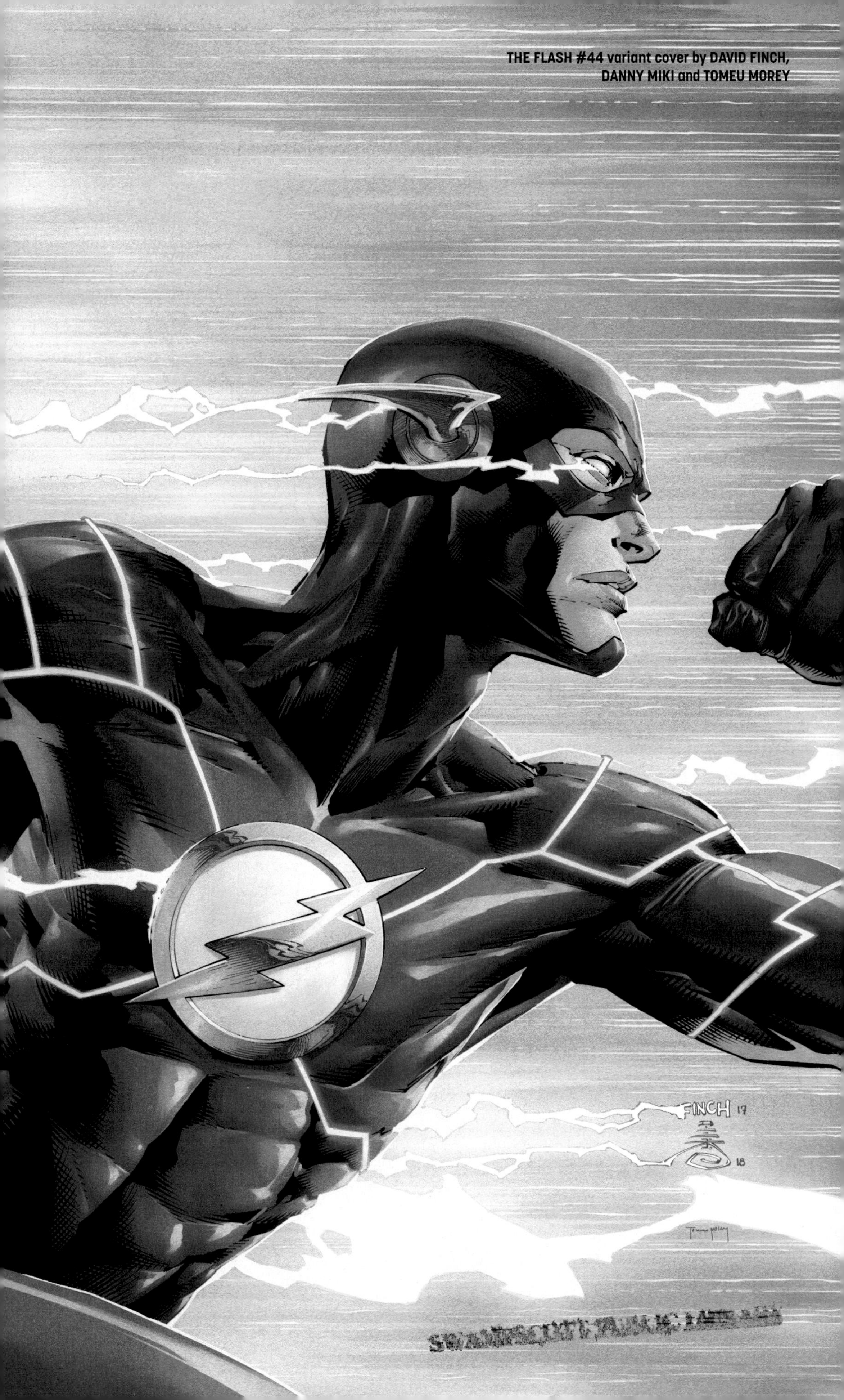
FINCH 17

THE FLASH #44 variant cover by DAVID FINCH, DANNY MIKI and TOMEU MOREY

THE FLASH #45 variant cover by DAVID FINCH
and ARIF PRIANTO

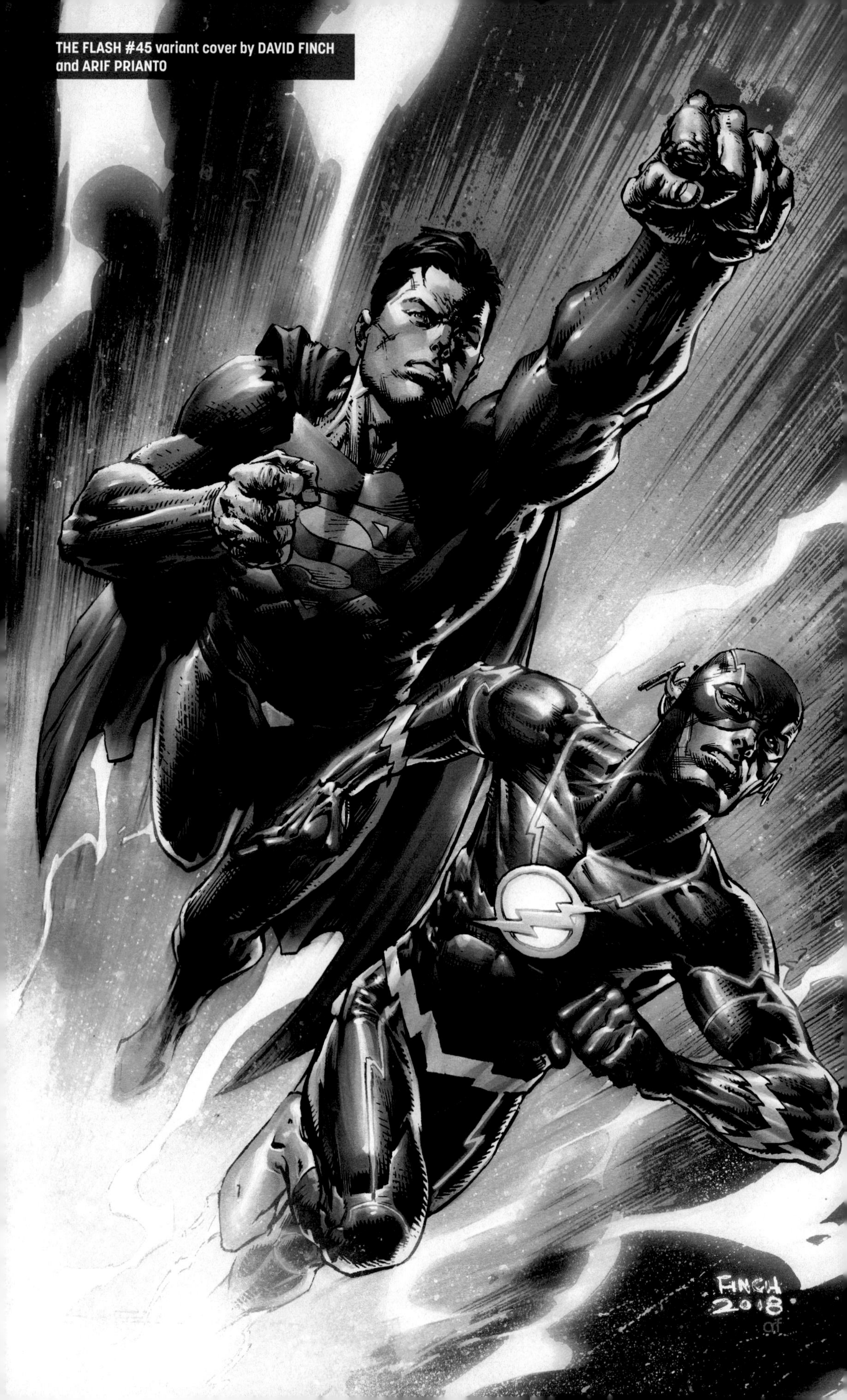
FINCH
2018

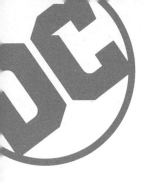

'Joshua Williamson's writing is on point."
- NERDIST

'Williamson makes [The Flash] as accessible as ossible to new readers."
- COMIC BOOK RESOURCES

C UNIVERSE REBIRTH

THE FLASH

OL. 1: LIGHTNING STRIKES TWICE

JOSHUA WILLIAMSON
vith CARMINE DI GIANDOMENICO
nd IVAN PLASCENCIA

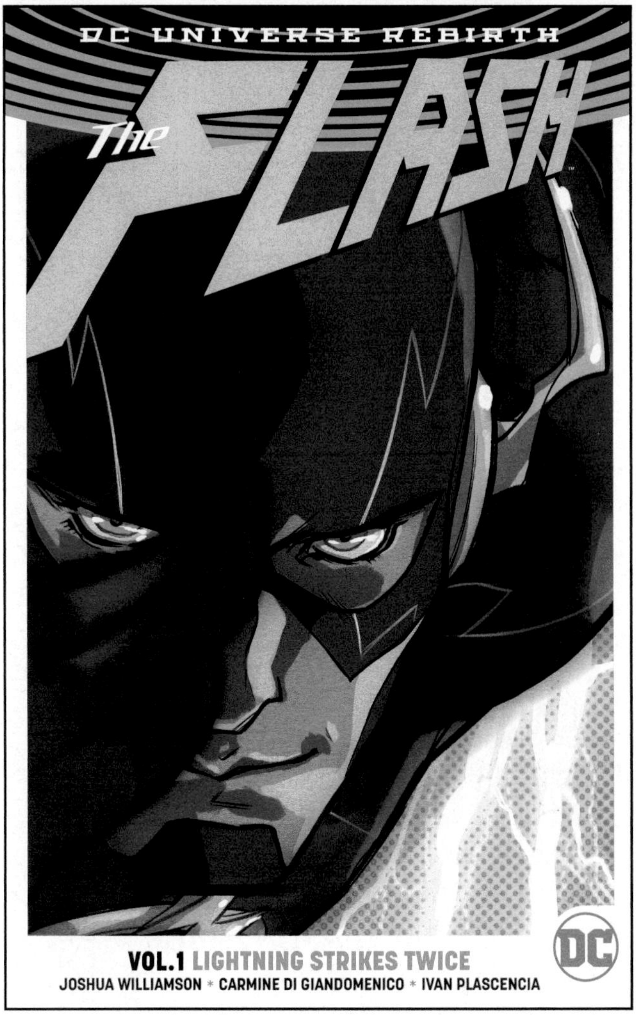

DC UNIVERSE REBIRTH
The FLASH
VOL.1 LIGHTNING STRIKES TWICE
JOSHUA WILLIAMSON * CARMINE DI GIANDOMENICO * IVAN PLASCENCIA

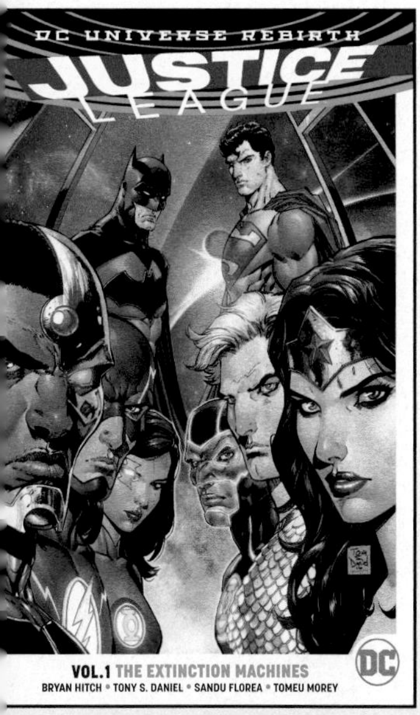

DC UNIVERSE REBIRTH
JUSTICE LEAGUE
VOL.1 THE EXTINCTION MACHINES
BRYAN HITCH • TONY S. DANIEL • SANDU FLOREA • TOMEU MOREY

JUSTICE LEAGUE VOL. 1: THE EXTINCTION MACHINES

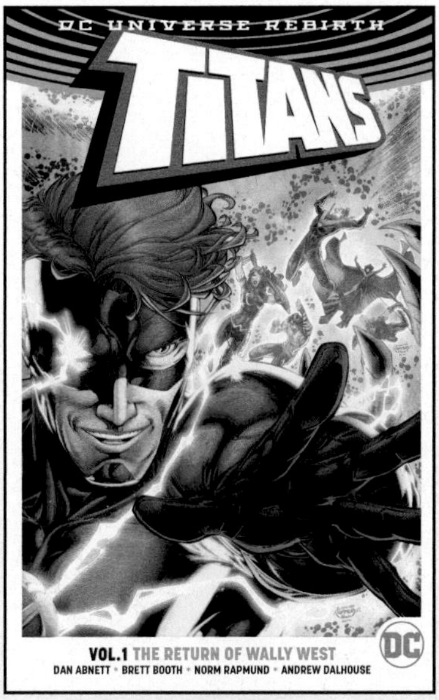

DC UNIVERSE REBIRTH
TITANS
VOL.1 THE RETURN OF WALLY WEST
DAN ABNETT • BRETT BOOTH • NORM RAPMUND • ANDREW DALHOUSE

TITANS VOL. 1: THE RETURN OF WALLY WEST

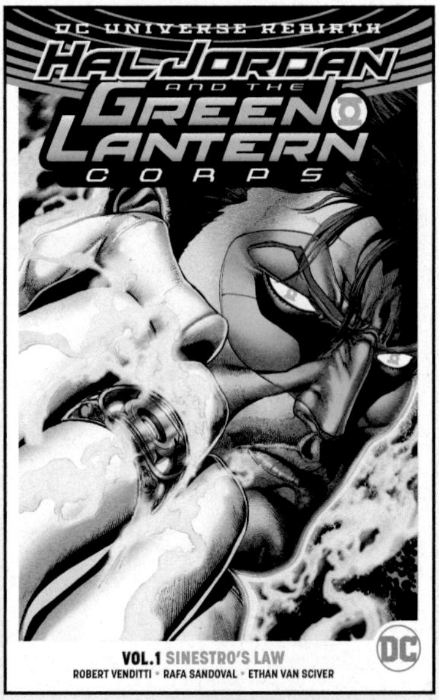

DC UNIVERSE REBIRTH
HAL JORDAN AND THE GREEN LANTERN CORPS
VOL.1 SINESTRO'S LAW
ROBERT VENDITTI • RAFA SANDOVAL • ETHAN VAN SCIVER

HAL JORDAN AND THE GREEN LANTERN CORPS VOL. 1: SINESTRO'S LAW

Get more DC graphic novels wherever comics and books are sold!